It's about Time

It's about Time

COUPLES AND CAREERS

Edited by **Phyllis Moen**

ILR Press
an imprint of
Cornell University Press
Ithaca and London

First published 2003 by Cornell University Press
First printing, Cornell Paperbacks, 2003

Printed in the United States of America

Library of Congress Cataloging-in-Publication Data
It's about time : couples and careers / edited by Phyllis Moen.
    p. cm.
Includes bibliographical references and index.
   ISBN 0-8014-4080-7 (cloth : alk. paper)—ISBN 0-8014-8837-0 (pbk. :
alk. paper)
    1. Time management—United States. 2. Dual-career families—United
States. 3. Family—Time management—United States. 4. Work and
family—United States. I. Title: It is about time. II. Moen, Phyllis.
   HD69.T54 I87 2003
   640'.43—dc21   2002011388

Cornell University Press strives to use environmentally responsible
suppliers and materials to the fullest extent possible in the publishing
of its books. Such materials include vegetable-based, low-VOC inks
and acid-free papers that are recycled, totally chlorine-free, or partly
composed of nonwood fibers. For further information, visit our website
at www.cornellpress.cornell.edu.

Cloth printing   10 9 8 7 6 5 4 3 2 1

Paperback printing   10 9 8 7 6 5 4 3 2 1

Contents

Part Three **Community, Organizational, and Policy Contexts**

Foreword

Americans feel stressed. Conventional wisdom says that longer working hours cause this pressure. But the best data show that the number of hours most individual Americans work has changed little. Yet adults in many dual-earner families genuinely do feel pulled in too many directions. Work alone is usually not the reason. The reason, rather, is that the fundamental arithmetic of the family has changed. The traditional family operated with two jobs and two adults. The husband had a full-time paid job in the world of work while the wife had a full-time unpaid job—bringing up the children, developing ties with the community, taking physical care of the home, and tending emotionally to extended family and friends. In today's two-career family, one more paid job has been added and nothing subtracted. This problem is usually discussed in terms of gender equity, as women typically do much more than half of the unpaid job. But there would still be too much work even if there were perfect gender equity and each person did one paid job and the half of the unpaid one.

What can we do? Traditionalists argue that women should return home, restoring the traditional ratio of two jobs, two adults. Others push for government or employer-subsidized child and elder care services, that would, in effect, outsource part of the unpaid care work.

We believe that what is needed are better opportunities both at home and at work, so that families can chart their own directions. Some families will want to spend more of their time on work. For women in many of these families, professional status and separate earning streams are important. These families need ways to simplify or outsource many aspects of their home jobs. Others will want to spend more of their time on family and will need to have reduced-hour careers to facilitate the roles they want to play at home. This is especially likely for some of the most stressed families—those with young children. Moreover, many families will want one arrangement at one time in their life and something else at another.

While the arithmetic of the family has changed fundamentally, the institutions of the workplace, home, and neighborhood have not. Workplaces mainly have the structure they had when all employees were full-time males. They are intolerant of part-time employees, who often function without benefits and without reasonable career paths. They provide few opportunities for people to work hours that vary from the traditional full-time arrangement.

Phyllis Moen and her colleagues at the Cornell Employment and Family Careers Institute, which was the first of the Sloan Centers on Working Families, have written a powerful book on how these families manage their multiple responsibilities over different time frames—ranging from minutes of commuting to hours of leisure to weeks of work over the course of a year. Furthermore, they use time to situate individuals, couples, and families by stage of life.

Perhaps most important, their book captures the time lags between how the workplace was structured in terms of career paths, workweeks, and work years at the beginning of this past century and how out of date many of these practices and policies are in light of the realities of the lives of today's dual-earner families. At the heart of this book lies compelling evidence that it is about time for American society to confront the realities and needs of contemporary working couples.

KATHLEEN CHRISTENSEN AND RALPH GOMORY
ALFRED P. SLOAN FOUNDATION

New York City
June 2002

Acknowledgments

This book and, indeed, its institutional underpinnings, the Cornell Employment and Family Careers Institute, would not have been possible without the vision of the Alfred P. Sloan Foundation and especially Ralph E. Gomory and Kathleen E. Christensen, who not only recognized the mismatch between today's changing workforce and the unchanging rules governing work but also have provided leadership in fostering an environment conducive to promoting understanding of its many implications. I thank the foundation, and especially Kathleen and Ralph, for their leadership in defining a new working family agenda and for supporting not only the Cornell Careers Institute, but all the other centers they have established in universities across the nation.

Neither could this book, and the institute which made it possible, have been possible without the support of Cornell University, particularly Dean Francille Firebaugh, Dean Patsy Brannon, Provost Don M. Randel, and Provost Biddy Martin. Located within the Bronfenbrenner Life Course Center, the Cornell Careers Institute has been successful in carrying out a productive research, training, and outreach mission that has culminated in the writing of this volume. The staff of the Careers Institute over the years since 1996 have worked well with the staff of the Bronfenbrenner Life Course Center and the Department of Human Development (including Anne Dickinson, Theresa Pollard, Kimberli Fenner, Carrie Chalmers) in making it possible to fulfill our research, outreach, and training agendas. In fact, *It's about Time* is not only about the experiences of the couples in our survey, it is also about collaboration. Since 1997, graduate and postgraduate fellows and faculty associates have met regularly to identify key research issues, design sample selection procedures, survey instruments, coding schemes, analysis strategies, and writing projects. Most chapters in the book reflect this fruitful collaboration between faculty and fellows, research partnerships that have indeed proved synergetic. Fellows have made invaluable contributions to every stage of the research process, and many of them have published in this volume. Predoctoral fellows participating in some way in this enterprise include: Kristine Altucher, Noelle Chesley, Emma Dentinger, Mary Ann Erickson, Heather Hofmeister, Kathryn Hynes, Hyojin Kang, Kimberly Kopko, Youngok Lim, Janet Marler, Stacey Merola, Hyunjoo Min, Steven Mock, Joy Pixley, Heather Quick, Rosern Rwampororo, Mary Still, Linda Tolan, Monique Valcour, Ronit Waismel-Manor, Sonya Williams. Postdoctoral fellows include Paul Callister, Marin Clarkberg, Stephan Desrochers, Judith Galtry, Andrew Hostetler, Jungmeen Kim, Robert Orrange, Susan Singley, Raymond Swisher, Bickley Townsend, and Yan Yu. But the backbone of the data collection, preparation and reports has been with the institute staff and with Yasamin DiCiccio's wonderful Computer Assisted Survey Team (CAST), all of whom have been committed to excellence. We have been blessed over the years with two wonderful project directors: Dr. Patricia Roehling and Dr. Stephen Sweet; talented and dedicated research associates: Veronica V. Banks, Kristin Campbell, Deborah Harris-Abbott, Shinok Lee, Lauren Meritt, Vandana Plassmann, and Wipas Wimonsate; three exemplary executive coordinators: Noelle Chesley, Liane O'Brien, and Lisa Dahl, and extremely hard-working, conscientious assistants: David McDermitt, Sarah Jaenike Demo, Joanne J. Kenyon, and Carrie Chalmers. Undergraduates have also played an important role; I especially want to recognize Caren Arbeit, Akshay Gupta, Musarrat Islam, Lisa Kahn, and Sarah Yeung. Larry Clarkberg and Susan Lang provided important editorial assistance. The people at Cornell University Press have been most helpful, especially Ange Romeo-Hall, the manuscript editor and Julie Nemer, the copyeditor. I appreciate Fran Benson taking the time from her busy schedule as editor-in-chief to offer early and invaluable encouragement and advice.

Most important to recognize of course, are the participating employers who gave us access to their workforce as well as to their human resource personnel. Since we use pseudonyms in this volume, we can never thank you publicly, but will do so privately. And the workers and couples who graciously participated in focus groups, in-depth interviews, and surveys—you are the ones who are the pathbreakers, who have taught us about creative strategies to manage two occupational careers along with family careers in an uncertain world. We thank you for your participation and your patience with our too-long surveys.

Writing and editing a book about time requires considerable time, graciously provided to me by Dean Brannon at Cornell University. I could not have completed this volume without a fellowship from the Radcliffe Institute for Advanced Study (2000–01). I thank Drew Faust, Annemette Sorensen, and Paula Rayman for making it possible, and my other friends at the Radcliffe Institute (and its wonderful Murray Center and Public Policy Center) for their support (especially Connie Ahrons, Roz Barnett, Irene Padavic, Nance Goldstein, Deborah Belle, Dhooleka Ray, Kathleen Coll, Sarah Kuhn, and the late Al Nagao). Appreciation as well goes to Dean Steven Rosenstone of my soon-to-be new home at the University of Minnesota for encouraging me to take the time to step back for the larger view. Finally, I would like to thank Sarah Demo and Donna Dempster-McClain who have both given unstintingly of their time on this project, as has my husband, Dick Shore.

1

Introduction

Phyllis Moen

Karen Hughes became a headline and a media talking point in 2002 because she decided to leave her job. Hughes, arguably one of the most powerful women in government, was more than White House counselor; she was also George W. Bush's confidant, adviser, and close friend. Her access to and role in the policy-making process had not come easy, but she finally had made it; her candidate was ensconced in the White House, and she was at his elbow. What on earth would make her leave this prominent, long sought-after, influential position?

When Hughes gave the "family reasons" explanation, social commentators on both the right and the left could be seen nodding sagely: women are finding it difficult, if not impossible, to do it all. Is this a personal failing or a policy issue? No one would argue that Karen Hughes's job was not demanding and exhausting. But neither would anyone argue that she was not up to it. Hughes was the topic of columns and cable talk shows precisely because she embodies the strength, the skills, the resources, and the determination to succeed at work and at family life. The media spinned this as part of a larger story: of women valuing family more, work less, in light of the unremitting challenges of both, even for professional, high-powered women like Hughes. This notion was reinforced by the publication of Sylvia Ann Hewlett's book *Creating a Life: Professional Women and the Quest for Children*, in which she argues, in effect, that women have to choose between career success and family success. If people such as Karen Hughes, part of

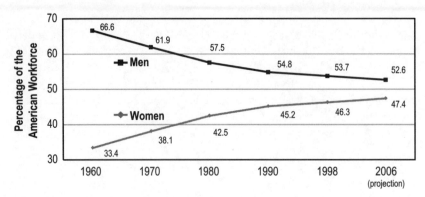

Figure 1.1 Women now constitute nearly one-half of the American workforce. Data are from U.S. Census Bureau (1999, 413, table 652). Data for 2006 are a projection taken from U.S. Census Bureau (1999, 411, Table 650).

the most capable, most advantaged segment of the female workforce, couldn't manage, how on earth could women without high-powered spouses or high-level connections, much less her financial wherewithal, do so? But note the conventional cast to this story: social commentators (frequently women public intellectuals or policymakers) in the media and in the press describing the circumstances of women *not* able to manage, choosing to stop trying, or at least to scale back[1] (for Hughes, to a long-distance consulting role). Like these social observers, many scholars also fall unwittingly into the trap of blaming the victims, that is, the women doing the scaling back. Karen Hughes is not unique; neither are the obstacles she faced in synchronizing the multiple strands of her life.

The fact is, we in the United States are all experiencing radical—and uneven—transformations in the nature of careers, work, families, communities, gender values, and the life course. Today, most workers—men and women—are married to other workers. Most children have working mothers. Indeed, almost one-half of the workforce is now female[2] (see fig. 1.1). Moreover, the members of this new workforce tend to be older than ever before. Most workers are, like Karen Hughes, in their forties, and the leading edge of the baby boom generation will begin turning sixty in 2006. This reconfiguration of the contemporary workforce, along with increasing longevity, the aging of the baby boomers, technological advances, and the globalization of the economy, is at odds with the script of the traditional life courses of everyone: men, women, and children—regardless of age, ethnicity, gender, education, or occupation.

It's about Time examines this mismatch between outdated structures and scripts and the contemporary reality experienced by dual-earner couples. It aims to broaden our understanding of the range of occupational career and family career strategies couples use in light of the widening gap between real lives and outdated work-hour and career-path roles, rules, and regulations. Hughes's story is not simply one of a woman seeking work-family balance, of the conflicts between the pull of an exciting career and the demands of raising a teenage son. This high-powered woman has a husband who followed her career path to Washington, D.C., but was unable to reconfigure his own career there. She had a community of family and friends in Texas and no time to be with them. She is a baby boomer contemplating the future from the vantage point of middle age. And most important, she is a victim of the dearth of choices in work hours and career paths available to her, just as they are unavailable to members of working families throughout the nation. What Hughes faced, realistically, were but two options: continue her long-hour, high-demand, but also high-status and high-impact job as is or else quit cold turkey. That she chose the latter is startling precisely because it reminds us all of the starkness of the choices she—and we all—face.

Time Matters

Can we even imagine other scenarios? Or is Sylvia Ann Hewlett right: women simply, and still, have to choose between work careers and their family careers? I believe there *are* other scenarios for working men and women, but only if we change our minds and our institutions—the ways we think about and organize time. Existing work-hour and career policies and practices developed in response to the needs of the first workforce of mostly young, mostly white working-class and middle-class men, located for the most part in blue-collar (unionized) and white-collar jobs in the manufacturing sector in the first half of the twentieth century. These taken-for-granted rules of the game about work time and nonwork time (such as the notion of a weekend, a two-week vacation, sick days, a five-day workweek, and a standardized retirement) are out of step with the new workforce that consists as much of women as men from a range of cultural backgrounds, of workers (men and women) without homemakers to manage their child-care and elder-care responsibilities, of people of all ages and stages, including growing numbers of older workers wanting to scale back on hours and demands but not actually retire; and, increasingly, of workers who are either currently married to other workers or will be so at some point in their life course. The average worker today is a member of a two-earner couple, trying, like Karen Hughes, to synchronize two occupational careers: his and hers, along with their family careers—but without Hughes's resources and connections. This new workforce faces additional challenges at home and at work, but policy response has been minimal at best. We can think of other possibilities for Karen Hughes, her husband, and the millions of Americans like her with too much to do and too little time to do it, often with the need and desire to be at two places at once. But to reframe her (and all of our) options requires understanding what has changed, what has not changed, and what needs to change. Let me be clear: This book does not offer any quick fix or simple solutions. Major work-hour and career policy innovation is a long-term project, involving governments, organizations, employers, unions, the media, communities, families, employees, and retirees. What is required is recognition that the culture and infrastructure of time embedded in work and in career paths can be changed. What is required is recognition of the need to begin.

What creates the contemporary career dilemmas faced by so many in today's workforce is the fact that occupational career paths remain predicated on a single-earner per family (breadwinner) template: a continuous, linear, full-time march up a career ladder or at least toward seniority and security. Key to this formulation is the backup provided by full-time homemakers who, in the past, managed the nonwork aspects of workers' lives. This outdated lockstep template is slowly changing but not always in ways that benefit the growing numbers of single-parent and dual-earner families. Moreover, moving to a global, highly competitive information economy has meant that career ladders and prospects are now less predictable, secure, or stable than was the case since the Great Depression of the 1930s. The old contract between employers and employees (the often informal trade-off awarding security to workers with seniority in return for their hard work and commitment) is quickly disappearing for all workers, in all occupations, and in all sectors of the economy.

This book is about couples and careers, about how members of two-earner families manage their two (paid) work careers along with their conjoint family career, given the hidden infrastructure of time embedded in jobs and occupational paths, a rigid and arcane network of ideas and institutions that permeate virtually every aspect of contemporary culture. I call this culture and infrastructure of time—around the workday, workweek, workyear, and life course—*hidden*, precisely because it is so deeply embedded in our taken-for-granted systems of meaning: the ways we act and the ways we expect others to act. We literally take as givens all the timetables providing order and routine to our lives: commute time, school time, work time, lunchtime, family time, holiday time, vacation time, overtime, free time, dinnertime, sleep time, and (as my three-year-old grandson says) wake-up time. The career path is itself a time belt: people feel on- or off-time in completing their schooling, in occupational entry and reentry, in promotions, in job shifts, in plateaus, in retirement. We present findings from the *Cornell Couples and Career Study*[3] to show how working couples strategize to manage two jobs and a family in a political and organizational climate better geared to life in the middle of the twentieth century (and the single-earner family) than the beginning of the twenty-first. We show that in doing so these vanguard couples—mostly middle-class professionals not unlike the Hughes family—experience both successes and strains. Moreover, we find—even among this front-line group most apt to endorse gender equality and most advantaged in terms of status, earnings, and opportunities—that they commonly reproduce neotraditional (dual-earner) variants of traditional gender divisions and long-standing gender inequalities. We document specific business policies and work conditions that expand or constrain the options available to contemporary couples at all stages of the life course, finding that working in different organizational environments affects both employees and their spouses. Our evidence pointing to the importance of the organizational environment in shaping dual-earner families' strategies, strains, and successes provides a backdrop for considering various policy innovations (policy leads) as well as existing policy lags in both the public and private sectors.[4]

While single mothers and singles also confront the mismatch between prevailing policies and their needs or goals, we focus here on the largest segment of the changing workforce: members of *working couples*—those in which both spouses (or partners) are in the labor force—drawing on data from telephone interviews conducted (separately) with both members of 835 middle-class dual-earner couples in 1998–99 (for an overview of the study and a description of the sample, see the appendix). The study includes 811 heterosexual couples, both married and cohabiting couples in marriagelike relationships (we treat them as if married but also look for potential differences)—and a small sample ($n = 18$ couples) of same-sex couples. Each of these couples has a partner working at one of seven organizations in upstate New York. This sampling strategy enabled us to link couples with specific workplace policies, practices, and cultures. To flesh out the survey findings, we also conducted fourteen focus groups at the participating organizations ($n = 112$ workers) and undertook intensive interviews with an additional 160 people (of whom seventy-eight were members of couples). These provide a deeper understanding of individuals' values, beliefs, and expectations from their own vantage point.

This book is not about time *use*; we have no time diaries charting the details of daily life minute by minute, hour by hour. But it is about *time*. Time frames are mostly created by people. It is true that the twenty-four-hour day is one revolution of the earth, the month is tied to lunar phases, and the year is the time it takes the earth to circle the sun. But the seven-day week is a social invention, as is the five-day, forty-hour workweek (which is itself a product of the Fair Labor Standards Act, enacted in 1938). The lockstep march through the life course— from schooling to adult work and family roles to retirement—simply reflects the invention and establishment of institutions: universal education, occupational career paths, occupational status hierarchies, the positions of breadwinner and full-time homemaker, gender divisions of labor, and retirement. Time is a commodity—to be saved, spent, lost, used, savored, counted, allocated, given away, billed, and traded for money. Time is both a resource (when we have it) and a constraint (when we have to spend it on things we do not like, have too little, or too much of it). Time is subjective as much as it is objective, passing all too slowly or flying by. There are cultural norms about timing—the right time to get married, get a job, have a child, retire, and also to start the workday, eat lunch, commute, and take time off. Norms about time itself exist as well—about using it effectively, not wasting it, scheduling it, organizing it, and filling it with activities. But people do not, as economists suggest, always allocate their time in the ways that they desire. We show that members of dual-earner couples have time preferences at variance with their own experiences—for less work (see Clarkberg and Merola, chap. 3; Hutchens and Dentinger, chap. 16 in this volume)—and for having a child (Altucher and Williams, chap. 4). People locate subjective turning points in time (Wethington, Pixley, and Kavey, chap. 11), see themselves as managing time (Orrange, Firebaugh, and Heck, chap. 10), and find strains and positive emotions "spilling over" from one time, one setting to another time, another setting (Roehling, Moen, and Batt, chap. 7).

The ways people spend time change over time. Marin Clarkberg and Stacey Merola (chap. 3) along with Phyllis Moen and Stephen Sweet (chap. 2) show that leisure time and paid work time vary over the life course. Clarkberg and Merola find that when wives put in long hours on workdays, both spouses have more leisure on nonwork days. Moen and Sweet show that, in contrast to their wives' experiences, there is little change in men's work hours, regardless of their life stage, prior to retirement. Sonya Williams and Shin-Kap Han (chap. 6) chart various time trajectories of occupational patterning from conventional, static, and steady to intermittent and volatile. Time past is reflected in prior choices, as Joy E. Pixley and Phyllis Moen (chap. 12) chronicle in their analysis of career priorities, and in prior experiences, as Elaine Wethington, Joy E. Pixley and Allison Kavey (chap. 11) capture in their study of turning points.

And, most significant for policy innovation, institutions structure time, often creating or exacerbating, and occasionally lessening, couples' time binds. Janet Marler, Pamela S. Tolbert, and George Milkovich (chap. 15) show how time is structured in both regular and alternative or nonstandard work schedules. Robert Hutchens and Emma Dentinger (chap. 16) depict the way retirement has traditionally been structured as an all or nothing exit. Heather Hofmeister and Penny Edgell (chap. 13) demonstrate the way religion structures nonwork time. Noelle Chesley, Phyllis Moen, and Richard Shore (chap. 14) show how information and communication technologies are reorganizing the distribution and meaning of time. Monique Valcour and Rosemary Batt (chap. 19), along with Mary C. Still and David Strang (chap. 18), discuss innovative ways to refashion work-time policies and practices.

In this book we first show that, regardless of income, time is a scarce commodity in dual-earner households. With two jobs, two commutes, often long work hours, high job demands, business travel, several cars, children, ailing relatives, and/or pets, time is always an issue.

Second, we demonstrate that time is built into jobs and career paths in ways that make continuous full-time (forty or typically more hours a week) paid work the bedrock of social organization, social advancement, and security. The rhythms of days, weeks, and years, traffic, coffee shops, and television schedules, as well as production plans, timelines, work design, the provision of health insurance, pensions, and other benefits—all reflect the primacy of full-time (at least) work continuously throughout adulthood. Part-time, reduced-hour jobs with health insurance and other benefits are hard to come by; those with real prospects for advancement are rarer still. And few employers offer opportunities for phased retirement or postretirement employment.

Third, we show that the very notion of career connotes the unfolding of occupational trajectories as well as individual and family development over time. Members of couples move through their life courses in tandem, with early choices—to have children or not, to work long hours or not, to switch jobs or not, to relocate for his or her occupational advancement or not—having long-term consequences.

Thus *It's about Time* considers multiple temporal perspectives—minutes of commuting time; hours of leisure on workdays and nonwork days; the work week of individuals and couples' life biographies. We use time as a way of locating individuals and families by life stage (based on age and the presence and age of children). Time is also about the timing of experiences and expectations—of having a child or another child or of retirement; the synchronizing of two occupational careers along with a family career; and occupational career progression and trajectories.

This brings us to the fourth and final way this book is about time: we capture time lags, the mismatch between outdated occupational, corporate, and public-policy regimes and the realities of life in dual-earner households. The evidence from this study suggests that it is about time for the United States to confront the realities and needs of contemporary working couples and indeed, all members of the new workforce. To do so requires more than Band-Aid, short-term (and often shortsighted) policy remedies. We believe it is essential to reimagine and reconfigure work hours, workweeks, and occupational career paths in ways that address the widening gaps between the time needs and goals of workers and their families at all stages of the life course on one hand and the time available to them on the other.

Organization of the Volume

The book consists of three sections, each addressing various temporal dimensions of work careers, family careers and gender in a sample of middle-class, dual-earner households. The first part focuses most explicitly on time as units ranging from minutes, hours, days, and weeks to life biographies. Chapter 2 (Moen and Sweet), chapter 3 (Clarkberg and Merola), and chapter 5

(Hofmeister) chronicle the daily and weekly clocks ticking off work hours, leisure time, and commuting time. Chapter 4 (Altucher and Williams) incorporates biographical and biological clocks in analyzing the timing of parenthood. Chapter 6 (Williams and Han) documents the biographical pacing of occupational career paths as they unfold over the life course.

The second part of the book considers the personal meanings tied to time, including subjective assessments of daily spillover (Roehling, Moen, and Batt, chap. 7), and perceived control over work time and its implications for psychological well-being (Kim, Moen, and Min, chap. 8). It moves on to peoples' temporal interpretations of their own individual and couple biographies. In chapter 9 (Moen, Waismel-Manor, and Sweet), the reflections are about success in various domains. Chapter 10 (Orrange, Firebaugh, and Heck) turns to reflections concerning time management in households and its implications for success. Chapter 11 (Wethington, Pixley, and Kavey) views time from the vantage point of perceived turning points at work. This chapter, and indeed all of part two, reminds us that time is not only a simple string of events in a certain order but also people's assessments of their days, weeks, years, and lives. Chapter 12 (Pixley and Moen) underscores the significance of these assessments, as well as couple-level discrepancies in them, when depicting how married couples view the relative priority of his versus her occupational career.

The third part of the book locates individuals' and couples' time—in units of days and weeks and also in life stages and occupational career stages—in community, organizational, and policy contexts. Chapter 13 (Hofmeister and Edgell) moves to the weekend and to the neglected work-family-religion interface epitomized in the Sunday-morning rush hour. Chapter 14 (Chesley, Moen, and Shore) turns to the work-family-technology interface, assessing whether the new information technologies save time or take time. The temporal horizon then broadens even more in chapter 15 (Marler, Tolbert, and Milkovich) to consider the implications of alternative work arrangements as potential solutions to the time squeeze of working families.[5] Chapter 16 (Hutchens and Dentinger) underscores the temporal dimensions of occupational careers, considering the preferences for, but often impossibility of, reduced work hours for individuals approaching retirement. This emphasizes our core theme of time-related policy lags—institutional arrangements around work hours and career paths that have failed to keep pace with changing realities. Another lag is in the recognition of same-sex couples as a growing component of the workforce. How they manage two occupational careers and a family career in a world of invisibility or outright discrimination is the topic of chapter 17 (Mock and Cornelius). The final two chapters further flesh out the book's central message, showing how existing policies and practices no longer fit with the realities of a changing workforce. Most workers in the early twenty-first century are married to other workers. They must manage three time-absorptive careers: one at home and two at work. Chapter 18 (Still and Strang) takes time into account in the form of the time it takes to change policies to become more family friendly. Chapter 19 (Valcour and Batt) and the epilogue (Moen) conclude with what is our bottom line: in light of a changing workforce and the mismatch between it and existing policies and practices, it is about time for fundamental changes in the organization, design, and reward structure of work, work hours, and occupational career paths.

The authors of these chapters are all affiliates of the Cornell Careers Institute, an Alfred P. Sloan Center for the Study of Working Families. Together, we designed *The Cornell Couples and Careers Study* to incorporate the distinctive interests and contributions of outstanding sociologists and demographers (David Strang, Elaine Wethington, Pamela S. Tolbert, Shin-Kap Han, Phyllis Moen, Penny Edgell, Lindy B. Williams, Robert M. Orrange, and Stephen Sweet); psychologists (Steven Cornelius, Patricia Roehling, Jungmeen Kim, and Richard P. Shore); economists (Robert M. Hutchens, Francille Firebaugh, George T. Milkovich, and Ramona K. Z. Heck); and labor and industrial relations and human resources specialists (Rosemary Batt and Bickley Townsend). As important, this interdisciplinary group of both established and young scholars is collaborating with a new generation of equally interdisciplinary predoctoral fellows at the Cornell Careers Institute (Kristine A. Altucher, Noelle Chesley, Emma Dentinger, Heather Hofmeister, Janet H. Marler, Stacey S. Merola, Steven E. Mock, Hyunjoo Min, Joy E. Pixley, Mary C. Still, P. Monique Valcour, Ronit Waismel-Manor, and Sonya Williams) to broaden the framing of careers, work-family, gender, and time. As a consequence, *It's about Time* is not a collection of unrelated chapters but instead tells a story.

Key Life Course Themes

The work-family interface in dual-earner couples consists of fluid, ever-changing relationships: his job changes, her job changes, their family changes, and they both grow older (if not wiser). Our life course theoretical framework captures this dynamic aspect of work and family careers,[6] emphasizing roles, relationships, and how they intersect with gender and with the outdated infrastructure of time undergirding contemporary experiences of work, work hours, and careers. The book highlights five important life course themes. Part one, with its focus on clocks and careers, introduces the concepts of linked lives, adaptive strategies, and work and family career dynamics. The second part examines concepts related to personal meanings in the form of role quality, spillover, overloads, and other subjective assessments. Part three emphasizes the multilayered contexts in which dual-earner couples operate, a fundamental theme permeating the entire volume. We focus especially on four contexts: gender, life stage, the political and cultural climate in the seven participating organizations from which we drew our sample, and the societalwide mismatch between the new workforce and out-of-date rules and regimes. This broader policy context forms the basis for the suggestions in the epilogue, which lays out the need to join the career dilemma issue in both public and corporate arenas. We believe the agenda should not be about women and work, or work and family, or even work life, but on the infrastructure of time as it is embedded in work-hour and career-path policies and practices that constrain all workers' options, along with the options of all families, at all stages of the life course.

Linked Lives

The degree to which the study of the work-family interface and of careers has focused on the circumstances of individuals is surprising. Our theme of linked lives illustrates the ways in which career decision making is always a social-relational process. We focus in this book on how the decisions of husbands and wives in middle-class, dual-earner households impinge on each other's life chances and choices.[7] Together, couples choose jobs, homes, parenthood, work hours, leisure, geographical moves, and commutes. But, as we show, this continues to be a gendered process. Other members of people's social networks—their children, parents and other relatives, friends and neighbors, coworkers, and employers—also shape their life paths. Because there is such a strong tradition of women as the family kin keepers and care providers, women's biographies tend to be embedded in, and structured by, the experiences and expectations of husbands, children, and aging parents, as well as coworkers and employers. Motherhood and other forms of dependent caregiving epitomize the linked lives of women. Having a first, second, or third child or having an ailing or infirm parent often leads to changes in women's work hours and their psychological investment in their jobs.[8] Being part of a two-earner couple also shapes women's life courses. For example, as Sonya Williams and Shin-Kap Han show in chapter 6, husbands' occupational paths have enormous consequences for women's own career trajectories.[9]

Men's lives are also embedded in the lives of others. Breadwinner norms along with coworker and employer expectations often propel men into working long hours on the job. And having wives who work only part time or even drop out of the workforce to take care of family and household responsibilities tends to facilitate men's own career development.[10]

Part one emphasizes the importance of locating the idea of linked lives within the context of gender. Even when both spouses subscribe to the value of gender equity, couples must still juggle two paid careers along with their family career, often reconstructing conventional gendered distributions of paid work, house-work, leisure, and life course patterns."[11] One spouse's opportunities and con-straints invariably affect the choices and options of the other. The notion of linked lives captures this gendered interdependency between partners as they experience—and negotiate—their work hours, free time, housework, geographical moves, and occupational paths, as well as whether and when to become parents.

Adaptive Strategies

The strategies couples adopt to manage their multiple obligations constitute another key theme of *The Cornell Couples and Careers Study*. By "strategies" we mean the choices individuals and couples make (as workers and as family members) under conditions of constraint. A household is a "role budget center,"[12] operating as a unit to allocate family members' time and energy.[13] In periods of social stability, the choices about whether and when to have children, work for pay, move for a promotion, and work long hours are taken-for-granted decisions based on conventional cultural (and gendered) templates. But in times of rapid social change, these conventional templates frequently become out of date. This means that couples must devise their own modes of adaptation. One adaptive strategy documented by Kristine Altucher and Lindy B. Williams (chap. 4) is postponing or choosing not to embark on parenthood or to have a second or third child. Other strategies may mean unexpectedly following neotraditional gender paths. For example, Stephen Sweet and Phyllis Moen (chap. 2) find that even the egalitarian couples in this study sample may decide that the woman and not the husband will reduce her work hours when they have children, based on the man's comparative advantage in earnings and advancement, a comparative advantage whose roots can be traced to, among other things, the fact that husbands are still more apt to follow the lockstep breadwinner model of continuous, full-hour (or even long-hour) employment throughout adulthood.[14] Marin Clarkberg and Stacey Merola (chap. 3) describe similar gendered choices around leisure, as do Heather Hofmeister about commute time and Joy Pixley and Phyllis Moen about career priorities. And Sonya Williams and Shin-Kap Han (chap. 6) track the long-term (and gendered) consequences of work force and occupational continuity and change. But decisions in this domain are made in an environment fraught with gender expectations and structural constraints about breadwinning and caregiving, along with the fact that women typically earn less than men and are less likely to advance occupationally. These realities color couples' decision-making processes, and individual decisions in couple settings are often made in the context of the other partner's decisions.[15] We seek to capture this complex tension between choice and constraint in family strategies in the chapters of part one.

Work and Family Career Dynamics

"Career" connotes the orderly flow of persons through a variety of institutions,[16] but it most frequently describes occupational pathways. Most people think of a career as systematic movement either up a job ladder or through various tiers of seniority, a progression characteristic of white, middle-class or skilled blue-collar men in the booming economy emerging in the years following World War II. But the typical career paths of women, immigrants, and minorities have always involved moving in and out of the workforce, in and out of various types of jobs.[17] In this book we use the term "career" to chronicle the dynamic progression of individuals and couples along various role pathways. The very notion of career captures the importance of time, as individuals and couples move through life. Work-family researchers traditionally study what amounts to snapshots of data on individuals or families at single points in time. Occupational researchers tend to focus exclusively on the world of work. Family researchers concentrate on marriage and parenting in the cross section or, more rarely, over time. These studies of single life paths, such as occupational careers or marriage careers, neglect the dynamics of the multiple, interdependent pathways related to work, family, education, leisure, religion, and community that individuals—and couples—follow.[18] In chapter 6, Sonya Williams and Shin-Kap Han use fine-grained life history analysis and sophisticated methodology to capture the forked, but linked, roads of husbands and wives.

Personal Meanings

Roles—institutionalized blueprints for behavior for those occupying certain positions (for example, as employee, parent, husband, wife)—also exist in both shared societal and personal interpretations and expectations about work, family, careers, and the life course. Roles provide social contacts, social identity, and social status, giving purpose, meaning, and guidance to life.[19] Members of couples where both partners are paid workers as well as spouses (and possibly parents) may enjoy enhanced economic security, purchasing power, and life quality. But occupying multiple roles also raises the odds of people experiencing role conflicts and spillover as one set of role obligations contests with or carries over into another. The very nature of work and family roles can produce incompatible pressures.[20] In the chapters that follow, we address a number of questions about couples' work and family roles: What are the strategies that couples use to manage the multiple dimensions of their lives? How do they deal with the interdependency and the interlocking nature of their job and family roles over the life course? What are the meanings of various role arrangements in terms of people's sense of success and well-being? Meanings can also take the form of a sense of personal control over one's life; individuals and couples experience cycles of control as they respond to changing needs, goals, and resources over their life courses, seeking to match one with the other.

Contexts

A life course approach investigates people's life paths as they play out in historical context as well as in the situational circumstances and chance events shaping them. Contemporary dual-earner couples are living in a historical time period when they are the norm. Recall that over half the workforce is currently married to (or partnered with) another worker. This represents an enormous societal and workplace transformation. Still, jobs, career paths, community services, and family life remain structured in ways that assume that workers have someone else to take care of households, personal affairs, children, and aged or infirm relatives. In middle-class families in the middle of the twentieth century, this typically was the wife. The realities of today's workforce—workers with working spouses, single parents, single workers, aging workers—make the old rules of the game (at home and at work) out of date. For a while, society defined this as a dilemma confronting the women moving into or remaining in the workforce in the 1960s, '70s, and '80s. Today we recognize that most workers—men and women—have to cope with the career dilemma embedded in old ways of thinking about and structuring time. Outdated policies and practices in both the public and private sectors are crucial contexts in which to locate dual-earner couples who constitute the majority of the new workforce.

The Policy Context

Having both spouses employed alters the traditional family budgeting of time and energy, as well as the organizational arrangements responding to them. Eventually, new blueprints for living will become part of the institutional landscape. But this is a time of policy lag when the infrastructure of policies and practices defining work time and occupational careers is at odds with the time needs of workers associated with other, nonwork dimensions of their life courses.[21] Because of this lag, employees, be they men or women, have to adapt to a system that assigns the highest priority to paid work, largely ignores unpaid family work, and provides only a one-way, lockstep march to a one-way retirement. Schools, medical services, and community activities continue to operate as if an adult is available in every family during the workday and on call at all times. And, in line with the outdated breadwinner-homemaker blueprint, domestic life remains largely the province of women. Work itself is changing; there is growing evidence that workers are putting in more hours on the job than in the 1950s or 1970s, and more are engaged in contingent or contract work.[22] Long hours are encouraged by a culture of occupational attainment equating time on the job with productivity and by an environment of mergers, downsizing, and bankruptcies that both instills job insecurity and increases the burden on workers who survive with jobs intact.[23]

To date, corporate, union, and government policy initiatives addressing the needs and values of the new workforce have been remarkably unimaginative, even among otherwise visionary CEOs, organized labor leaders, chief executives, and legislatures at both the state and national levels. Evidence from our focus groups and in-depth interviews shows that even workers themselves define the dilemmas of working families, of older workers confronting retirement, and of the growing numbers of workers on uncertain and insecure career paths as private troubles rather than as societal issues. In the middle of the twentieth century the nation fashioned bold solutions to the challenges confronting the primary (white, male, middle class or unionized) workforce—Unemployment Insurance, Social Security, work and hour laws, health insurance, disability benefits, Medicare, the G. I. Bill, OSHA protections, private and public pensions, and security linked to seniority. Similar imaginative innovations for the challenges confronting the new workforce are conspicuously absent from the contemporary policy agenda at any level (public, union, or corporate; local, organizational, or national). Moreover, even existing, established supports to workers, families, and communities portend to unravel. At the same time, a changing economy serves to reinforce policy prescriptions about working longer, working harder, working smarter in order to move ahead or even to retain one's job, creating a real career dilemma for working families. *It's about Time* chronicles the implications of this failure of imagination to address the fundamental mismatch between the needs and goals of the new workforce, on the one hand and arcane time (day, week, year, career) policies on the other. We show, even among middle-class, dual-earner families (arguably the best equipped to deal with the mismatch), evidence of persisting gender inequality in earnings and attainment, but also persisting gender inequality in hours on the paid job at work and the unpaid job at home, in strain, spillover, and psychological well-being; and we show evidence as well of hard choices to have fewer children or even to remain childless, to retire cold turkey or not, to move across the state or nation or not, to scale back on hours and commitment or not, to consider a new job or not, to prioritize his or her job, or neither—all in order to better manage work and family career exigencies.

Findings throughout this volume suggest that simple assumptions about the work-family interface portray a very limited snapshot of a much more complicated, variegated phenomenon. *The Cornell Couples and Careers Study* offers insight into the life-course challenge to contemporary thinking and courses of action. We demonstrate the need for new social inventions, new theoretical and policy models better geared to a world undergoing profound sociocultural shifts in virtually every dimension and segment of the life course. The chapters in this book provide windows at different angles and levels from which to view couples' contemporary lives as well as the dearth of policies addressing their time needs and preferences.

PART ONE

TIME STRATEGIES

2

Time Clocks: Work-Hour Strategies

Phyllis Moen and Stephen Sweet

> I returned to work full time when my daughter was 10 weeks old. I worked full time for about four months, five months maybe, and I said, "I'm sorry, this isn't working." [laughs] But the thing is, when my husband and I got married, we both got married with the understanding that we would work and have a child, and I couldn't very well go back on my understanding that I had with my husband, and financially we were not in a position for me to not work at all. So I now work 30 hours.
>
> —a twenty-eight-year-old marketer at a manufacturing company married to a forty-three-year-old director of a human services organization (they have a three-year-old child and a fourteen-year-old stepchild from his previous marriage)

In contemporary society, family and work roles are at odds with one another.[1] As a consequence, many dual-earner couples adapt to the demands of their two jobs by postponing childbearing and reducing family size. A few couples (those who both prefer and can afford it) hire surrogate "wives" in the form of nannies, au pairs, or domestic help.[2] All of these strategies share in common a bending of family structure or functioning to accommodate workplace demands in a world where organizations still operate on a breadwinner template of occupational paths.

We focus here on another form of adaptation: partners' strategic choice of work hours to manage the challenges of their dual-earner lives. We investigate the likelihood of couples adopting various work-hour arrangements in light of their gender orientations, occupational career demands, family obligations, and life stage. We also assess the degree to which work-hour arrangements predict partners' experiences inside and outside the workplace, including various strains and resources (energy levels, free time, workload, and satisfaction with family and marital relationships). But this also works in reverse—strains and resources shape work hours as well. For example, one spouse's high income may permit the other spouse to scale back on his or her own hours on the job.

Couples negotiate and adopt various work-hour strategies in an attempt to manage the demands imposed by each of their job and career prospects, and their family. They do so in terms of their goals and values related to gender, work, community, and family. Thus, the choices they make reflect (1) each spouse's own personal preferences, power, and occupational opportunities; (2) prevailing cultural expectations (regarding gender, work, community, and family); and (3) the reality of the hidden infrastructure of the labor market: the continuous forty-hour-plus work week for "good" jobs and career attainment.[3] Having both spouses work long hours leaves little time for anything else, including raising children. But raising children remains a gendered activity. We therefore expect different work-hour choices for each spouse at various life stages, given their changing gender expectations, resources, and obligations at various points in the family cycle. These different work-hour strategies, in turn, may have varying effects on each spouse's workload, free time, energy, and satisfaction with family relationships, again depending on shared meanings and couples' stage in the life course. Given the outdated structure of work and occupational career paths, there is likely no single "best" adaptive strategy for all couples but rather a variety of strategies that offer mixed rewards and costs and that may well shift throughout the life course.[4]

In this chapter, we address issues central to understanding couples' work-hour strategies. First, we chart diversity of work-hour strategies among dual-earner, middle-class couples in *The Cornell Couples and Careers Study*. Second, we investigate couple-level factors that predict particular strategies. Specifically, we focus on the combined influence of (his and her) jobs, gender values, and life stage. Third, we assess possible life quality correlates of different work-hour strategies. We conclude with an overview of implications for policy and for future research.

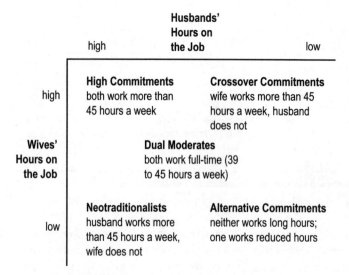

Figure 2.1 Potential work-hour strategies of dual-earner couples.

Types of Work-Hour Adaptive Strategies

"Strategy" implies a means to an end, given specific opportunities and constraints. In the middle of the twentieth century, couples who could afford to do so adopted the taken-for-granted strategy of managing potentially conflicting work and family obligations by decoupling them, adopting the breadwinner-homemaker template, with husbands doing the breadwinning and wives doing the homemaking. But this (now outdated) blueprint provides little guidance for contemporary couples who want or need to have both spouses in the workforce. Given the lag between the realities of two-earner households and the conventional model of occupational career development (continuous forty-hour-plus work throughout adulthood), couples in the twenty-first century are having to devise their own stop-gap solutions.

Figure 2.1 offers a typology of hypothetical arrangements. *High commitment* couples are heavily invested in workplace activities, with both partners putting in long hours on the job. These couples are typically in high-powered occupations, on the fast track of professional or managerial careers.

Both partners in *alternative commitment* couples, either by choice or because they lack the opportunity, devote comparatively less time as a couple to paid work. These couples have one partner who works at most a regular full-time workweek (not long hours), and the other working even less. These couples hypothetically have more time to invest in activities outside their jobs, including family care and personal pursuits.

Table 2.1   Dual-Earner Middle-Class Couples' Work-Hour Strategies[a]

Work-Hour Strategy	His Work Hours	Her Work Hours	Percentage	N
High commitments	45+	45+	21.2	170
Dual moderates	39–45	39–45	13.0	104
Neotraditionalists	45+	<45	38.5	308
Crossover commitments	<45	45+	10.7	86
Alternate commitments	One partner works less than 39 hours, the other works no more than 45 hours		16.6	133

[a] From *Cornell Couples and Careers Study*, 1998–99. N = 801.

Based on prior research on a national sample,[5] we place *dual moderate* couples at the central point in this typology; these are couples with both partners working full-time, but not more than forty-four hours a week. Spouses in these couples allocate roughly equal time to their jobs. Having both partners work regular hours means each spouse has a job with benefits and possibly opportunities for advancement. However, neither partner in this category works long hours (forty-five hours or more a week), which is increasingly what employers expect of committed employees.

The previous three strategies are symmetrical, in that both partners are investing in their jobs to roughly the same degree. By contrast, neotraditional and crossover commitment couples represent compensatory strategies, with partners dividing commitments. In both types, one spouse invests in more hours in paid work while the other remains less engaged. *Neotraditional* couples adopt a variant of traditional gender divisions, with husbands working longer hours and their wives working fewer hours. Research finds, not surprisingly, that wives in neotraditional arrangements assume greater responsibility for family tasks, as well as carrying more of the emotional burdens at home.[6] In contrast, *crossover commitment* couples invert traditional gender schema, with wives putting in more hours than their husbands.

We move away from simple part-time/full-time distinctions, given that so many workers are putting in long hours at work. We base our dividing points using a grounded theoretical approach,[7] examining distributions in the data and testing alternative approaches before arriving at the typology presented in table 2.1.

Most typically dual-earner middle-class couples adopt a neotraditional strategy. Husbands in the *Cornell Couples and Careers Study* work on average 8.9 hours more than their wives, revealing the continued salience of gender in the configuration of work-hour arrangements. Almost two in five (38.5%) dual-earner couples follow a neotraditional model, with husbands working approximately

54.1 hours and their wives 33.8 hours a week. This produces an average discrepancy of 20.3 hours a week between spouses, almost equivalent to three eight-hour workdays each week.

But there are a wide variety of arrangements. One in five (21.1%) are high commitment couples, with both partners working more than forty-five hours a week. This represents an average of approximately fifty-six hours for husbands and fifty-four hours for wives. Combined, these couples are working on average 110 hours per week, nearly the equivalent of three full-time workers.[8]

Few (16.6%) couples have one or both spouses working fewer than thirty-nine hours a week, with neither putting in long hours, following an alternative commitment path. This also is a gendered pattern, with husbands in this category putting in almost 40.4 hours on average and their wives working approximately 28.4 hours a week. This twelve-hour difference between spouses makes it clear that typically the wife, not the husband, works a reduced-hour workweek. But note that husbands in this category, by defintion, put in fewer hours than most husbands in our sample.

Although our culture maintains the fiction of a forty-hour workweek, only a surprisingly small proportion (13.0%) of these couples can be characterized as dual moderates, with both spouses working "regular" (between thirty-nine and forty-five) hours. Among those who do, wives work an average of 42.4 hours a week and husbands 43.1, a difference of less than one hour.

Least prevalent are crossover commitment couples—wives working longer hours than their husbands (10.7%). In these couples, husbands average only 40.1 hours a week and their wives work on average over 54.6 hours a week. These women typically work about fifteen hours more than their husbands, a smaller difference than in neotraditional couples but large nonetheless.

Clearly there is no prevailing dual-earner work-hour strategy among middle-class couples in *The Cornell Couples and Careers Study*. But almost two in five adopt the neotraditional approach.[9] Somewhat less common is the high commitment strategy; one in five couples have both partners working long hours. What is relatively scarce are the dual moderate couples, with both partners working "regular" full-time schedules. Rare also are crossover commitment couples, who invert gender norms with wives working longer hours than their husbands, and the alternative commitment couples in which both partners combined put in the fewest hours (on average fewer than seventy hours a week).

Predicting Work-Hour Strategies

We theorize that couples adopt particular work-hour strategies in response to their preferences and values, as well as in light of institutional and gender expectations and possibilities. Given that most jobs are organized around full-time or more hours, there are few reduced work-hour options for those seeking occupational advancement, health and other insurance benefits, or even job security. But, as we have seen, many couples opt for one spouse to work long hours at a "good" (one with benefits) job and for the other to work less. Still, most workers and most couples would like either one or both partners to work less (on average 12.4 fewer hours for husbands and 11.9 fewer hours for wives). We concentrate on three sets of factors predicting couples' actual work-hour arrangements: occupational demands and rewards, both partners' gender values, and couples' life stage. To assess which couples are most apt to adopt particular work-hour strategies, we performed a series of logistic regressions.[10] We include in our model four key couple-level predictors: both spouses' occupational levels, job prestige, gender orientations, and life stage.

Occupational Career Demands and Rewards

Choosing jobs and choosing work hours are both strategic adaptations on the part of couples seeking to mesh two lives together and to mesh these lives with lives of their children. Some occupations necessitate considerable time commitments, acting as a usurper of couples' time. Such is the case with managers, who tend to work longer hours than other professionals. When both partners are managers, we expected couples to pursue a high commitment strategy. Contrary to our expectations, we find that they are twice as likely (compared to when she only is a manager or neither are managers) to follow a neotraditional lifestyle (a visual representation of these findings is available at www.life-course.cornell.edu/about_time.html, table 2.2). In other words, in some cases both spouses are managers, but the husband works long hours and the wife works considerably less. Couples in which she is a manager and he is not are much less likely than dual managers to pursue a neotraditionalist work-hour strategy. This makes sense, given the heavy demands her career imposes and the likely lower demands of his career. Couples in which he is a manager and she is not are only one-third (0.33) as likely to adopt a crossover commitment work-hour arrangement that prioritizes the wife's career in terms of work hours. In the case in which neither partner is a manager, couples are more than twice (2.20) as likely to adopt an alternative commitment strategy compared to dual manager couples.

We also expected job prestige to dictate certain work-hour strategies. High-status, highly rewarding jobs can act as time magnets, both requiring and fostering high levels of commitment and, correspondingly, long hours (even if not necessarily mandated by job tasks). Whether both spouses have high-prestige jobs should figure into their work-hour adaptive strategies.[11] We find that partners who both have high-prestige jobs are almost three times more likely (than other couples) to follow a high commitment work-hour arrangement. By contrast, couples in which he has a high-prestige job and she does not are almost twice as likely to follow a neotraditional strategy and slightly less likely (1.69) to adopt an alternative commitment work-hour strategy. Couples in which the wife has a high-prestige job and the husband does not tend to adopt dual moderate or alternative commitment strategies. When neither spouse has a high-prestige job, couples are nearly twice as likely (1.86) (as those who both hold high-prestige jobs) to follow a crossover commitment strategy. Compared to couples who both hold high-prestige jobs, couples in which she has a high-prestige job and he does not are nearly twice as likely (1.81) to adopt a dual moderate strategy, and over one and one-half times as likely (1.69) to adopt an alternative commitment strategy. Clearly, occupational circumstances matter for couples' work-hour strategies, reflecting both prior opportunities and choices along with the hidden infrastructure of various occupations and positions that virtually dictate long or at least full-time hours on the job.

Gender Orientations

To borrow a metaphor first offered by Max Weber,[12] values and norms operate like switchmen guiding the responses of couples down tracks in accordance with deep underlying beliefs of what is a "right" or "wrong" path of action. In the case of dual-earner couples, one of the primary values that could influence their work-hour arrangements is the degree to which each partner subscribes to traditional or egalitarian gender orientations. Such values may limit or expand the horizon of possible strategies that each partner even considers. For example, couples with traditional gender orientations are expected to be most likely to adopt the neo-traditional strategy.[13]

To capture both spouses' values, we divide the gender ideology index at the mean, identifying respondents as being more or less traditional or egalitarian in their orientations. This results in a fourfold typology of couples. As table 2.2 reveals, couples' gender orientations are strongly related to work-hour strategies. Compared to couples in which both partners hold egalitarian attitudes, we find couples in which one or both partners have traditional values are by far more likely to adopt neotraditional or alternative commitment work-hour strategies. By contrast, those with traditional gender attitudes are unlikely to adopt high commitment, dual moderate, or crossover commitment strategies.

From these analyses, it is difficult to determine which partner's gender orientation has the stronger effect or how these effects play out in relationships. The most important finding is that couples' work-hour arrangements are associated with at least one partner holding a traditional (or egalitarian) attitude and in the expected direction. Couples' own value systems play out within a broader cultural context that reaffirms gendered norms for work and family careers, prioritizing work roles for men and family roles for women, even while endorsing the notion of equality of opportunity for men and women in jobs, pay, and advancement. Thus, when both partners in dual-earner households hold traditional gender orientations, they are more than twice as likely (2.41) as couples with egalitarian attitudes to adopt a neotraditional work-hour arrangement.

Life Stage

The responsibilities and commitments associated with couples' stage in their life course can have a profound impact on their work-hour strategy. As discussed in chapter 1 and the appendix, we conceptualize life stage as reflecting age, developmental, cultural, and structural expectations and circumstances, dividing couples into seven stages based on their ages and the presence and ages of children.

What we see among younger child-free couples (under forty) is a heavy emphasis on their occupational careers, commonly adopting a work-hour strategy that usurps a great deal of each partner's time. Their strategy appears to be to devote time to maximizing both partners' occupational career development. By contrast, couples just launching their families, that is, with young children at home, are unlikely to invest long hours in both partners' jobs. In fact, couples with preschoolers are only one-fifth (0.20) as likely as those without children to adopt a high commitment strategy; those with grade-school-age children are approximately one-third (0.31) as likely, and those with high school age children are only one-half (0.48) as likely to adopt a high commitment strategy. Note as well that couples with adult children in the home (many of whom are in college) are also less likely (0.36) to be in high commitment arrangements than are those without children. It seems then, that having both spouses work long hours is a lifestyle more common to the DINCS (double income, no children) than to couples at any other life stage.

Couples who decide to have children find that child-rearing responsibilities have profound effects on their work-hour arrangements. We find couples with children at home are far more likely than nonparents to have the greatest discrepancy in husbands' and wives' work hours because wives scale back to accommodate to their families' care needs, are the least likely to adopt a demanding work-hour strategy, and are more inclined to retool their work-hour configuration to adapt to increased family demands.[14] Those with children in primary school (early establishment stage) and secondary school (late establishment stage) adopt work-hour strategies similar to those with preschoolers.

Differences in work-hour strategies by life stage are readily apparent in figure 2.2. The high commitment strategy occurs most frequently among couples with no child-rearing responsibilities regardless of age, namely the nonparent and empty nest stages. Fully two out of five (41.5%) of nonparents under age forty have a high commitment work-hour strategy, making it the most common strategy for these child-free couples in their twenties and thirties. In comparison, those

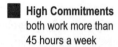

High Commitments
both work more than
45 hours a week

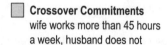

Crossover Commitments
wife works more than 45 hours
a week, husband does not

Dual Moderates
both work full-time (39 to
45 hours a week)

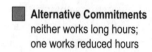

Alternative Commitments
neither works long hours;
one works reduced hours

Neotraditionalists
husband works more than 45
hours a week, wife does not

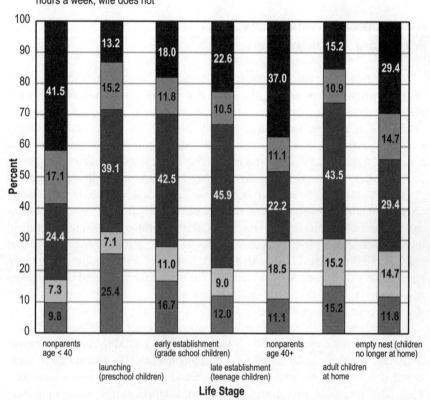

Figure 2.2 Couples' work-hour strategies by life stage. Source: *Cornell Couples and Careers Study* 1998–99. $N = 801$, $p < .01$.

with child-rearing responsibilities tend to adopt the neotraditional work-hour strategy. Approximately two out of five couples with young children have husbands working long hours and wives working shorter hours. Those with preschoolers are also the most likely to adopt an alternative commitment strategy, with neither spouse working long hours and one working reduced hours.[15]

These findings suggest the considerable impact of family circumstances on couples' work-hour arrangements.[16] They highlight the couples' shifting cycles of control (see Moen, chap. 1; Roehling, Moen, and Batt, chap. 7 in this volume); as resources and obligations change throughout the life course men and women allocate time differently. Parenthood is a real watershed transition, often pushing dual-earner couples to neotraditional arrangements, with husbands putting in long hours on the job and their wives putting in considerably less. Once children grow up and leave home, work hours may shift once more.[17]

Life-Quality Correlates of Various Work-Hour Arrangements

Thus far we have painted a picture of considerable heterogeneity in dual-earner couples' work-hour strategies. We show that part of this variation can be explained by both spouses' occupational levels and prestige, as well as their gender values and life stage. But which strategy is "best" in terms of life quality? Research on work and family typically draws on two broad theoretical approaches: role enhancement and role strain. The role enhancement perspective follows a long tradition linking involvement in social roles with emotional and physical well-being. From this perspective, men and women in dual-earner couples should have high levels of well-being regardless of their work-hour arrangements. This conforms to research linking unemployment (mostly of men) to poor mental and physical health and to research on the beneficial effects of paid work for women (compared with full-time homemaking). Moreover, research on dual-earner couples (such as that by Rosalind Barnett) demonstrates that occupying both work and family roles is positively linked to both men's and women's psychological well-being.[18]

An alternate theory, the role strain perspective, emphasizes the costs rather than the benefits of multiple roles.[19] One of the most striking portrayals of role strain and conflict can be found in Arlie Hochschild's *The Second Shift*, highlighting how the combined demands of work and family drain women's energy.[20] The role strain perspective underscores the limited time, energy, and commitment that individuals have available. From this viewpoint, couples seeking to mesh both partners' job demands along with home demands should experience conflict, overload, and strain, especially when both put in long hours. Thus, those in neotraditional or alternative arrangements should experience the least stress.

Most of existing work-family research literature assumes that the work-family interface is invariably stressful. One reason is that workplace rules and routines (the hidden infrastructure) presume that workers are free from family responsibilities. The lockstep template assumes that workers are either young and without family responsibilities or else breadwinners (men) with someone else (a wife) to take care of demands on the home front.[21] But, given that most workers today are combining work and family roles and responsibilities, the issue is not whether doing so is stressful, but the circumstances under which it is.

With the exception of the investigations by Phyllis Moen and Yan Yu and by Rosalind Barnett and Caryl Rivers,[22] few studies have looked at the effectiveness of the various work-hour adaptive strategies of dual-earner couples. Under which arrangements are members of working couples most apt to experience the highest life quality? Which arrangements at work and at home are conducive to men's, women's, and couples' well-being? How does the effectiveness of various strategic actions vary by life stage and/or by gender? Previewing the chapters in part two of this volume, we highlight here the ways in which work-hour strategies correspond with personal experience. We examine two broad sets of outcomes: effects on time demands and relationship effects on family satisfaction.

We hypothesize that strategies most closely reflecting the traditional gendered division of labor at home and at work are the most adaptive for men (with their wives doing the accommodating), given that this best fits with the male-breadwinner template embedded in the infrastructure of work, occupations, and career paths. We have no a priori expectations about the couple strategies most effective for women's life quality, but we believe that women might best benefit from arrangements providing the greatest family-related resources and supports, especially in terms of time and income.[23]

Our analysis in this chapter (as well as those throughout the book) is framed around two general assumptions. First, we believe that men and women should be studied separately (given the gendered nature of men's and women's biographies), but that husbands' and wives' careers can only be understood in tandem. Accordingly, we view work hours as a strategic couple arrangement, while simultaneously recognizing that the life-quality correlates of these arrangements will probably be very different for husbands and for wives. Second, we believe that effects are not uniform or even necessarily linear but vary by couples' location in the life course. Work-hour arrangements may have different implications for peoples' life quality depending on whether they have young or school-age children in the home, whether they are just starting out in their occupational and family careers, or whether they are moving toward retirement.

Workload

We expect a complex, two-way dynamic between workload and work hours. Some jobs simply have (or employers expect) high demands and long hours. Alternatively, the decision to scale back the amount of work time can create a compression of the time available to accomplish the many obligations imposed by an individual's job, thereby increasing the perceived workload, using an index based on three five-point Likert-scale items indicating the degree to which an individual's job requires working very hard, working very fast, and doing excessive amounts of work.

We find that both life stage and work-hour strategy predict men's assessment of their workload. Younger (under 40) child-free men, who are not yet (or may never become) parents, report the highest workload, but men's workload does not drop dramatically across the life course. Men in alternative commitment couples report the lowest workload, whereas men in both high commitment and neotraditional arrangements have the highest workload. For men, then, long work hours appear to go hand in hand with a heavy workload.

For women, too, both work-hour strategies and life stage matter for workload, each with distinctive effects. In general, workload appears to decrease throughout the life course, as indicated by comparing those at younger life stages with those at later stages. This effect is most pronounced for child-free women who are in their twenties and thirties adopting a crossover commitment strategy that is, working more hours than their spouses. But women who work more than their husbands at later life stages report significantly lower workloads. As we predicted, women in couples adopting an alternative commitment work-hour strategy report the lowest workloads throughout most of the life course. But even for this group, workloads are highest for younger child-free women.

It appears that, for both wives and for husbands, couples' work-hour strategies matters for workload regardless of life stage and that life stage matters regardless of work-hour strategy. The evidence suggests that workload tends to be highest for couples at the beginning of their work and family careers, remains quite high when children are in preschool or early school years, and declines as children leave the family and as work careers mature.[24]

Free Time

Recall that work-hour strategies reflect dual-earner couples' efforts to accommodate and satisfy both work and family demands. Because it is actually very difficult to satisfy all these demands, we expect to see three general trends related to discretionary time. First, leisure should vary according to family responsibilities, with dual-earner parents of preschoolers having less free time than those with no children, regardless of couples' work hours. Similarly, both dual-earner couples whose children are grown and child-free couples in their 40s, 50s and 60s should have more leisure time. Second, we expect women in dual-earner households to have less free time compared to husbands, given their heavier family obligations. Third, people with the highest work hours (such as couples following a high commitment strategy of both spouses working over forty-five hours a week) should report the least free time.

Our analysis supports all these proposed relationships (see also Clarkberg and Merola, chap. 3, in this volume). Women do, in fact, report having less free time on workdays (on average 1.1 hours per day, compared to 1.44 hours per day for men). Free time is lowest for women with young children (preschool, 0.66 hours; grade school, 0.61 hours), but is higher for childless workers over forty (1.9 hours) and for those whose children are grown and gone (1.9 hours). Childless women over age forty who adopt a dual moderate work-hour strategy report the most free time (2.75 hours each workday), whereas those with preschoolers and long hours (crossover commitments and high commitments strategies) report the least (0.45 and 0.65 hours, respectively).[25]

Similar shifts in free time across life stage categories hold true for men. In general, men with long hours (following high commitment and neotraditionalist strategies), report the least free time (on average 1.5 and 1.2 hours on workdays, respectively).

Work-hour strategy and life stage in combination with gender help to account for variations in free time. Women in dual moderate couples have seventeen minutes less free time each day than men following this strategy, when both spouses put in long hours. Women in high commitment couples have twenty-one minutes less free time each day. Free time is especially scarce for women with grade-school children, when the demands of children are especially high. These findings demonstrate that different work-hour strategies are associated with different leisure time for men and women (see also Clarkberg and Merola, chap. 3 in this volume).

Vitality

The obsolete breadwinner-homemaker template, which still shapes the organization of jobs, families, communities, and career paths, suggests that working women in dual-earner couples are more apt to experience stress than are working men in the same circumstance, given that women typically retain most of the family obligations in addition to the demands of their paid jobs, producing the very real possibility of conflicts, overload, and strain. We expect, therefore, that the women in this two-earner middle-class sample (especially those with children), should experience a lower sense of vitality, particularly if they have adopted a highly taxing work-hour strategy. We asked respondents to rate (on a scale of 1–10) how much energy they have had lately and found (as shown in figure 2.3) that energy levels vary considerably by life stage for women, with a slight upward trend in energy levels later in life. But this depends on work-hour strategies. Contrary to role strain theory, comparing women with preschoolers to those under age forty without children, we find that mothers of preschoolers working at least full-time hours or more (in high commitment, dual moderate, and crossover commitment couples) report higher energy levels. This suggests that being active as a parent and an employee may produce energy, in line with the role enhancement thesis. But it could well be a matter of selection. Women

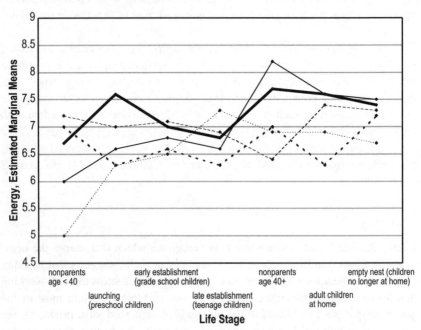

Figure 2.3 Women's assessment of energy by life stage and work-hour strategy. Source: *Cornell Couples and Careers Study* 1998–99. *N* = 801. Life Stages *p* < .01; Work.

in highly demanding jobs who have preschoolers and little energy may well shift to another work-hour strategy, leaving only those with high energy in long-hour strategies. Consistent with aspects of both the role strain and role enhancement perspectives, childless women over forty following high commitment or dual moderate strategies report the highest levels of energy (7.6 and 8.1).

Unlike women, men report similar energy levels regardless of their life stage (an average of 7.38). What matters in predicting men's energy ratings are their work-hour strategies. Specifically, men following a dual moderate strategy report the lowest energy levels (6.9), whereas men in couples adopting neotraditional, crossover commitment, and high commitment strategies report the highest energy levels (7.4, 7.4, and 7.5.). Men who work at most a forty-hour week may be doing so because they have less energy. Alternatively, their jobs may be insufficiently challenging to generate energy.

Note our findings should be interpreted with caution, in that we cannot actually track couples as they move from life stage to life stage. For example, it is entirely possible for instance, that women with preschoolers who work full time or longer hours are doing so precisely because they have high vitality. Those with less energy may have scaled back on their work hours or even left the workforce when they became parents. Our data underscore the distinctive occupational career paths of men and women, with women shifting their involvements over their life course (see Williams and Han, chap. 6 in this volume).[26]

Satisfaction with Relationships

Role enhancement and role strain may also explain any links between various work-hour strategies and partners' satisfaction with their family and marital relationships. We measure both family and marital satisfaction on five-point scales, with 5 indicating "completely satisfied" and 1 indicating "completely unsatisfied." Role strain theory posits family and marital satisfaction to be lowest for women and men with long work-hour strategies and for those with children in the home. Family and marital satisfaction should be highest for those following strategies with lower time commitments.

Figure 2.4 shows how work-hour strategies correspond with women's family satisfaction at different life stages. Women in neotraditional arrangements tend to report the same levels of family satisfaction regardless of whether they are under forty and child-free or have children at home. But women in neotraditional arrangements in later life stages, both those without children and those whose children are gone (or at least grown), are the most satisfied with their family lives.

By contrast, women in high commitment arrangements with adult children still at home report, by far, the lowest family satisfaction. Neither role strain nor role enhancement theory predicts these variations by life stage. One possible explanation could be that living with adult children poses a strain in these couples; both spouses put in long hours and perhaps expected to be free of child-related responsibilities once their children were out of high school.

Both life stage and work-hour strategies also matter for men's family satisfaction, but separately, not in combination. Men putting in relatively fewer hours (those in crossover commitment and alternative commitment arrangements) tend to report the lowest family satisfaction (4.1 and 4.0), but so do men in high commitment arrangements (4.1). In contrast, men in dual moderate and neotraditional arrangements tend to report the highest family satisfaction (4.2 and 4.2). Child-free men, regardless of age, report the highest family satisfaction, whereas those

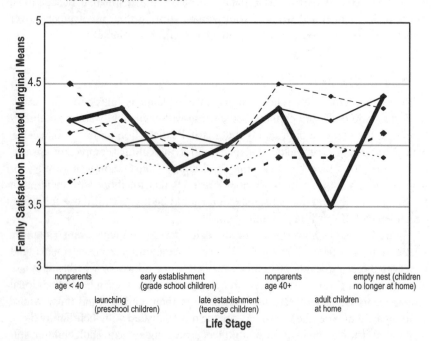

Figure 2.4 Women's family satisfaction by life stage and work. Source: *Cornell Couples and Careers Study* 1998–99. *N* = 801. Life Stages *p* < .01; Work Hours *p* < .01; Interaction *p*-not significant.

with teenage children report the lowest (3.9). It appears that people without children tend to be most satisfied with their family lives!

Work-hour strategies predict women's, but not men's, satisfaction with their marriages. Specifically, women in dual moderate and neotraditional arrangements are most satisfied with their marriages (87.0 and 87.2, on a scale of 0–100), whereas those in crossover commitment and alternative commitment arrangements have lower marital satisfaction (82.2 and 82.9).

This body of evidence suggests that work-hour strategies are correlated more with women's than men's family and marital satisfaction. This is consistent with the key theme of this book: the legacy of the infrastructure founded on the breadwinner-homemaker template perpetuates adaptive strategies that prioritize women's relationships with their children and spouses, even in dual-earner households, often at a cost to women's occupational and income attainment.

Summing Up

In this chapter we examine the types of work-hour strategies that dual-earner couples adopt, the factors predicting who is likely to adopt these strategies, and some personal experiences related to them. What we see are a range of work-hour strategies across dual-earner households, depending on life stage. Most common is the neotraditional strategy, a modification of the breadwinner-homemaker template developed in industrialized economies of the nineteenth and twentieth centuries. This strategy reflects the ways many contemporary couples accommodate to the policy lags in the hidden infrastructure manifest in the social organization and expectations related to paid and unpaid work, occupational career paths, community services, families, and child-rearing.[27] It is easiest, in light of these lags, for couples to adopt a slight modification of the preexisting breadwinner-homemaker template, with husbands putting in far more hours than their wives and wives working less on the job and more in the second shift at home. The prevailing view of dual-earner couples—two people spending long hours on their jobs (high commitment strategy)—is common only for those without children.

Given the weight of the prevailing infrastructure of work life and family life, women in couples adopting the neotraditional strategy tend to be among those reporting the highest family satisfaction, lowest workload, highest energy, and most free time throughout the life course. However, it is important to recognize that this adaptive strategy also is likely to have deleterious effects on women's occupational careers, with possible long-term consequences in terms of their status, advancement, and job security (see also Hutchens and Dentinger, chap. 16 in this volume). Joy Pixley and Phyllis Moen (chap. 12 in this volume) describe the ways in which giving priority to one spouse's occupational career often reproduces conventional gender schemas. In light of the evidence in this and the remaining chapters, we believe public- and private-sector policies and practices need to foster a range of alternative life-course paths, organizing both work and careers in ways that do not penalize the growing number of workers with both job and family interests and responsibilities.

What we show here and in part two is that simple assumptions about positive or negative ties between employment and well-being portray a very limited snapshot of a complicated relationship. For example, people who do not have children report the greatest family satisfaction, and mothers of preschoolers in high commitment work-hour arrangements rate themselves high on energy. We obviously need new theoretical models that move beyond the limited role strain and role enhancement orientations, a model focusing on the trajectories of couples' career paths, work hours, and well-being over the life course. Understanding the linkages between partners' careers and how couples strategically respond to the challenges of synchronizing work and family responsibilities in a world geared to their strict division is key to shaping policies that work for the twenty-first century.

3

Competing Clocks:
Work and Leisure

Marin Clarkberg and Stacey S. Merola

It is a familiar refrain: an increasing number of Americans report that they are "rushed," "stressed," or otherwise "crunched for time."[1] Yet studies of trends in work hours conflict as to whether U.S. workers are actually working more hours and experiencing less leisure than they were two or three decades before.[2] The disparity between Americans' impressions of increasingly frenetic lifestyles and the data, which show no substantial increases in work hours for the average individual, may stem, in part, from the great demographic shift away from breadwinner-homemaker households described in chapter 1.[3] Since the 1960s, U.S. society has changed from one in which most workers had a partner at home who was dedicated primarily to the tasks of household and family maintenance to a world in which only a small minority of workers do. Instead, workers are increasingly married to other workers. Debates that center on the measurement of individual-level averages are missing the point—the time squeeze is largely a family-level phenomenon.

By focusing on the couple household as the unit of analysis, *The Cornell Couples and Careers Study* gives us a new and unique opportunity to understand the relationships between work time and leisure in a population of those most susceptible—and perhaps most afflicted—by the pressures of competing clocks: dual-earner couples at the top of the occupational hierarchy.[4] By examining the interrelationship of work hours, leisure time, and perceptions of not having enough time, we can begin to understand how the level and balance of work hours between partners contributes to the sense of long work hours, the desire to cut back, and the amount of time allowed for leisure in families at various stages along the life course.

Conceptualizing Time Use: Work, Overwork, and Leisure

Scholars have documented—and hotly debated—aggregate trends in work hours with a variety of data sources. The question is straightforward: Are Americans working more than they have in the past? But the answer is not as clear and contradictory findings have been hotly contested. For example, Juliet Schor contends in her best-selling 1991 book *The Overworked American* that working women were putting in 305 hours per year more in 1987 than in 1969 and working men 98 hours more per year. Replying directly to Schor's work but with different data, researchers John Robinson and Geoffery Godbey find that employed men and women worked less in 1985 than in 1965; employed women dropping from approximately thirty-seven hours per week in 1965 to only thirty-one in 1985, and men dropping from forty-six to forty hours per week, on average.[5]

The debate over the trend in work hours has centered on differences in the kinds of data researchers use and, in particular, on the quality of the data. Schor draws on large annual surveys administered by the government, whereas Robinson and Godbey make comparisons from a small handful of studies that use the far more exacting time-diary method (in which respondents log how they spent every fifteen-minute period of a day).[6] The debate has tested the limits of researchers' capacity to measure historical time-use trends, and the limits of data collected decades in the past provide obstacles that are difficult, if not impossible, to overcome in contemporary research. Although these debates will, we hope, move us toward better measures and increased accuracy in this type of research, a continuing battle of competing estimates of the average worker's work hours may miss the point. No matter how precise, objective, or representative, these estimates can only provide a limited explanation of the time squeeze in contemporary U.S. society if they continue to ignore the context of these work hours in individuals' lives and workers' families.

For example, as already mentioned, these studies typically ignore the fact that workers are increasingly married to other workers. The fact that the family work-week has increased[7] means that the time available for other activities in the family has decreased. Family context could be even more salient than accurate measures of individual work hours in shaping peoples' perceptions of work time, overwork, and the appropriate or desired amounts of leisure.

Objective measures of average work hours also fail to capture how workers feel about their time on the job. Even if work hours have remained constant, workers may increasingly wish they could work less. We must account for not only how much people work, but also how much they want to work and how institutional constraints shape people's use of time, to better understand the rising sense of a time famine.

We should also recognize that although work hours have apparent implications for time use more generally, work may not be the only structuring activity in Americans' lives. Specifically, conclusions about leisure and its decline need to be based on data on leisure per se rather than on assumptions that leisure is literally the time remaining when we subtract daily work hours from twenty-four.[8] Work and leisure seem to constrain one another arithmetically—as one goes up the other must go down—but even here, Robinson and Godbey suggest that there is often a "more . . . more" principle at work: people who work long hours also tend to participate more in active leisure pursuits. Scholars need to reexamine the assumption that work hours alone adequately explain time-use patterns and that leisure is simply an inconsequential residual not worth studying in its own right.

In short, the contemporary time bind may be a function of changing work hours since the 1960s, as Schor and others have argued, but analyses of aggregate trends in work hours, no matter how well specified, cannot tell the whole story. First, we have to account for family context and how that shapes people's perceptions of time use. Second, we need to consider how workers would prefer to spend time and how institutionalized definitions of jobs and work constrain them. Third, studies of time use must also focus on time spent outside paid labor, specifically on time spent at leisure, to glean a comprehensive understanding of time-use and the contemporary perception of a time famine.

Measuring Time Use

In studying time use, researchers generally rely on surveys with simplistic one-item questions such as: "How many hours did you work last week, at all jobs?" This, in turn, might be complemented with questions about time spent at housework, and, less frequently, a question about leisure time. Such simplistic measures are easy to ask, easy to code, and easy to analyze. But is there a price to such simplicity? Robinson and Godbey have argued that respondents in these surveys find it very difficult to tally weekly hours, especially if work schedules are irregular, change frequently, and/or are not carefully logged. Survey measures clearly reveal evidence of this difficulty, with many responses clustered around round numbers such as 40, 50, and 60. More significantly, however, Robinson and Godbey argue that these simplistic summary measures reflect more than harmless measurement errors, but represent systematic exaggerations of work hours, making survey measures virtually meaningless.[9]

In an innovative study designed to address exactly this claim, Jerry Jacobs compared self-reports of weekly work hours with a measure of work hours calculated from the depart-and-return-from-home times on the previous day. Jacobs found that the two measures provide similar estimates of work hours (correlating at 0.8), belying Robinson and Godbey's contention that weekly summaries promote the tendency to exaggerate and that more proximate recall (e.g., yesterday) is substantially more accurate that longer-term recall (e.g., last week). Jacobs concludes that self-report measures are reliable and accurate and, in most settings, provide researchers with reasonable data for understanding time-use patterns.[10] Although questions about data accuracy will continue to be part of the time-squeeze debate for some time, there is almost certainly more to the contemporary feeling of a time squeeze than measurement issues.

Accounting for Time: *The Cornell Couples and Careers Study*

In *The Cornell Couples and Careers Study*, we built on the standard survey method used in numerous other studies, this time asking respondents several questions about how they use their time. First, we asked about work time, distinguishing between contractual time and actual time at work.[11] We asked, "How many hours a week are you officially supposed to work?" followed by, "On average, how many hours a week *do you actually* work, including any paid or unpaid extra hours that you put in beyond your official work week?" The first question merely allowed respondents to signal that they worked, for example, full-time (or forty hours per week), whereas the second question invited them to respond with more reflection and, we hope, precision. We focus here on responses to the latter question only. We also asked about preferences for work hours: "If you could do what you wanted to do, ideally how many hours would you like to work each week?"

In addition to time at paid work, we asked about family maintenance, another important aspect of work time that is unfortunately often neglected. Specifically, we asked: "On average, on days when you are working, about how much time do you spend on home chores—things like cooking, cleaning, repairs, shopping, yard work, and keeping track of money and bills?" and, in a separate item, we asked about time spent doing child care. Finally, to capture time spent at leisure, we distinguished between days in which the respondent was working (at their paid job) and not working, asking, "On average, on days when you are [not] working, about how much time do you spend on your free-time activities?"

How Good Are Our Self-Reports?

In light of the heated debates over the quality of self-reports of time use, do our data make sense, or have face validity? One way to address this question is to look at the total time accounted for in a day, aggregating all four of our measures of time use. Are respondents exaggerating their daily load, reporting absurdly long days?

In principle, our four categories of time use account for everything people do in a day, with the major exception of tending to self-care tasks including sleep, eating, bathing, and grooming. With surprising consistency, time-dairy studies—including the three waves of the Michigan-Maryland time-diary studies as well as a handful of other small studies—indicate that, on average, people spend between ten and eleven hours a day tending to these physiological needs, including sleep.[12]

Largely consistent with the time-diary results, we find an average of just less than ten hours a day unaccounted for with our measures of paid work, housework, child care, and leisure in our sample of dual-earner couples. This suggests that our data represent reasonable and not grossly overestimated accounts of time use. Further, we find that these plausible reports are highly typical: the reports of more than three-quarters of the sample imply that respondents spend between eight and twelve hours per day sleeping and in other self-care activities. The self-report measures in *The Cornell Couples and Careers Study* appear to represent reasonably accurate measures of actual time use.

Outlines of Time Use in Dual-Earner Couples

Figures 3.1 and 3.2 describe the allocation of time on workdays among husbands and wives, respectively, at different positions in the life course. Recall (see chap. 1 and 2) that our life-stage measure captures family development, but stages of career development are frequently coterminous, with the most intense career-building stages often occurring exactly when young children require intensive time and attention. The life stages we use here are nonparents under age 40, launching (children under age 6), early establishment (youngest child is age 6–12), late establishment (children 13–18), nonparents ages 40 and above, adult children (children over age 19 at home), and empty nest (children no longer at home).

Figure 3.1 indicates that the men in our sample report working, on average, close to ten hours a day at their jobs, or almost fifty hours per week, substantially longer than the typical forty-hour contractual workweek. Recalling that our sample is one of professionals, this is not surprising; other studies also find that professionals tend to work more hours than those who hold other occupations. The gray area across the bottom of figure 3.1 shows very little variation in paid work hours by life stage among men. Apparently, these husbands in professional couples maintain this pattern of long daily hours at employment throughout their life course.

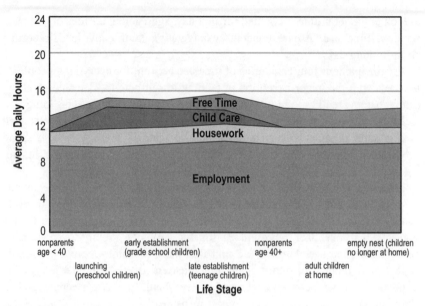

Figure 3.1 Husbands' daily time use on work days. Source: *Cornell Couples and Careers Study*, 1998–99.

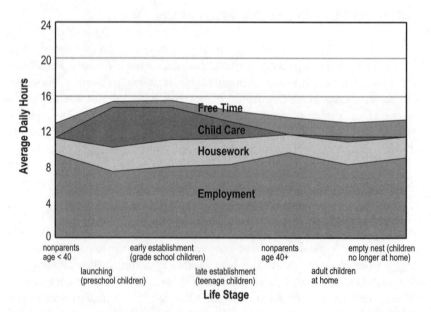

Figure 3.2 Wives' daily time use on work days. Source: *Cornell Couples and Careers Study*, 1998–99.

The other major component of the workday—housework—also shows little variability over the life course for men, as shown by the second band from the bottom in figure 3.1. Men under age forty without children do the least, whereas young fathers in the launching stage do the most, but the difference is relatively minor, ranging from about one and one-half to two hours per day on workdays.

In contrast to the consistency in the paid work and housework day, husbands in our sample experience substantial variation in the amount of time they spend taking care of children and engaging in free-time activities with the entrance and exit of children from the household. Fathers average at least two hours and as many as 2.6 hours a day on average among launching-stage fathers on child care when children are in the household.

The increase in time spent caring for children appears to take a bite out of men's leisure time. Men in the launching stage experience huge decreases— 50 percent or more—in their leisure compared to men at other stages and experience only fifty-five minutes of leisure per day on average. In contrast, older men who have never had children (nonparents over age forty) average more than two hours per day for their own free-time activities. Even though leisure itself remains a fairly small proportion of the entire day, it may be a salient and highly appreciated portion, and a 50 percent decline associated with having children may have a tremendous impact on perceptions of overwork during the child-rearing years.

Although *The Cornell Couples and Careers Study* does not directly measure time spent on physiological needs, the unshaded portion of figure 3.1 implies that sleeping, eating, and other self-care activities may be shortchanged during the launching and establishment life stages. Young nonfathers and those men with grown children appear to spend over eleven hours a day in unaccounted for activities, including sleeping, bathing, and eating, whereas fathers appear to average as few as nine hours a day tending to their own physiological needs. Although such a small figure could result from a tendency among parents to overreport time spent at other activities, qualitative evidence collected by the Cornell Careers Institute and studies by other researchers support the contention that parents are often underrested.

Although the life course appears to play an important role in structuring the use of time among men, with fathers of small children, in particular, experiencing declines in leisure and perhaps in sleep, the structure of time use among women (figure 3.2) appears to be much more strongly shaped by events in the life course. Consider, for example, employment. Childless women under age forty work, on average, more than forty-eight hours a week (9.7 hours per workday) in our sample—a number statistically indistinguishable from their nonparent husbands. However, once children enter a household, women's time at work dips more than two hours per day, to an average of approximately seven and one-half hours a day. Even in this highly select sample of employed dual-earner professional couples, women appear to scale back at work to a substantial degree when they have children.[13]

Time spent on household tasks also varies with the presence of children for women, in contrast to the relative stability among husbands. Young nonparent women report doing approximately one hour and fifty-five minutes of housework on an average workday—a figure quite comparable to the amount done by their husbands. And older women without children in the home average less than two and one-half hours a day—again, a figure not far from their husbands'. But women in all the other life stages, when children are in the household, report over three hours of housework on workdays, approximately 50 percent more than their husbands do.

By far the biggest difference in husbands' and wives' behavior in our dual-earner professional couples concerns child care. In the launching life stage, wives do an average of 5.3 hours of child care on a typical workday—fully double the amount their husbands perform. Mothers' participation tapers off as children enter school, but even in the late establishment stage, wives report performing three hours of child care on a daily basis, or approximately 50 percent more than their husbands.

Although it is the case that mothers spend less time at work during the child-rearing years, presumably to accommodate family needs, the increased time they spend doing child care and housework during those years more than compensates for the cutback and appears to encroach on the amount of time available for their own leisure. Women in the launching stage report approximately forty-five minutes a day of free time—almost 15 percent less than their husbands, and less than one-half than nonmothers (those in the nonparent stages and those whose children have left home). Similarly, establishment mothers average just under one hour of free time—approximately 25 percent less than their husbands and again substantially less than those without children in their home.

As in our results for husbands, the unshaded portion of figure 3.2 implies that time spent at self-care may be severely cut back among mothers. Women without children in the home average nearly twelve hours a day for unaccounted for activities such as sleeping, eating, bathing, and grooming—a figure slightly higher than their nonparent husbands. Women with children under the age of twelve in home, however, average less than nine hours per day in all self-care activities. Again, this is consistent with the claim that mothers of young children—and especially working mothers—cut back on sleep and minimize time spent grooming and eating.

These simple estimates of time use suggest a few broad and related conclusions. First, both husbands and wives in our sample of dual-earner couples tend put in very long hours at their jobs, even when they are parents of young children. With many wives and most husbands reporting fifty hours a week on the job or more, these couples appear to be working the equivalent of two and one-half full-time jobs outside the home between them, while trying to manage their family lives at the same time. Second, although the relatively career-oriented couples in *The Cornell Couples and Careers Study* have opted not to follow the traditional breadwinner-homemaker mold, distinct gender differences remain: husbands tend to work longer hours at paid employment and wives put in more household and child-care hours. The average mother of a small child in our sample works a bit less than forty hours a week, but puts in eight and one-half hours a day on housework and child care. In contrast, fathers of small children average forty-eight hours a week of paid employment, but just four and one-half hours on their workdays tending to the home and children. Third, the progression of the life course and presence of children in the home have a far larger impact on women's time allocation than on men's. Whereas men maintain a relatively steady course of long workdays over their lives, these professional women appear to cut back on both their careers and free time to accommodate a substantial increase in the second-shift responsibilities accompanying motherhood.

Work Hours: Actual and Preferred

Many studies of time use have tended to assume that the hours worked reflect the preferences or desires of individual workers: if work hours have increased, it is because workers want to work longer hours. However, our data indicate a substantial gap between the number of hours husbands and wives in dual-earner couples say they *would like* to work and the number of hours they *actually do* work. Figure 3.3 illustrates this gap between actual and preferred hours (where positive values above the dotted line indicate working more than our sample would like).

These box plots illustrate the central tendency as well as the variability in the data for each of the six life stages, separately for men and women. The median gap is illustrated with the solid line running through the middle of each shaded box. The shaded boxes, in turn, delineate the interquartile range, a range that excludes 25 percent of the more extreme observations from both the high end and low end of the distribution, resulting in a truncated range containing one-half of all the cases. The Ts extending above and below the shaded boxes indicate the full range observed among our respondents.

Figure 3.3 suggests three important conclusions. First, for both sexes and at every life stage, three-quarters or more of the individuals in our sample are working more than they would like. Second, the data suggest that the average gap is fairly large, with a median between nine and fifteen hours too much work per week across all the groups. Third, in many cases, the gap is more static across life stage than actual behavior. For example, mothers in the launching stage work more than ten hours a week less than nonmothers under age forty, but, because launching mothers

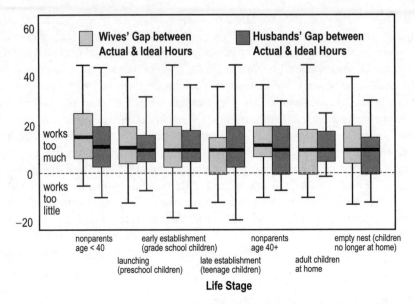

Figure 3.3 Gap between actual and ideal work hours for husbands and wives, by life stage. Source: *Cornell Couples and Careers Study*, 1998–99.

have adjusted their preferences as well as their behavior, the gap between actual and desired work hours is reduced but by no means closed. Thus, young nonmothers average fifteen hours more per week than they would like, whereas wives with children under the age of six—who have often cut back their work hours substantially—still typically work eleven hours more per week than they prefer.

To explore the pervasive sense of overwork, or the disjuncture between ideal and actual work hours, *The Cornell Couples and Careers Study* asked respondents who were not working the number of hours they wanted what factors drove them to work the hours they do work. Consistent with the idea that work hours are bundled with the infrastructure of jobs and largely nonnegotiable, 65 percent of men and 51 percent of women simply responded that those hours were built into the job or the kind of work they were in. Indeed, evidence from the qualitative data collected at Cornell suggests that these professional employees often did not even imagine that they might have a choice about their work hours, let alone actually try to negotiate for a changed schedule with their employers. Also important, but to a much lesser degree in this sample, were financial concerns: one-quarter of wives and 15 percent of husbands said they did it for money.

Relationships in Time Use

Time spent in one activity cannot be spent at another, but studies that have explicitly examined the issue suggest that time at work and time for leisure may

Table 3.1 Correlations between Time Use Variables for Men and Women[a]

| | | Men | | | | | Women | | | |
| | | Work Days | | | | Off-Day | Work Days | | | |
		Work Hours	Chores	Child Care	Free Time	Free Time	Work Hours	Chores	Child Care	Free Time
Husbands	Chores, work days	−.03								
	Child care, work days	−.18**	.24**							
	Free time, work days	−.15**	.10**	.10*						
	Free time, off-days	−.04	−.04	−.04	.45**					
Wives	Daily work hours	.08*	.08*	.00	.12**	.14**				
	Chores, work days	.07†	.01	−.02	−.05	−.11**	−.20**			
	Child care, work days	−.03	.03	.00	−.05	−.10*	−.22**	.24**		
	Free time, work days	.03	.01	−.12*	.23**	.19**	−.04	−.05	−.04	
	Free time, off-days	−.03	.00	.07	.20**	.27**	.15**	−.13**	−.12*	.56**

[a] The sample sizes for the correlations vary. Correlations with the child-care questions are calculated from data on approximately 400 couples with children; correlations involving other measures are based on data from approximately 800 couples. † indicates $0.05 < p \leq .10$; * indicates $0.01 < p \leq .05$; ** indicates $p \leq 0.01$.

not necessarily be zero-sum game. How strongly related are time spent at work and time spent at leisure? Are there intracouple effects such that, for example, the time a spouse spends at work shapes his or her partner's time for leisure? Table 3.1 presents correlations between five of our measures of time use measured separately for husbands and wives: the boxed coefficients present intra-couple correlations and the two triangular matrices represent intra-individual correlations.

Turning first to individuals, the zero-sum view of time suggests that the correlation between work hours and free time on workdays should be nearly perfectly negatively associated, but the correlations here in our data are far from −1. Specifically, the correlation among husbands (−0.15) is significant but only moderate in size, and the correlation for wives is statistically indistinguishable from 0. Time spent at chores and child care could also be seen as subtracting from available leisure, but the evidence here supports this claim even less: among wives, there is no association between leisure and either workday chores or workday child care, and, among husbands, those who do more child care and chores during the week actually report more workday leisure.

Clearly, time spent at paid work and at family and household labor are not the only determinants of free-time hours on workdays. Rather, table 3.1 suggests that free time is a product of some other process. For example, both husbands and wives with more free time on workdays also have more free time on nonwork days (correlations of 0.45 and 0.56 for husbands and wives, respectively), perhaps because they strive to carve out leisure for themselves as a lifestyle choice. There is also suggestive evidence that wives who put in long hours at paid work are more likely to set aside time for leisure on their weekends (the correlation between work hours and free time on off-days is 0.15 and statistically significant), whereas wives who do lots of child care and unpaid housework during the week have less leisure on weekends (correlation of −0.13), perhaps because their household and family responsibilities carry over into the weekends. These patterns of overflow from the workweek to the weekend do not hold true for husbands, however.

What about intracouple factors? Do couples enjoy leisure together, or does his leisure come at her expense and vice versa? The evidence in table 3.1 suggests that although there is a slight tendency for couples to work similar numbers of hours (i.e., his hours and her hours are significantly correlated, but only at 0.08), there is a stronger tendency to have similar levels of leisure (the correlation between his leisure and her leisure on workdays is 0.23 and the correlation on nonwork days is 0.27). This similarity between partners suggests that there are high leisure couples and low leisure couples. Further, contrary to the idea that husbands' leisure is made possible by women's chores, table 3.1 indicates that the more housework wives do, the less free time husbands enjoy (correlation of −0.11). Indeed, it is actually the husbands of women who spend more time at work who enjoy more leisure: wives who work long days are not only more likely to save leisure for themselves on their nonwork days, as previously described, but their husbands also enjoy more leisure as well. Conversely, husbands of women who do lots of chores and child care during the week get less free time on the weekend. We also find that both men and women married to partners working long hours tend to do more housework and that the relationship is about the same whether it is the husbands or wives who are working more (correlations of 0.08 and 0.07).

A more complete analysis of these interrelationships using multiple regression can be found on our website (www.lifecourse.cornell.edu/about_time.html); this generally replicates the pattern of findings in table 3.1 and suggests a number of general conclusions. First, although many bemoan that there are only twenty-four hours a day, our analysis indicates that there is considerable slippage between time use in various domains. For example, the amount of leisure individuals report is shaped by their own work hours only to a fairly minimal degree—it is not even a statistically significant association among women. Further, contrary to the expectation that men enjoy leisure instead of pitching in around the house, we find that men with more leisure time are also the ones who do more housework and child care. Second, we find that the way spouses use time is related. For example, the extent of wives' labor-force participation has a strong effect on husbands' use of time; wives who work long hours are married to men with more free time, whereas wives who do more housework and child care are married to men with less free time. Third, contrary to the claim that one spouse enjoys leisure at the expense of the other, we find that when one spouse enjoys more (or less) leisure, the other tends to as well, suggesting that leisure is often a jointly consumed (or forgone) commodity.

Summing Up: Time as a Couple-Level Commodity

In this chapter, we have examined both the measurement of time use and how couples in *The Cornell Couples and Careers Study* report using their time. We find that couples appear to be fairly accurate in their self-reports of time use, with the sum of their estimates of hours spent on paid work, chores, child care, and free time and likely estimates of time spent on physiological needs being approximately twenty-four hours a day. Time spent in these activities varies by life stage, but far moreso for women than for men.

We also find that couples work more hours than they would prefer. Feelings of overwork so often voiced in contemporary society and prevalent in our sample may be shaped as much by this disparity than by objective measures of time-use trends. Indeed, most of our respondents say that they work the hours that they do simply because their jobs require it, not because of a conflicting personal motivation or household-level demand.

At the same time, however, we also find work hours, although no doubt providing some constraints on time use as generally conceived, play a fairly minimal role in shaping how much time the couples in our sample spend on chores or leisure. Our data suggest that important lifestyle choices may be operating—some couples place a priority on free time, whereas other couples do not—and that leisure is not simply a residual left over after other uses of time have been accounted for.

Taken as a whole, our results suggest that time use, although in some senses conceptually easy to analyze, is a complex phenomenon. Although clearly the men and women in our sample feel they do not have enough time, time use is at the same time not necessarily a zero-sum game. The contemporary time squeeze is apparently more than a direct function of long work hours; it also reflects profound life-stage effects on time use, disparities between ideal and actual work hours, and couple-level effects in time use that, together with the hidden infrastructure of work and occupational career paths, conspire to create households in which both partners put in long hours and enjoy little free time together.

4

Family Clocks: Timing Parenthood

Kristine A. Altucher and Lindy B. Williams

When Charlotte Perkins Gilman wrote *Women and Economics* in 1898, on the eve of the suffrage movement, she was concerned with the vast changes industrialization was wreaking on the family and on the role of women in society. Many of these social changes echo in the current transformations of society as shifting configurations of the U.S. family clash yet again with political and cultural conceptions of what constitutes a family and the appropriate place of women in the family and the workplace. Gilman writes, "In reconstructing in our minds the position of women under conditions of economic independence, it is most difficult to think of her as a mother."[1] It is exactly that paradox that we address in this chapter by looking at how family formation decisions—whether or not to have children, when to have children, and how many children to have—are made within the context of two-career families.

As women have entered the workforce and taken on new roles, they have retained their position in the family as the person responsible for bearing and frequently raising the children. The question of who works, who takes care of the children, and how whoever this is will manage to fulfill these tasks is still contested and in flux as shifting cultural expectations come into conflict.[2] This is a sociocultural process, but also part of a larger global process. Consistent with the neoliberal economic framework that increasingly dominates social thought, both in the United States and globally, this process is generally characterized as one of individual actors making their own choices.[3] Perhaps as a consequence of this perception, women are expected to reconcile the conflicting demands of work and family with limited infrastructural support, creating individual solutions for what is essentially a wide-scale social transition.

The potential for conflict is inherent in the gender-specific expectations for women and men. On the one hand, Melissa Milkie and Pia Peltola argue that it is a "gendered 'must'" that "mothers must be all-giving to their children."[4] Their roles as mother, wife, and labor-force participant are independent and likely to be in conflict. Men, on the other hand, experience their roles as father, husband, and labor-force participant as interdependent and easier to combine. Whereas men have been found less likely to adjust their schedules to accommodate others, women may, when facing work-family conflict, reduce their attachment to the paid labor force or leave it entirely.[5]

In general, however, the difficulty of managing work and family obligations remains a greater problem for women than for men. Expectations of child care remain focused disproportionately around women (see Clarkberg and Merola, chap. 3 in this volume) and as a result, women continue to be disproportionately affected in terms of their "choice of occupations, their time spent in paid employment, their work commitment, and their allocation of effort to household and workplace activities."[6] Ultimately, many argue that women tend to self-select positions that are less at odds with family obligations. In this chapter, we attempt to better understand just how couples integrate their family formation with work.

Work versus Children

Which Came First, the Job or the Egg?

Researchers have had contradictory results when trying to establish a causal relationship between fertility and female employment (see fig. 4.1). Using a dynamic model that incorporates change over time to ascertain unambiguously ordered behavioral sequences, James Cramer finds that fertility influences employment in the short run, whereas employment affects fertility in the long run.[7] In other words, women who have children are less likely to engage in (paid) work in the short term, whereas working women are less likely to have children (or are more likely to have fewer children) overall. Using longitudinal data, Cramer finds that the amount of time women spend in the labor force each week affects the stability of childbearing intentions over time and that a reduction in hours is linked to more volatility in childbearing plans.[8]

As we do in this book, Frans Willekens describes motherhood and employment as two parallel career processes, interdependent and continuously interacting.[9] But we broaden this approach to consider three interdependent processes; two (his and hers) occupational careers along with a family career. How family

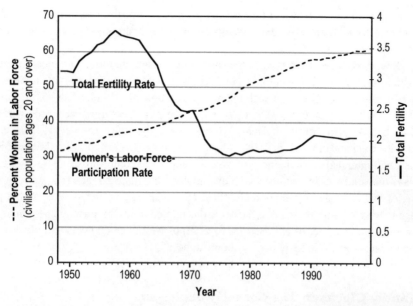

Figure 4.1 Women's labor-force participation and total fertility rates, 1948–99. Source: U.S. Bureau of Labor Statistics (2000); U.S. Census Bureau (1975, 2000c).

formation and labor-market involvement are intertwined is still unclear. What causes people to make their choices about work and family? What do they see as more mutable and what is beyond the realm of their control?

Does Later Mean Never?

Although most people say they want children, more and more women are remaining childless or postponing having children.[10] By 2000, the percentage of childless women between the ages of forty and forty-four had reached 19 percent, up from 15.7 percent in 1992.[11] Declines in fertility for women in their teens and early twenties have meant more first births for women in their thirties and forties, as some of the women who delayed having children catch up later.[12] This, in turn, portends a greater potential for conflict between the already established careers of women and the demands of children, as well as a higher potential for infertility.

Research shows that delayed childbearing may eventually lead to forgoing children. Jane Menken has explored the phenomena of postponement, age-related infertility, and the consequences for intergenerational obligation. Clearly these issues catch the attention of the general population. Menken also highlights the widespread media response to postponement and infertility, frequently reporting stories of "high-powered career women, who postponed childbearing until they thought themselves ready to take on the joy and responsibilities of motherhood, and then found themselves far less successful in the bedroom than they had been in the boardroom."[13]

Nevertheless, women continue to postpone having children. The median age at first birth in the U.S. went from 21.3 in 1969 to 24.6 in 2000, and this increase was greatest among women with the most education. Nearly one-half (45.5%) of women with sixteen or more years of education were over thirty years old when they had their first birth in 1994.[14] But what are the processes behind delayed childbearing and childlessness? Are these consciously elected, preferred lifestyles or the unintended consequences of time demands and compromises of daily life? Says one study, "Most women who eventually are childless reach that state by a series of decisions to postpone childbearing rather than by deciding at a young age to have no children."[15] Are the decisions related to family formation—timing, spacing, and number of children—a function of well-planned goals and ideals or of decisions made in response to circumstances?

Family Clocks in *The Cornell Couples and Careers Study*

We draw on data from ninety-four in-depth semistructured interviews with working men and women at different stages of the life course, conducted as part of *The Cornell Couples and Careers Study*.

From a pool of 149 interviews, we selected all interviews in which the respondent discussed either having children or issues related to having children. We omitted interviews that made no mention of children ($n = 55$); most of these participants were either young and childless or older with no children present. These interviews offer human voices and faces to the themes of family formation and work.

In approximately one-half of our subsample ($n = 44$ couples) both members of the couple were interviewed. The spouses were interviewed separately, except in one case. Because we include both members of a couple, there is a potential for overrepresentation of certain experiences, but we do not quote both members of any couple in the analysis that follows.

The subsample we describe in this chapter consists of more women than men (fifty-three and forty-one respectively). At the time of the interview, the mean age of the respondents was thirty-eight; the average age for women was thirty-six and for men forty-three. Most of the respondents were married ($n = 76$) or cohabiting ($n = 9$), and only nine were single and not cohabiting; 74 percent of the respondents had at least a college degree. Approximately one-third of the sample had no children ($n = 32$), but more than one-half who did had two children ($n = 36$). Approximately 75 percent of the subsample were white, close to 7 percent were ethnic minorities, and the remaining people were of unspecified race or ethnicity. There were four people who described themselves as in committed lesbian relationships, although sexual orientation per se was not asked about during the interview.

Establishment and Shifting Gears Stages: Completed Families

Women and men who have the number of children they had intended speak eloquently about the compromises they made in their work and about family formation issues. Surprisingly, almost one-half of those with completed families (twenty out of forty-three people) express some regret that they did not have more children. Of these, one-third attribute this directly to the difficulty of combining work with raising children, specifically a lack of time, lack of resources, and age. Family disagreements about family size are also a problem.

Time   Many people speak of problems with finding enough time to fulfill the demands of their jobs and still having time with their family. The director of a child-care program at Lake University[16] says, "Thinking about having a third child. It was something we decided against. . . . If I didn't have a career, I think I would have had another baby. . . . But to be the kind of parent I wanted to be, and that I was, and wanting to work and needing to work, I just couldn't do justice. . . . It was me deciding that I didn't have enough left over, I didn't have the time to be with my kids if I was going to have more" (39-year-old mother of two).

Even respondents who do not express a preference for more children mention the impact of their employment on family-size decision making. Answering a question about whether her career influenced her decision to have children, an executive assistant at Utilco says, "As far as the number, yeah. I don't know if I could psychologically handle more children—the guilt is already there that I never see these two!" (35-year-old mother of two).

Almost all the people who say that their work limited their family size are women, although several men with children describe family or commitment to time with the family as a barrier to career success. When discussing how he manages his family and his job, a machine parts buyer responds, "My aspirations have changed. When I started with General Corporation I expected to be an executive vice president by the time I was 35, but that was before kids and a lot of other things. I plan to head towards the corporate end with Transco, but I do not expect to be an executive vice president! I think I have a fuller understanding of what that means and entails, so I have different aspirations" (42-year-old married father of three).

Resources   With more money, many respondents say, one partner could stay home with the additional children or other resources that would help in raising children would be more accessible. A teacher's assistant married to a manufacturing representative says, "I always wanted to have children. I really thought he [her spouse] was in a position where I didn't have to work. . . . I wanted a big family but financially we couldn't afford it" (43-year-old mother of three).

For a mental health therapist at Citizen's Health whose wife is a high school teacher, lack of resources is expressed in terms of winning the lottery: "If you asked my wife she would probably say if we won Lotto that she would have another child and stay home" (38-year-old father of two).

A quality assurance manager at Vantech married to a dental hygienist frames the resource conflict in a different perspective, "There obviously have been times when I would say if I didn't have any children I would be able to do something, probably be able to own a Ferrari if I was still single, but that was not really a regret because I wouldn't rather have a Ferrari than my wife or children" (father of two in his fifties).

Age   Because the people who say they do not expect to have any more children are generally older, they often couch the acceptance of their existing family size in terms of the interaction between age and work. A woman who works in administration at Lake University, married to a computer programmer, says, "If I were younger, I would have more children, and if I didn't have to work, I would have more. So as a working mother, two children is about as much as I can do. Ideally I would like to have more children" (43-year-old mother of two).

Men also raise age as an issue. A physician at Citizen's Health describes the impact of his career on the size of his family:

> I put off having my child until I was 40 years old, because it's difficult to think about having kids when I was in my training period. . . . We have been married for twenty years. We got married young. Well, my family life is pretty ideal. I have a really wonderful wife and a wonderful son. I cannot ask more. I probably won't have any more children [since] we are getting up [in] years. I guess no more children. This is it. (43-year-old father of one)

When Spouses Disagree   Respondents also say they have fewer children than they want because of their spouses' wishes; four women and two men wanted more children than their spouse did, and in all but one of these families the final decision was to not have another child. A production worker married to a customer service worker, both working at Transco, talks about spousal differences in preferred family size: "My wife wanted to have another one. . . . I said no. Not that it really made a big difference, but I had asked not to have another one. I figure, you've got one of each, why go messing with nature, you know? Both of them are healthy, they don't have any problems, so . . ." (39-year old father of two).

This is consistent with other studies that show that when a disagreement over family size exists, the lower preferred family size takes preference.[17]

Although a number of people had children earlier than planned, very few say they have a larger than ideal family.[18] This may be due to the acceptance and rationalization of actual family size, but there is no evidence of this in the interviews. Rather, it probably reflects the high degree of family planning in this highly educated population.

Launching Stage: Families Still in Formation

People who have not yet completed their families at the time of interview talk about these issues from a different perspective. These people can be divided into three subcategories: those who see having children as a somewhat abstract idea for the future, those who are actively in the process of creating or enlarging their families, and those who are struggling with finding a time to fit children into their educational or career trajectories. The timing of having children is a key concern for all of these groups, but they see different dimensions of timing as most important.

Age is one facet of timing, but age encompasses several different time-related concepts. These include not only the biological clock (which is generally discussed in reference to women's bodies) and related health consequences of having children at a more advanced age, but also the presumably youthful energy needed to cope with young children and the potential negative impact of a large age gap between parent and child. Because they are at varied stages of planning and thinking about having children, members of each of the three groups tend to focus on different aspects of timing and age.

Family Sometime in the Future   Most of the people who plan on having children someday, but not soon, do not discuss or anticipate incompatibility between work and having children. Many are still single and talk about planning to get married and then at some point having children, usually two. Having children is not a major preoccupation for them. Many younger married women and men see childbearing as something distant and abstract. Men and women are similar in their discussions of work and family matters. A director of human resources at Citizen's Health focuses on the present: "I like being a manager, and just think I want to go up the career track. I might think differently once I have kids, but I don't know. Not having kids I think makes it easier to make those decisions and plans now" (30-year-old married woman).

When asked to describe his ideal family, a manager at Citizen's Health responds, "Two kids, when we're in our early 30s. I don't have a sex preference.

We don't have a timeline worked out. We both feel that right now we couldn't handle [children]. I think a lot of times we feel that we don't manage to keep the carpet vacuumed, I don't know how we'd find time to raise a child. She would probably work half time or not at all. I think we're both people who would be comfortable in either role" (married man in his late twenties).

Starting a Family Now   The second group sees age as pressing. The biological clock is a real concern for them, but other aspects of age are mentioned as well—especially parental energy and an age difference between parent and child. When asked why he wants to have children by the time he is thirty, a research assistant at Lake University replies:

Well, because a woman's best, when it's easiest on a woman's body, my understanding is the earlier the better. My understanding is that the risks of birth defects, I guess it's pretty stable all the way through till 36 and then there's really rapid increases in different risks of birth defects. So the biological aspects are my biggest concern. But next, and pretty close, is my wanting to be young and to really enjoy my kids as long as possible. (25-year-old married male)

A lab technician who is asked about her plans for starting a family raises a number of age-related concerns:

Hmm, well, we're planning on having kids pretty soon, like within a year. . . . well, my clock's ticking and I want to have one before I'm 30 anyway. I'm 27. Be 28 in May, and wait 9 months to have it. . . . [*Why do you want to have one before the age of 30?*] It reduces breast cancer risk, and cervical cancer. . . . I guess because I don't want to be too old before the child grows up. I want to get that out of the way. Not out of the way, but you know what I mean. I want to get started because I don't want to be 50 when the kid is still in high school or something (laughs). (27-year-old married woman with no children)

Trying to Find the "Right" Time   Timing means something different for the people who are struggling to fit children into their lives. Their calendar is not set by age but by educational or career paths. People trying to find the right time to have children speak of a "buffer year" in which a baby would be less problematic or of how to have a child without compromising their resumés. The challenge of coordinating work and family careers is most pronounced for them because they have not yet reached a solution for the problem of fitting it all in. Over one-half of the people planning on having children speak of work or school as the main reason they have not yet achieved their ideal family size.

A manufacturing engineer describes the difficulty in finding time to have children: "The timing is never right. Once in a blue moon, you almost wish birth control was not invented, because then you wouldn't have an excuse not to have kids. Don't get me wrong, its very, very necessary [to use birth control] but if it doesn't just happen [having kids] then the timing never seems right" (27-year-old married woman with no children).

In addition to finding the right time to have a child within the broader context of a career or education, the daily dimension of time, just finding enough hours in the day, is an issue as well. A graduate student in a same-sex relationship who is considering having children says, "By sheer force of necessity, I just have to work all the time at the moment . . . and . . . the prospect of trying to negotiate those, sort of . . . external demands placed on you by one's advisor, or boss, or whatever versus a child, I think would be quite difficult to negotiate" (33-year-old partnered woman with no children).

Behind the frequent mention of time as a problem lies the apprehension that work may actually be incompatible with children. In answer to a question about when she and her husband plan to have children, an agricultural technical advisor says:

> We've talked about it. I think we'd prefer sooner rather than later, but I also don't, with this job, I don't see how it can work out. . . . I don't see how I could for example, go out in the field with farmers and expect them to take me seriously if I were eight months pregnant. That just wouldn't work. . . . I wouldn't want my opinions or my expertise about cover crops or cultivation . . . to be lessened by who I am or what gender I am. I want to be able to say what I want and do my job without having someone think, oh she's a woman, she can't say that . . . or she's having kids and so she doesn't really care about her work. I would just not want it to matter just the way I wouldn't want skin color to matter, but I know it does. (27-year-old married woman with no children)

This woman raises the theme of perceived commitment to work, or professionalism, being called into question by having a child, in addition to the issue of timing. How can people be seen as serious about their work when they are undertaking something that will clearly distract their attention from what "should" be their priority? For obvious reasons, women usually bring up this issue, which is a central part of the gender difference in managing work and family.

Similarly, some men who have not yet had children feel that their career would have a negative impact on their children, because of time demands. When asked what impact not having children has had on his career, an assistant professor observes, "[I haven't] . . . had to worry about making a permanent impact on another human being as they are growing up. . . . 'a lot' of senior [employees] have told me that they regret what they did to their family, which is, essentially, neglect them in order to be successful in their career" (a 34-year-old married man with no children).

Childless Families Do delays cause unwanted childlessness? Although other studies[19] and popular perception lead us to believe they do, we do not find evidence of that in this sample. The few people who have no children and are past childbearing age speak of the positive aspects of childlessness, especially with respect to their work. In response to a question about how to manage work and family a professor answers, "Oh, I think a lot of people, a lot of women have horrible problems. And I've been lucky, I've not had children, so I've been relatively free to make a commitment to work. This is the big thing, when you have children" (46-year-old woman with no children).

Another woman working in sales at Transco says, "I don't know. . . . I don't know how to balance it. The only thing that isn't happening in my life is that I don't have kids, thank God" (50-year-old woman with no children).

None of the people who are childless and expect to remain childless speak of it as a negative or involuntary condition; however, those who are involuntarily childless may not have mentioned infertility or children at all during the interview and are therefore not included in this analysis. Also, a few people do mention infertility problems as the reason for their smaller-than-ideal family size. This may also reflect the tendency to rationalize past events, especially fertility outcomes, in light of current realities.[20]

Summing Up

Our findings offer evidence that this sample of professional workers perceive work as inhibiting family size and delaying childbearing. One of most important ways that many people coordinate work and family is by having fewer children. This is consistent with the declining birthrates since the 1970s and may shed some light on the process through which people arrive at smaller families. Perhaps smaller families are not only a result of delayed childbearing; perhaps time delays and smaller families are both outcomes of the compromises inherent in coordinating work and family. And although many people with completed families speak of how they delayed having children for a variety of reasons, delays in and of themselves are not explicitly described as a cause of childlessness in this particular population.

Structural lag in the hidden infrastructure of work and career paths is most evident among those struggling to have a family because institutional arrangements have failed to accommodate the realities of women and couples in the workforce. These people are attempting to find individual solutions to something that is not easily addressed on an individual level. Because as a society we tend to view family issues as a private matter to be resolved by each family alone, a lag occurs between public conceptions of what the family should be and the existing realities with which each family must struggle.

Women are expected to maintain their professionalism, their commitment to their careers and often their schedules, while simultaneously taking on what is essentially a second career of motherhood. When they or their spouses foresee this as an impossible expectation, they may respond by postponing or having fewer children because they believe that controlling family size is more feasible than controlling career demands. But recall that women who choose to control career demands by leaving the labor market are not in our sample.[21] Although many women want to work while raising a family, economic constraints force many women to stay in the labor force who would rather have the option of staying home with their children, at least temporarily. Limited resources result in limited choices, and, even though our sample population is largely professional and middle class, respondents often express a desire for enough money to have the options of either staying home or hiring adequate assistance.

Our results show that workers, especially women, often compromise their ideals to adapt to the realities of a world in which work is often necessary or desired but not always compatible with family-formation preferences and goals. This is clearly the case not only in terms of family-building strategies, as we have indicated in this analysis, but also in terms of career trajectories, as the other chapters in this volume indicate. Even though some employers attempt to provide a more flexible workplace, the structure and culture of work, especially of professional work, is often based on the outmoded (male) breadwinner–(female) homemaker template. But the changing dynamics of work and family exact a cost in children postponed or never conceived, a cost neglected in policy deliberations.

5

Commuting Clocks:
Journey to Work

Heather Hofmeister

The distance between home and the workplace has been increasing since the 1970s. The building of ever more highways allows workers to forgo slow two-lane roads and still get to work, even if they live far away.[1] Workers live in suburbs instead of cities for the larger homes, homogenous neighborhoods, better schools, and lower crime rates.[2] And in households in which both spouses work for pay, the residence is likely to be farther from one spouse's workplace than the other's.[3] U.S. workers spend, on average, twenty-four minutes traveling to work each day, which means they spend nearly a week of twenty-four-hour days per year just in work-related transit.[4] Thus, commuting consumes a sizeable (and widely varying) portion of time, financial resources, and commitment.

Couples' choices of home and workplace locations are influenced by other commitments, including the ages and needs of children, the stage and prioritization of their careers, and the potential or actual commute of each spouse.[5] In this way, commutes reflect work and family career dynamics. Yet the commuting patterns of U.S. workers are usually discussed as an individual phenomenon, without considering couples' linked lives and linked careers. This chapter examines the journey to work in its household context and the patterns that emerge based on the relative times spouses travel to work. Are couples in which both spouses have short commutes versus couples in which both have long commutes versus couples in which only one spouse has a long commute different?

The commute is not only a demand on workers' time, but it is also a time and resource commitment borne by other family members. Commute time is potentially distributed between working spouses as a part of couples' division of labor, in a sense like paid work, washing the dishes, or preparing dinner. Thus the spouse with the longer commute may, for example, do less housework. Commute differences between spouses may reflect earnings differences; often a long commute is part of the price paid for a higher salary. In a sense, the higher salary justifies the long drive, and so high earners are willing to go farther, literally, for the money. A longer commute on the part of one spouse may be a sacrifice so that the family can live in a more desirable neighborhood or so that the other spouse can be closer to his or her workplace.

Historically, commuting has had a gendered pattern.[6] Men have tended to commute longer distances than women, but this difference has rarely been examined within households.[7] If, indeed, commuting is part of couples' division-of-labor equation, in what ways is it a gendered decision? This chapter asks how might the commute be a family strategy,[8] one of the compromises couples make between their two careers. Among couples in which only one member works close to home, is one spouse—the husband or the wife—more likely to work closer to home based on income, job tenure, job prestige, or life stage? Do outcomes of family satisfaction, perceptions of success, or work-family spillover vary by commuting pattern?

Why Care about the Journey to Work?

For many, the commute is a private, unexamined daily necessity. But its impacts are far-reaching, with implications for the environment, the way urban space is built and maintained, and families' stress levels.

As a result of most Americans driving to work in private cars rather than taking public transportation,[9] the entire country is affected by high pollution levels, overuse of fossil fuels, expensive road infrastructure, less wilderness, and reduced access to places other than work because of work-related traffic and congestion.

The gendered preferences for commuting length, distance, and the responsibilities a commute represents have relevance for companies' decisions to relocate, retailers' decisions to open or close a store in a particular area, and developers' and renovators' decisions to build or improve certain neighborhoods over others.

Just as work stress can spill over into home life and home stress spill over into work (see Valcour and Batt, chap. 19 in this volume), it is reasonable to anticipate that the commute can affect family relations and work experiences. Because commuting occurs between work and home, couples and those who work with couples (including therapists, day care centers, family members, supervisors, and employees) can benefit from understanding the overt and nuanced ways in which commuting permeates family life. The quality as well as length of the commute may have consequences for family relationships and well-being.

Theories Influencing Couples' Commutes

Role Quality, Conflicts, Strains, and Overloads

Roles in one sphere tend to influence roles in another.[10] Some roles are bundled together, especially in married men's and women's households, in which role sets come with (often gendered) meanings about identity and contributions to the household.[11] For example, a spouse who works part time may take on more household responsibility to make up for the lack of income, thus forming a bundle of roles from both the work and home spheres. In this example, the role bundle is typically a female-gendered pattern and it is unclear which comes first, the part-time job or the majority of housework. Each facilitates and reinforces the other. In some role situations, a long commute may be seen by both partners as a normal part of (male) breadwinning. Regardless of whether it makes rational sense for one or the other spouse to bear an extra long or short commute, gender expectations, not logic, determine the commuting structure. Given the hidden infrastructure of work and career paths built with a breadwinner-homemaker template, a long commute may be a defining aspect of what it means to be a good breadwinner, and a short commute that meets the children's needs may be part of the definition of a good mother. In one study of women working close to home (within ten minutes), those in female-type occupations were twice as likely (32%) to say they wanted to be able to get home quickly for children or emergencies compared to women in nonfemale type occupations who lived equally close to home (15%).[12] If a shorter commute is viewed as a feminine role marker, wives with longer commutes may feel a role conflict from the inconsistency between their actions and the expectations for them in their role, in addition to bearing the physical and psychological stress of being in transit for a long period each day. The degree of stress associated with a longer commute may vary by life stage, with long-commuting mothers of younger children feeling greater stress than women without children or with grown children.

Couples may also arrange their commuting patterns according to (apparently) nongendered household choices. The spouse whose career is more personally salient or higher earning may get the first choice of job and the "best" commute, with the other spouse arranging employment around the first spouse's job. But according to a 1977 study, even between men and women with equal job investments, earnings, occupational statuses, and family circumstances, women are far less likely than men to maximize their job prospects by relocating the family.[13] By extension, wives may also be less likely to inconvenience the family by having a long commute or to require a long commute of their husbands for the sake of their own jobs.

On the other hand, the commute arrangement may be a concession of one spouse to the other as a trade-off for the ideal job. The spouse with the better (higher earning, more personally salient) career may compensate for getting job priority by taking on the more arduous commute and allowing the job-compromising spouse the first choice of residential location. Or the longer commute may be the price paid for having less responsibility around the house, an idea borne out in qualitative interviews with forty French couples in the Paris region in the late 1980s. In a study by Jeanne Fagnani of dual-earner couples' housing and job decisions, it was found that dual-earner couples with middle-range incomes must decide between two compromises: to live in smaller dwellings with less privacy and less green space (within the city) close to work or to live with more space, home ownership, and privacy (within the suburbs) but withstand a long commute into the city for work and cultural activities.[14] Fagnani found that wives have the ultimate voice in where the family lives because wives bear the greater burden of responsibility for child and home care (and the greatest sacrifice of sleep and leisure). One of the strategies the wives in this study use to maintain their dual commitments is to have the family live closer to their work than their husbands' work, both within and outside the city. Husbands, for their part, put up with long commutes and even suburban living, sometimes against their own preferences, because not to do so would mean doing more housework, something that the husbands in Fagnani's study say they are reluctant to do.

Adaptive Strategies, Choice, and Constraint

Couples may use the length of each spouse's commute as a strategy to maximize the family's best interest, even though risking each spouse's individual best interest. They choose their home to minimize the distance to both spouses' jobs within the constraints of finding a neighborhood that meets the family's and children's needs (affordability, quality schools, safety, and being located between the two jobs). Other constraints on housing-work proximity include jobs and homes without access to public transportation, shopping areas and residential areas placed far apart, and industries located far from the residential areas where their employees prefer or can afford to live. In an imperfect decision-making situation, such as the housing market, couples will sometimes make housing decisions based on limited information, including not knowing where both jobs will be in the future, whether or how many children they will have, whether school quality will change, and whether caregiving for elderly relatives will be part of the equation. Any of these could affect the housing decision. Lives and needs change over time. The commutes resulting from earlier housing decisions are a function of the imperfect decision-making process and available housing options (choice within constraints) at the time of the move and home acquisition and may bear no reflection on the relative job values for each spouse.

Just as the locations of home and work can be seen as resources, time is a scarce and finite resource, especially in dual-earner couples. Members of rationally acting couples make trade-offs with one another, their time, and the locations of work and home to maximize the benefit to the household. For example, the worker who earns the most may specialize in the work domain and be best able to afford a longer commute. This person's overall time investment in work, even considering the commute time, makes it worthwhile to the family to lose that worker to the road for those hours every workday. The average twenty-minute commute[15] (which sums to over three hours every workweek) is not a trivial amount. The morning commute time is traded for sleep time or getting children prepared for their day; the evening commute time is exchanged for family time— time for dinner preparation, time spent with a spouse, time spent with children, and time for leisure. Individuals and families must weigh commute time relative to the sacrifices to arrive at a livable solution.

Work and Family Career Dynamics: Life Stage and the Journey to Work

Another important explanatory factor for travel time is life stage. According to David Levinson, life stage (which he measured by the age of the oldest child and number of adults in the household) explains 10 percent of the variation in the duration of time spent at home, at work, and in other activities (although this figure does not consider gender).[16]

One husband in our study explains how closely linked his and his wife's commutes are to their changing life stages:

> She began a long commute. . . . And she did that until we decided to start a family. And virtually the moment she became pregnant, in 1984. . . . There was never a question that she wouldn't continue her career. So it became clear that for that to happen, in part because of the way the world is constructed and in part the way work was structured in her workplace versus mine—that I just had a much more flexible life—we decided that it would be better for us to move nearer to her work. And we moved to [Metro City] at that time and . . . I started to do the commuting. And we've done that now for thirteen years in August, living somewhere in the [Metro City] metropolitan area, with me commuting to [small town an hour away]. (forty-two-year-old husband with three sons)

An interview with a twenty-seven-year-old married woman who is planning to have children in the future reveals how the combination of life stage and job opportunities enhance the attractiveness of a long commute. She and her husband had been enjoying short commutes after buying their first house near their workplaces, but she was offered a more distant opportunity:

> I was so impressed with the people, the business plan, and the position they offered me—I just couldn't resist, despite the big commute. The commute is 67 miles each way; about 1 hour 15 minutes when I interviewed, hopefully less if I leave really early and come home late (or early, on occasion). . . . I really doubt I'd be willing to take this on at any other point in my life, so I want to seize the opportunity now while it is before me.

She reveals a sense of timing with her career and her family planning—at another stage in her life she would not be so willing to take on such a long commute, but for now, while she can focus on her career instead of her family, she will.

Couples "do gender" in their homes through the ways they divide work, avoid work, and create work.[17] Whatever way couples divide their labor, they can think about it as either maximizing the best interests of the household or as part of "what we do here." It may reinforce traditional gender schema or forge new ways of behaving. Commuting can be seen as a form of household labor that couples enact in a variety of ways.

The Journey to Work: *The Cornell Couples and Careers Study*

Couples may use various decision-making strategies to decide where to live in relation to work and how much of a commute to work they are willing to make. This section describes the sample used for the commuting analysis, comparing the different types of commutes of dual-earner couples in *The Cornell Couples and Careers Study*. I first describe couples with one partner working at home (no commute) and couples that have one or both members with such variable commutes that they cannot report a commute time. The remainder of the chapter examines fixed-length commuters and at-home workers, comparing couples with short (less than twenty-five minutes one way) and long (twenty-five or more minutes one way) commutes.

At Home, at the Office, or in Between: What Are the Differences among Couples by Commuting Type?

There are three strategies for commuting. The first is to avoid a commute and work out of the home. The second is to take a job with a varying commute, such as sales or contract work, in which "going to work" means meeting clients at their workplaces. Finally, and most commonly, commuters may travel to the same work location each workday. In our sample of 811 dual-earner couples, eighteen husbands and twenty-five wives work at home (their commute is zero minutes). In each case, when one spouse works at home, the other works outside the home and has a commute. In another twenty-nine couples, one spouse's commute varies and cannot be pinned down (in approximately one-half the husband's commute varies, in one-half the wife's commute varies). The remainder of the couples, 771 wives and 779 husbands, have fixed-length commutes (see table 5.1). Note how this reflects the hidden infrastructure of work: we take for granted that we go to work at a different location from where we live, and telecommuting full time remains the exception, not the rule.

Wives who work at home for pay earn far less than their husbands and than other wives in the sample, and they are less likely to have college degrees. But overall household income is no different for these households, suggesting that their husbands make up the difference. Home-working wives are significantly less likely than other wives to have professional-level jobs,[18] and their husbands are significantly more likely to be professionals (see figure 5.1) and to work at least four more hours a week on average than other husbands. Wives working at home or at varying work sites work fewer hours, on average, than wives working at a fixed site. Spouses are no more likely to work at home, a fixed distance away, or at varying sites based on their job tenure, neighborhood tenure, age, or marriage length.

Wives' gender attitudes are closely linked to husbands' and wives' commute types. Wives working at home hold more traditional values compared to other wives. Husbands working at home or at varying work sites have more egalitarian-oriented wives than husbands working a fixed distance from home.

Wives working at varying sites experience the most positive work-to-family spillover and the least negative family-to-work spillover compared with wives working elsewhere. Their husbands also report the most positive family-to-work spillover. Wives working at home have low negative *work*-to-family spillover, but among the highest negative *family*-to-work spillover. Bear in mind that those same women working at home report high levels of perceived success and family satisfaction (although the differences are not statistically significant).

Commuting as a Couple-Level Pattern

Couples in our sample work in a variety of locations—from their own dining room table to a work site three hours away. In some couples, both partners travel a similar distance to work. In other couples, one spouse works nearby and the other works far away. Are these couples with different commutes different from one another? For these analyses of couples' commuting patterns and how those patterns affect family life, we compare couples with fixed-length commutes and

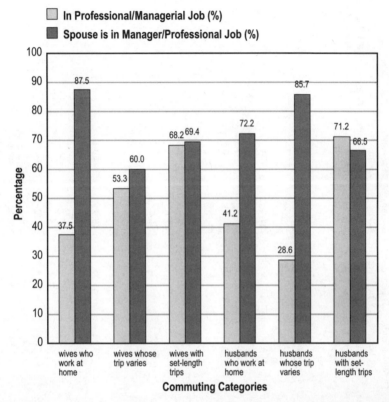

Figure 5.1 Professionals and managers by commuting categories. *The Cornell Couples and Careers Study*, $N = 811$ couples. Own professional status is statistically significant for wives at $p < .001$. Spouse professional status is statistically significant for husbands at $p < .001$.

at-home workers because working at home is a strategy to reduce commuting length that may relate to family life. We exclude couples with varied-length commutes because their commutes are unquantifiable. The remaining couples fall into four groups: (1) both spouses work within a twenty-five-minute drive of home (termed short commuters), 323 (41.2%) of our couples; (2) the husband works within a twenty-five-minute drive and the wife travels twenty-five minutes or more each way (a commuting pattern termed nontraditional because it is the wife who is traveling longer), 152 (19.4%) of our couples; (3) the wife works closer to home (within 25 minutes) and the husband has a long commute (termed neotraditional commuting pattern), 151 (19.4%) of our couples; and (4) both spouses have long commutes, 157 (20%) of our couples.

We find these couples are not all alike. Elements of their personal lives, professional lives, and life histories covary by the commuting pattern they occupy (see table 5.2).

Table 5.1 Commuting Strategies[a]

	Variable, N (%)							
	Wives Who Work at Home 25 (3.1)	Wives Whose Trip Varies 15 (1.8)	Wives with Set-Length Trips 771 (95.1)	Husbands Who Work at Home 18 (2.2)	Husbands Whose Trip Varies 14 (1.7)	Husbands with Set-Length Trips 779 (96.1)	P-Value, Wives	P-Value, Husbands
Commute (minutes each way)								
Individual's commute	0	varies	22.4	0	varies	23.1		
Spouse's commute	26	20	22.5	29.5	25	21.5		
Annual income (in $1,000s)								
Household average	92.7	90	104.7	104.3	107.4	104		
Individual income	16	31	40.5	62	54.5	64.8	$p < .001$	
Spouse income	75	63	64.3	42	51	39.3		
Proportion of total contributed by wife	0.17	0.29	0.38	0.42	0.51	0.37	$p < .001$	$p < .05$
Education and job prestige (%)								
College degrees	56.0	80.0	68.7	61.1	64.3	74.8		
Spouse has college degree	84.0	80.0	73.9	77.8	78.6	68.2		
Professional/managerial jobs	37.5	53.3	68.2	41.2	28.6	71.2	$p < .001$	
Spouse has professional/managerial job	87.5	60.0	69.4	72.2	85.7	66.5		$p < .001$
Work hours (per week)								
Average work hours	32.5	33	40.95	46.25	49.9	49.1	$p < .1$	
Spouse work hours	53.5	47.5	49	39.8	41.9	40.83	$p < .05$	
Timing								
Years in current job	6.7	8	6	5	5	7.8		
Range of years in current job	<1–28	1.0–24	0–37	<1–15	0–12	0–39		
Average number of jobs so far	3	3.5	3.7	4	4.2	4		
Date of last geographic move	Mar-87	Nov-84	Jul-86	Oct-88	Apr-85	Jul-86		
Age	41.5	43.5	42.9	44.9	42	44.8		
Spouse's age	42.5	45.6	44.9	42.8	40.4	42.9		
Number of years in current marriage	18	18	16.8	14	14.6	16.9		

Life stages (%)

Nonparents, wives under age 40	4.0	6.7	5.1	5.6	0	5.1	
Launching (kids under 6)	36.0	26.7	24.0	33.3	42.9	23.9	
Early establishment (kids 6–12)	32.0	0	28.3	16.7	21.4	28.2	$p < .05$
Late establishment (kids 13–18)	8.0	20.0	16.9	5.6	28.6	16.7	
Nonparents, wives ages 40 and above	8.0	20.0	6.6	16.7	7.1	6.7	
Adult children (kids in home 19+)	0	6.7	5.8	5.6	0	5.8	
Empty nest (kids no longer at home)	12.0	20.0	13.4	16.7	0	13.6	

Attitudinal measures

Wives' gender attitude score	−0.84	0.30	0.02	0.45	0.43	−0.02	$p < .001$
Husbands' gender attitude score	−0.38	−0.18	0.02	0.04	−0.02	0.00	$p < .05$
Wives' overall success (0–100)	85.00	81.44	80.70	79.87	78.62	80.91	
Husbands' overall success	80.50	79.20	78.83	79.76	80.36	78.84	
Wives' family satisfaction (1–5)	4.29	4.05	4.05	4.00	4.10	4.06	
Husbands' family satisfaction	4.35	4.21	4.12	4.16	3.97	4.13	
Wives' positive work-to-family spillover	2.88	3.50	2.87	2.72	2.89	2.88	$p < .01$
Husbands' positive work-to-family spillover	2.70	2.63	2.51	2.78	2.46	2.52	
Wives' negative work-to-family spillover	2.46	2.70	2.76	2.72	2.79	2.75	$p < .1$
Husbands' negative work-to-family spillover	2.96	2.63	2.73	2.81	2.43	2.74	
Wives' positive family-to-work spillover	4.00	3.93	3.82	3.69	3.54	3.84	
Husbands' positive family-to-work spillover	3.90	4.13	3.69	3.81	3.86	3.70	$p < .05$
Wives' negative family-to-work spillover	2.44	2.07	2.44	2.47	2.68	2.42	$p < .1$
Husbands' negative family-to-work spillover	2.16	2.43	2.36	2.36	2.18	2.35	

[a] From *Cornell Couples and Careers Study*, 1998–99. $N = 811$ couples.

Table 5.2 Commuting Patterns[a]

	Variable N = 783 (100%)				
	Both Have Short Commutes (<25 min.) 323 (41.2)	Nontraditional (Wife Commutes Long, Husband Short) 152 (19.4)	Neotraditional (Wife Commutes Short, Husband Long) 151 (19.4)	Both Have Long Commutes (25+ min.) 157 (20.0)	P-Value
Annual Income ($1,000s)					
Annual salary, wives	$37,749	$41,228	$34,022	$46,838	***
Annual salary, husbands	$65,507	$59,517	$67,589	$65,857	+
Total household income	$103,027	$100,550	$101,727	$112,777	*
Proportion of total contributed by wife	0.36	0.42	0.32	0.41	***
Education (%)					
Wife is a college graduate	0.34	0.26	0.40	0.25	*
Husband is a college graduate	0.24	0.29	0.26	0.25	
Work contexts					
Hours/week, wives	40.7	40.9	39.7	42.4	
Hours/week, husbands	49.4	48.0	50.4	48.4	+
Number of jobs, wives	3.6	3.7	3.7	3.7	
Number of jobs, husbands	4.1	4.0	4.3	3.7	
Years of current employment, wives	6.5	6.0	5.9	6.6	
Years of current employment, husbands	8.3	7.1	7.2	7.9	
Job prestige, wives	51.51	54.04	51.17	55.96	***
Job prestige, husbands	55.16	53.61	55.64	55.29	***
Ratio, wife's job prestige to husband's job prestige	0.97	1.06	0.95	1.06	
Timing					
Date of last geographic move	Dec-85	Dec-87	Feb-85	Jan-88	**
Wife's age	43.4	41.9	43.3	42.3	
Husband's age	45.4	44.4	45.2	43.8	
Years married (current partner)	17.4	15.0	18.5	15.9	**

Life stages (%)					
Nonparents, wives under age 40	0.07	0.06	0.03	0.04	
Children under 6	0.18	0.34	0.22	0.30	***
Youngest child is 6–12	0.30	0.29	0.27	0.27	
Youngest child is 13–18	0.17	0.13	0.18	0.16	
Nonparents, wives age 40 and above	0.07	0.06	0.05	0.08	
Adult children (children in home 19+)	0.06	0.03	0.10	0.04	*
Empty nest (children no longer at home)	0.15	0.10	0.16	0.11	
Gender and household roles					
Wives' progressive gender attitude score	-0.10	0.16	-0.24	0.21	***
Husbands' progressive gender attitude score	-0.05	0.15	-0.19	0.16	**
Wives' total minutes on chores/workday	168	139	170	149	**
Husbands' total minutes on chores/workday	108	128	102	119	+
Perceived success					
Wives' overall success	81.93	79.34	82.10	79.14	**
Husbands' overall success	79.36	79.17	79.02	77.43	*
Wives' satisfaction with family	4.13	4.00	4.08	3.97	
Husbands' satisfaction with family	4.18	4.15	4.10	4.06	
Measures of spillover					
Wives' positive work-to-family	2.81	2.96	2.85	2.90	
Husbands' positive work-to-family	2.59	2.50	2.50	2.42	
Wives' negative work-to-family	2.71	2.82	2.65	2.88	**
Husbands' negative work-to-family	2.71	2.73	2.79	2.79	
Wives' positive family-to-work	3.83	3.80	3.83	3.86	
Husbands' positive family-to-work	3.73	3.70	3.72	3.60	
Wives' negative family-to-work	2.41	2.46	2.39	2.49	
Husbands' negative family-to-work	2.29	2.36	2.34	2.47	*

[a] From Cornell Careers I data: 811 couples selected through one spouse's employment in a targeted organization, 1998–99. +indicates $p < .10$; *indicates $p < .05$; **indicates $p < .01$; ***indicates $p < .001$.

Income

David Levinson suggests that higher income is linked to a longer commute because those with more income are more selective about where they live and they can buy more housing and land with their earnings. Larger homes and more land are generally located farther from workplaces, and people are willing to commute farther if they have incentives, such as getting paid more.[19] A life stage view says that people who earn higher wages are likely to be a little older and better established in their careers, which suggests that they may have lived in their current home longer than they have had their current job. If that is the case, home and work may be farther apart because they prefer not to uproot their home and family, opting instead to have a longer commute. Either explanation accounts for people with higher wages traveling farther to get to work.

A counterargument is that those with more income can afford to buy housing closer to work because price is less of an obstacle. These families populate the wealthy inner-ring neighborhoods of cities and inhabit high-price condos and apartments closer to their workplaces. Less affluent families must drive great distances from work to arrive at housing in their price range or settle for substandard inner-city housing.

In our sample, we find partial support for the more money–longer commute theory: wives who travel farther have better-paying jobs, whether or not their husbands work near home. Wives who travel twenty-five minutes or more to work receive, on average, $4,000–$10,000 more per year than wives who travel less than twenty-five minutes each way. Husbands in nontraditional commuting patterns (with a shorter commute then their wives) receive lower paychecks than husbands in all other commuting patterns. Husbands with short commutes whose wives travel farther may exchange a lower paycheck for the convenience of living closer to work. Their wives, who earn higher salaries on average for their longer commutes, thus contribute a greater proportion of income to the household (see figure 5.2).

Job Prestige, Education, and Occupational Type

Job prestige predicts commuting patterns in the same way income does: a more prestigious job is a greater enticement to travel farther from home at least for the wives in our two-earner sample. Specifically, wives who travel twenty-five or more minutes to work have higher occupational prestige scores, on average, than wives who work closer to home. Wives who travel longer distances are also likely to have prestige scores that exceed their husbands' scores. Husbands' prestige scores do not predict their commute length as wives' scores do.

Couples with one or both partners working as managers show different commuting patterns than do other couples, tending to work closest to home, on

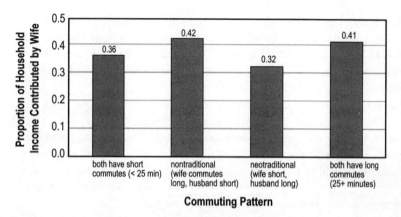

Figure 5.2 Proportion of total income contributed by wife by commuting pattern. Source: *Cornell Couples and Careers Study*, 1998–99.

average. However, wives who are managers are much more likely to work farther from home than other wives. Husbands who are managers and whose wives are not are more likely to display the traditional pattern: commuting a long distance themselves while their nonmanager wives work closer to home.

Work Hours

Work hours are positively linked to husbands' commutes, suggesting the longer they spend somewhere, the more worthwhile the trip. For a job that demands long hours, a few extra minutes in a commute may seem irrelevant in the grand picture. However, note that work hours are only predictive of husbands' longer commutes, not wives'. Husbands with long commutes whose wives work close to home put in 50.4 hours a week on their jobs on average, an hour more than husbands who travel under twenty-five minutes to work. But husbands in a nontraditional pattern (he has the short commute) also work two hours more than do husbands in a neotraditional pattern (she has the long commute), suggesting that there are no simple markers (such as work hours) of time spent commuting. Life stage and spouses' work hours may explain some of these relationships.

Age, Length of Marriage, and Life Stage

Age and length of marriage combined provide an interesting picture and a possible explanation for the different commuting patterns couples adopt. Age itself does not vary by commuting pattern for husbands or wives; length of marriage does. Couples who have been married longer tend to have wives with shorter commutes; wives with short commutes have been married two to three years longer than wives with longer commutes. Because the ages of the couples do not differ among commuting types, this finding suggests that the couples who married earlier in their lives or who have stayed married to the same partner are more likely to have wives working close to home and may be more traditional in their gender attitudes. (We look at the relationship between gender attitudes and commute pattern explicitly in the next section.)

Life stage is related to commuting patterns, but in unexpected ways. Previous research suggests that wives work closer to home when they have children.[20] Instead, we find that wives in the launching stage (those with preschoolers) are equally or more likely to have long commutes (52.4%) than short ones. One explanation could be that launching-stage wives have not yet fully adjusted their careers to the presence of children. One launching-stage mother in our study describes a three-hour commute during her pregnancy:

> I commuted back and forth to Albany during my pregnancy. The last time I made the trip, my own physician said, "I don't think you should make this trip." And I said, "Oh come on, you know, it's only a couple hours, I have three weeks before the baby is due." He said, "You want to have the baby somewhere along the route?" I said, "Oh, there's no signs of that." So I went, and I felt horrible the whole time, a lot of pressure and stuff. Got back and . . . had her! So I almost had her in Albany. She was two weeks early and it sort of surprised me. So I worked right through.

Nonparents and empty nesters are actually the most likely to have short commutes and are especially likely to have both partners with short commutes. This phenomenon is probably due to their ability to live in cities, close to work, instead of choosing a home based partly on their children's needs (e.g., for schools and parks).

Gender Values

Previous research suggests that gender attitudes could be a primary influence on the commuting distances of wives, with more traditional wives taking their household responsibilities more seriously than their work responsibilities and thus prioritizing being near home over landing a well-paying or prestigious job that might be farther away.[21] As figure 5.3 suggests, even in this sample of middle-class, financially comfortable, dual-earner couples, gender values still help describe their commuting patterns. In households in which wives work closer to home, both spouses' hold more traditional gender attitudes than average; in households in which wives travel farther to work, couples are more progressive in their gender values. These orientations, in turn, probably exert an influence on each spouses' income and job-prestige attainment goals.

Household Roles   Gender ideologies are often reflected in household chores. The time spent on household chores may be linked to gender, not commuting pat-

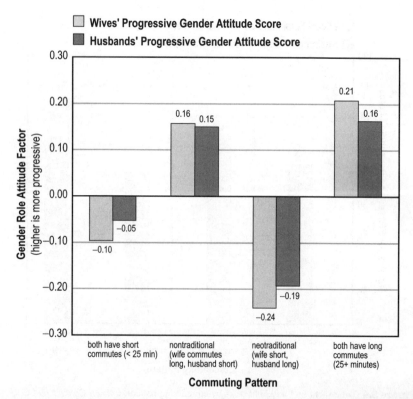

Figure 5.3 Gender attitudes by commuting pattern. *The Cornell Couples and Careers Study*, $N = 811$ couples. Wives' gender role attitudes significant at $p < .001$. Husbands' gender role attitudes significant at $p < .01$.

terns, with wives doing more household tasks than their husbands. Or the time each spouse spends on chores may be linked to the time available, with spouses who commute longer distances putting in less time (fitting with the classic household dinner distribution rule: whoever arrives home first starts dinner). In this sample, gender plus commute time explains time spent on household tasks (see figure 5.4). Husbands routinely do less housework than their wives, especially husbands whose wives have shorter commutes. But even in couples in which both spouses commute long distances, husbands do thirty minutes less housework per day than wives. The smallest difference between spouses is among couples in which wives travel longer distances and husbands work close to home. These couples are most egalitarian regarding chores, with wives spending only twelve minutes more per day than husbands. The couples with the largest gap in chores (one hour and ten minutes difference, on average) have the most traditional-looking commute pattern: husbands travel twenty-five minutes or more and wives travel less.

One husband in our study gives a sense of how housework is distributed over the week and in the end admits that his longer commute has something to do with it:

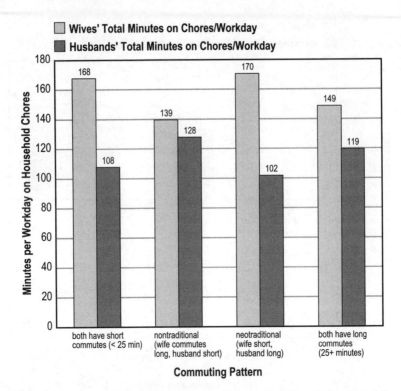

Figure 5.4 Time spent on household tasks by commuting pattern. *Cornell Couples and Careers Study*, $N = 811$ couples. Wives' household task time significant at $p < .01$. Husbands' household task time significant at $p < .1$.

I would say that, um, the weeks [my wife] owns. And does a lot for the kids. I do *some* things, but much more limited. So she does a lot during the week. I pretty much handle the weekends. Whatever has to be done. Driving here, driving there, wherever. She doesn't but I do most of that. That seems to work. Because of my commute—she has a commute which is only about 10 minutes, I'm 30 to 35 minutes, I'm 26 miles away—she is closer, she has somehow been able to flex her time, and also we have depended, from time to time, on parents.

Time available for free time was tested by commuting pattern but was not statistically significant.

Possible Outcomes of Commuting Patterns on Family Life

So far, we have looked at family circumstances that may contribute to the way couples' commuting patterns evolve. Now we look at some psychological consequences of the various commuting patterns, particularly the ways in which the commuting pattern is linked to family satisfaction, feelings of success, and work and family spillover.

Satisfaction with Family

How does the time spent traveling to work relate to contentment with family life? Even though wives work more around the house than their husbands even when they have long commutes, wives' satisfaction with family is actually higher when wives work closer to home, and it is the highest of all in households in which both spouses work close to home. Couples in which both have long commutes are the least satisfied with family life. However, husbands' satisfaction does not vary appreciably by commuting pattern.

Feelings of Success

Husbands' feelings of overall success in life do not vary by commuting pattern, but wives' feelings of success do. As with family satisfaction, wives with shorter commutes report higher levels of overall success than wives who work farther from home.

Spillover between Work and Home

Can the journey to work operate as a buffer zone between work and home? If so, we expect a longer commute to be associated with less negative work-to-family and family-to-work spillover because the commuter has time to decompress and adjust between the spheres during transit. But, in fact, wives with longer commutes report more negative spillover from work to home in a pattern much like family satisfaction. Husbands report more negative spillover from family to work, not due to their own commute buffer but to their wives' long commute. Husbands in couples with two short commutes report the least negative family-to-work spillover. One likely explanation is that husbands whose wives work close to home have fewer worries because their wives are able to get home more quickly for emergencies. In addition, husbands in couples in which both spouses can get home quickly feel the least negative spillover from family to work because either member can rush home in an emergency.

Summing Up

Decisions that individuals and couples make about where to live relative to work and where to work relative to home are influenced not only by length of commute but also by life stage, education, income, managerial and professional status, job prestige, hours spent at work, gender ideologies, and the ages of the youngest children. Commuting time also carries with it some consequences, such as work-to-home and home-to-work spillover, feelings of success, and family satisfaction. Causal directions are suggested but not verified by these data.

We find that couples with no commute or varying commute lengths are significantly different from one another and from couples with fixed-length commutes. Wives who work at home make less money, work fewer hours, and live in more traditional households, but enjoy feelings of success and family satisfaction, although not always. One telecommuter in our study says that:

> When my boss told me that I could telecommute, . . . I didn't realize that it was a compromise. But what I find now that I'm here . . . I'm in a community that I don't know. What I've given up is a sense of community, an area that I know. This would happen to anyone who moved, but what I am finding is telecommuting . . . working out of your home—everyone thinks [it] is such a great deal, and maybe it is, but what the compromise that I've found is that I've given up a lifestyle. . . . the problem is, when you're telecommuting, it's out of sight out of mind. . . . you are out of the gossip mill, you are out of the network. So it makes it harder to stay connected, to stay plugged into what is going on.

By contrast, wives whose husbands work at home or whose husbands' have variable commuting times earn a higher proportion of the household income, are more likely to be professionals or managers at work, put in more work hours, and have progressive gender attitudes. Wives of husbands whose commute length varies feel the least positive family-to-work spillover and are the only group of wives who report lower feelings of overall success than their husbands. Husbands whose trip length varies are the least likely to be in managerial or professional jobs, but put in among the highest work hours and have the lowest family satisfaction (and are the only group of men whose wives report higher family satisfaction than they do).

Wives' income and job prestige are higher for couples in which wives have longer commutes, especially when their husbands have long commutes as well. Commuting pattern also varies by life stage: couples in which both commute a short distance are the least likely to have children—they can choose their housing exclusively to be near their own jobs rather than choosing housing, as parents do, to be near parks and schools. Couples with wives who have long commutes and husbands who have short or long commutes are the most likely to be in the launching stage (to have children under age six) and the least likely to have adult children. This pattern probably reflects the need for parents to make stops before and after work, particularly to day care. Those women who remain employed while their children are young are also likely to be invested in their jobs or their income; thus the job provides incentive to commute longer.

Gender schemes and gendered behavior show similar trends by commuting pattern. The most traditional couples, in which both spouses or just the wife has a short commute, also have the widest gap between spouses in housework contributions. Yet these wives have the highest family satisfaction, feelings of overall success, and the lowest levels of negative spillover.

Accounting for each of these predictors simultaneously (results not shown), husbands are more likely to travel longer to work when their household income is high or when their children are in school, suggesting that a long commute may be an extension of fathers' "good provider" role. They take on the long commute to provide children with a good school district, to buy a better home for the family, or to escape housework. Here's a 35-year-old wife and mother of two young children, talking about these kinds of trade-offs: "Yeah, he works really long days. So dinner is my responsibility and all of that stuff. We could have moved closer to his job but it wasn't a location that we wanted to be in. I also thought my opportunities would be better to stay in the [Metro City] area, and the opportunities for the kids as well. So he chose to keep the commute. It would be nice to have him home at breakfast, but you make those sacrifices".

Wives with more prestigious jobs or whose incomes are a larger proportion of the household total are more likely to commute longer distances (almost regardless of the husbands' commutes). It appears that an individual's station in life predicts commuting behavior much more accurately than attitudes do—gender attitudes are not as important at predicting commuting patterns as are life stage and social class.

Clearly, lifestyle trade-offs both reflect and operate through couples' commuting patterns. Wives who commute longer tend to have higher prestige, more income, and more professional accomplishment than wives who work closer to home, but they also experience lower family satisfaction, lower feelings of success, and more spillover stress than wives with short commutes. Although the journey to work alone is not wholly responsible for these differences, the potential relative costs and benefits of long and short commutes point to the interdependence of work and home and to the way each is valued within couples in a unique and revealing way.

6

Career Clocks: Forked Roads

Sonya Williams and Shin-Kap Han

> Living is like working out a long addition sum, and if you make a mistake in the first two totals you will never find the right answer. It means involving oneself in a complicated chain of circumstances.
>
> —Cesare Pavese, *The Burning Brand:*
> *Diaries 1935–1950*[1]

I magine two scenes, twenty-five years apart. First, imagine Carol and Lynn at their college commencement where they promise to keep in touch with each other, and, most important, to show up at the twenty-fifth reunion no matter what. Now, twenty-five years later, despite their intentions, they have not kept in touch. What do Carol and Lynn expect to see in each other? They were like two peas in a pod when they parted—same gender, same race, same age, same cohort, same region, and same education. Do these factors predict where they end up?

The answer is both yes and no. The affirmative answer rests on the typical practice of sociodemographic mapping: scholars use distinctions among genders, cohorts, racial and ethnic groups, educational backgrounds, and so forth to explain differences in particular outcomes. This line of reasoning, however, leads to a prediction that Carol and Lynn will find each other in rather similar situations. Perhaps. But the prediction is at odds with common sense intuition. A lot could happen in the intervening years; the twenty-five-year period after the college, in particular, is when many critical life events, both in work and family, occur. Although Carol and Lynn started out at the same place, different pathways and events have very probably taken them to vastly different places.

The problem with sociodemographic mapping is that it is static, ignoring the dynamics of the interval between the start and finish lines. This chapter directly addresses this dimension through a life course approach, with a particular focus on the concept of career. The notion of career intersects both microlevel (e.g., individual choices and family constraints) and macrolevel (e.g., organizational and institutional settings and the larger opportunity structure) events and processes.[2] Career also evokes time, the temporal nature of life course processes, demonstrating how prior choices, institutional arrangements, and chance events shape life paths and life chances.[3] Our main purpose in this chapter is to demonstrate a way to operationalize the concept, charting the employment career pathways of men and women in dual-earner families from *The Cornell Couples and Careers Study*. We also examine several mechanisms that operate to sort individuals into career pathways and consider differences in outcomes that individuals with different career pathways experience.

Conceptual Approaches to Career Pathways

The concept of career is based on a central tenet of the life course perspective: to understand behavior at any one life stage requires knowledge of prior transitions and trajectories.[4] Transitions are always embedded in the trajectories that give them distinctive forms and meanings.[5] Life events, such as returning to work, changing jobs, or retirement, therefore should be viewed as transitions occurring in the context of overall career trajectories, reflecting biographical pacing.

Career pathways are typically thought of as a shorthand for occupational mobility. Yet they can be conceptualized and operationalized in a variety of ways.[6] Career pathways may differ in terms of level of overall mobility and may, similarly, vary in terms of their relative continuity in employment. Taking career pathways to be series of positions, we may expect an orderly and hierarchical progression of jobs[7] or individual achievement[8] to be the norm. The extent and shape of the deviation from this norm are of crucial importance, however, and need to be examined empirically.[9]

In fact, whether continuous full-time employment with few interorganization moves and increases in occupational prestige and/or hierarchical authority remains the "normal" career pathway should be questioned in light of labor market and demographic changes occurring over the past thirty or so years. Many employers have sought to move away from the traditional model of mutual obligation, the implicit contract, toward a more contingent form of employment.[10]

Changes in the industrial structure at the aggregate level, such as the shift from manufacturing to service industries and occupations, globalization, and increased competition, have also altered the labor market.[11] These economic transformations have made employment more uncertain, both increasing job turnover (voluntary and involuntary) and reducing job security.

On the demographic front, one of the most significant changes has been the large increase in labor-force participation of women, particularly married women and mothers of young children. These fundamental shifts in the economy and the labor force (fewer younger workers, more women, and more workers with dependent children or aging parents) provide the underlying rationale to reappraise the traditional paradigm of careers as well as the organization of the life course in terms of the work-family interface so that they better address the changed and changing social reality. Instead of focusing on occupational status or mobility at particularly points of time, we shift the frame of reference to trajectories over the life course, including movements in and out of the labor force, in addition to the usual referents in career studies such as job changes or occupational mobility.

Career Pathways: *The Cornell Couples and Career Study*

The data for this analysis are drawn from *The Cornell Couples and Careers Study*, looking at each job respondents have held from age thirty to the time of the interviews. To have sequences of sufficient length for analysis, respondents who were younger than forty-four at the time of the interviews (in 1998–99) are not included in the analysis. We also exclude cases with incomplete job spell information. This results in a sample size of 829.[12] Compared to the full *Cornell Couples and Careers Study* sample, the subsample used in this analysis is slightly more female, better educated, and slightly older.

Our analysis of career pathways focuses on five dimensions of a respondent's employment history: work status, occupation, type of employer, multiple employment in each year, and the number of employers during the observation period. Tables 6.1 and 6.2 (available at www.lifecourse.cornell.edu/about_time.html) show the status set (the possible states for each year of each person's history) for these dimensions. For those who have had multiple employment in a given year we have coded work status, occupation, and type of employer for the job they held for the longest time for that year. We have coded the number of employers in reference to employer changes; in any given year, respondents working for their first employer have been coded 1, those who are working for their second have been coded 2, and so on.

Using years as the unit of time, we transformed the data into sequence data format; the minimum sequence length is fifteen (ages 30–44) and the maximum length is set to thirty-one (ages 30–60). An example of sequence data is also presented in tables 6.1 and 6.2. This hypothetical respondent, Susan, was not employed from ages 30–33 (thus all dimensions have been coded 0) and began working part-time as a sales clerk in a large department store at age thirty-four (work status = 1, occupation = 23, employer type = 1, multiple employment = 1, and number of employers = 1). Twelve years later at age forty-five, she began working full-time as a secretary at a government agency (work status = 1, occupation = 27, employer type = 2, and number of employers = 2) without leaving the part-time sales clerk position (multiple employment = 2). Then, at age fifty, Susan moved to an organization participating in our study (employer number = 3) and ended the part-time sales clerk employment (multiple employment = 1). Two years later, at age fifty-two, she was promoted to administrative supervisor (occupation = 25) and continued in this position until the time she was interviewed in 1999.

To chart the regular patterns in employment history, we employ a sequence analysis technique known as optimal matching or optimal alignment.[13] This is a new method for old ideas; sequences of events or phenomena have been a concern of a wide variety of research areas in the social sciences.[14] Life course researchers, in particular, have been interested in this issue over the past two decades, because it is at the core of the life course perspective's two key constructs—trajectories and transitions—both conceptually and methodologically.[15] However, the methods developed and used thus far have mostly focused on individual events, not the sequence as a whole, that is, sequence qua sequence. Event history analysis is a typical case in point, in which individual spells are the unit of analysis, with transitions between spells being the events of interest.[16] By contrast, we consider each respondent's whole sequence, examining the overall patterning of career trajectories. Specifically, we take into account the incidence, timing, and duration of diverse events and their sequence across multiple domains of career.[17]

Our analyses[18] reveal six distinct pathways. Figures 6.2–6.4 (later in the chapter) show the age profiles of each career pathway on each of the career dimensions included in the analysis. Table 6.3 (available at www.lifecourse.cornell.edu/about_time.html) contains additional summary measures, which further describe each pathway type in terms of the various career dimensions. Figure 6.1, along with table 6.3, also presents the relevant data for the entire subsample used in the analysis, to serve as a basis for comparing the six pathway types.

Career Pathway Types

The figure 6.1a displays both the employment status-level distribution (left axis) and incidence of multiple employment (right axis) for all cases used in the

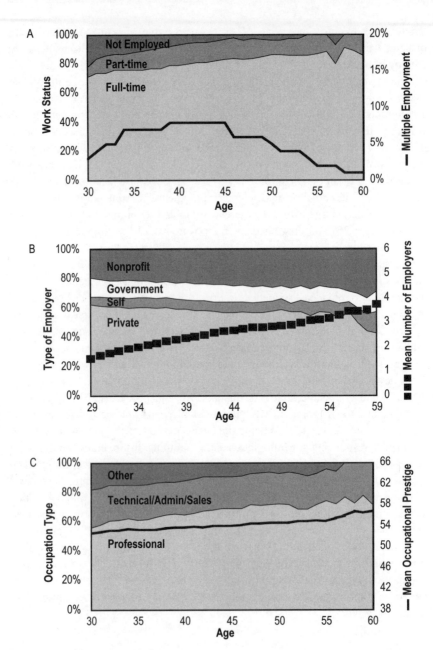

Figure 6.1 Age profiles of the analysis subsample (*N* = 829). Source: *Cornell Couples and Careers Study*, 1998–99.

analysis. The majority of respondents were employed in every year of the observation period and most of those employed worked full time. The average (mean) age at first employment (after age thirty, our starting point) was thirty-one (table 6.3, row 1, column 1), but approximately one-third of the sample changed their employment status (row 2) and the average proportion of time out of the labor force (not employed) between age thirty and the time we interviewed them was 8 percent. On average, 15 percent of the respondents' work was part-time and approximately one-quarter of the respondents experienced a change in employment level (in other words, they moved from full-time to part-time work and/or vice versa). Most of the people in *The Cornell Couples and Careers Study* worked for only one employer in every year of the observation period. Overall, only 21 percent of the respondents have had multiple jobs at some point, and those who have spent on average approximately 37 percent of the observation period with two or more jobs.

Figure 6.1b shows the age profile of those with different employer types (private firm, self/family business, government/military, or nonprofit organization) on the left axis and mean total number of employers on the right axis. (The percentage employed in each employer type was calculated with the number of respondents employed as the denominator.) Not surprisingly, given the organizations from which we drew the sample, employment at private firms dominates, except for a few years at the end of the observation period. Nonprofit organizations (including universities and health-care facilities) are the next most common type of employer, followed by government or military employers and self/family employment. Over the course of time, the percentage working for private employers declines, the percentage at nonprofit organizations increases, and the percentage working for the government remains steady. The percentage of self-employed remains steady until the last few years, when it increases in tandem with the relatively sharp decline in the percentage employed at private firms (see also table 6.4 available at www.lifecourse.cornell.edu/about_time.html). Respondents spent, on average, more than one-half of their employment time working for private companies, and 44 percent of them worked exclusively for this type of employer. Close to one-third of the respondents (31%) worked for a nonprofit organization at some point in their careers, whereas 20 percent worked for the government and 13 percent were engaged in self/family employment. In addition, only approximately one-third of the respondents (33%) ever changed type of employer. However, respondents did change who they worked for an average of three times (see table 6.3), with the average (mean) number of employer changes at each age increasing steadily during the observation period (figure 6.1b).

Figure 6.1c displays the distribution of occupation types (left axis) and the average (mean) occupational prestige (right axis) at each age in the observation period. (The percentage holding each type of occupation and mean prestige were calculated using the number of respondents employed as the denominator.) At each point, most of the respondents held professional or managerial occupations, with the percentage increasing during the observation period. One in five respondents are in technical, sales, or service occupations at each age. A smaller proportion are in other types of occupations, but the proportion declines over the observation period. Over three-quarters of the respondents (77%) remain in professional or managerial occupations over the course of their careers; over two out of five (44%) hold only professional or managerial positions from age thirty on. Technical, sales, and service occupations are less common in our sample; still over two out of five respondents (44%) were in this occupation type at least once. Only 12 percent of the sample worked exclusively in this type of occupation. Occupation type appears to remain fairly stable in this middle-class sample of dual-earner couples; only 39 percent of the sample have had more than one type of occupation over their careers. Average occupational prestige increases slightly over their careers, but only 64 percent of the sample experience any mobility during their careers. Of those that do, 84 percent make upward moves (mean change 11.8) and 69 percent make downward moves (mean change 10.9).[19] Over the course of their employment careers (in other words, the difference between their prestige score at age thirty and their prestige scores at the time we interviewed them in 1998–99), almost one-half of the respondents (43%) have no change in mobility, with approximately one in three (35%) experiencing an increase (mean change 12.8) and approximately one in five (22%) experiencing a decrease (mean change 10.5) in occupational prestige.

Figure 6.2 displays the work status and multiple employment age profiles by career pathway type, figure 6.3 shows the employer type and number of employers by age for each career pathway, and figure 6.4 shows the occupation type and prestige age profiles. One hundred five respondents follow a conventional career pathway. We designate this pathway *conventional* because its members have employment histories that conform with the usual definition of career—that is, these respondents have been continuously employed, working full-time hours (or more), and are likely, compared to the analysis sample, to have experienced changes in either their work hours or employment status. On average, respondents with conventional careers have had three employers and most of the changes in employer occurred relatively early in the career. Most of these respondents' careers are spent in professional or managerial occupations; not quite one-half (49%) worked only in these types of occupations. Although this group differs from the analysis sample in terms of occupation type, its profile in terms of occupational mobility is similar. Likewise, its type of employer profile is also similar to that observed for the entire subsample. However, this pathway exhibits a markedly different age profile for multiple employment, with higher levels of

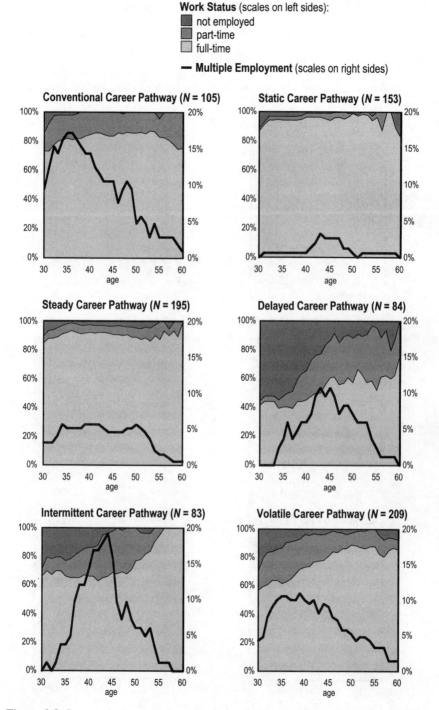

Work Status (scales on left sides):
- ■ not employed
- ■ part-time
- □ full-time

— **Multiple Employment** (scales on right sides)

Figure 6.2 Career pathway age profiles: work status and multiple employment. Source: *Cornell Couples and Careers Study*, 1998–99.

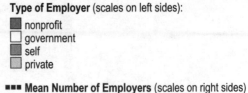

Type of Employer (scales on left sides):
  ■ nonprofit
  □ government
  ■ self
  ■ private

■■■ Mean Number of Employers (scales on right sides)

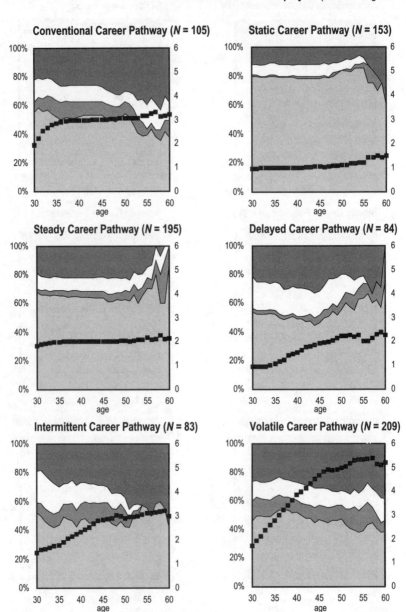

Figure 6.3 Career pathway age profiles: employer type and number of employers. Source: *Cornell Couples and Careers Study*, 1998–99.

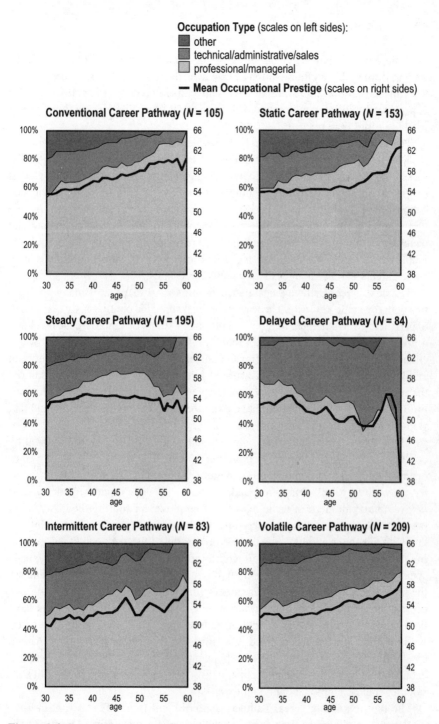

Figure 6.4 Career pathway age profiles: occupation type and prestige. Source: *Cornell Couples and Careers Study*, 1998–99.

multiple employment occurring at early ages and the proportion of individuals with multiple jobs declining among those ages thirty-six and older. Compared to the full subsample, more individuals with conventional career pathways have experienced multiple employment and have spent more time during their careers working more than one job.

The next career pathway type is designated *static* ($n = 153$); it is characterized by relatively few changes on most of the career dimensions. Specifically, these respondents are less likely to have changed employment status (17%), level (6%), and employer (mean total number of employers: 1) or to have experienced occupational mobility (57%). These respondents have spent most of the observation period employed full-time (or more) in professional or managerial occupations in private firms and have experienced relatively little multiple employment (only 5% ever had more than one job). In sum, individuals with static careers can be thought of as having career jobs.

The next career pathway, designated *steady* ($n = 195$), shares many similarities with the static pathway. These respondents were also continuously employed, experiencing few changes in either employment status or employment level and a lower likelihood of occupational mobility. Respondents with steady pathways changed employers at least once (mean number of employers: 2), usually between employers of the same type (9% worked for more than one type). In addition, these respondents are more likely than those with static careers to have held multiple jobs and, for those that did have more than one job, to have maintained that status for a significant portion of their careers.

These three career pathways, conventional, static, and steady, are marked by continuous full-time (or more) employment with few changes in employer or occupational type. In contrast, the remaining three types are marked by instability in various forms. First, respondents with the career pathway designated *delayed*, have the highest mean age at first employment (during the observation period). These respondents are the most likely to have experienced a change in employment status and have the highest proportion of time not employed, reflecting the relatively long delay in their workforce entry. These respondents also have spent the highest proportion of their employment years working part-time and are the most likely to have spent their careers working in technical, sales, or service occupations. In addition, approximately one-quarter of these respondents have held more than one job at a time, spending approximately one-third of their working time at a second or third job. However, this career pathway is marked by stability of a sort, in that these respondents are the least likely to experience occupational mobility, change occupational types, and, compared to the full subsample, change employers and employer type.

The two remaining career pathways, *intermittent* ($n = 83$) and *volatile* ($n = 209$) have employment trajectories characterized by instability. These respondents are more likely to experience changes in employment status and level, with volatile career pathways having more changes than the intermittent ones. These respondents are also more likely to have worked for more than one type of employer, again with the volatile career pathway having a higher percentage. However, whereas the high level of change in type is accompanied by a high total number of employers for respondents with volatile careers, those with intermittent careers have the same average total number of employers as the analysis subsample. Whereas respondents with volatile careers are also the most likely to have held more than one occupation type and experienced occupational mobility, particularly upward mobility, those with intermittent career pathways are less likely to have changed occupation types and experienced occupational mobility. Finally, respondents with intermittent and volatile pathways are more likely to have held more than one job at some point in their careers.

The six types of career pathways are distinguished by the overall level of changes along all of the dimensions and the timing of the changes. Also, some types of changes, such as the change of employer or entry/exit from employment, matter more than others in distinguishing among career pathways. Approximately one-half of the respondents can be classified into two career pathways: 24 percent have had steady careers and 25 percent have had volatile careers. The remaining types can be seen as variations of the two dominant types, with the static and conventional pathways serving as variations of the steady type and the delayed and intermittent pathways serving as variations of the volatile type. These results indicate two opposing norms governing career pathways: stability versus instability. How do individuals get sorted into pathways of stability versus instability, and what are the implications of this variation in career pathways for the outcomes?

Factors Serving as Sorting Mechanisms

We examine descriptive measures regarding sociodemographic characteristics of the respondents by pathway type, which may operate as sorting mechanisms in the determination of career pathways (see table 6.4). Gender is a critical dimension shaping employment trajectories. Most of the respondents with steady and static career pathways are men, whereas most of the respondents with delayed and intermittent career pathways are women. However, a significant proportion of women do experience the predominately male career pathways, and a significant proportion of men experience what are the predominately female career pathways. Men and women experienced the remaining career pathways, conventional and volatile, more or less equally.

Education is also related to career pathway. Respondents with conventional career pathways are more likely to have college degrees than the total subsample, whereas those with delayed pathways are the least likely. Graduate degrees are also more common among those with conventional pathways and are least common in the static and intermittent pathways. However, including gender in the mix changes the picture. Most notably, men with delayed pathways are more likely to have both college and graduate degrees, whereas women with this career type are among the least likely to have either type of degree. Also, whereas men with conventional career pathways are more likely to be college-educated, women with this pathway type are less likely. Both men and women with conventional pathways are more likely to have graduate degrees.

The economic and demographic changes described in chapter 1 are expected to produce differences in the distribution of career pathway types across birth cohorts. Overall, respondents with static or intermittent pathways are more likely to have been born after 1945 (i.e., they are baby boomers), whereas those with volatile or delayed careers are the least likely. Gender differences also emerge in the relation between cohort and career pathway. Whereas women with delayed career pathways are less likely to be part of the baby boom or post–baby boom cohort, the proportion of men with this pathway is similar regardless of whether they are born before or after 1945. Men with steady pathways and women with intermittent pathways are more likely to be baby boomers (or younger), whereas men with conventional careers are less likely to be part of the older, pre–baby boom cohort. For respondents in the static and volatile pathways, the gender difference is not in direction but degree. The increase in the likelihood of baby boomers having a static career is greater for women than men; the decrease in the likelihood of baby boomers having a volatile career is greater for men compared to women.

These sorting mechanisms also interact with career pathway. For men in the delayed career pathway, those born as part of the baby boom after the second world war or later are more likely to have college and graduate degrees than those born before the war's end, whereas men in the conventional career pathway are much less likely to have graduate degrees compared to those baby boomer men born before 1946 (results not shown). For women in the baby boom generation and younger, those with steady careers are more likely to have college and graduate degrees compared to those born before 1946, whereas those with static and conventional pathways are less likely to have college or graduate degrees. In addition, the proportion of women baby boomers with graduate degrees is higher compared to those born before or during the war and earlier for respondents with a delayed or volatile career pathway and is lower for those with an intermittent pathway.

These results indicate that gender, education, and birth cohort both exert a direct effect and interact in a complex manner to sort individuals into different career pathways. On the one hand, women are more likely to experience unstable pathways; on the other hand, however, increased educational attainment leads to pathways characterized by stability for both genders. Interestingly, membership in a later birth cohort appears to move individuals toward a path of stability despite the economic and demographic changes that are thought to have increased the probability of employment instability over time. The interactions among these three sorting mechanisms appear to operate in complex ways, sometimes loosening and sometimes reinforcing the norm of stability or instability.

Employment, Family, and Work-Family Interface

In this section, we consider variation in various types of outcomes associated with variation in career pathway. Table 6.5 (available at www.life-course.cornell.edu/about_time.html) shows employment, family, and work-family interface outcomes of the respondents at the time of *The Cornell Couples and Career Study* interview by career pathway and gender. First, the median annual salary of the respondents is displayed. The three pathways typified by continuous full-time work and relative stability (steady, static, and conventional) all have higher median salaries, whereas the other three pathways have lower median salaries. Moreover, the median salary for men is higher than that for women in every type of career path. The gender difference is greatest in the delayed pathway, followed by the static pathway. The least gender difference occurs among those following a volatile career pathway.

The second section of table 6.5 displays the mean scores on two subjective measures of employment outcomes by career pathway and gender. The first measure is of perceived success at work[20] and the second is of job security;[21] both are measured on a one hundred-point scale. There is little difference among career pathways in terms of perceived work success. (See Moen, Waismel-Manor, and Sweet, chap. 9 in this volume, for further discussion of perceptions of success among the Cornell study respondents.) Controlling for gender reveals no difference on the work success measure, except that women with static and conventional pathways rate themselves slightly more successful than the overall sample of women. The respondents in the delayed, intermittent, and volatile pathways have a higher mean rating of job security compared to respondents with other pathway types; this relationship remains after controlling for gender. In addition, women with static and conventional careers have a significantly higher mean score on the job security measure compared to men with the same pathways.

Next, table 6.5 shows details of the family context in which respondents charted their career paths. Overall, the mean age at first marriage is twenty-four, with a standard deviation of five. Seven percent of the sample married at age nineteen or earlier (more than one standard deviation below the mean), and 13 percent married at age thirty or later (more than one standard deviation above the mean). Respondents with a volatile career were less likely to marry early and more likely to marry later; however, men with this career type married later and women with this career type married earlier. In addition, men with volatile careers were more likely to have divorced. Women with static careers were more likely to marry later. Respondents with delayed careers are the least likely to have been divorced, regardless of gender. However, gender differences in divorce percentages are apparent for those with steady and intermittent careers. Women with steady career pathways are more likely to have been divorced, whereas men in this pathway are less likely; the relationship is reversed for those with intermittent careers.

Overall, 10 percent of the analysis subsample has not (yet) had children. Women with static and steady careers and men with volatile careers are the least likely to have children, whereas men with conventional careers are the most likely to have children. Respondents with delayed careers are also more likely to have children, regardless of gender. Overall, the mean age of becoming parents is twenty-eight, with a standard deviation of five. Sixteen percent of the sample had their first child at age twenty-two or earlier (more than one standard deviation below the mean) and roughly the same percentage had their first child at age thirty-three or later (more than one standard deviation above the mean). Women with steady careers are the most likely to have had their first child early, whereas women with conventional careers and both men and women with intermittent careers are the least likely to have had their first child early. Men with volatile careers are the most likely to have had their first child late, whereas men with static or conventional careers and both men and women with steady careers are less likely to have had their first child late.

Finally, we consider the work-family interface. The last section of table 6.5 presents the percentage of respondents who report a job change that was family related. Overall, women are far more likely to cite family as an explanation for a job change. None of the men with a static career cite family as a reason for a job change (perhaps because so few of them experience any changes). Men with steady and delayed career pathways are also unlikely to have cited family, whereas men with volatile careers are the most likely to do so. Women with static careers are the least likely to have cited family, whereas women with volatile and conventional careers are most likely to cite family as a reason for a job change. However, there is little difference in perceived success with balancing work and family life among respondents when controlling for gender and career pathway (results not shown).[22]

Because our data include couples who are married to one another, we can examine how husbands and wives pair their career pathways. Due to the small number of couples ($n = 325$),[23] we group career pathways into two larger categories: predominately stable (steady, static, and conventional pathways) and predominately unstable (delayed, intermittent, and volatile). The most common pairing is husband stable/wife unstable (40%), followed by both stable (28%). In 21 percent of the couples, both partners have unstable career pathways; 12 percent consist of the husband unstable/wife stable pairing. We find the same pattern even after controlling for the birth cohort of the couple, with one exception: when both partners were born before 1946, the both unstable combination is the second most common combination (after husband stable/wife unstable) followed by both stable (results not shown). Controlling for the partners' education reveals the same pattern, except when the wife is more highly educated than her husband (results not shown): the both stable combination and the husband stable/wife unstable combination are equally common.

Summing Up

In this chapter, we have examined the employment career pathways (or trajectories) of men and women in middle class, dual-earner families in upstate New York. We characterize employment trajectories on multiple dimensions, including the duration and timing of employment (both absolute and relative to other life events), frequency of interorganizational moves, and changes in occupational status. Although continuous full-time employment with few interorganizational moves and increases in occupational status over time is the traditional definition of career and is usually the standard (implicit or explicit) against which all other types of employment are compared, it characterizes the life paths of an ever-smaller number of workers. Empirically examining variations in employment trajectories is important considering the transformations that have occurred in the labor market, the growing number of women participating in the labor force, the emerging dominance of dual-earner families, the decline of implicit contracts between employers and employees (bonds of mutual obligation), and the expansion of service sector employment.

We have found two broad possibilities: roughly one-half of our respondents experience careers centered on a norm of stability and the other half have careers centered on a norm of instability. This finding contradicts the notion of a single career path, commonly assumed in the employment careers literature. What makes our findings unique is that we have broadened the focus of the inquiry and expanded the definition of career to search for actual patterns (rather than imposing preconceived notions), allowing for a more diverse and theoretically interesting career typology.

We expected that younger cohorts, those entering the labor market at later periods, would have more unstable careers given the economic transformations of the labor market and the demographic changes in the labor force. What we observe among cohorts, however, are differences in types of stability or instability. This suggests that the norm of instability has not emerged as a response to macrolevel changes but instead has been operating, albeit unrecognized, for a period of time. If this is the case, it may be that macrolevel changes are shifting the form of both stable and unstable norms governing employment trajectories. In order to fully address this issue, further study, incorporating additional birth cohorts, is required.

The practice of sociodemographic mapping specifies individual characteristics, such as gender and educational attainment, as strong, invariant determining forces of career paths. And, in fact, women are more likely to experience instability, while more highly educated workers are more likely to have stable careers. However, a significant number of both men and women in the Cornell sample have experienced all six pathways, and the highly educated do not dominate any single type of career. In addition, we observe changes over time in the operation of these factors, indicating that neither the strength nor the direction of sorting mechanisms is invariant, but that they are, in fact, mutable.

In terms of outcomes, those with stable career pathways, on average, garner higher economic rewards. However, those with stable (as opposed to unstable) careers are not better off in terms of subjective measures. In fact, individuals with unstable pathways are slightly better off on noneconomic employment outcomes. This finding suggests that a purely economic motivation is not the only force driving individual employment choices. That is, some individuals may prefer intrinsic rewards over economic ones when assessing achievement or success in the employment realm. Hence, we should consider a diverse range of motivations.

Finally, what light does our analysis shed on the work-family interface that people in dual-earner families experience? Overall, both women and those with unstable careers are more likely to cite family concerns as a reason for job changes than are men and those with stable careers. At the couple level, husbands are more likely to have stable careers and their wives are more likely to have unstable careers. On the one hand, these findings support the neotraditional patterns described in Moen and Sweet (chap. 2 in this volume): gendered life trajectories arising from a modified version of the traditional division of labor (with husbands focused on the labor market and wives focused on family maintenance). However, the neotraditional approach to managing the competing demands of work and family is hardly universal. A significant portion of women experience stable careers and a significant portion of men experience unstable careers. This finding suggests a convergence in the ways middle-class men and women, at least, chart their employment pathways. That is, women's work patterns look more like men's full-time, continuous permanent attachment, and men, perhaps in response to the changing social organization of workplaces and families, increasingly show employment behaviors once ascribed solely to women.

The findings in this chapter show that incorporating a long view of time by examining the trajectory of employment careers provides insight into the complex pathways that individuals follow from one point in life to another. The life-course approach yields a richer and more diverse view of both the operation of institutional forces and the strategies that individuals and families use in constructing life courses in their own biographies.

PART TWO

STRAINS, SUCCESSES, AND SUBJECTIVE ASSESSMENTS

7

Spillover

Patricia V. Roehling, Phyllis Moen, and Rosemary Batt

> I can remember times in our marriage that I have said to
> her "this isn't work, this is home, this is family"; you
> cannot separate work and family totally but I have learned
> to come home and shake myself of everything.
>
> —Fifty-two-year-old teacher speaking about
> the difficulty his wife (who is a
> consultant) has in separating work
> and family

As we show throughout this volume, traditional customs and practices of societal institutions are out of step with the needs of contemporary couples. Work-family spillover, the transfer of mood, affect, and behavior between work and home,[1] is one of the consequences associated with this structural lag. The simultaneous management of work and family domains in a world that treats them as separate spheres can lead to strains and conflict. But it also offers the possibility of gains. In fact, spillover between work and family can be both positive and negative. Positive spillover occurs when satisfaction and stimulation at work translate into high levels of energy and satisfaction at home. Negative spillover occurs when problems and conflicts at work drain and preoccupy individuals, negatively impacting their behavior and experiences with their families.[2]

Work-family spillover has important ramifications for the functioning of the workplace as well as the well-being of employees and their families. For example, research shows that negative spillover and work-family conflict relate to higher rates of absenteeism, turnover, and exhaustion along with lower levels of productivity, job satisfaction, and job commitment.[3] High negative spillover and conflict are also associated with a lower quality of family life, greater marital conflict, poorer health, and higher levels of psychological strain, depression, stress, and problem drinking.[4]

The goal of this chapter is to promote a fuller understanding of the concept of spillover. In the first section, we review the research on the spillover between work and family; we discuss theoretical models of how people manage their work and family roles, highlight the most important empirical findings, and identify current limitations in the literature. In the second section, we draw on our findings from *The Cornell Couples and Careers Study*, focusing on the incidence of spillover among couples and over the life course: How do the characteristics of one spouse influence the spillover experienced by the other? How does spillover vary across life stage? What family and workplace variables affect the spillover of the worker and their spouse? To answer these questions, we draw on both quantitative (survey) and qualitative (focus groups and in-depth interviews) data.

Historical Overview of the Spillover Literature

Scholarly understanding of work-family spillover has grown significantly since the 1960s. Early research in the 1960s and 1970s focused on the correlation between the quality and satisfaction of work life and the quality and satisfaction of nonwork life.[5] Three major models help us understand this relationship: compensation, segmentation, and spillover. According to the compensation model, people compensate for dissatisfaction in one domain by trying to find more satisfaction in the other domain (i.e., work and nonwork satisfaction are negatively correlated).[6] The segmentation model posits that employees compartmentalize work and nonwork life so that emotions and stresses from one domain remain independent from the other domain (i.e., work and nonwork satisfaction have a correlation of zero).[7] The spillover model posits that experiences in one domain spill over into and influence the other domain (e.g., work and nonwork satisfaction are positively correlated).

Although research evidence exists for all three relationships, the majority of workers and families fit the spillover model.[8] For example, using data from the 1977 Quality of Employment Survey, a 1994 analysis found that 68 percent of workers met the criteria for spillover (work satisfaction and nonwork satisfaction positively correlated), 20 percent for segmentation (minimally correlated), and 12 percent for compensation (negatively correlated).[9] It is estimated that the correlation between work and nonwork satisfaction is between 0.40 and 0.48.[10] Segmentation and compensation, when they do occur, are more likely to characterize employees in nonprofessional occupations and workers who have encountered disappointments in their career.[11]

A major problem with correlational studies is the difficulty inferring causation from them. To circumvent this problem, scholars have developed measures of spillover that directly assess the transfer of emotions, stresses, and behaviors from one domain to the other domain (e.g., "job worries distract you when you are at home"). This permits the direct assessment of spillover rather than relying on a correlation to infer its presence. Moreover, scholars have moved away from simple correlational studies to more complex research designs and analyses (such as multivariate, longitudinal, and path analytic studies).

Work-Family Conflict and Interference

The work-family conflict and interference research is closely related to and has developed concurrently with research on spillover. Studies on conflict and interference are rooted in role theory, which argues that role conflict (and role overload) occurs when there is a "simultaneous occurrence of two (or more) sets of pressures such that the compliance with one would make more difficult compliance with the other."[12] Work-family conflict and work-family interference are the direct result of incompatible pressures from an individual's work and family roles. Both the conflict and interference research and the spillover research examine the transfer of emotions and behaviors from work to home and from home to work. However, the conflict and interference research also assesses the intrusion of tasks from the work role into the family and vice versa. A second difference between the spillover research and the conflict and interference research is that spillover denotes the transfer of negative and positive emotions from one domain to the other. This is in contrast to the conflict and interference research, which focuses solely on the deleterious nature of the work-family interface (analogous to negative spillover).

Because they are so closely related, we review here the evidence on both spillover and conflict and interference. For the sake of simplicity, we refer to this simply as spillover, but when discussing specific findings we employ the terms used by the researchers (conflict, interference, or spillover) to describe the work-family relationship.

Work and Family Career Dynamics: The Impact of Career on Family and of Family on Career

The extent and direction of the links between work and family are important issues for both employers and employees. A growing consensus finds that employment has more of a negative impact on family life than family life has on work life. Four studies—one using daily reports recorded at random intervals, and three using cross-sectional survey methods—show that, for both men and women, work interferes with family more than family interferes with work.[13]

One explanation for the greater level of work-to-family spillover is the relative inflexibility of work life compared to family life. In most cases, employees are required to work a set number of hours, with the scheduling and location of work relatively fixed. Family roles, however, have no external guidelines for the amount of time that must be devoted to family members or the location in which family interactions must take place. When work-family conflicts do arise, workers can hire others to perform many domestic duties (e.g., child care, cleaning, and cooking), which is rarely the case for workplace responsibilities. As a result of this relative inflexibility, demands at work tend to invade and dictate the pace and timing of family life.

A second explanation is that employees typically have less control over decisions in their work life than they do in their family life. For example, employers dictate and may alter the hours, location, or conditions of work without notice, whereas workers exert more control over such decisions on the home front. A 1995 study of health-care professionals (nonphysicians) showed that when employees have greater influence over decisions at work, they are more able to balance work and family demands.[14] Similar findings emerge in *The Cornell Couples and Careers Study*.

Factors Influencing Spillover

Role Involvement

According to the scarcity hypothesis, the more committed a person is to a particular role, the greater the chance of conflict or interference with other roles.[15] Consistent with this hypothesis, several studies have found that spillover is related to level of role involvement. Scholars have found that the more involved or the more central an individual's work role, the greater the reported level of work-family conflict.[16] Hours spent at work, typically viewed as an objective measure of role involvement, has also been positively related to work-family interference and negative spillover, particularly among women.[17] Involvement in the family role also predicts work-family conflict. Ego involvement in parenting (but not the actual hours spent in the parental role) and high levels of family involvement predict greater negative work-to-family spillover.[18]

Involvement in either work or family roles increases not only the likelihood of work-family conflict and negative spillover, but also the likelihood of positive spillover. In a study of Canadian managers and Canadian business school alumni, scholars found greater parental role involvement to be associated with workers' perceptions of greater benefits, both at home and at work.[19] Note, however, that such benefits are not linked to the amount of time spent in the parenting role. In fact, for this sample of business school alumni, time spent in active parenting is negatively correlated with positive spillover.[20] Thus, positive spillover appears to be a function of the value that workers place on the parenting role and the quality of the interaction between parents and children, not the amount of time that workers spend in parenting. This echoes the mantra that it is the quality not the quantity of the family time that is important.

Gender

The relationship between gender and spillover is complex and can best be understood by examining family-to-work spillover and work-to-family spillover separately. Given that women identify more strongly with the family role than do men[21] and spend more time with their children than do men,[22] we expect that women also experience more family-to-work spillover than do men. Empirical evidence regarding this hypothesis is mixed, however. A longitudinal daily diary study[23] and two cross-sectional surveys[24] found that men experience greater family-to-work spillover than women. However, two other studies, one of which was also a daily diary study, found that women experience greater family-to-work spillover than do men, particularly women with young children.[25] Three other studies show no difference between men and women on degree of family-to-work interference.[26] These studies lead to the conclusion that there is no definitive story linking gender with negative family-to-work spillover.

There is a clearer picture regarding the relationship between gender and work-to-family spillover. Four studies find women experience greater levels of negative work-to-family spillover and work interference with family than do men.[27] Three studies report no gender differences, and one provides evidence that men experience more time-based work-to-family conflict than do women.[28] Given that women report levels of work commitment similar to men[29] and that women spend more time than men engaged in housework and child care, it is not surprising that, in many studies, women report the highest levels of work-to-family spillover and interference.

Context: Work-Related Variables

The contexts in which employees work and live influence their experience of spillover. Several studies confirm that the more flexible and supportive the workplace, the less interference and negative spillover there is from work to home. Specifically, having a supportive supervisor[30] and having supportive coworkers[31] are related to lower levels of negative work-to-family spillover and conflict. Degree of autonomy at work,[32] work variability,[33] and employee control over decisions at work[34] are also related to less work-to-family spillover. Finally, substantial evidence suggests that the use of flextime is related to lower levels of work-family interference.[35] These supportive practices and policies clearly help employees to alleviate some of the stresses and conflicts associated with integrating work and family roles.

On the other hand, some workplace conditions lead to higher levels of negative work-to-family spillover. Not surprisingly, jobs that are high in stress and conflict are related to higher levels of negative spillover from work to home.[36] A heavy workload and time pressures are also related to more work-family conflict and spillover.[37] Finally, among men, schedule inflexibility is linked to greater work-family conflict.[38] Thus, a demanding, stressful, and inflexible job often results in the spillover of stresses and frustrations into the home.

Context: Family-Related Variables

An important part of the context in which an individual lives is the family environment. Several characteristics of the family have an impact on spillover. Not surprisingly, research suggests that employed parents experience greater negative work-family spillover than employed nonparents.[39] Problems with child care are a special dilemma that is linked to greater negative family-to-work spillover.[40] However, as children get older and the workload associated with parenthood decreases, the family-to-work spillover also decreases.[41] The number of children in the home is also related to spillover, with larger families reporting higher levels of work-to-family and family-to-work conflict.[42] Surprisingly, studies have not found greater levels of family-to-work interference among single parents compared to partnered parents.[43] Although single parents have less support than parents with partners, they also have one less role (the role of spousal partner). This trade-off may account for the similarity of family-to-work spillover among partnered and unpartnered parents. Meshing work and parenthood can also be a positive experience—a 1993 study found that parenthood was associated with more positive as well as negative family-to-work spillover, especially for women.[44]

The ways in which husbands and wives balance their work and family responsibilities also influences spillover. Men with nonemployed wives report lower levels of negative spillover from work to family compared to those in two-earner households.[45] This is not surprising—men married to full-time homemakers are likely to devote less time and attention to domestic tasks, which translates into less spillover between the two domains. Finally, the more perceived support individuals receive from family members, the less work-family conflict they report experiencing.[46]

Linked Lives: Marital and Parental Relationships

To fully understand the relationship between work and family, we need to incorporate the perspective of linked lives. People do not live in a vacuum. Rather, they are socially interdependent. Relationships with spouses and children impact workers' experiences and relationships at work and vice versa.[47] For example, a 1993 study of Boston-area dual-earner couples found that the strains associated with poor marital and parental relationships spill over into and negatively affect relationships and experiences at work. Conversely, workers who report having quality relationships with their children and spouse say that their family life enhances their experiences at work.[48]

Stressors and relationships at work can also influence the quality and tone of interactions with family members. Rena Repetti and her colleagues found that on days characterized by high workloads, both mothers and fathers are more behaviorally and emotionally withdrawn from their children when they return home from work. In addition, among fathers, unpleasant interactions with coworkers are often followed by more negative interactions with their children.[49]

Marital interactions are also affected by events at work. This is called crossover or stress contagion. Crossover occurs when the stresses that people experience at work lead to stresses for their spouse at home.[50] A 1989 longitudinal study of dual-earner couples found that on days when men report feeling overloaded at work their wives report feeling overloaded at home later that evening.[51] Wives' feelings of overload at work, however, did not appear to impact husbands' feelings of stress or overload in the home. Similarly, a 1993 study of dual-earner couples also found the crossover of stress from work to home occurs primarily from the husbands' job to their wives, but not vice versa.[52]

The mutual work arrangements of a couple matter as well. Jeffrey Greenhaus and associates have found that work-family conflict is greatest when husbands and wives have very different levels of job involvement. And conflict is lowest among couples in which both members have a high level of job involvement.[53] This suggests that if both members of a couple share a common orientation toward work, they may be less likely to put pressure on one another to change their arrangements. Problems also arise when one spouse reports that his or her career has higher priority than his or her spouse's career.[54] Finally, Phyllis Moen and Yan Yu found less conflict and stress among dual-earner couples if both members work approximately the same full-time hours but neither spouse puts in long (more than forty-five) hours.[55]

Spillover in *The Cornell Couples and Careers Study*

In our study, we extend the spillover research in several ways. First, we focus on workers who share a particular context: dual-earner middle-class couples. The demands of dual careers and professional work in our sample provide the opportunity to examine spillover when the range and intensity of spillover are likely to be high. We also examine gender differences between men and women who face quite similar professional demands at work.

Second, most of the conflict and interference and the spillover research has focused on the negative aspects, the strains, of integrating work and family roles, whereas we consider positive as well as negative spillover. We also identify the strategies that dual-earner couples employ to maximize the benefits and minimize the costs of meshing work and family life.

Third, by taking a couple-level perspective in our spillover analyses, we examine the linked lives of working men and women, a dimension most scholars have ignored. Couple-level research suggests that spousal behaviors, emotions, and characteristics are likely to play a significant role in the other spouse's experience of work-family spillover. We therefore use information gathered from both members of our dual-earner couples to understand the relative levels of spillover experienced by husbands and wives and how the work experiences of one member of a couple affect their partners' sense of spillover.

Fourth, we take a life course perspective, which gives us a snapshot of the work and family career dynamics that occur as men and women move through different work and family roles. Previous studies that have taken a life stage approach to understanding spillover have, with few exceptions, only defined two life stages: parenthood and nonparenthood.[56] Our seven life-course stages permit a better understanding of how the benefits and stresses associated with work and family vary across the life course for both men and women.

Finally, we examine the effect of a variety of work and family characteristics on spillover and the strategies that people use for managing work and family. We consider family constraints (such as the time spent in household chores and dependent care), as well as work-related variables (such as hours of work, workload, and control over scheduling). Of particular interest are family and work strategies (the use of computer technology, telecommuting, and flextime) for increasing the efficiency of running the home and/or to increase the flexibility of work. Each of these characteristics is measured for both self and spouse.

Methods

Our respondents are dual-earner couples ($N = 811$) in *The Cornell Couples and Careers Study* (see app.). We analyze the data using basic descriptive techniques as well as repeated-measures analysis of variance (ANOVA) and ordinary least squares (OLS) hierarchical regressions. We use a repeated-measures analysis of variance rather than one-way ANOVAs because husband and wife spillover scores are not independent of one another. With a repeated-measures ANOVA, the couple is treated as the unit of analysis and husband and wife spillover scores are treated as separate observations within the same unit. Previous studies have not compared the spillover scores of husbands and wives; rather, they have compared the scores of employed men and women, without taking into account the specific employment circumstances of their spouse.

Measures

Spillover We use a shortened version of the spillover scale developed by the John D. and Catherine T. MacArthur Foundation Network on Successful Midlife Aging. The scale assesses four types of spillover, measuring each type with two questions (scored on a five-point scale where 1 equals all the time and 5 equals never). Items were recoded so that a higher score represented greater spillover. The items were then averaged to form an index.

Life Stage Recall, the seven life stages consist of

two nonparent stages: young nonparents (ages 25–39) and older nonparents (ages 40+)

four stages with children in the home: launching, preschool-age children (ages 0–5); early establishment, young school-age children (ages 6–12); later establishment, adolescents (ages 13–18); and adult children (over 18 in the home)

one stage that includes parents of children who are grown and have left home: empty nest[57]

Variables Used in Regression Equations To predict work-to-family spillover, we examine several work-related variables. Flexible work strategies include whether the respondent utilizes (1) flexible technology that allows workers to communicate with work while at home (whether respondents regularly use technology to work at home, including email, fax, beeper or cell phone, and a portable computer or home computer), (2) telecommuting (the ability to work at home for some portion of work time), and (3) flextime (the ability to arrange a work schedule to meet family or personal needs).

We assess three dimensions related to work conditions: workload, schedule control, and average weekly hours.

Workload. This is assessed by asking respondents whether their job requires them to work very hard and very fast and whether they are asked to perform excessive amounts of work. Responses are recorded on a four-point scale (from 1, strongly agree, to 4, strongly disagree).

Schedule control. This is assessed by a shortened version of a measure of control over areas at work.[58] The eight-item scale measures whether respondents are able to determine when to begin and end their workday, the number of hours they work, whether work can be done at home, the timing of vacations, the amount and timing of work that must be taken home on evenings or weekends, when to take a few hours off, and whether they are able to make or receive personal phone calls and emails while at work. Items are scored on a five-point scale (from 1, very little choice, to 5, very much choice).

Average number of hours worked per week. This is assessed by the respondents estimate of the amount of time, on average, spent at work, combining all jobs.

When predicting family-to-work spillover, we consider four family-related variables: the amount of free time, the time spent on dependent care, the time spent on household chores, and the time spent caring for infirm family members.

Work-to-Family versus Family-to-Work Spillover

Our findings on the relationship between work-to-family spillover and family-to-work spillover are consistent with previous studies. Specifically, even in this middle-class sample, we find that work has more of a negative impact on family than family has on work (see figure 7.1) for both women and men. Most employees in our study bring more worries and stresses home with them from work than they take from home to work. To function effectively at the workplace, most people compartmentalize their family concerns while at work. By contrast, family members are less effective at shielding their concerns at work from home. Note, however, that on average respondents report negative work-to-family spillover somewhere between rarely and sometimes, meaning that for most people in our sample, negative spillover from work to home (or vice versa) is not a major issue.

Moreover, respondents in our study also report that, for the most part, the benefits of combining work and family outweigh any drawbacks (see figure 7.1). On average, respondents report that positive spillover from family to work occurs more frequently (between sometimes and most of the time) than negative spillover. Thus, family life enhances more than it hinders an individual's performance at work. Further, the couples in our sample report that home life enhances work life to a greater degree than work life enhances home life.

Spillover between Husbands and Wives

Previous research on gender differences in family-to-work spillover has been conflicting, with no clear pattern emerging. In our sample, we find that women report greater levels of negative family-to-work spillover and greater levels of positive family-to-work spillover than do men (see figure 7.1). Although relatively small, these differences are statistically significant. The added statistical power of our couple-level analysis may have allowed us to detect a significant difference that was too subtle for other studies to detect. We are not surprised to find women reporting slightly higher levels of family-to-work spillover than men. In our sample, women spend more time on household chores (2.6 hours vs. 1.9 hours on workdays) and, among parents, on child care (3.9 hours vs. 2.2 hours on workdays) than do men. The added roles in the home, combined with their work role is likely to translate into greater levels of both positive and negative spillover.

We do not find a significant difference between husbands and wives in negative work-to-family spillover. This contradicts prior studies that tend to show that wives display greater levels of negative work-to-family spillover than do husbands. It may be that the context for working women is changing. Middle-class female workers may be becoming more adept at leaving the concerns of the workplace behind when they are home, decreasing negative work-to-family spillover. At the same time, as middle-class men begin to invest more in the roles of parent and spouse, they may be experiencing an increase in work-to-family spillover.

We do find a small, but significant, difference between men and women on positive work-to-family spillover (see figure 7.1). Middle-class wives, when compared to their husbands, have a greater tendency to feel that being involved in work outside of the home enhances their effectiveness and emotional well-being in the home. Still, the small, and even nonsignificant, differences that we found between middle-class husbands and wives on spillover levels are consistent with a general trend in the work-family literature. As societal attitudes shift to reflect the changing demographics of the workforce, the differences between men and women in their orientation to work and family are disappearing.[59]

Patterns of Spillover

Previously, researchers have treated positive spillover and negative spillover as separate processes and have not explored how positive and negative spillover

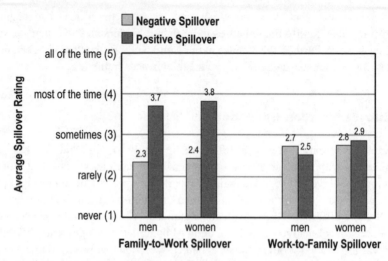

Figure 7.1 Work-to-family and family-to-work spillover among middle-class men and women in dual-earner couples. Source: *The Cornell Couples and Careers Study*, 1998 ($N = 1642$). Significant differences occur between negative work-to-family and negative family-to-work spillover ($t = 19.0, p < .01$); between negative family-to-work spillover and positive family-to-work spillover ($t = 53.6, p < .01$); and between men and women on positive work-to-family spillover ($t = 9.3, p < .01$), positive family-to-work spillover ($t = 2.5, p < .05$), and negative family-to-work spillover ($t = 3.4, p < .01$).

relate to one another. To identify the frequency of patterns that could occur between positive and negative spillover, we place respondents into categories based on whether they report a high level (average between 4 and 5, meaning they report experiencing spillover all or most of the time) or a low level (average between 1 and 2, meaning they report experiencing spillover rarely or never) of each type of spillover. Workers who report spillover sometimes (an average of 3) are not included in either of the high or low categories and are therefore excluded from these analyses. We then place respondents into categories based on their level of both negative and positive spillover.[60]

Figure 7.2 shows how our middle-class families are distributed in these categories. Happily, the Family Optimal category is by far the most common pattern of spillover, with the majority of workers reporting high positive and low negative family-to-work spillover. Work Segmented is the second most common category. These workers report very little spillover from work to home, suggesting that they are able to compartmentalize experiences at work and not let them influence emotions and behaviors in the home. Approximately 10 percent reported Work Strain, with high negative and low positive work-to-family spillover. Family Strain, representing high negative and low positive family-to-work spillover, is a relatively rare category, representing only 1 percent of our sample. Most of our

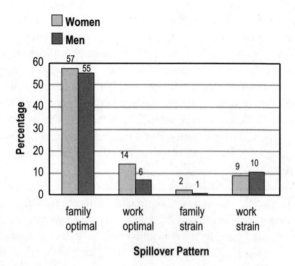

Figure 7.2 Distribution of types of spillover. Source: *The Cornell Couples and Careers Study*, 1998 (*N* = 1604, 803 couples).

respondents find that their work lives are enhanced by their family lives. Few feel that family is a detriment to their work.

Spillover by Industry Sector

We next examine how the work context is related to spillover. We operate under the premise that various industrial contexts, or sectors, experience different competitive pressures, which might translate into different levels of work and family spillover. Our sample is divided into four primary sectors: manufacturing, health care, higher education, and utility (see app.). For these analyses, we only use respondents who work in one of our seven participating companies. Because a significant portion of respondents in our sample fall into the Family Optimal, Work Optimal, or Work Strain categories, we use chi-square analyses to examine whether workers in various sectors are more or less likely to display these patterns of spillover.

Family Optimal spillover is consistently high for both men and women who work in higher education (66% of men and 44% of women in higher education fall into the Family Optimal category). Many of these respondents are faculty members, who have unusually flexible work hours. When not in the classroom, faculty have a great deal of discretion regarding their work schedule. This flexibility may allow them to mesh work and family needs more easily than other workers.

We also find that a large number of men (67%), but fewer of the women (44%), who work in the health-care sector report a Family Optimal spillover pattern. This gender difference may be due to the different types of positions that men and women in our health-care sector hold. Most of the women are in support or technical health-care positions (e.g., nursing and lab technicians), whereas most of the men are in management positions. Women in these nonmanagement positions tend to have fixed schedules, often including shift work, which may be less flexible and more difficult on the family. Employees in the utility and manufacturing sectors were the least likely to report a Family Optimal pattern of spillover (between 35% and 54%).

We find no significant differences among sectors on the Work Optimal pattern of spillover. However, we do find a significant difference among sectors on the Work Strain category. A greater percentage of men and women in the manufacturing sector report high levels of negative work-to-family spillover and low levels of positive work-to-family spillover (15% and 14%, respectively, in the manufacturing sector compared to 5%–9% of men and women in the other sectors). This may be because both of the organizations in our manufacturing sector were downsizing their workforces during our survey (see app.). Our focus-group interviews reveal that professional employees at these organizations are concerned about the security of their jobs and are also taking on the work and responsibilities of those who have been laid off. Thus, the context of downsizing, rather than the sector itself, is a plausible explanation for the higher work-to-family strain employees in the participating manufacturing firms experience. However, these firms are part of the competitive and hard-driving global economy, with (according to the focus-group interviews) demands and uncertainties clearly spilling over into the family lives of their employees.

Linked Lives between Husbands and Wives: Patterns of Symmetry in Family-to-Work Spillover

Curious about whether there are common patterns of spillover between husbands and wives, we categorized couples' spillover relationships as being either symmetric, asymmetric, or independent. A symmetric relationship is one in which both members of a couple experience similar levels of spillover from family to work. An asymmetric relationship exists when one spouse reports high levels of negative spillover and his or her spouse reports low negative spillover. A 46-year-old computer technician and mother of two children explains how, even among couples who share family responsibilities, the experience of spillover can be asymmetric: ". . . he [her husband] told me last night that he was headed to Buffalo today and wouldn't be back until tomorrow night and could I meet the sitter, stay late, all that kind of stuff. The routine has been that I get out the door

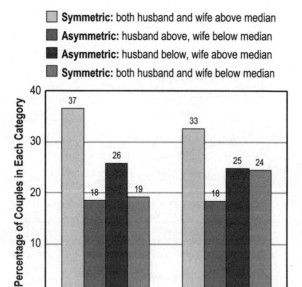

Symmetric: both husband and wife above median
Asymmetric: husband above, wife below median
Asymmetric: husband below, wife above median
Symmetric: both husband and wife below median

Figure 7.3 Distribution of couple-level family-to-work spillover scores. Source: *Cornell Couples and Careers Study*, 1998 (*N* = 803 couples).

first and he waits until the sitter arrives and then he leaves so it's like no advance notice and all of a sudden this morning I had to stay."

Similarly, a 40-year-old accountant with two school-age children describes her experiences regarding day-care arrangements: ". . . had someone very good, but whenever there was a problem, I'd mention it to 'Charlie' and he'd say, 'Oh, just hire somebody else.' Like you could just go out on the street. Another thing I think is hilarious is that they have both phone numbers at school, you know, mommies and daddies. And they never call the daddy."

To get a fuller understanding of the relationship between husbands' and wives' family-to-work spillover, we divide couples into four categories (two symmetric and two asymmetric) based on whether each member of the couple is above or below the median score for men and women on negative family-to-work spillover. Figure 7.3 illustrates the percentage of couples falling into each category of symmetry for negative and positive family-to-work spillover (the differences between groups was significant at the .01 level for both positive and negative family-to-work spillover). Overall, we find that a majority of couples are symmetric in their reports of family-to-work spillover. Over one-half of the couples are either both above or both below the median on positive and negative family-to-work spillover, meaning that they have a similar level of spillover experiences. When

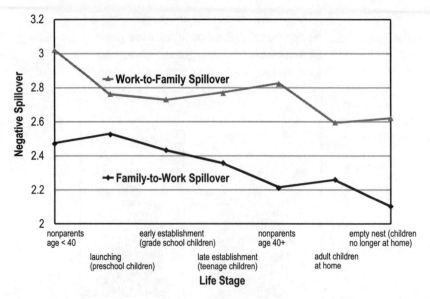

Figure 7.4 Negative spillover by life stage in middle-class dual-earner couples. Source: 1998 *Cornell Couples and Careers Study* (men $N = 802$, women $N = 802$). Family-to-work spillover difference between life stages: $F = 14.9$, $p < .01$. Work-to-family spillover difference between life stages: $F = 12.5$, $p < .01$.

there is an asymmetric relationship, it is typically the wife who reports high family-to-work spillover and the husband who reports low spillover. These findings suggest while family-to-work spillover in this sample of husbands and wives is best characterized as symmetric, there are families in which the wife bears the brunt of the negative spillover.

Work and Family Career Dynamics: Life Stage and Spillover

For each form of spillover, negative and positive, family-to-work and work-to-family, we perform an analysis of variance to assess whether spillover scores differ across life stages for both men and women. We are particularly interested in the impact of parenthood on spillover.

Family-to-Work Spillover

Our analyses reveal that the level of negative family-to-work spillover does vary significantly by life stage, for both men and women (both significant at the .01 level). Negative family-to-work spillover is relatively high for workers who have young children in the home and decreases as children get older (see figure 7.4). This

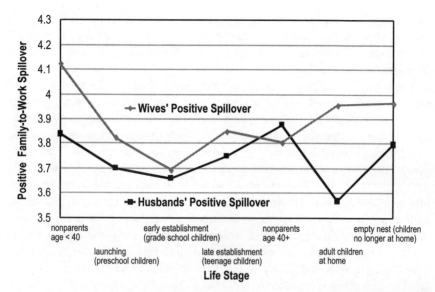

Figure 7.5 Positive family-to-work spillover across the life course in dual-earner couples. Source: 1998 *Cornell Couples and Careers Study* (men N = 802, women N = 802). Life stage F = 14.9, p < .01. Life stage × gender interaction: F = 3.2, p < .01.

is consistent with the scarcity hypothesis,[61] which predicts that combining the roles of employment and parenting is associated with higher levels of negative spillover. One unexpected finding is the relatively high negative spillover among young married men and women without children. This may reflect the struggles these young people face as they simultaneously adjust to both their marriages and their occupational careers.

Regarding positive family-to-work spillover, we find a statistically significant difference by life stage for women, but not men (see figure 7.5). Although positive family-to-work spillover scores are generally high (averaging close to 4 on a scale from 1 to 5), positive spillover is generally lower when children are in the home, but increases by the time the youngest child reaches his or her teen years. Taken together, we see that, as children become older and better able to care for themselves, they have less of a negative and more of a positive impact on women's and men's work life.

Work-to-Family Spillover

Negative work-to-family spillover varies across the life course (significant at the .01 level). The effect of life stage on negative work-to-family spillover is similar for men and women. As figure 7.4 illustrates, negative spillover from work to family is greatest for younger workers without children. This is the life stage at which men and women begin launching their careers but have not yet moved into launching families. In our sample of young married couples without children, work evidently intrudes into the home at a relatively high rate. These men and women have few family commitments and tend not to separate their jobs from their home lives.

Interestingly, among dual-earner couples, parenthood is associated with less negative work-to-family spillover compared to men and women of comparable ages without children (young nonparent and older nonparent stages). We speculate that the presence of children may act to buffer parents from the stresses at work. Parents may be less willing to let the hassles and pressures from work invade their life at home, making a conscious effort to separate their work life from their family life. Children may also act to distract parents from the issues that they face at work. The bottom line, however, is that parenthood appears to help men and women achieve a greater separation of work from home (but not vice versa). Overall, negative work-to-family spillover tends to gradually diminish across the life course. As employees settle into their careers, they may learn how to juggle work and family so that they do not interfere as much with one another. Life stage is statistically unrelated to positive work-to-family spillover for both men and women.

Predicting Spillover

To identify which work- and home-related factors predict spillover, we perform eight separate hierarchical regressions—four for men (positive and negative work-to-family spillover and positive and negative family-to-work spillover) and four for women. Each regression equation has three steps. First, we control for psychological disposition (negative affect) and life stage. For family-to-work spillover, in the second step we assess whether the respondents' home-related variables and flexible work strategies influence spillover. Third, we examine whether the spouse's behaviors at home and flexible work strategies influence spillover. This third step allows us to discern how spouses' orientations to work and family are linked to the respondents' own experience of spillover. For work-to-family spillover, we follow these same steps, except that in the second and third steps we examine the impact of work-related variables and flexible work strategies on work-to-family spillover.

Predicting Family-to-Work Spillover

The more tasks and roles that individuals perform in the home, the greater the negative family-to-work spillover. Specifically, men who spend more time on household chores, and men and women who spend more hours at work (leaving fewer available for the home) report higher negative family-to-work spillover. In the same vein, the more free time that husbands and wives report having at home, the lower their reports of negative family-to-work spillover (recall we control for negative mood and life stage).[62]

Roles in the home also have implications for positive spillover. Husbands whose wives care for an infirm relative report lower levels of positive family-to-work spillover than husbands whose wives do not have this additional role. It is likely that women who care for an ill relative are less available to perform household tasks and to meet the needs of their immediate family, leaving their husbands to perform some of these tasks, which then detracts from their experiences at home. As the population ages and elder care becomes more prevalent, the impact of caregiving on worker and family well-being will become a more acute issue.

Work strategies also impact family-to-work spillover. The more hours that a wife works, the more positive spillover reported by her husband. This is consistent with previous research that shows that when husbands and wives have similar high levels of commitment to work, husbands report lower levels of work-family conflict.[63] It may be that wives who work relatively long hours are more supportive of their husbands' work and more willing to discuss work-related issues in the home, resulting in more positive home-to-work spillover. The opposite seems to be true for women. Wives whose husbands work relatively long hours report greater negative family-to-work spillover. Because of their husband's long hours (recall that the men in our sample work longer hours than the women), these women may shoulder a larger burden of home-related tasks, resulting in greater negative family-to-work spillover.

Flexible work strategies have a paradoxical relationship with family-to-work spillover. Women who bring work home report higher levels of both positive and negative spillover. They feel both enhanced and burdened by this strategy. In contrast, men who bring work home report greater positive family-to-work spillover only. Among men, working at home is a strategy that enhances their work life, without the corresponding downside that we find with women. Women, who are responsible for the majority of household tasks, may be overburdened at home when they also have to perform work-related tasks, leading to greater fatigue and stress in the workplace, which is not found among men.

Predicting Work-to-Family Spillover

Several work-related conditions significantly affect work-to-family spillover.[64] First, for both husbands and wives, control over when and where an individual works is associated with higher positive spillover. On the down side, a greater workload is associated with higher negative work-to-family spillover. In addition, husbands whose wives have heavy workloads tend to have lower levels of positive work-to-family spillover. High workloads and a lack of control at work are both sources of stress for employees, which appears to negatively affect workers' experiences at home.

A more complicated picture emerges when we examine the relationship between spillover and workplace strategies that are designed to facilitate the meshing of work and family. For husbands and wives, bringing work home has the paradoxical effect of increasing both negative and positive work-to-family spillover. Further, wives whose husbands bring work home tend to report lower positive work-to-family spillover. The use of telecommuting, another strategy touted as an aid for working families, is related to lower levels of positive spillover among wives and also among wives whose husbands' telecommute. The use of flextime also has some negative consequences. When husbands use flextime, wives report lower levels of positive work-to-family spillover. Interestingly, the use of these family-friendly policies appears to have more of a detrimental effect on the wive's spillover than on the husbands'. In addition, wives appear to be negatively impacted by their husbands' use of these family-friendly policies, but husbands are not impacted by their wives' use of the policies.

Although flexible work strategies seem to help workers cope with the multiple demands of work and family, they are not a panacea for the working couple (especially for the wife) but seem to be a double-edged sword. Strategies such as bringing work home are simultaneously related to enhancing and detracting from husbands' and wives' experiences at work and at home. Other flexible work strategies, such as telecommuting and flextime, are related to decreases in positive spillover for women and for wives whose husbands use these strategies.

Summing Up

In this chapter, we build on and extend prior research on spillover in several ways. We use a unique sample of dual-earner middle-class couples to show how shared contexts and linked lives of couples promote an understanding of positive and negative spillover between work and family. First, the most common pattern of spillover is Family Optimal; that is, almost 60 percent of respondents report high levels of positive family-to-work spillover and low levels of negative family-to-work spillover. Although negative family-to-work spillover does exist, it is not a major concern of workers in our middle-class, largely professional sample.

Second, most couples fit a symmetric model of spillover (e.g., low negative spillover for both husbands and wives), with husbands' and wives' experiences with spillover linked to a greater degree than we expected. These findings suggest that as women become more integrated into the workforce, differences in experiences between men and women are becoming smaller. The structural lag between the demography of the workforce and the social organization of work may be similar for both men and women. There are, however, a significant number of couples who have asymmetric spillover. For example, some husbands report low negative spillover from home to work, whereas their wives experience relatively high negative spillover. Our interpretation is that in a substantial minority of cases the traditional relationship of asymmetry still exists; that is, the wives bear the brunt of negative spillover for both partners.

Third, life stage plays a significant role in how much spillover working spouses experience. Life stage captures the dynamic interplay between individuals' work careers and family careers. Husbands and wives with the greatest family demands are more likely to report higher levels of negative family-to-work spillover. This is particularly true for the wives in our study. Both spouses in later life stages tend to report less negative work-to-family spillover. Surprisingly, however, among husbands and wives under the age of fifty, having children in the home is related to less negative work-to-family spillover. These findings suggest that children may buffer their parents from the stresses of work.

Fourth, home conditions, work conditions, and flexible work strategies are significant determinants of spillover. Control over work schedules appears to enhance positive spillover, whereas heavier workloads predicts negative spillover. Flexible work strategies have complex effects that vary for men and women. For both husbands and wives, bringing work home acts as a double-edged sword, related to higher levels of both positive and negative spillover. Wives who telecommute and wives whose husbands telecommute, use flextime, and/or work at home tend to experience less positive spillover from their work and home lives. Thus, not only do women's own use of flexible work policies influence spillover, but their husband's use of those policies also affects spillover. Therefore, although these strategies make it easier for couples to combine work and family responsibilities, they may come at a cost to wives' (and a lesser extent to husbands') sense of spillover.

Note that our findings should be interpreted in the context of the sample population. Our sample does not include single individuals or single parents—that is, individuals who have opted not to marry or who have more challenges as single parents in balancing work and family. In addition, although a sample of middle-class couples is expected to have high work demands, these professionals also have more resources than do lower-income families. Future research, therefore, should include a wider range of workers to test whether our results can be generalized to individuals in other household and economic circumstances.

Our analysis of positive and negative spillover among dual-career couples at different life stages provides important insights into the complexities of work-family relationships. The effects of spillover from family to work and work to family heavily depend on the characteristics and strategies of the household as well as the circumstances at work, for individuals and for their spouses.

8

Well-Being

Jungmeen E. Kim, Phyllis Moen, and Hyunjoo Min

For most adults, having a paid job provides not only economic but also psychological and social benefits. In this chapter, we draw on a life course approach to investigate the relationships among personal resources (such as education, perceived income adequacy, and subjective ratings of health), the work environment in dual-earner households (work hours, control over work circumstances, and workload), and the psychological well-being of men and women at various life stages. We propose that personal resources operate through the work environment, predicting the well-being of middle-class men and women in dual-earner households. Specifically, people with good health, a sense of an adequate income, and more education are more apt to choose, remain in, or be allocated into particular work environments. The characteristics of these environments (work control, work hours, and workload) are significantly related to psychological well-being. Moreover, we expect these work circumstances also shape the quality of family life, which, in turn, predicts well-being.

We are especially interested in workers' perceived control over their work. A large literature documents that having a sense of control is related to better well-being.[1] Job control has been linked to fewer physical health problems and better psychological functioning.[2] For example, Linda T. Thomas and Daniel C. Ganster find that, among a sample of working women (on average, thirty-five years old), higher work control relates to lower work-family conflict, which, in turn, predicts lower depressive and somatic symptoms.[3] Control of their work schedules can be one way members of dual-earner couples manage the multiple dimensions of their lives in light of the mismatch between their time preferences and the outdated infrastructure of work time.

Life Course Model

We propose that the links between resources, the work environment (especially control over work schedule), family quality, and psychological well-being can best be understood through the lens of a life course perspective.[4] As we show throughout this book, the life course approach highlights the dynamic processes of development and change over the life span. From the vantage point of our life course model, we focus on two main themes: process (mechanisms) and context (gender and social-relational resources).[5]

Process

In this chapter we investigate the possible mechanisms through which personal resources might operate to shape the work environment, family quality, and psychological well-being. Specifically, we test whether personal resources predict perceptions of control over work schedules and other work circumstances and test whether the quality of relationships operates as a link between the work environment and well-being.

Research suggests that marriage and family relationships are important resources, facilitating individuals' adjustment to stress.[6] Studies have shown that emotional support from a spouse helps individuals come to terms with stressful life events, thereby sustaining their psychological well-being. For instance, using data from a 1989–90 national study of older (over sixty-five) men and women, Jason T. Newsom and Richard Schulz found that less social support is an important predictor of lower life satisfaction and more depressive symptoms.[7] And in their study of late midlife retirees and workers (ages 58–64 years) Elizabeth Mutran and colleagues found that being married predicts positive attitudes toward retirement, possibly buffering the uncertainty around it.[8]

Context

We first consider the context of gender, given that women and men have different work histories, employment opportunities, and general life experiences.[9] Life course patterns are distinctive for men and women, with gendered life scripts and options throughout the life course. For example, women are more likely than men to experience discontinuity in their career paths, moving in and out of the labor force and in and out of part-time work in tandem with shifting family responsibilities.[10]

Investigators have found women's psychological well-being is more heavily influenced by marital quality than is men's. That marriage and family relationships matter more for women's psychological well-being is consistent with their typically greater involvement in marital and family roles over their life course, as well as their greater focus on interpersonal relationships. We suggest that family and marital quality serves as an important mediator of the work control and well-being linkage and that it will be more influential for the psychological well-being of women in dual-earner households than of men.[11]

Second, a life course, ecological perspective reinforces a couple-oriented view by emphasizing that lives are interdependent. Thus, we consider the work environments of both spouses.[12]

We investigate the following possible relationships:

Personal resources and life stage predict well-being by operating through work conditions.

A sense of control over the time and timing of work is significantly related to psychological well-being, whereas long work hours and a heavy workload reduce well-being.

Any negative effects of work hours and workload may be moderated by a high sense of work control.

The effects of work circumstances on well-being may operate through positive and supportive family and marital relationships.

Family and marital support may be more critical for women's well-being than for men's.

Workers' levels of control over the time and timing of work, other work circumstances, family relationships, and psychological well-being are different at different stages in the life course.

Both spouses' work environments may have significant effects on each person's psychological well-being.

Methods

To assess whether or not conditions at work, and especially control over one's work schedule, and support at home mother for emotional well-being, we draw on data from the 811 men and 811 women in *The Cornell Couples and Careers Study*. Recall that the average age of individuals in this sample is 44.8 years (SD = 8.0) for men and 42.8 years (SD = 7.3) for women. (Descriptive statistics for the sample and the measures are presented in the appendix.)

We focus on two indicators of well-being: a sense of personal growth and a measure of negative emotional affect. We gauge personal growth with a three-item scale (based on a scale of psychological well-being by Carol D. Ryff)[13], including

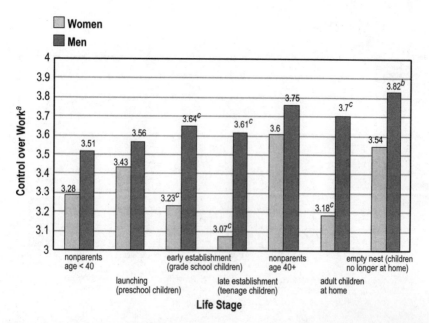

Figure 8.1 Control over work by gender and life stage, 1998. [a]Significant difference by gender, life stage, and the interaction by gender and life stage ($p < .05$). [b]Significant life stage difference with the first category as a reference group ($p < .05$). [c]Significant difference between spouses within a life stage ($p < .05$). On a five-point scale, with a higher rating reflecting greater perceived control over work hours and workload. Source: *Cornell Couples and Careers Study*, 1998–99.

items such as "For me, life has been a continuous process of learning, changing, and growth," and "I think it is important to have new experiences that challenge how I think about myself and the world." Negative affect consists of a scale (based on a scale used in Mid-Life Development Inventory as part of the McArthur Survey of Midlife Development in the U.S., MIDUS) with five items, such as "How much of the past month did you feel so sad that nothing could cheer you up?" and "How much did you feel nervous?" (see app.). Consistent with our life-course focus, we used a life stage variable based on age and parenting stage (see discussions of life stage and other variables throughout part one and app.).

Work Characteristics and Well-Being by Gender and Life Stage

Figures 8.1–8.5 provide graphic representations of variations in people's sense of work control and psychological well-being by gender and life stage.[14]

In figure 8.1, what is most evident is the gender difference in control at work; at every life stage men in dual-earner households report having more

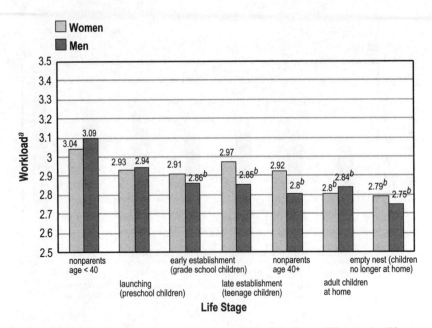

Figure 8.2 Workload by gender and life stage, 1998. [a]Significant difference by life stage ($p < .05$). [b]Significant life stage difference with the first category as a reference group ($p < .05$). On a four-point scale, with higher rating reflecting greater workload. Source: *Cornell Couples and Careers Study*, 1998–99.

work control than do the women in the study. Men who are in the empty nest stage (whose children are grown and no longer living at home) report the highest levels of work control, with men under forty with no children having the lowest work control. By contrast, childless women ages forty or older report the highest work control, whereas women with school-age children report the lowest control at work. Husbands report significantly higher work control than wives when couples are raising school-age children, as well as when they live with their adult children.

Figure 8.2 shows a considerable variation in workload across the life course, with young couples who have not yet had children reporting the highest work load. Men who are under age forty with no children and men who are fathers of preschoolers report significantly higher workloads compared to all other groups. By contrast, midcourse women (whose children are over 18, either living at home or having left home) report significantly lower workloads compared to all other groups.

Figure 8.3 depicts each spouse's work hours by gender and life stage. Note that there is very little difference in men's work hours across the various life stages (see Moen and Sweet, chap. 2 in this volume). Note as well that women

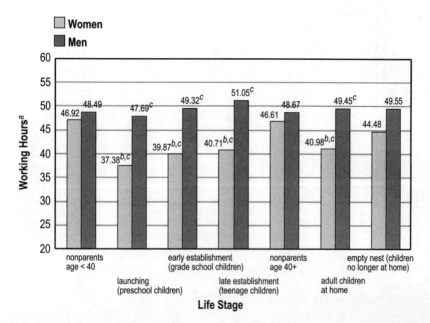

Figure 8.3 Work hours by gender and life stage, 1998. [a]Significant difference by gender, life stage, and the interaction by gender and life stage ($p < .05$). [b]Significant life stage difference with the first category as a reference group ($p < .05$). [c]Significant difference between spouses within a life stage ($p < .05$). Source: *Cornell Couples and Careers Study*, 1998–99.

in dual-earner couples report fewer work hours than their husbands at every life stage, with the greatest discrepancies occurring for those with children in the home. For men, those in the late establishment stage with adolescent children work the longest hours; for women, those under forty without children work the longest hours.

Turning to psychological well-being, we find women report significantly higher personal growth than men. Although differences across the life course are rather small, younger women (under age forty) without children and older men (ages forty and above) without children tend to report the highest levels of personal growth (see figure 8.4). In younger couples (under age forty) with no children and older couples in the empty nest stage, husbands tend to report significantly lower levels of personal growth than do their wives. In figure 8.5, we see significant life course differences in negative affect, with younger childless men and women reporting the most negative affect and those whose children are grown and gone the least. Among couples with elementary school children, wives tend to report lower negative affect than do their husbands.

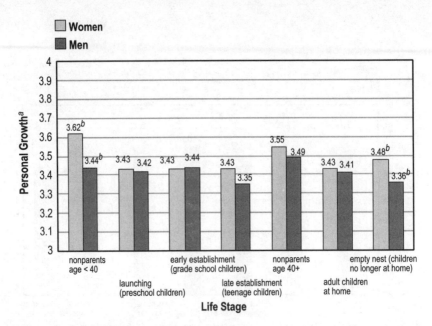

Figure 8.4 Personal growth by gender and life stages, 1998. [a]Significant difference by gender ($p < .05$). [b]Significant difference between spouses within a life stage ($p < .05$). On a four-point scale, with higher rating reflecting greater personal growth. Source: *Cornell Couples and Careers Study*, 1998–99.

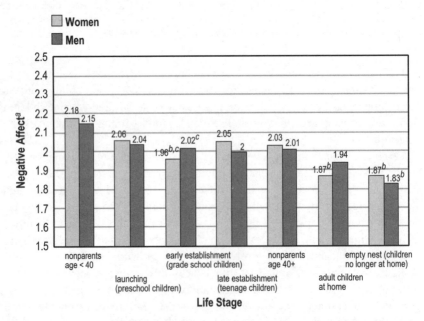

Figure 8.5 Negative affect by gender and life stage, 1998. [a]Significant difference by life stage ($p < .05$). [b]Significant life stage difference with the first category as a reference group ($p < .05$). [c]Significant difference between spouses within a life stage ($p < .05$). On a five-point scale, with higher rating reflecting greater negative affect. Source: *Cornell Couples and Careers Study*, 1998–99.

Testing Direct and Mediational Models

To better understand the relationships among personal resources, work characteristics (work control, workload, and work hours), family quality, and psychological well-being, we test a series of hierarchical regression models. Because we believe that work characteristics and family relationships contribute to psychological well-being in distinctive ways for men and women, we analyze all data separately by gender.[15]

Actual statistical data shown in table 8.1 (available at http://www.lifecourse.cornell.edu/cci/about_time) reveal, not surprisingly, that two key resources—educational level and perceived income adequacy—predict men's sense of personal growth. Men with higher workloads tend also to score higher on the personal growth scale. The effects of these two resources appear to operate through men taking on demanding jobs with heavy workloads, and these jobs provide a work environment conducive to personal growth.[16] Once the characteristics of the work environment are entered into the equation neither educational nor income resources remain as significant predictors, suggesting that the work environment plays a mediating role. Neither family nor marital quality nor conditions at work—control and hours on the job—predict men's sense of personal growth.

For women, having a higher level of education is also an important resource related to personal growth, regardless of their family or work environments. Women with children at home—especially in preschool and grade school—report significantly less personal growth compared with those in their late twenties and thirties without children (the reference group). None of the work environment factors are related to women's personal growth. As predicted, however, higher levels of family satisfaction are positively related to personal growth among the women in our sample. Family factors—life stage and family relationship quality—matter for women's sense of personal growth, but not for men's.

Negative Affect

Feeling that their incomes are adequate for their needs is an important factor for emotional well-being. Both men and women with a higher sense of income adequacy have lower negative affect scores. Life stage is also a key predictor, with men and women whose children are adults (at home or living elsewhere) being less likely than those in their twenties and thirties to score high on the negative affect scale.

Conditions at work—hours, control, workload—matter for men's emotional well-being, and greater workloads predict greater negative affect for both men and women. For men, there is a significant interaction between work control and work hours: men who work long hours are more apt to report greater negative affect when their control over their work is low. Thus, having a high sense of

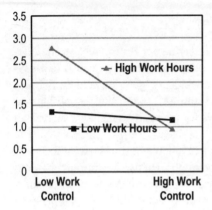

Figure 8.6 Men's negative affect (mood) is related to low work control and long work hours. Source: *The Cornell Couples and Careers Study*, 1998–99.

work control appears to act as a protective factor for men who put in long hours (see figure 8.6).[17]

We find that both family and marital satisfaction matter for men's and women's negative affect. Those most satisfied with relationships at home tend to have less negative affect.

Both Spouses' Work Environments

To investigate the possible effects of both spouses' work environments on each one's psychological well-being, we have conducted a series of regression analyses. In the regression models, we include the covariates of education, income adequacy, subjective health, and a set of life stage variables. Both the respondents' work environments and their spouses' work environments are included to test the effects of both spouses' work environments on well-being. Separate regression analyses involving each work environment variable (i.e., work control, workload, and work hours) have been conducted. Because most of the included variables overlap with the models reported in tables 8.1 and 8.2, we describe findings related to the effects of both spouses' work environments on well-being.

Recall that men's work control, workload, and work hours are positively related to their personal growth ($p < .05$). Their wives' workload is also positively related to men's personal growth ($p = .06$), whereas their wives' work control is negatively related to men's personal growth ($p = .06$). For women's personal growth, only their own work control, workload, and work hours are positively related to personal growth ($p < .05$). In other words, characteristics of their husbands' jobs do not predict women's own personal growth.

Regarding men's emotional mood, having high levels of workload ($p < .05$) and low levels of work control over their schedules ($p = .07$) predict greater negative affect. But having a wife in a job with high work control also predicts men's negative affect ($p = .08$). Both women's own high workload and long work hours matter for their negative mood ($p < .05$). None of their husbands' work circumstances is a significant predictor of women's negative affect.

Summing Up

This chapter underscores life course themes of process and context in the links between personal resources, work and family circumstances, and the psychological well-being of members of middle-class dual-earner households. We show how both work circumstances and well-being vary across the life course, and they frequently vary by gender as well.

Our findings underscore the importance of personal resources in the form of education and perceived income adequacy for well-being. Educational attainment appears to play out in middle-class men's lives by their following paths to demanding jobs with high workloads, which in turn provide opportunities for personal growth. On the other hand, men who have a greater workload may choose such work because they already have high levels of personal growth. In this cross-sectional study we cannot disentangle the direction of the effects between workload and men's personal growth, but it suggests that having a demanding job may have positive outcomes. But having high a workload also predicts negative affect (depressive symptoms) for both men and women in dual-earner couples. In fact, all measures of the work environment—low control, high workload, and long work hours—matter for men's negative affect. By contrast none of the measures of women's work environment predicts women's personal growth, and only having a heavy workload relates to women's negative affect.

Although there is a link between workload and negative affect for both men and women (with higher workload related to poorer emotional health), overall the work environment is more consequential for men's depressive symptoms (as measured by negative affect). This evidence is consistent with previous findings that demonstrate significant links between work conditions and well-being, and we find this to be particularly true for men.[18] Moreover, men who work longer hours on the job are more likely to report more depressive symptoms when they have low levels of control over their work schedules. For men with control over their worktime and scheduling, however, working long hours is not related to negative affect.

Our hypothesis that women are more influenced by family circumstances than are their husbands is supported in the case of personal growth, with women's (but not men's) personal growth significantly related both to their life stage (lower for those with young children) and their family satisfaction. However, high family quality in the form of family and marital satisfaction matters for the emotional health (negative affect) of both women and men.

We further examine whether their spouses' work environments, in conjunction with individuals' own work environments, matter for individuals' psychological well-being. Our data provide evidence that wives' work environments may well predict men's psychological well-being. Specifically, men are more likely to report higher personal growth when both their wives and the men themselves have heavy workloads. For men, having wives who feel they have higher work control seems to be detrimental to their psychological well-being; husbands with wives reporting higher work control tend to report both lower personal growth and higher negative affect. Note that there is no significant impact of spouses' work environments on women's psychological well-being. It appears that in our sample of middle-class dual-earner couples, only husbands' well-being is related to their spouses' work conditions, a topic worthy of future research.

Finally, our findings do not support the notion that social support (as gauged by family and marital satisfaction) is the link between conditions at work and well-being. Rather, work circumstances have a direct effect on (especially) men's well-being, regardless of the quality of their home lives. Nevertheless, family and marital relationships do appear to make a unique, separate contribution to the psychological well-being of both women and men in dual-earner households.[19] Strong and satisfactory relationships at home may well help members of dual-earner households sustain their emotional well-being.

Once again we see that time matters: men who work long hours with little control over their work schedules and in highly demanding jobs report higher levels of depressive symptoms. Demanding jobs (those with high workloads) are associated with such negative affect for women as well. But family relationships also matter for life quality for both men and women in dual-earner couples. Focusing on just one dimension of the work-family equation tells only half the story. Still, from a policy perspective, the importance of the work environment for workers' well-being has obvious implications for the organization of work: the factors increasingly associated with today's jobs—long hours and heavy workloads—appear to take a psychological toll. And for men, high control over their work time and timing is an important predictor of emotional health and an important moderator of any potentially deleterious effects from long hours on the job.

9

Success

Phyllis Moen, Ronit Waismel-Manor, and
Stephen Sweet

One of the newest U.S. Internet magazines is called *Failure*. The editor says he envisions a major shift in contemporary notions of success, with "failure" in conventional terms no longer having the stigma it held when "success" meant climbing an occupational status ladder, earning a rising income, and building seniority. Notions of success may be changing, as well, because both spouses and single parents are increasingly in the workforce, meaning that most workers—men and women—now have to manage both work and family goals and responsibilities. They are seeking effectiveness, or "success," not only in the occupational sphere, but also in the private aspects of their lives and in integrating the two.

In this chapter, we develop a framework for understanding perceptions of success in both work and family domains, as well as in their integration. We examine how conditions at work, but also at home, predict perceived success, as well as how couple-level circumstances relate to the perceived success of husbands and wives in dual-earner households. Do husbands in dual-earner couples feel more successful generally than do their wives? Do wives rate themselves higher on success on the family front than at work? Do demands and resources at work and at home predict who feels most successful?

We also address the interrelatedness of various aspects of success. Specifically, we assess whether success at work comes at the cost of family success (or vice versa) or whether success in one domain is positively linked to success in another, creating an overall sense of successful living. Finally, we want to know whether one spouse's perceived success at work and at home comes at the cost of the perceived success of the other spouse or whether there is crossover in the successfulness of both spouses in dual-earner couples.

The Concept of Success

Scholars traditionally measure success by simply equating it with objective economic attainment and/or occupational mobility up a career ladder.[1] But the degree of successfulness also constitutes part of individuals' personal meanings, their beliefs about how well they have done or are doing in particular domains.[2]

For men, success at work has also meant success as a family breadwinner, suggesting that, for men at least, being successful at work spills over into their success at home.[3] Husbands' earnings have meant families can buy more, possibly translating into wives' sense of family success as well. As John Clausen and Martin Gilens point out, for most women, success in the past was derivative, the result of marrying an occupationally successful man.[4] But as women have entered, remained in, or reentered the workforce in unprecedented numbers, this breadwinner-homemaker model of success has become increasingly obsolete.[5] Today few workers (male or female) have family members at home to manage the nonwork aspects of their lives and to facilitate their occupational achievements. Nevertheless, the structure and culture of work life and family life continue to be seen (by employers, governments, and the media, as well as by many husbands and wives) as a women's issue; if women cannot fit into the existing (male-breadwinner) template of work and career paths, many observers and women themselves see this as a private trouble, a personal failure. A case in point is Sylvia Ann Hewlett's recent book, which encourages women to give primacy to the family side of the work-family equation.

This raises the issue of whether women feel successful at work only at a cost to their sense of family success (and vice versa).[6] If women's success at work is bought at the cost of their success on the home front (as Hewlitt suggests) we maintain it is precisely because of the culture and structure of time in U.S. society. The obsolete breadwinner-homemaker blueprint still undergirds notions about work, occupational careers, family responsibilities, and success. The fact is that men as well as women are caught in the mismatch between the breadwinner-homemaker career template and the realities of the new workforce. Is men's success on the home front simply a function of their "bringing home the bacon"? Or do contemporary dual-earner couples trade off success, with husbands' success at work bought at the cost of their wives' work success? Do husbands and wives have a division of success, with men feeling more successful at work and women feeling more successful on the family front?

Success and Cycles of Control

To understand why some members of dual-earner households rate themselves more or less successful in their work and family roles, we develop a model based on the role demands they face and the resources they have with which to meet them. Our model underscores the life-course notion of cycles of control, as workers strive for a fit between demands and resources.[7] As family and occupational environments change across the life course, workers experience corresponding shifts in both demands and resources. When demands outstrip resources, individuals' assessments of their own effectiveness (success) should be low; conversely, when their resources meet or exceed demands, workers should feel successful in various life domains.

This framework suggests that family and occupational circumstances predict assessments of success precisely because they produce gaps between resources and demands, as well as a corresponding decline in individuals' sense of control (see also Kim, Moen, and Min, chap. 8 in this volume). Bandura points out that an individual's having little ability to influence the circumstances of his or her life can produce feelings of anxiety, futility, and despondency.[8] Similarly, Leonard Pearlin and his colleagues define mastery as "the extent to which people see themselves as being in control of the forces that importantly affect their lives."[9] Catherine Ross and John Mirowsky underscore that a "sense of powerlessness arises from the inability to achieve one's ends, from inadequate resources and opportunities, from restricted alternatives, and from jobs in which one does not choose what to do and how to do it."[10]

William Goode's theory of role strain provides support for a cycles of control model of success. Role strain theory points to the potential conflicts and overloads associated with conflicting role obligations and goals. Factors related to role strain, "the felt difficulty in fulfilling role obligations"[11] should be at odds with perceptions of success, especially in terms of integrating work and family objectives and obligations. Goode points out that the "values, ideals, and role obligations of every individual are at times in conflict."[12]

Goode's theory has spawned considerable research on role conflict and strain in the work-family interface.[13] By adopting this approach, scholars have focused on how problems and conflict at work drain and preoccupy the individual, making it difficult to achieve a successful or satisfactory family life. (See also the discussion of role conflict in relation to work hour adaptive strategies in Moen and Sweet, chap. 2 in this volume.) Other researchers have distinguished between positive and negative spillover, as in Kevin Williams and George Alliger's study of the ways that satisfaction and stimulation at work are correlated with high levels of energy and satisfaction at home.[14]

The difficulty with much of the existing evidence on work-family strain, conflict, and spillover is that scholars rarely consider the historical and temporal

136   It's about Time

nature of the objective circumstances and subjective experiences they study. Goode anticipated the dilemmas of the contemporary work-family interface by pointing out that norms are not always adequate guides for individual action. The rules and expectations related to the now-outmoded breadwinner-homemaker template have not been replaced by new norms for successfully meeting both private (family) and public (work) role commitments. And, although Goode emphasized the fact that individuals "take part in many *different* role relationships," he did not examine the dynamics of role interconnections.[15] Both conflicts between and spillover across public and private domains may shift in intensity over the life course in tandem with shifts in demands or needs on the one hand and available resources on the other.

Combining the role strain and life-course theoretical approaches provides a way of linking perceptions of success with the fact that, given the prevailing culture and infrastructure of time and career paths, both occupational and family demands and resources are structured to change over the life course.[16] Previous research indicates that family responsibilities rise dramatically with the arrival of children.[17] Given the culture and organization of occupational career paths and of child care (seen as principally a family or maternal obligation), when family responsibilities are high, the likelihood of conflict between work and family domains is also high, particularly for those invested in their jobs. Moreover, challenging occupations may be especially demanding during the child-rearing years as managers and professionals strive to move up occupational or company ladders established by the market, by the professions, and/or by corporate actors.[18] Institutionalized resources with which to cope with domestic and occupational demands also vary over the life course (e.g., with income rising with age and men with preschoolers more apt to have the resource of a spouse at home or working reduced hours) and by occupational status (with higher income and greater job autonomy more characteristic of managerial and professional occupations). Both role strain theory and the life-course theory of cycles of control suggest that periods when there is a disjuncture between responsibilities and resources should be times of feeling less effective or successful.

We can envision shifts in perceived success over the life course as occupational and family demands exceed an individual's economic and time resources at various life stages, or vice versa. Consider, for example, the model[19] presented in figure 9.1, which charts hypothetical differences in demands and resources at four (normative) life stages: anticipatory (those in their twenties and thirties, without children), launching (those just starting their jobs and families); establishment (those actively building their careers and their families), and shifting gears (those whose children have left home and who may be considering retirement or second careers). This stylized model attends to the intersections of work and family as they change in conjunction with age as well as with changing circumstances and options. Given the biological, social, and cultural imperatives

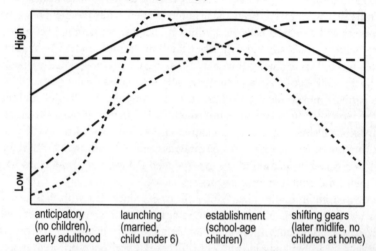

Occupational Demands (time, energy, involvement)
Family Demands (time, energy, involvement)
Temporal Resources (24 hours in a day)
Financial Resources (earnings, savings)

anticipatory (no children), early adulthood launching (married, child under 6) establishment (school-age children) shifting gears (later midlife, no children at home)

Figure 9.1 The disjuncture between demands and resources at various life stages, a hypothetical model. Source: *Cornell Couples and Careers Study*, 1998–99.

shaping both occupational careers and family careers, the gap between resources and needs is expected to be especially pronounced in the child-rearing (and career-building) years.

Previewing this perspective in the 1960s, Harold L. Wilensky suggested that low worker morale would be especially prevalent among workers (male in the 1960s) with preschoolers. It is in this period that demands are most apt to outstrip resources (whether the resource is time or money) on the home front and the demands of building a career and/or achieving job security are greatest.[20] Accordingly, we expect that the greatest overload and, hence, the lowest sense of success at work, at home, and certainly at balancing the two would occur for those raising preschool children who are typically also in their early career building years. But life stage cannot be considered separately from the cultural schema and institutional structures shaping the biography of gender.[21] Although working men and women in their twenties and early thirties—just starting their adult lives—may be similar in assessing their successfulness, this is apt to diverge with age as experiences, choices, and opportunities in the work place and in their private lives follow distinctively gendered paths.

A note of caution in considering the hypothetical model in figure 9.1: although time is constant, in terms of the twenty-four-hour day, we know that time is socially structured. Individuals can rarely choose how many hours of a day or week they spend at their jobs. Consequently, the resource of time is not necessarily available for discretionary use. The same holds true, in less obvious ways, for other resources. And in some cases one resource can substitute for another, as when families use income to eat out or buy prepared meals, thereby freeing up time that would have been spent in the kitchen. Thus the distinction between resources and demands is easier to draw in the abstract than in everyday experience, with families strategizing about the time-income trade-offs husbands and wives make. For example, time at work is frequently negotiated by couples, in terms of comparative advantage or socially structured norms of exchange, with one partner (most typically the husband) investing more in the job and the other (most typically the wife) investing more at home (see discussion on strategic adaptations in Moen and Sweet, chap. 2 in this volume).[22] Employed wives and mothers may therefore have fewer time demands at work than do husbands and fathers precisely because they have responded to family time demands by reducing their time commitments at work.

Albert Bandura holds that "self efficacy is concerned with judgments about how well one can organize and execute courses of action required to deal with prospective situations containing many ambiguous, unpredictable, and often stressful elements."[23] Individuals in different life stages experience different demands in both their work and personal lives; they also have different expectations as well as different amounts of rewards and resources. Consequently, they may well interpret their success in their work and family roles differently.

There may also be a cumulation of advantage in perceived success over time.[24] This is obvious in the way career paths and economic resources have been structured, but it is also true with regard to abilities. For example, work can shape patterns of stress management, patterns that are sustained over time and that carry over into other domains of life. Robert Karasek and Tóres Theorell have found that job conditions (such as autonomy and demands) influence patterns of stress both on and off the job. In support of this, Rosalind Barnett and Robert Brennan found evidence of links between time pressures at work and psychological distress.[25] And Jungmeen Kim, Phyllis Moen, and Hyunjoo Min (chap. 8 in this volume) show that high workload, low work control, and long work hours are negatively related to men's well-being.

Workers at different life stages have different skills, different responsibilities, different resources, different opportunities, and different prospects for the future. They can be expected, therefore, to also have different perceptions of success. For example, younger, child-free employees just beginning to anticipate their work and family careers may be investing a great deal of time and energy in preparing for occupational achievement, but feel successful in neither work nor personal/family domains. Those in the launching stage (with young children in the home), who are working hard at building their jobs and their personal lives, are apt to feel the most strained and the least successful, given their time demands at work and at home. Similarly those in the establishment stages (with children in school) may feel more successful at work but less so at home because the raising of school-aged children and adolescents continues to require an investment of time, energy, and attention. For example, Robert Cournoyer and James Mahalik found that middle-age men (averaging forty-one years of age) are less conflicted about occupational success than college-age men, but are more conflicted about combining work and family responsibilities.[26] But men and women in their forties and fifties without children may be better able to feel successful about their public and private lives than those at similar ages raising children. People in the shifting gears stages (those with children in college and those whose children are grown and no longer living at home) are often at the height of their earning capacity and also looking toward retirement, second (or third) careers, or some combination of both. With few domestic demands and more stable (or even declining) job demands, they may well experience a heightened sense of control, with resources meeting or exceeding their needs. Workers in their fifties and sixties may also have scaled back on their expectations and aspirations, thus making it easier for them to feel successful.

Resources, Demands, and Success

We anticipate that, regardless of gender, perceptions of both occupational and family success are highest for those in late midlife and for those with greater incomes and in higher-status occupations (both are in line with a traditional objective model of success). But, given the gendered distribution of resources and obligations at home, at work, and in the larger society, corresponding with the still-prevailing structural and cultural template of the lockstep breadwinner model of career paths, husbands in dual-earner households should experience higher levels of both occupational and family success than their wives. Employed wives, on the other hand, are apt to experience the conflicts and overloads that Goode describes as accompanying the enactment of two demanding roles,[27] resulting in their having lower assessments of success in one or both domains. Employed wives in the launching stage, traditionally shouldering the additional time demands and tasks accompanying having preschool children at home while trying to meet the expectations (and frequently inflexible hours) of their jobs, can be expected to report the lowest levels of success at work, at home, and at balancing.

The biggest discrepancy between experiencing success at work versus at home should revolve around time. Temporal and psychological investments in paid work necessarily have opportunity costs in terms of investing in the family. We therefore expect that long hours on the job and a strong work ethic would be positively linked to occupational, but not family/personal (or balancing), success and that more time spent in family work would be positively linked to success on the home front (and to balancing both roles).

Our argument in brief is that the breadwinner-homemaker template of U.S. success has privileged men's typical career trajectories (see Williams and Han, chap. 6 in this volume) as the route to economic resources, status, power, and, hence, perceived success.[28] In tandem with the breadwinner career template, workers' incomes should be key to their perceptions of success. But, given that more wives and mothers are now entering, reentering, or remaining in the workforce, along with the shifting social contract between employers and employees making all jobs more insecure, we believe that contemporary Americans may well be in a process of redefining the norms and values associated with success (see Roehling, Moen, and Batt, chap. 7 in this volume). Since the majority of workers (male and female) are married to other workers, time is an increasingly salient resource. Time at work and time spent in family activities (as well as other time-related resources and constraints) represent a bounded resource—what is spent in one domain is lost in the other. Time put in at work and at home (whether by choice or by constraint) and other time-related factors (such as workload, parental leave, flexibility, and control) reflect workers' cycles of control (in terms of resources and needs) and can therefore be expected to predict perceptions of success.

Success in *The Cornell Couples and Career Study*

Testing the factors that predict success requires situating individuals in the context of their work and family environments, linking their situations with those of their spouses, and anchoring respondents in their life courses. *The Cornell Couples and Careers Study* was structured to provide just this type of ecological information.

We investigate success using interrelated, but distinct, measures. Respondents were asked to rate their perceived success with three questions.[29] "On a scale of 0–100, where 0 means 'not successful at all' and 100 means 'absolutely successful,' how successful do you feel about your work life? How successful do you feel about your family life? How successful do you feel about "balancing" work and family life?" As previously discussed (see Moen, chap. 1 in this volume), the notion of balance is not necessarily the only way to capture the work-family connection, and strategies (see Moen and Sweet, chap. 2 in this volume) probably vary across the life course in achieving balance or, more accurately, the "satisficing" of the often competing demands of work and family. Nonetheless, the term "balance" was used in *The Cornell Couples and Careers Study* to conform with existing measures[30] and because it fits the parlance familiar to respondents living in a culture encouraging workers, especially women workers, to balance the multiple dimensions of their lives. (But note how this fosters a view of the career dilemma as a private trouble rather than a public issue.)

A number of factors probably influence perceptions of success. Generally taken-for-granted, traditional, objective predictors of success include education, income disparity, job prestige, and work hours. We include these measures, but also examine the degree to which asymmetric configurations in couples affect husbands' and wives' levels of success.

Job circumstances have an impact on resources and constraints, and, consequently, are likely to influence perceptions of success. Of paramount importance, theoretically, is the degree of job security, the degree of control offered in an individual's job, and degree of perceived income adequacy.[31]

Family circumstances also influence resources and obligations and therefore may predict success for husbands and wives. To gauge these effects, we include measures of minutes spent on chores each workday, whether the respondent helps to care for an ailing or infirm relative, and the couple's life stage (based on age and child-rearing responsibilities).

Family-friendly benefits constitute a theoretically important resource as well. Specifically, whether the husband or wife (or both) use parental family leave, flextime, or telecommuting can potentially influence the ability of individuals and couples to chart a successful work-family interface. As such, we expect that using these programs would show the strongest relationships with balancing success, but not necessarily with a sense of family or work success.

As already discussed, success is not something that is imposed solely by external forces but instead is also likely to be influenced by an internal sense of agency and perhaps a deeper condition of emotional well-being. Given this synergistic relationship, we include measures of psychological resources: the degree to which the husband and wife report feeling constrained in their options, their sense of mastery, and negative affect.[32]

Findings

Ratings of the various dimensions of successful living in terms of feeling successful in work, family, and balancing for dual-earner men and women at various life stages show first that most workers in our sample typically report feeling reasonably successful in the various aspects of their lives. (Actual statistics are available in table 9.1 at www.lifecourse.cornell.edu/about_time.html.) But, at all stages, husbands and wives report higher levels of family success (84.5) than work success (79.3). Respondents in the empty nest (or shifting gears) stage assess themselves highest in terms of work success (82.1) and those with children in college (also shifting gears) rate themselves highest in terms of family success (87.2). As expected, young (under age forty) childless workers (anticipatory stage) rate themselves the lowest on these two measures of success (82.7 and 75.1). These findings suggest some age-related advances (and cumulation of advantage) in perceived effectiveness on the job and in individuals' personal life.

We asked people in in-depth interviews how they define success for themselves. One woman answered this question by saying first "that [the definition of success] has certainly changed over my life." She is both a Ph.D. student and a director of database services, and her husband holds a degree in computer science. They are expecting their first child soon. She continues, "The main thing right now is a focus on a healthy family, a healthy relationship with my husband is very, very important to me, a healthy relationship with our new baby that's coming. And success at work means still being a major contributor to the company and a major influence on the company, but not needing the power, like I needed in the past."

This woman offers a succinct description of a concern facing most of the respondents in *The Couples and Careers Study*, as well as those in the nation as a whole—namely, how to maintain both work and family obligations. She also highlights how priorities can shift with changing experiences over the life course. As shown in previous research, our survey data reveal that both men and women in dual-earner couples report less success in balancing work and family (75.6) than they do in either of these separate domains. Older, childless workers (wife forty or older) are more apt to see themselves as more successful at balancing (79.2) than are those at any other life stage.

Surprisingly, women tend to report higher levels of success in their work life, family life and in balancing than do men. Interpreting this finding is thorny, however, in the light of gender differences that result in time squeezes, second-shift work, and strategies of scaling back, which, as we have seen in part one of this volume, fall disproportionately on the shoulders of women. Wives in dual-earner families may use a different metric than do their husbands when assessing the successfulness of their lives. Note, however, employed women with young preschoolers (launching stage) report being less successful at their work lives than do men at this stage. This conforms to the notion of control cycles, with the periods of early child-rearing being times when demands exceed resources, especially for women.

These relationships provide compelling support for the cycles of control theory as applied to success, but are only a step in the process of understanding what is in fact a much more complicated dynamic. Recall the observations depicted in figure 9.1—demands and resources are not constants, nor are they randomly distributed among men and women or across the life course. Changes in family demands are captured, to a great extent, through our use of life stages, which divide couples into groupings based on age and child-rearing responsibilities.

There is also considerable variation in couples' work hours by life stage and gender. Wives put in the fewest hours when there are preschoolers in the home; husbands at this stage put in over forty-seven hours a week. In fact, no matter what life stage they are in, U.S. men in dual-earner households tend to work more hours than their wives. Only women without children work almost as many hours as do their husbands (an average of forty-seven hours per week, with their husbands working an average of forty-eight hours per week). This reflects the strategic choices couples make in adapting to a world in which the culture and structure of careers, communities, and families lag behind the realities of dual-earner (and single-parent) households.

There are also significant life-stage differences in workload (requiring individuals to work very fast, very hard, or do excessive amounts of work). Young nonparents experience the highest workload, whereas older shifting gears employees (empty nest stage) are the least apt to describe their jobs as very demanding. The job prestige of men and women in the Cornell study is roughly the same across life stages and is atypically high, reflecting the high percentage of managers and professionals (66% of the women and 69% of the men) in this sample of daul-earner middle-class households.[33] But there are significant differences in earnings, both by gender and by life stage. There is a clear age trend for men with children: those who are older, whose children have become adults, typically earn the most; men without children earn less than men with children. Women show the opposite trend: they earn more when they do not have children.

Women and men (in this dual-earner, middle-class sample of couples in upstate New York) tend to see their incomes as more than adequate to their needs. And, although their actual earnings differ considerably, there are no statistically significant differences between men and women's sense of income adequacy. Both men and women, however, are least apt to feel satisfied with their incomes when they have preschoolers or children in school. Women tend to report higher levels of job security, as do those further along in their life course, when children have left the household.

These findings highlight how resources and obligations fluctuate throughout the life course, coinciding with some of the variation in the levels of work, family, and balancing success experienced by U.S. workers in dual-earner, middle-class couples. Because these variables are probably confounded with one another, we extend the analysis, examining how jobs, family circumstances, family-friendly benefits, and psychological outlook predict success, net of other traditional predictors of success.

What Predicts Success?

Traditional Predictors of Success

We now assess multivariate models of successful living, looking at the degree to which traditional markers of objective success and other resources and demands predict men's and women's perceptions of success at work, at home, and in balancing the two.[34] For actual analysis see table 9.2 (available at

www.lifecourse.cornell.edu/about_time.html). We find that traditionally hypo-
thesized factors do predict success, but not always to the same degree for men
and women, nor do they predict success in all three domains but rather show
differing effects on work, family, and balancing success.

Resources, at times, are best conceptualized in relative terms (such as in the
concept of relative deprivation, when individuals compare themselves to others)
than as absolutes. Illustrating this dynamic, we find that husband-wife disparities
in educational attainment, income, or prestige are associated with elevated and
deflated appraisals of success. For example, in couples in which only the wife
has a college degree, husbands report significantly lower balancing success.
Although women report higher levels of work success in couples in which the
wife earns more than the husband (as is expected), in these same couples husbands report lower levels of work success. Women who outearn their husbands
also tend to report considerably lower levels of balancing success, implying
that for these types of couples the wife's economic prosperity may come at
the expense of her success at effectively managing her work-family obligations.
Wives who have higher job prestige than their husbands tend to also report higher
levels of work success.

Couple work-hour arrangements predict considerable variation in success
ratings for both husbands and wives. As expected, compared to dual moderate
couples (in which both work at, at most, full-time jobs), partners who both work
long hours (over forty-five hours per week) tend to report lower balancing success
(−4.7 and −7.9 points lower for women and men, respectively). Husbands in these
high commitment (long-hour) couples also feel less family success, while their
wives report considerably higher levels of work success compared with wives in
couples where both work about forty hours a week. When one partner works long
hours and the other does not, both partners report lower success in family and
balancing. Women who work longer hours than their husbands (crossover commitments) have considerably lower ratings of family success (−6.6) and balancing
success (−9.7) than do women in dual moderate relationships. Similarly, men who
work long hours, but whose wives do not, report lower levels of balancing and
family success. These findings offer compelling support for the cycles of control
theory. One group, however, is an anomaly. In couples in which one partner
(almost always the wife) works fewer hours, both partners tend to report lower
levels of family success and, for husbands, lower levels of work success. But this
could reflect the low value of part-time work in U.S. society, as well as the fact
that those working fewer hours frequently do the bulk of the work at home.

Job Circumstances

Job circumstances are commonly linked with conceptualizations of work
success, but our findings also reveal their linkages with family and balancing

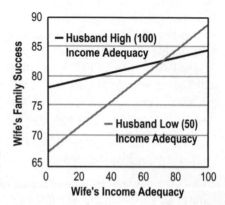

Figure 9.2 Wife's family success as influenced by husband's and wife's income adequacy. *The Cornell Couples and Careers Study*, 1998–99 ($N = 810$). Main effects: $p < .01$; Interaction: $p < 0.01$.

success. These relationships offer support for our thesis about different meanings of success by gender; the resources of job security, control over work, and income adequacy are almost all uniformly positively associated with different types of success. Among the most important factors for husbands is the certainty that they will keep their jobs, which predicts husbands' feelings of success at work, family, and balancing. Wives' job security has no relationship to their levels of success, but offers a modest predictive value for their husbands' sense of success.

Individuals' sense of control over their work is not associated with their perceived success at work, but does correspond with balancing success for both husbands and wives. We believe that that control in the workplace matters for balancing success by increasing the flexibility of workers in reacting to family demands. Wives' sense of income adequacy corresponds with their higher levels of work, family, and balancing success. By contrast, husbands' own appraisal of income adequacy predicts only their work success.

Figure 9.2 points to the importance of husbands' and wives' combined appraisals of income adequacy for wives' family success. Both are positively related to wives' family success, but when husbands report a lower sense of income adequacy, the wives' own ratings have a significantly stronger effect on their own family success. This is to be expected from a cycles of control perspective, emphasizing the importance of perceptions of the relative presence or absence of a resource (in this case a sense of an adequate income), and how an individual's own assessment of resources can make a remarkable difference in their appraisals of success, especially when the other partner feels less well off. Similar relationships are found for job security (not shown): Wive's feelings of job security matter more for their perceived success when their husbands feel less secure.

Clearly, successful living is tied to a sense of economic adequacy and job security. These statistical results mirror what we find in in-depth interviews with some workers in dual-earner couples. In one interview with a first-line Vantech supervisor, a 54-year-old woman, without children and married to an engineer who also works at Vantech, defines success as "... being able to meet all of our financial expenses, number 1."

Similarly, a married (second marriage) engineer at Vantech, a man whose two children are now grown and living elsewhere reports, "Salaries and promotions are more important in terms of whether you are successful or not. You will not feel very successful if you don't have reasonable salary to go along with."

Family Circumstances

As we have shown, job circumstances matter for people's feelings of both family and balancing success. But family circumstances matter as well, predicting all three—family, work, and balancing success. These effects are not always, however, in the direction suggested by the life-course notion of cycles of control. For example, the amount of time wives and husbands spend on chores each workday is positively related to their sense of work success and (for women) family success, but has no influence on either partner's balancing success. We expected the opposite effect. It is possible that the time an individual has to spend on chores is a reflection of the relative time pressures at work and at home. Chore time may be a marker of control over an individual's life—at least at the microlevel. Hiring outside help or forgoing regular cleaning routines may, on the other hand, signal a time crunch making such outsourcing necessary. Or else people who do farm out domestic chores may feel less successful in managing the multiple dimensions of their lives.

Another anomaly is that, although caring for an infirm or aging relative corresponds with an enhanced appraisal of wives' sense of family success, it is also positively correlated with feelings of balancing success of both husbands and wives in this sample of dual-earner couples.

The life-course theory of cycles of control is supported in the analysis of the effects of life stage on the success husbands feel in balancing work and family. Success in balancing tends to be highest among husbands who have older children or who are themselves older and without kids. This latter group of men also reports significantly higher levels of work success. Wives report the highest levels of work success when their children are grown and no longer at home. However, compared to younger wives who have not had children, women with school-age children report significantly higher levels of work success. One possible explanation, requiring a longitudinal analysis not possible here, is that at the point when children enter school, working women achieve an elevated level of success compared to their previous condition of heavy responsibilities of raising a preschool age child. If supported, this life-course dynamic is consistent with the cycles of control argument.

Family-Friendly Benefits

Theoretically, family-friendly benefits should have the greatest impact on balancing success. Complicating the issue is that these benefits are disproportionately available to and, used by workers who experience the cumulative advantages of education, control, income satisfaction, and so on. Accordingly, we assess any effects of family-friendly benefits net of these other factors.

We find, to our surprise, that using parental leave has a stronger relationship to work and balancing success if the husband uses it rather than the wife. Husbands who use parental leave report significantly higher levels of work success, and both they and their wives report higher levels of balancing success. One possible explanation for the differential impact of men's and women's use of parental leave is that men's use of parental leave recasts gender dynamics and potentially influences family adaptive strategies to more effectively bridge the work-family divide of the twenty-first century. These findings, at least, suggest a need to consider the unique situations that influence couples' use of parental leaves and to study the ways in which this strategy influences each partner's success in fulfilling work and family roles. (Note also that many of the men saying they have used parental leave in fact only took vacation time off.)

Flextime and telecommuting have effects opposite to what we expected. Although women's use of flextime is positively associated with their balancing success, it corresponds with significantly lower levels of balancing success for their husbands. Similarly, husbands' use of flextime is associated with lower levels of family success for their wives. When both partners telecommute, balancing success is low for husbands. These findings are, admittedly, puzzling, but there may be an explanation consistent with the cycles of control theory. In *The Time Bind*, Arlie Hochschild suggests that the workplace is increasingly a place where workers with stressful circumstances on the home front want to be. Therefore, being "at work," whether in the office or the home office alleviates them from thinking about other pressing family commitments and concerns.[35] When partners use flextime or telecommuting, the boundary between work and family becomes increasingly blurred as activities in one domain spill over into the other. In contrast, workers who establish strong boundaries between what occurs at work and what occurs at home may be in a more advantageous position to restrict the degree to which work and family roles compete. Such an interpretation is consistent with the cycles of control theory; telecommuting may well be an adaptive strategy (albeit not necessarily a productive one) that enables workers to escape to work while at home, restricts obligations and demands imposed from the family sphere, or at the very least blurs the boundary between work and nonwork (see also Chesley, Moen, and Shore, chap. 14 in this volume).

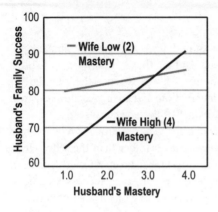

Figure 9.3 Husband's family success as influenced by husband's and wife's mastery. *The Cornell Couples and Careers Study*, 1998–99 (*N* = 810). Main effects: *p* < .05; *p* < .10. Interaction: *p* < 0.05.

Psychological Outlook

We also investigate the degree to which correlates of individual agency (perceived constraints, personal mastery, and negative affect) predict success. We find that wives who have a sense of high perceived constraints limiting their options tend to report lower work, family, and balancing success. For husbands, perceived constraints have a negative relationship with family and balancing success, but not work success. A sense of personal mastery operates in the opposite manner, although not with the same consistency. One notable finding is that both spouses' feelings of mastery over their lives matter for men's family success (see figure 9.3). In couples where there are discrepancies between husbands' and wives' levels of mastery (i.e., when the husband reports low mastery and the wife reports high), husbands have a low rating of family success. This suggests that both spouses' psychological outlooks matter for men's perceptions of success in the family domain. For example, when both spouses report low feelings of personal mastery, husband's assessments of their family success is much higher than when only his is low.

Negative affect (depressive symptoms) consistently operates in the predicted manner predicting lower assessment of success on all three dimensions for husbands and wives. Women with higher negative-affect scores report lower work success, family success, and remarkably lower balancing success. The same relationships hold for men with higher negative-affect scores. Women with high negative-affect scores also tend to have husbands reporting lower family success, but the reverse is not true (husbands' high negative-affect scores do not predict wives' scores).

Taken together, these findings indicate that the assessments of success in various domains by husbands and wives are intricately related. Each spouses' perceptions of success is associated in a direct relationship with their own socio-economic circumstances, work conditions, family conditions, and psychological

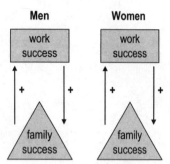

Figure 9.4 Spillover in perceptions of work and family success among individuals in dual-earner households.

outlook. But their sense of success is also associated with crossover effects, whereby the conditions of their spouses' work situation and psychological outlook matter for their own successes as well.[36]

Does Success at Work Come at the Cost of Success at Home?

Popular conceptions tend to equate work success at the cost of family success, as if excelling in one domain automatically means faring less well in the other. This zero-sum notion of success lies at the heart of a whole literature on work-family balance, such as assumptions that success at family life requires a scaling back on work life goals and aspirations.[37] But our findings do not support this view at all. After controlling for all our objective measures of success and including one measure of success as a predictor of the other, we find that, for both men and women in our dual-earner sample, a sense of success at work is positively related to a sense of success at home, and vice versa (see figure 9.4). Thus, contrary to popular conceptions, we see positive spillover in various aspects of successful living.

One mother working in marketing and training in a software firm, whose husband is a manager of a large nonprofit organization, summarizes this positive spillover: ". . . Having demonstrated success in your career tends to coincide with some of your personal growth anyway."

If One Spouse Is Successful, What about the Other Spouse?

We also are interested in crossover success: Does one spouse's report of success in a particular domain translate into the other spouse's similar success? Or does one spouse's success come at the cost of the other spouse? Again,

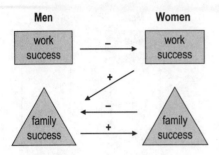

Figure 9.5 Crossover in perceptions of work and family success among individuals in dual-earner households.

controlling for all objective measures of success, we introduced the other spouse's ratings of successfulness at work and at home as predictors. The results (shown in figure 9.5) suggest negative, not positive, crossover. Specifically, having husbands who rate themselves high on work success is negatively related to women's assessments of their own work success. Similarly, wives' ratings of family success are negatively related to men's family success. But women's work success is positively related to their husbands' family success. It appears that, given the way jobs and occupational careers are constructed, men's success at work comes at the cost of not their own family success but of their wives' work success. And, given the gendered norms about family and the divisions of household power and labor, women's family success comes at the cost of their husbands' family success.

Because both scholars and social commentators use the term balance to mean managing the interface between work and family domains we included our measure of balancing success. The fact that women's sense of success at balancing both roles is affected by their husbands' family success suggests that women can be more effective at managing both work and family roles if their husbands see themselves as successful on the home front (see figure 9.6). Note also that, contrary to popular belief, feeling successful in both work and family domains contributes to high ratings on balancing success for both men and women.

Summing Up

The findings discussed in this chapter suggest that in dual-earner, middle-class couples personal assessments of success at work are not at odds with personal assessments of success at family life. Rather, feeling successful in one domain predicts feeling successful in another. And successfulness in each is related to a sense of balancing success. This is important because it identifies the fundamental problem in the balancing metaphor, which implies trading off one domain for the other. What we see instead is a certain synergy across domains, producing a sense of successful living overall.

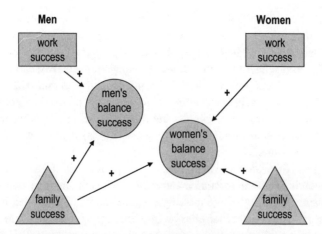

Figure 9.6 Crossover in perceptions of work, family, and balancing success among individuals in dual-earner households.

A case in point is the way a marketing manager with two children, ages eight and ten, in the process of divorcing her husband, defines success as "Having a very well-rounded personal life as well as a professional life."

But the term "balancing" remains a popular way of discussing the work-life interface. Another working mother, a strategic information systems consultant, also with grade-school-age children, working for a company that manufactures industrial equipment (Vantech), and married for fifteen years to a medical doctor, defines it this way: "Success for me would be balance. Balance and happiness. I think if you can balance then you do get happiness. And that means on all fronts— on being a parent, on being a spouse, on being career-oriented, driven people."[38]

Another key finding is that, regardless of gender, work hours matter— positively for success at work and negatively for men's success at balancing home and work. This underscores the time squeeze that many married employees experience as they strive to meet employers' long-hour expectations and the difficulty as employees begin to bear and raise children. Couple-level factors are also important predictors of successful living. For example, when both spouses work regular work hours (39–45), they are each most apt to rate themselves high on all measures of success.

Our evidence generally supports a cycles of control theoretical model: those with more resources and fewer demands tend to see themselves as successful at work, at family life, and at balancing both. The strong ties between measures of a sense of individual agency (perceived constraints, personal mastery, negative affect) and assessments of all three forms of success reinforce the cycles of control model.

Although individuals' seeing themselves as successful at work and at home is not a zero-sum game, what is surprising is that success in various domains within couples may be. Specifically, men's perceived success at work is negatively related to their wives' feelings of work success, and women's sense of family success is negatively related to their husbands' ratings of success on the home front. This could reflect the neotraditional arrangements discussed in Moen and Sweet (chap. 2 in this volume), with husbands typically emphasizing their roles as breadwinners and wives continuing to focus on the domestic aspects of their lives, even in dual-earner households. But there may also be some nontraditional trading off, given that husbands' family success is positively related to wives' ratings of their own success at work.

In this time of profound social change and policy lags in the institutions of work, the labor force, the economy, and the family, contemporary perceptions of success may well be both more multifaceted and more complex than in the past. U.S. workers in dual-earner families are not only trying, one couple at a time, to refashion traditional life patterns, they are also reconstructing their visions of success, seeking a sense of biographical coherence by optimizing their intersecting public and private worlds, given the existing infrastructure of time, in ways that move beyond the traditional income and prestige views of success.

10

Managing Households

Robert M. Orrange, Francille M. Firebaugh, and
Ramona K. Z. Heck

A key theme of the life-course perspective and of this volume is
adaptive strategies. This chapter examines how couples strategize
ways to manage their households on a day-to-day basis. We examine the extent
to which household management practices reflect couples' responses to external
organizational work demands and internal family dynamics, in addition to individual differences among household managers. Given the serious challenges that
dual-earner couples face in meshing their work and family responsibilities, we
need to know more about how couples actually manage household work so that
scholars might begin to identify whether and how good management practices
lead to positive outcomes such as greater levels of satisfaction or perceived
success in coping with the often competing demands of work and family life.

A major body of research exists in the social sciences focusing on the household division of labor and particularly its gendered dimensions. Although there has
been some important in-depth research on managing households,[1] research on this
topic does not take into account the importance of household management but
instead focuses only on household tasks.[2] Perhaps this is in large part because a
primary interest is to track changes in the sharing of household tasks between
husbands and wives, especially as wives have moved into the labor force in
ever-greater numbers. Given that family members engage in a host of diverse
activities and involvements outside the family itself and most families no longer
have the benefit of full-time homemakers, we know little about how contemporary

couples manage their ongoing household chores and responsibilities. What are the factors that push or pull the household manager to take a consciously managerial approach to getting home-based work done?

Our life-course approach, with its emphasis on linked lives, life-stage shifts in both occupational and family demands and responsibilities, and family adaptive strategies amid changing cultural norms, helps us to identify the differing contexts in which the management of daily household activities takes place. We also draw on the family economics–home management perspective in order to conceptualize the dimensions of managing. Uniting these two approaches can promote an understanding of the managerial role, as well as the mediating links between effective management and positive outcomes such as satisfaction and perceived success.

We can only speculate as to how the nature and demands of household management have evolved. We do know, however, that the environments in which middle-class households now are managed seem strikingly different from the environments in which couples operated during much of the postwar era. Consider the different kinds of challenges couples have faced within each era. During the period 1945–75, large segments of professional middle-class families adapted to an external environment (economy) in which they had to make accommodations to the more stable, formalized, and predictable, yet demanding schedules and job requirements associated with the male-provider role while having the benefit of full-time homemakers at home. Many middle-class men worked in manufacturing firms characterized by stable employment, long-term investment, intricate and detailed (yet rigid) planning, and stable production. Many middle-class women engaged in full-time homemaking that revolved around, first, meeting the formal, predictable, demanding schedules of their husbands' jobs and, second, cultivating, feeding, or providing for the practical and emotional needs of family life in accordance with (idealized) standards and practices.

In contrast, contemporary middle-class families are coping with the demands of an external employment environment that is fast paced, unpredictable, and focused short term, without the benefit of a full-time homemaker to manage the household. Dual-earner households may see managing effectively as being even more central to keeping the household operating successfully on a day-to-day basis. And although concerns have been raised about certain excesses associated with taking a managerial approach to family and personal life,[3] as well as about the seemingly contradictory requirements of meeting market demands while living up to the cultural requirements of good motherhood,[4] managing well seems to be an essential component of middle-class life in a society that is heavily organized around formal organizations (e.g., his job, her job, schools, child care, boy scouts, and soccer).

The Family Economics–Home Management Approach

A family economics–home management perspective assumes that individuals and couples can direct their family-based activities using effective management practices to achieve desired outcomes or family-defined goals.[5] Scholars use a family resource management framework to explain the nature of family activities directed toward the achievement of family goals.[6] Much of the field has been defined by a systems perspective, one that views families as dynamic systems involved in interdependent relationships with other systems or social institutions.[7] With its focus on dynamic and interdependent relationships, the family resource management approach provides a highly useful framework for conceptualizing how an activity, such as care of a child or of an aging infirm relative, which seemingly takes place within the self-contained unit of the family, exists in an interdependent relationship with the external demands confronted by family members.

Although families clearly engage in productive (although unpaid) activities producing valuable goods and services, the process of systematically identifying whether and how families engage in conscious, outcome-oriented managerial behavior has posed a formidable challenge within the field, despite efforts to elaborate on the concept managing.[8] Yet some advances have been made in determining whether people can distinguish between managerial behaviors and other kinds of things that families do. For instance, Mary E. Betsy Garrison, Sarah H. Pierce, and Vicky Tiller, in their study of 151 mothers of school-age children, demonstrate that mothers readily distinguish between managerial and coping behaviors. "Coping" implies a passive orientation to family challenges in which change is forced on the family and in which its members, in turn, respond in a reactive manner. "Managing," in contrast, implies a proactive approach to life's challenges, whereby family members intentionally or purposefully initiate change in order to meet these challenges.[9]

We assume that to some extent, family life is managed and that the members of working couples in our study identify certain formal managerial behaviors in their own family-based activities. We use a cluster of ten items based on Ruth E. Deacon and Francille M. Firebaugh's conceptual framework for family resource management, defining the family system as containing personal and managerial subsystems.[10] Although the focus of our research is on the managerial subsystem, keep in mind that it receives inputs from the personal subsystem, which involves a host of wider interpersonal relations and involvement that, in turn, feed back into the managerial subsystem, supplying it with value orientations and aspirations on which people act. In fact, we expect that a blending of these activities and a blurring of their boundaries occurs in everyday life, and we also expect that our middle-class respondents will acknowledge these managerial components in their daily activities to a greater or lesser extent. And as we have emphasized, the managerial subsystem also responds to various demands from the external environment.

The managerial subsystem encompasses four major components: input, planning, implementing, and output. Each of these contains one or more subelements (see table 10.1 for a description of each subelement). These components form a continuous managerial cycle whereby the household manager responds to demands from the external environment as well as to values and aspirations generated in the course of ongoing interpersonal relationships among family members, converting these into goal-directed behaviors, the accomplishment of which involves varying degrees of planning and implementing. After any household-related job or task is planned (the front end of the managerial process) and those plans are subsequently carried out or implemented (the tail end of the managerial process), the manager then monitors and evaluates the outcome of these activities, the results of which then become new inputs into the managerial subsystem.

Garrison and colleagues rely on a version of the Deacon and Firebaugh approach developed by Ramona Heck and colleagues.[11] Heck and colleagues examine how extensively a group of 482 home-based (paid) workers (predominantly women) who also self-identify as being the primary managers of their own households identify with various dimensions of managing in each of the two domains. They find that respondents score higher overall on managerial activity in their (paid) home-based work than on their (unpaid) family work. Overall, they find that the scores for the management of (unpaid) family-based work are highest on managerial concepts relating to checking how a job is going, making adjustments as needed, and assessing how well respondents like the results associated with a given task. Their evidence suggests that respondents do not conceptualize the family-managerial process in a manner neatly congruent with the Deacon and Firebaugh approach.[12]

Karen A. Duncan, Virginia Zuiker, and Ramona Heck do a factor analysis of the managerial behaviors for a sample of 673 business-owning households, which they separate into two groups: solo-role holders, who manage solely in the (unpaid) family sphere and dual-role holders, who manage in both (unpaid) family and the (paid) business spheres. They find that neither group's family-managerial behavioral conforms neatly to the Deacon and Firebaugh framework but that people combine their own managerial behavior in somewhat idiosyncratic ways.[13]

Scholars in the field continue to raise concerns about the widely held assumption that effective family management leads to desired outcomes, an assumption that has not been adequately tested with respect to the overall management process.[14] The limited number of studies in this area has produced only a few, highly qualified findings.[15] In effect, before the intricacies of the managerial

Table 10.1 Description of Family Managerial Subsystem

Components	Description
Inputs	
Goals	Indicating the extent to which family activity is consciously directed toward the realization of certain values or aspirations.
	Each week you decide something specific you can do for your family.
Planning	
Standard setting	Identifying the level of quality desired in the accomplishment of any given household task.
	Before starting a complex task, you have a firm idea about how to judge the outcome.
Demand clarification	Thinking through a plan of action to ensure that the goal/end product is clearly defined such that the means (how to do the job) and the ends (the final product) are in alignment.
	When planning a task at home, you think the plan through so that your goal is clear before you begin doing the task.
Resource assessment	Defining the amount of time, energy, and resources (such as money) available to complete a specific job/task.
	Before you begin a task, you figure out how much of your time, money, and energy you can devote to this particular task.
Action sequencing	Assessing, within the broader repertoire of jobs/tasks, when and in what order any given job/task will be done.
	You think about when to do a task at home and not just how much time it will take.
Implementing	
Actuating	Defining when a task is typically initiated, ranging from early/ahead of time or late/at the last minute.
	When there is a task to be done at home you wait until the last minute to do it (reverse coded).
Checking	Examining during the course of a job/work project whether things are going as planned.
	As you work at home, you check whether things are going as you want them to.
Adjusting	When things are not going well, willingness to change plans in midstream and figure out another way to get the job done.
	When things are not going well you figure out another way to do it.
Output	
Demand responses	Identifying how well respondent likes the results associated with a given job/task.
	When a task is done, you think about how well you like the results.
Resources changes	Extent to which respondent evaluates the effectiveness of work processes employed to achieve a given outcome or complete a task/job.
	You are pleased if the work just gets done; you do not spend time thinking about how effectively it was done (reverse coded).

process beyond the general trends can be explored, managing the household must be established as a meaningful endeavor—one that can lead to desired outcomes.

Family Management as Adaptive Life-Course Strategies

Drawing on Phyllis Moen and Elaine Wethington's framework,[16] we conceptualize household management as a microdimension of a broader repertoire of family adaptive strategies that couples employ to meet family career and occupational career-based goals and demands. Moreover, following the theme of linked lives, we approach the career and employment strategies of husbands and wives as interdependent, mutually referential, and ultimately having some impact on how daily household activities are managed. For instance, the managers and professionals in this study, like large segments of the broader society, pursue careers without the benefit of a full-time unpaid worker (typically a housewife) at home. As a result, they must adapt to the added burden of managing his career, her career, and their family career simultaneously. It is clear that although unprecedented numbers of wives are now in the workforce husbands' involvement in household and child-care responsibilities has barely changed. Accordingly, although husbands have become more involved in family-related care work, wives still bear overwhelming responsibility both for doing family care work and managing it.[17]

Furthermore, family adaptive strategies and their associated external environments are not impervious to change and, therefore, need to be placed in a life-course framework that takes account of the dynamic interplay of lives over time. Account must also be taken of the fact that individual lives and their institutional contexts are historically embedded in unique cultural and structural circumstances. We also expect couples at various points in their adult lives to experience different levels of work and family demands. As Phyllis Moen and Yan Yu confirm, the overall demands that couples face at different life stages vary significantly—those in the earliest (anticipatory) stages without children and just starting careers face the least demands, whereas those just starting families and careers (the launching stage with preschoolers) experience the greatest demands.[18] Over time, couples experience modest reductions in demands until their children begin leaving home and they begin making serious preparations for retirement (shifting gears), when their demands decline significantly (assuming that both partners remain healthy).

As we examine how couples manage household work in the context of broader family adaptive strategies, we are reminded of the interdependence between the family and other institutional realms and are led to investigate how shifting circumstances in the external environment may lead (pull factors) household managers to make adjustments in their home-based managerial efforts. Similarly, we must also take into account that some individuals are more oriented toward managing (or to certain subcomponents thereof) than others and, therefore, are more likely to exhibit managerial behavior more extensively across a variety of situations. In order to understand how couples manage their household work activities, we must consider how a host of factors associated with the internal familial environment, other factors associated with the external organizational or work environment, and individual qualities such as cognitive complexity and social competency form the broader context in which the microprocesses of managing household work develop.

We define the broader context to include such factors as husbands' and wives' employment circumstances, which include their individual and household incomes, work hours, job demands, and employment environments. Also we examine factors associated with family life, including number and ages of children, current investment in household chores, and gender ideology. These along with generation/cohort differences form much of the life-course context for developing adaptive strategies and household management approaches. In addition, we examine the interface between home and work, focusing on communication technologies used to bridge the two life domains. We also consider the interface between the household and the market to identify the extent to which certain key household chores get contracted out, which may, in turn, affect managing. Finally, we expect that certain factors associated with individual differences in propensity to manage the household along formal managerial lines might be associated with an individual's sense of personal mastery, as well as belief in his or her abilities to deal with the problems of life. We also consider certain kinds of cognitive complexity, either developed through extensive education or certain forms of work that allow ample decision-making autonomy to be associated with proactive managerial behavior.[19]

Research Questions

Building on the broad contours of the changing work-family dynamics highlighted in the introductory section of this chapter, we address several questions with respect to the middle-class couples' family resource management activities and how they manage daily chores and tasks in their environment. We examine these in relation to the Deacon and Firebaugh framework.

To what extent do wives and husbands report that formal family management practices reflect their own household management activities? And on which components of the managerial framework do they place the greatest emphasis?

Given the lack of empirical evidence linking family resource management and success, we seek to establish some basic (bivariate) relationships between family resource management activities and desired outcomes, such as personal satisfaction or perceived success with certain aspects of work and family life. This provides an important justification for social scientists and practitioners taking an interest in family resource management: Is there a simple bivariate relationship between family management activity and desirable outcomes such as perceived success at work, home, and balancing both or satisfaction with close relationships?

Finally, once we have established a link between family resource management activities and desired outcomes, we examine factors (ranging from work and organizational characteristics to family and individual ones) associated with overall managerial behavior to determine the conditions under which our middle-class respondents are most likely to incorporate such practices into their family-based work related activities. What organizational/work-, family-, and individual-based factors are associated with respondents placing greater emphasis on overall managerial behavior?

Methods: Research, Sample, and Data

We use survey data from *The Cornell Couples and Careers Study*, 1998–99, work-related module that includes a subsample of 260 couples from the larger study. Because respondents were randomly assigned to answer questions from one of three modules, our subsample does not differ greatly from the broader sample of respondents. These couples are not representative of dual-earning couples in the United States overall. They are middle-class, with many being business managers and professionals. Furthermore, the sample is primarily white. Therefore, our analyses focus on this subsegment of the U.S. population, and our findings are generalizable only to similar middle-class dual-earner couples.

Measures

Family management scale. We use items developed by Ramona Heck, Mary Winter, and Kathryn Stafford to reflect the major subcomponents of the Deacon and Firebaugh family resource management framework (see table 10.1).[20] In addition, in treating family management as an outcome or dependent variable, we use the overall scale, as opposed to subcomponents thereof, in keeping with the findings of Heck and colleagues and Duncan and colleagues that support this approach.[21] The cluster of ten items based on the Deacon and Firebaugh framework are not intended to capture all aspects of the managerial process extensively but, instead, focus more heavily on the planning and implementing (throughput) elements of the overall managerial process. The managerial focus of this research seeks to assess the impact of the nuts and bolts phases of the managerial process in more detail than, say, the goal-value clarification aspects of family management. We can still examine, however, the extent to which respondents emphasize each of the four phases of the managerial process.

Life stage. We draw on a modified version of the life stage model as a predictor to examine whether being in the launching stage (with preschoolers) or early establishment stage (with elementary school children) has the effect of pulling respondents into the managerial role. We base our rationale on Moen and Yu's finding that couples in the early child-rearing phases of the life course face the greatest overall demands.[22]

Work hours. We also draw on a modified (dichotomized) version of a fourfold couple work hour variable to see if couples in which one member works long hours (more than forty-five hours per week) also experience a pull into the managerial role.[23] We assume that different dynamics exist for couples in which spouses work over forty-five hours each week and for those in which both spouses work regular hours (forty-five hours or less) at most.

Work load. We also include measures of supervisor support, decision-making autonomy, personal mastery, and perceived constraints. All are described in the appendix.

Findings

Our respondents self-identify with taking a managerial approach to getting household work done. Table 10.2 shows the overall spread of responses for men and women on each of the family management items. For seven of the ten items, well over 50 percent of the women and men identify with managerial behavior. The items are based on a five-point scale in which a score of 1 indicates that the item does not describe the respondent at all, and a score of 5 indicates that the item exactly describes the respondent. We use the top two responses as indicative of respondents identifying with a given item. The item for goals is rated higher for women (57%) than men (46%); the orientation of the statement was specifically focused on the family. Women (49%) also rate actuating somewhat higher than men (41%), suggesting that men are more likely to wait until the last minute to do a task at home. Men rated resource changes more highly than women, indicating that these men value doing a task effectively, not just getting it done. Holly Hunts and colleagues, reporting research using the same scale for household management, found that men, compared to women, "show significantly more 'efficient' behavior, including setting goals for work, setting standards, clarifying what is needed, assessing resource needs, checking and adjusting."[24]

Table 10.2 Frequency of Responses to Family Management Items by Gender[a]

	Women (N = 270)					Men (N = 260)				
Management Concepts	Not at All 1	2	Somewhat 3	4	Exactly 5	Not at All 1	2	Somewhat 3	4	Exactly 5
Input										
Goals (%)	6.3	12.2	23.7	30.0	27.8	4.2	16.7	32.7	26.6	19.8
Planning										
Standard setting	.7	5.9	22.1	45.4	25.8	1.1	4.9	19.4	42.6	31.9
Demand clarification	3.0	11.8	24.0	32.8	28.4	1.5	9.1	19.8	36.1	33.5
Resource assessment	3.7	11.4	24.4	38.0	22.5	4.9	12.5	20.2	36.5	25.9
Action sequencing	7.4	8.5	20.0	35.9	28.1	5.0	8.1	25.4	43.1	18.5
Implementing										
Actuating	5.5	17.0	28.4	21.0	28.0	7.6	20.5	30.8	22.4	18.6
Checking	1.1	2.6	24.4	46.7	25.2	1.1	2.7	23.0	47.5	25.7
Adjusting	0.0	2.6	14.4	45.4	37.6	0.4	2.3	11.4	46.0	39.9
Output										
Demand responses	0.7	1.1	11.8	37.3	49.1	0.8	1.1	11.0	40.7	46.4
Resource changes	10.3	19.2	27.7	26.2	16.6	6.1	18.3	22.4	34.6	18.6

[a] *Cornell Couples and Careers Study*, 1998–99. For each item the respondent was asked: "Think of a scale from 1 to 5, where 1 means the statement does not describe you at all, and 5 means it exactly describes you." Specific items appear in table 10.1.

Table 10.3   Bivariate Relationships between Family Management and Success or Satisfaction[a]

	Family Management Scale[b]			
	Women		Men	
	Low	High	Low	High
Satisfaction with family life	3.89	4.26**	4.01	4.12[tt]
(1–5 scale)	(.57)	(.52)	(.61)	(.52)
Perceived work success	78.7	84.8**	81.1	82.3
(0–100 scale)	(12.3)	(10.9)	(11.5)	(13.1)
Family success	83.1	88.8**	84.4	87.8**
(0–100 scale)	(13.5)	(11.6)	(13.4)	(11.8)
Success balancing work and family	73.6	79.4**	76.0	76.7
(0–100 scale)	(15.6)	(17.0)	(16.4)	(16.4)

[a] *Cornell Couples and Career Study*, 1998–99. ** indicates $p < .01$; [tt] indicates $p < .19$.
[b] High equals an average score of 4 and above for the 10 items of the scale, and Low equals a score less than 4.

Both men and women seem most likely to employ certain subelements of the managerial framework, particularly the items of checking, adjusting, and demand response, which straddle the implementing and output dimensions of the managerial framework. Therefore, we propose that they are emphasizing adjustment strategies in getting their household work done, which seems to mirror many of the changes that have occurred with respect to the work-family interface. Families must continually make adjustments in their household work to cope with all the demands associated with the fast-paced and rapidly changing society. In effect, both men and women in the family are responding to the changing world of work and to a highly complex external environment overall.[25]

Linking Family Management to Measures of Success/Satisfaction

Table 10.3 reports bivariate relationships between the overall family management scale and various measures of satisfaction and perceived success for both men and women. These relationships represent a significant starting point for establishing a link between overall family management and well-being. These four measures are satisfaction with family life, perceived success at work, perceived success in family life, and perceived success at balancing work and family. What we observe in the bivariate relationships between these items and the family management scale are fairly strong, statistically significant relationships for women (but not men) on all four items. These relationships are all very positive for the women, suggesting that women's effective management impacts their well-being.[26]

Table 10.4 Logistic Regressions for Estimating High Family Management: Odds Ratios for Wives[a]

Independent Variables	Model 1	Model 2	Model 3	Model 4	Model 5
Respondent/couple/family					
Age	.994	1.00	1.01	1.01	1.01
Respondent income	.916	0.95	0.90	0.90	0.83
Household income	1.44[†]	1.28	1.30	1.33[††]	1.26
Household chores (min.)	1.00[††]	1.003[††]	1.003[††]	1.003[††]	1.003[†]
Young children at home[b]	1.49[††]	1.73[†]	2.05*	2.15*	2.20*
Work characteristics					
Couple work hours[c]		1.95*	2.04**	2.17**	2.34**
Work load		1.45[††]	1.51[†]	1.62[†]	1.55[†]
Supervisor support		1.25	1.25	1.24	1.26
Wife's decision-making autonomy		1.72*	1.69*	1.69*	1.70*
Work-family interface–technology					
Use email: contact family			2.18*	2.24**	2.50**
Use email: contact work			0.78	0.82	0.74
Family-market interface					
Use shortcut/prepared food				0.50*	0.52*
Personal resources					
Education (years beyond high school)					1.06
Personal mastery					2.25*
Perceived constraints					0.92
−2 log likelihood	362.79	331.54	324.53	319.82	309.54
Model significance (df)	.145 (5)	.005 (9)	.001 (11)	.0004 (12)	.0002 (15)

[a] From *Cornell Couples and Careers Study 1998–99.* ** indicates $p < .01$; * indicates $p < .05$; [†] indicates $p < .10$; [††] indicates $p < .19$.

[b] Dichotomous variable for couples in launching (with preschoolers) or early establishment (with grade school children) stages versus all others.

[c] Dichotomous variable for couples with one member working over 45 hr/week.

Factors Associated with Family Management

Given its link to well-being, we now turn to a multivariate analysis of factors predicting women's home management. In keeping with a major focus of this book, we examine couple-related factors that may have an impact on managing. We estimate logistic regression models of family management, transforming the scale into a dichotomous variable. An average score of 4 or better for each of the ten items making up the scale indicates that a respondent is in the high (versus the not high) category (see table 10.4).

Model 1 examines relationships among factors such as age, individual and household income, time spent in chores, and the presence of young children, and family management scale. Model 1 as a whole is not statistically significant, suggesting that these characteristics are not good predictors of women's degree of home management. In model 2, we incorporate factors related to the wives' and the couples' work arrangements, finding strong, positive, statistically significant relationships between couples' work hours and women's family management. Having either member of the couple working long hours (greater than forty-five hours per week) is associated with higher management. Similarly, wives in jobs with high decision-making autonomy are more likely to be managers on the home front.

Model 3 incorporates factors associated with the work-family interface. Controlling for these factors, the presence of preschool or school-age children matters, with mothers in these life stages being more apt to engage in greater household management activities. Using email at work to contact home is also positively related to management, with women using email in this way being twice as likely to score high on the management scale (compared to those who do not use it for family purposes). By contrast, women who use convenience foods are less likely to engage in household management activities (see model 4, table 10.4). Those who use convenience foods to save time in the kitchen at home are only one-half as likely to score high on family management, compared to those who seldom use frozen dinners and other prepared foods.

We might assume that household management simply reflects a take-control personality, so in model 5 we include two measures of perceived control (personal mastery and perceived constraints), along with educational level. We find a very positive and statistically significant relationship with the family management scale. But the significant relationships for the presence of young children at home, couples' work hours arrangements, wives' decision-making autonomy at work, the use of email to contact family while at work, and using shortcuts/prepared foods all hold, even controlling for these measures.

Summing Up

As our findings show, members of dual-earner couples tend to have high scores on the family management items, indicating that they readily identify with the managerial elements of their household work.[27] These members of dual-earner couples also tend to score highest on the same items as do respondents in studies of home-based workers and dual- and single-role managers.[28] The people in our study tend to report various activities, checking (whether things are going as planned), adjusting (by changing plans when things are not going well), and asking themselves how well they like the results of particular tasks (demand response). They also do a great deal of managerial standard setting, seemingly an essential component of good management. This represents adaptive responses to the complex demands faced by household managers in dual-earner households in their efforts to adjust to the demands of two paid jobs along with the intricacies of unpaid family care work.

We also show some significant bivariate relationships between measures of satisfaction and perceived success at work, in family life, and in balancing the two, especially for women. Of course, these relationships suggest the value of effective management practices at home. These findings also point to the need for scholars to devote more attention to the issue of family resource management because of its importance in helping families adapt to and exert some control over their environments.

Typically, wives in dual-earner households remain the managers of their households. By integrating a life course approach with the family economics–home management perspective, we begin to identify factors associated with these wives having a managerial approach to household work. We have identified a number of pull factors, especially the presence of young children, that seem to draw wives into using more managerial practices more extensively. Mothers of preschoolers and grade-schoolers are twice as likely to score high on the family management scale. The increased demands at home from having younger children around most likely put pressure on wives in dual-earner households to manage more extensively in order to get housework done. Furthermore, wives in couples in which one partner works long hours are more than twice as likely to score high on the management scale. This suggests that couple-level demands at work (as evidenced by one member, typically the husband, working long hours), leads wives to become more managerial-minded in order to keep their households running smoothly.

Managing the household also takes place beyond the front door. Wives who use email at work to contact home are two and one-half times more likely to score high on managing. But, contrary to what we expect, using shortcuts in the kitchen, such as buying already-prepared meals, is associated with low levels of managing. It could be that respondents view managing as reflection of their own involvement and commitment to family life and that the use of such shortcuts is not so much an effective managerial tool as a consequence of the absence of such managing. This fits with Sharon Hays's view about the cultural contradictions of motherhood,[29] and, indeed, the cultural contradictions of trying to be both a wage-earner and homemaker.

We also identify certain characteristics that predict effective managing. First, wives whose jobs offer a good measure of decision-making autonomy are more likely to score high on family management. As Melvin L. Kohn has argued with respect to work and personality, the skills of competent, self-directed solvers of complex problems at work spill over into the home.[30] Women who have a strong sense of personal mastery over their lives are twice as likely to score high on managing, suggesting that they take proactive approaches to getting household work done and managing family life.

Given these findings for women, one area that should prove fruitful in future research is research on gender differences in management. Little work has been done in the area of gender and family management, partly because wives overwhelmingly continue to take responsibility for daily activities within the family realm. But, given that dual-earner households are now the rule, not the exception, with women having moved into the labor force, we may begin to see some interesting relationships emerge between how men and women approach managing. In future research, measures also need to be developed to capture not simply an individual's approach to managing, but also the extent to which he or she manages in any given household domain.

11

Turning Points in Work Careers

Elaine Wethington, Joy E. Pixley, and Allison Kavey

A perceived turning point at work is a period or point in time when people have undergone a transformation in their views regarding their job or a major change in direction in their work or career. In this chapter, we explore perceptions of work turning points, their perceived causes, and their psychological impact among married couples in *The Cornell Couples and Careers Study*. We also test whether couples are likely to report the same or related turning points at work. This chapter contributes to the study of the constructed life course, which focuses on how people believe choice and circumstance shape their work careers.[1] People's descriptions of meaningful changes in their lives and the roles they have in making those changes may shift over the life course.[2] Although social and environmental factors shape individual choice and the collective life course, people's views about how they can shape and control their work and other environments have an important influence on their well-being.[3] Critical events and transitions affecting a major role in life may particularly heighten consciousness of choice and control.[4] Events and transitions that pose a redirection or other major change in a work career may provoke the experience of a turning point in the life course.

Following John Clausen's definition,[5] we define a *turning point at work* as a point or period in time when people perceive that their work or career has taken a different direction. Other investigators have defined the turning point as the event that redirects people's lives or as events that bring about the "potential for long-term psychological change."[6] In the latter two definitions, the investigator identifies what events or transitions may provoke a turning point and examines the consequences of those events and transitions. In our definition, the investigator asks study participants to describe a situation in which a redirection took place and then classifies the self-reported causes and consequences of those experiences.

Our analyses in this chapter combine Clausen's emphasis on self-report with an investigator-based life events approach. Clausen's approach takes advantage of a major characteristic of self-report, namely that it captures "information that no one else knows."[7] We pose five basic questions: Who reports a turning point at work? What types of situations are reported as turning points? Do members of couples frequently report the same or related turning points? To what causes (e.g., work, family, or education) do people attribute those turning points? Among people who experience these types of work, family, and other events, what proportion come to define them as turning points?

Theoretical Approaches to Turning Points at Work

We approach the analysis of turning points at work from two related theoretical perspectives. The first derives from research on stressful life events and chronic difficulties. This life event approach assumes that work and career turning points are consequences of significant critical changes in the work environment.[8] The meaning of the turning point results, at least in part, from the objective characteristics of the situation itself. The report of a turning point is thus just a different way of assessing the impact of certain types of life events and difficulties, focusing on understanding the characteristics of situations that provoke the redirection of work trajectories.

The second approach to analyzing turning points derives from autobiographical memory research. This approach assumes that people construct turning points by a process of assigning meaning to past events in the context of the present.[9] Clausen uses the second approach in his studies of turning points.[10] He observes that many people designate internal psychological changes or reinterpretations of commitments to activities and roles as where their lives "took a different direction,"[11] even if no visible change in trajectory occurred. (Investigator-based approaches to turning points assume that all important changes in trajectory are visible to observers.) This autobiographical approach assumes that the turning point is an individual experience. Although life events may provoke turning points, whether people see an event or transition as a turning point depends on individual factors that may have little to do with the event itself. As well, perceptions of an event as a turning point may change over a person's life course, depending on intervening events. What may appear to be an important turning point in early adulthood (e.g., the first career job) may later appear less significant as a result of intervening events (e.g., changing to another career).

The Cornell Couples and Careers Study provides an opportunity to apply both life event and autobiographical memory perspectives. The availability of employment and family career history data from participants makes it possible to examine whether certain types of events are likely to trigger the perception that a turning point has occurred and whether that perception is related to life course factors, such as family and career stage.

The fact that *The Cornell Couples and Careers Study* interviewed both members of couples provides another opportunity to assess the life event and autobiographical memory approaches. The life event approach implies that partners might tend to report similar, related, or even the same turning points relatively frequently. The reasoning is straightforward. Members of couples are frequently exposed to the same situations. These situations may have similar implications for the future of both or for plans they have made together. Even when the event or difficulty affects only one person directly, the situation may cause the other to make adjustments that have serious impact and create joint turning points.

Situations likely to trigger joint turning points are events that affect both members of the couple in life-changing ways. Examples are having a first child, career changes that involve major adjustments, job loss, and retirement. This does not imply that members of couples react identically to these changes. Rather, it implies that either is likely to report a turning point in response to an event or difficulty that poses a serious threat or challenge to the future and plans of both. This approach also suggests that the likelihood of experiencing a turning point increases after specific types of events or difficulties. Situations that pose severe threats or challenges to future plans presumably create the demand for large adjustments in other areas of life and may also provoke emotional difficulties.[12]

The autobiographical memory approach proposes that the post hoc perception of a turning point is less related to a particular type of event occurring than to factors that affect the construction of a story about the meaning of the past. For example, a traditional life events as change approach suggests that the birth of a first child will probably lead to a (paid) work turning point for a new mother.[13] A more up-to-date contextual life events approach locates events in the context of prior experiences and orientations. It suggests that different types of preexisting work commitments will cause new mothers to experience the parenthood transition in ways consistent with their commitments.[14] Those less committed to their jobs may scale back their work commitments and reflect on the change as a positive turning point in their lives. Those more committed to their jobs, who find that caring for their child interferes with work commitments, may interpret the parenthood transition as a negative work turning point. Other mothers very committed to their jobs, but who are able to maintain that commitment (perhaps by finding high-quality child care), may not interpret the parenthood transition as a turning point at all.

By contrast, the autobiographical memory approach starts with an entirely different premise. This perspective focuses not so much on prior commitments as it does on post hoc reinterpretations of events. For example, a woman will report a birth as a work turning point if she later comes to perceive the event as having changed her emotional commitment to her job. Those who perceive no change will not report a turning point.

The autobiographical memory perspective also makes a different prediction about the propensity for husbands and wives to experience the same situation as a joint turning point, holding that members of couples are not especially likely to report joint turning points. From this vantage point, the reconstruction of the past is individual, even in the context of a close relationship and frequent shared experiences. Although the same events and difficulties may directly and indirectly affect both members of a couple (as emphasized in the linked lives theme throughout this book), the meaning each member assigns to such situations differs. Spouses share only part of their life history; they may not share the same aspirations and plans for the future; and they may well interpret the same situation as posing very different levels of threat or challenge to them personally.

Turning Points at Work in *The Cornell Couples and Career Study* and a National Sample

Method: Sample and Data

In this chapter we draw on data from a subsample of *The Cornell Couples and Careers Study*, the Life Transitions module. The subsample consists of the 308 married or partnered couples in which both spouses were interviewed. Because people were randomly assigned to various modules, the Life Transitions module subsample participants are very similar to the overall Cornell study sample.

The study, although not representative of the United States, is likely to resemble a national sample of middle-class couples in which one or both spouses are professionals and managers (see app.). To compare with dual-earner couples more generally, we compare the Cornell study respondents to demographically similar participants in the John D. and Catherine T. MacArthur Foundation Psychological Experiences Study (PTP). The PTP study reinterviewed 724 participants in the MacArthur Foundation National Survey of Midlife Development in the U.S. (MIDUS).[15] The study asked multiple questions about turning points in different areas of life, including work and career. The participants in the PTP study represent Americans living in the forty-eight coterminous states, who were interviewed from January to September 1998, at approximately the same time as *The Cornell*

Couples and Careers Study data. Among the 724 PTP participants, 267 (160 men and 107 women) were currently or recently employed (in the previous five years) as professionals and managers. These respondents make up the national comparison sample. For selected comparative analyses, we include only those PTP members who were currently working and living with a spouse or partner.

Measures

In this study, we use one question series to assess perception of a recent turning point involving work or career. In the PTP study, the most commonly reported turning point involved job or career.[16] The Cornell study asked, "The next question is about a turning point you may have had in the recent past, involving your job or career. This would be a *major* change in the way you feel or think about your job or career, such as how *important* or *meaningful* it is to you, or how much *commitment* you give it. Have you had a turning point like this in the last 3 years?" (If the answer was yes, the follow-up question asked, "What was that turning point about? Was anything special happening in your family or personal life at that time?")

In the Cornell study, these questions were posed only to those currently in the labor force. This strategy led to an important selection bias, with the majority of the sample for analysis consisting of dual-career couples with both members currently in the labor force. Couples in which one of the spouses was temporarily out of the labor force, such as for the birth of a child, long-term unemployment, disability, or education, are not included. Because of the selection criterion, the work turning points reported underestimate the probability of reporting a recent turning point involving the birth of children, unemployment, retirement, disabling illness, or full-time education.

In the PTP study, all respondents were asked about work turning points, whether or not they were currently in the labor force. The recall period for turning points was five years (rather than three years). In addition, the probe questions after the turning point question were different (if the answer was yes, the follow-up question asked, "What was that about? When did that happen? What impact did this have on you?").

Life Events, Transitions, and Difficulties

The question on work turning points was embedded in a longer interview that included a review of life history and role transitions. Many of the transitions correspond to categories of experiences that Clausen observes as "major life turning points"—parenthood, career and job changes, and educational transitions.[17] The life event perspective implies that some events are associated more than others with a higher probability of experiencing a turning point. Previous research on turning points at work suggests that job changes, moving, marital-status transitions, education and training, and parenting transitions may be associated with reporting a turning point involving work.[18]

Classifications of Turning Points

The first and third authors both coded responses to the work turning point questions in the Cornell and PTP studies. The code captured the major perceived cause of the turning point, as reported by the participant. This code was based on Clausen's classification of the causes of self-reported turning points.[19] The attributed cause could originate from the job or from other aspects of life. Many Cornell study and PTP study respondents provided long descriptions about conditions at work. Our code includes work-family conflict, family situations having an impact on the meaning of work, promotions and other honors, changing job or career, layoffs, decisions about retirement, job insecurity, other negative work conditions, other positive job conditions, and aspects of self-employment. These codes are useful for examining reports of what work and other conditions are associated with reporting a turning point. Many respondents reported multiple causes. For our analyses, we coded up to three mentions for each narrative.

A second code for turning points classified types of adaptive strategies, choices, and constraints that the respondent associated with the turning point. The five types are cutback in career involvement, increase in career involvement, job changes attributed to external events, job changes attributed to internal decisions (self-initiative), and other (unattributed) job changes.

The purpose of the code for cutback in career involvement was to identify turning points that capture, at least in part, the process of scaling back in a career. Scaling back is defined as "strategies that reduce and restructure the couple's commitment to paid work over the life course, and thereby buffer the family from work encroachments."[20] Penny Becker and Phyllis Moen find that women are more likely than men to report scaling back to accommodate their family lives.[21]

The code for increase in career involvement was applied to reported turning points that involved increasing emotional or time commitments to career. For an event to be classified as an increase in career involvement, respondents had to mention that the action was taken to further career or personal aspirations. This code is based on Arlie Hochschild's observations that success and opportunities at work are emotionally significant to both men and women.[22]

Many respondents reported job changes rather than changes in career involvement in response to the turning point question. Although cutbacks and increased involvement are also job changes, the turning points classified in the job changes categories were not reported as involving changes in career. Rather, these involved changes in "my job." These job changes are divided into three categories, according to the agent that the respondent mentioned as initiating the change. Some respondents emphasized the role of employer and external events (they were forced to change). Others emphasized their own initiative in making the change (they made the change before disaster struck or in response to changing preferences for work). Still other respondents reported job changes without specifying who or what caused it.

Analysis Strategy

First, we examine the distribution of reported turning points by gender, education, age, and life-course stage. Following this, we analyze the gender distribution of the various self-reported causes of turning points, focusing particularly on whether men and women report consistently different causes for a perceived turning point at work or different strategies at the turning point. We draw on both the Cornell study and PTP data in these analyses.

Next, we examine the associations of perceived work turning points with measures of well-being using the Cornell study sample only.[23] We consider not only whether perceived work turning points predict well-being, but also whether they predict the respondent's partner's well-being.

Another important theoretical issue is whether couples report the same, similar, or different turning points. We conduct a qualitative analysis to examine whether members of couples both report work turning points, connected turning points, or independent turning points.

As a final step, we address yet another question: Do certain types of life events increase the probability of perceiving a turning point at work? To answer this, we estimate the probability of experiencing a work turning point in the context of key-job and other role-related events.[24]

Findings

Distribution of Work Turning Points by Demographic Factors

Fifty-eight percent of *The Cornell Couples and Careers Study* participants report having had a work turning point in the previous three years. Women are as likely as men to report a work turning point. Among men, 56.5 percent report a turning point, and, among women, 60.2 percent report a turning point. These estimates do not differ significantly by marital status.[25] Results are comparable in the PTP study—60 percent of men and 62.3 percent of women report having a work turning point in the previous five years. Considering marital status, 58.5 percent of married, 78.6 percent of partnered, and 84.9 percent of single respondents in the PTP sample report a work turning point. Married people are significantly less likely to report a turning point at work.

Overall, educational attainment is not significantly related to reporting a turning point for either men or women in the Cornell study (although the relative homogeneity and high educational attainment of the sample may account

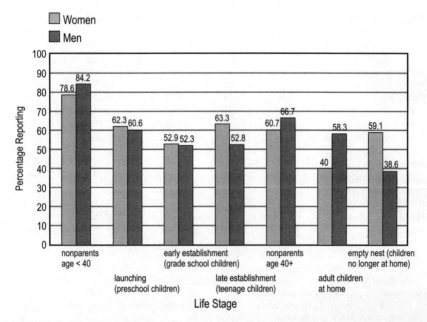

Figure 11.1 Turning points by life-course stage. Source: *The Cornell Couples and Careers Study*, 1998–99.

for a lack of relationship). In the PTP study, however, educational attainment is significantly related to reporting a work turning point, with those with at least some college education being more likely to do so.

In the Cornell study, life-course stage is significantly related to the proportion of men who report turning points, but not for women (see figure 11.1). Specifically, child-free men under forty are significantly more likely to report a turning point at work than are older men whose children are grown and gone (the empty nest stage).[26] The propensity to report a turning point does not differ significantly by gender except for those in the empty nest stage, in which women are more likely than men to report a turning point. The effect size, however, is very small.

In the PTP study, life stage is not significantly related to reporting a turning point at work; no life stage group contrasts are significant. If we take the two samples together, however, nonparents under age forty are more likely to report a turning point at work in both data sets.

Classification of Turning Points by Gender

Both men and women tend to describe turning points as arising from conditions or situations at work (see table 11.1). In fact, in the Cornell study the over-

Table 11.1   Reported Causes of Perceived Turning Points at Work by Gender[a]

	CCCS[b]		PTP[c]	
	Men	Women	Men	Women
Work-family issues	14 (8.0)	39 (21.7)	11 (11.5)	20 (32.3)
Education	3 (1.7)	6 (3.3)	5 (5.2)	3 (4.8)
Own illness	2 (1.1)	7 (3.9)	6 (6.3)	4 (6.5)
Quest for identity	11 (6.3)	10 (5.6)	7 (7.3)	4 (6.5)
Job or career changes	62 (35.6)	78 (43.3)	49 (51.0)	35 (56.5)
Layoffs, downsizing	12 (6.9)	9 (5.0)	10 (10.4)	11 (17.7)
Job insecurity	31 (17.8)	13 (7.2)	4 (4.2)	0 (0)
Work reorganization	13 (7.5)	11 (6.1)	5 (5.2)	2 (3.2)
Other negative job	19 (10.9)	19 (10.6)	11 (11.5)	11 (17.7)
Return to work	0 (0)	5 (2.8)	1 (1.0)	1 (1.6)
Promotions, honors	15 (8.6)	23 (12.8)	8 (8.3)	0 (0)
Retirement	5 (2.9)	4 (2.2)	14 (1.0)	6 (9.7)
Other positive changes at work	10 (5.7)	11 (6.1)	1 (1.0)	2 (3.2)
Self-employment	13 (7.5)	5 (2.8)	5 (5.2)	3 (4.8)

[a] Column percentages add up to more than 100 because up to three mentions were coded per respondent. Values in parentheses are percentages.

[b] CCCS (*the Cornell Couples and Careers Study*) percentages based on reports from 174 men and 180 women who report perceived turning points at work.

[c] PTP (Psychological Experiences Study) percentages are based on 96 men and 62 women.

whelming majority of turning points (76.3%) are primarily attributed to work conditions (e.g., 83.3% for men and 69.4% for women). Recall the sample design of the Cornell study; focusing on workers in middle-class jobs may play a part in this finding. Still, in the full PTP national sample, 70.8 percent of men and 54 percent of women report work conditions as the primary cause of work turning points. Among the currently employed, married, or partnered members of the national PTP study (a fairer comparison sample for the Cornell study), 74.6 percent of men and 57.5 percent of women attribute the cause of their work turning points to work-related situations.

Women more often mention work-family issues as causing turning points in both the Cornell study and PTP study. Yet nearly 80 percent of women in the Cornell study do not spontaneously attribute work turning points to work-family issues. In the PTP study, 11.5 percent of men and 32.3 percent of women attribute work turning points to work-family issues. These differences between the two samples probably result from sample-selection issues related to career commitment.

In sum, people in the Cornell study overwhelmingly point to job-related events and work situations as the causes of turning points, and this seems borne out in our national comparison sample. The majority of these situations are negative (e.g., overload at work because of corporate downsizing), but many are also positive (e.g., promotions). For example, in the Cornell study 35.6 percent of men

.

and 43.3 percent of women, (in the PTP study, 51% of men, and 56.5% of women) attribute their turning points to job changes. Some of these are job changes brought about by company layoffs, downsizing, work reorganization, and job insecurity, four other frequently mentioned causes of turning points. (Some of the job changes are involuntary and others are voluntary, a strategy to avoid a likely layoff in the future.)

Self-Reported Strategies at Work
Turning Points

Next we examine gender differences in the strategies people report using at work turning points. We believe that these are more sensitive to marital and employment status than the causes attributed to turning points. Accordingly we compare the Cornell study data to a comparable group in the PTP study. The PTP group consists of all sample members employed in professional or managerial positions during the previous five years and who are also married (or partnered) and employed at the time of the interview.

We observe two major differences when comparing the two samples. First, respondents in the Cornell study sample report strategies that are more consistent with strong career involvement. Men in the PTP study are more likely than men in the Cornell study to report cutting back on their careers (20.9% versus 13.3%). Women in the Cornell study are more likely than women in the PTP study to report increasing involvement in their careers (21.4% versus 4.8%).

Second, respondents in the Cornell study sample seem to have been more affected by involuntary job changes, most likely due to regional differences in the relative health and expansion of employment opportunities for professionals and managers. Men in the Cornell study are more likely than men in the PTP study to attribute job changes to external causes (43% versus 22.4%). Men in the PTP study are more likely than men in the Cornell study to attribute work turning points to self-initiative (40.3% versus 26.6%).

Turning Points and Well-Being

Perceived turning points are, by definition, significant cognitive events. As a cognitive event (or, alternatively, as life situations that lie behind the cognitive perceptions), reporting a turning point should be related to psychological well-being. Most Cornell study participants who report work turning points describe negative situations, although many respondents report situations that should result in positive emotions (e.g., promotions and honors) or mixed emotions (e.g., job changes that prevent unemployment but result in increased demands at work).

We have calculated the association between respondents' perceiving a turning point of particular content with five psychological outcomes: negative affect,[27] personal growth,[28] success at work, success in family, and success at balancing work and family.[29] We have also calculated the correlations of the perceived work turning points of respondents with their partners' well-being, separately for men and women. For men, reporting any turning point is marginally related to higher negative affect ($r = .099$) and significantly related to higher personal growth ($r = .119$). For women, reporting any work turning point is significantly related to higher personal growth ($r = .162$), feeling less successful in family and personal life ($r = -.132$), and feeling less successful at balancing work and family ($r = -.171$). None of the correlations with partner's level of well-being are significant.

Joint versus Individual Turning Points

In the 308 couples in the Cornell study, both spouses in 66 of the couples (21.4%) report turning points involving work in the previous three years. However, very few of the turning points they report are joint turning points (similar or related situations involving their careers). Only four couples report turning points that both members attribute to the same or a related cause. One couple said that the birth of their child led to turning points involving work (and used very similar language to describe their turning points). Another couple volunteered that their joint planning for retirement was a work turning point for both. A third couple reported that one partner's diagnosis with a life-threatening illness triggered work turning points for both of them. A fourth said that one partner's layoff was a career turning point for both of them. Of the remaining 62 couples in which both reported work turning points, each spouse attributed unrelated causes for their own turning point.

Turning Points and Recent Life Events

One weakness in relying on self-reported attribution of causes when analyzing turning points is that respondents may frame their answers to conform to what they think investigators expect.[30] For example, some respondents may believe that attributing the turning point to an event outside work is an incorrect answer. Others may misidentify, misremember, or conceal the true cause.[31] Thus, another way to examine the relationship between perceived turning points and life events or transitions is to estimate how often those who actually experience an event perceive it as a turning point at work.

We address this issue by estimating the probability of people reporting a work turning point in the context of their recent life events. Although question probing was not extensive, we did get a good sense of the types of events that tend to be associated with turning points. Using life history data, we identify two major types of events that may well be related to experiencing a turning point: the birth or adoption of a child and job changes. Although other types of events are also

Table 11.2 Relative Risk of Reporting a Perceived Work Turning Point If Birth or Adoption of Child in Past Four Years[a]

	Men		Women	
	No Birth/Adoption	Birth/Adoption	No Birth/Adoption	Birth/Adoption
No turning point	61 (43.6%)	8 (23.5%)	74 (42.8%)	9 (29.0%)
Turning point	79 (56.4%)	26 (76.5%)	99 (57.2%)	22 (70.9%)
Relative risk	2.51		1.83	
Chi-square	$p < .05$		NS	

[a] Age forty-five or younger only. NS, not significant.
Source: *Cornell Couples and Careers Study*, 1998–99.

implicated as frequent causes of work turning points, such as health problems and worsening work conditions, the Cornell study interview did not ask all respondents about them.

Birth of a Child   Sixty-five participants in the Cornell study report that they had or adopted a child in the previous four years. What is the probability of their reporting a work turning point after this event? Here we consider all work turning points. It is possible that the birth of a child would have an effect on the emotional meaning or significance of other events, even if the participant had not nominated the birth as the cause of the turning point. For example, having a child might increase the stakes of losing a job or vying for a promotion.[32]

For these analyses we use the statistic of relative risk. The relative risk is the ratio of turning point probabilities in the two groups of interest—namely those who did or did not experience a probable trigger for a turning point. The numerator of the statistic is the proportion of those who experienced a particular event and report a work turning point. The denominator is the proportion of those who did not experience the event and who report a turning point. We calculate relative risks separately for men and women (see table 11.2), confining our analyses to those under age forty-five.

Our findings are somewhat unexpected from a life events as change perspective. Among men, the relative risk of experiencing a turning point at work is 2.51 more likely among those who had or adopted a child in the previous four years. For women, the relative risk for experiencing a work turning point after the birth or adoption of a child is lower, 1.83, somewhat less likely than it is for men.

Job Changes and Life Stage   Because the analyses for the birth or adoption of a child suggest that parenthood is a significant predictor for work turning points among men, we expand the analysis of relative risk to take into account different family life stages, hypothesizing that people with more family responsibilities are more likely to experience a work turning point after a job

Table 11.3 Summary of Relative Risk of Reporting Perceived Turning Point If Changed Jobs within Last Four Years[a]

	Men	N	Chi-square	Women	N	Chi-square
Nonparents <40	2.50	29	NS	1.98	46	NS
Launching	0.62	71	NS	2.54	61	$p < .10$
Establishment[b]	3.64	131	$p < .01$	1.80	128	NS
Later life stages[c]	4.88	87	$p < .01$	9.04	74	$p < .01$

[a] By four life stages and gender. NS, not significant.
[b] Combined early establishment and late establishment.
[c] Combined older children in household, empty nest, and nonparents above age forty.
Source: *Cornell Couples and Careers Study*, 1998–99.

change. Our more qualitative analyses of turning points suggest that participants report many different types of job changes as work turning points. To see whether, in general, job changes increase the risk of reporting a work turning point, we construct a variable from the life history calendar, combining all job changes in the previous four years. This includes all events such as layoffs, firings, promotions, work-hour changes, job changes within organizations, and retirements.

To test the possibility that job changes have different emotional impacts at different stages of life, we calculate relative risk statistics by gender and by life stage. Because of relatively small subgroup numbers, we consider four broad life-stage groups: nonparents under age forty, those with preschoolers (launching stage), those with school-age children (establishment stage), and older respondents (those with children over eighteen in the household, empty nesters, and nonparents older than age forty).

Table 11.3 presents the results of the relative risk analyses by subgroups. In general, older respondents are more likely to report a psychological turning point after a job change. The estimated relative risk of a work turning point for the older life-stage group is 4.88 for men and 9.04 for women. For those in the establishment stage (with school-age children), the relative risk is 3.64 for men and 1.80 for women, one-half that estimated for men. Note that younger people (e.g., nonparents under age forty) are more likely overall to report a work turning point. This suggests that events and situations other than job changes are more likely to trigger turning points among younger people, whose adult roles are less established.

Summing Up

Not only objective circumstances but also cognitive perceptions vary among workers. In this chapter, we compare the Cornell study to reports from similar respondents in the 1998 PTP study, a national study of perceived turning points in different areas of life. In the Cornell study, over one-half the sample (56.5%

of men and 60.2% of women) perceive a turning point at work in the previous three years. The majority of respondents, both husbands and wives, attribute these turning points to conditions at work, especially events involving job changes and job insecurity. Fewer respondents (both wives and husbands) attribute work turning points to the difficulties of combining work and personal life. Respondents in the Cornell study report experiences similar to those reported in the PTP sample, although job changes and job insecurity events are somewhat more prevalent in the Cornell study. We find it very unusual for husbands and wives to report the same or related situations as turning points at work.

Overall, our analyses in this chapter provide support for examining and understanding self-reported work turning points from the contextual life events and autobiographical memory perspectives. The major support for this conclusion is that family transitions do not greatly increase the probability of reporting a turning point at work. We also find, contrary to the prediction of the life-events perspective, that members of dual-career couples overwhelmingly report individual rather than joint work turning points. Even very closely linked individuals who share similar life experiences perceive very different types of events as forks in the road in their work careers. Among our predominantly middle-class sample (as well as the PTP study sample), turning points in job and career are overwhelmingly associated with job situations and changes rather than with family events. We expected to find that many respondents report turning points at work after family transitions and events that could affect work commitment, women more so than men. We do not find strong support for this expectation. Although women are more likely to attribute work turning points to family transitions than men, the majority of women reporting turning points attribute them to changes and conditions on the job. In sum, the self-reported causes of work turning points, for both men and women, center on work.

One explanation for this finding is that contemporary men and women focus on work as their primary source of identity and fulfillment in life.[33] This tendency might be particularly strong among professionals and managers, who dominate the Cornell study sample. For women in the Cornell study, leaving work for an extended period or putting their career on hold may not be a reasonable option, probably because of the major investments they have made in their education and career. These investments commit them to maintaining a stable career trajectory over their adult lives (see Williams and Han, chap. 6 in this volume).[34] The PTP data do not produce exactly comparable results, but because of the small number of cases in the exact comparison sample, the lack of consistency should be interpreted with caution.

A second possible explanation for the focus on career is the level of job insecurity among the target population in the Cornell study. The members of this sample are very likely to have changed jobs within the previous four years. Even when job changes are self-directed and voluntary, they consume energy and generate challenges and stress. Such situations are very memorable and most likely to come to mind when answering questions on turning points.

A third explanation for the strong focus respondents placed on work is methodological. Respondents may have thought that describing events or situations outside of work was an incorrect answer to the question. The sample selection may have also played a part because, by design, the questions in the Cornell study were asked only of those currently working. Marital status may be another important selection factor. Job changes that threaten the well-being and future of entire families may provoke turning points among older workers who are committed to jobs not only for personal reasons but for family ones. We find job changes are more likely to lead to perceived turning points among those older workers, who are in the later stages of their occupational and family careers.

12

Prioritizing Careers

Joy E. Pixley and Phyllis Moen

Understanding how dual-earner couples negotiate their work and family roles requires considering four intersecting roles: her family role, his family role, her work role, and his work role. Many family scholars focus on the two that relate to each individual: the intersection of women's work and family roles or, more rarely, men's work and family roles. Studies address such issues as how women juggle incompatible career and family responsibilities or how fathers' work-family stress is related to the time they spend caring for their children. Other scholars examine a third intersection, the relationship between his and her roles within the home, typically focusing on how spouses divide housework and child-care responsibilities. In this chapter, we focus on the fourth combination of roles: his work role and her work role as they intersect over time.

Increasingly, not only are both spouses employed at any given time, but many are employed for most of their adult lives.[1] The fact that workers are married to other workers plays out in the dynamic relationship between husbands' and wives' occupational careers over the life course. Specifically, decisions about career opportunities that require an individual's spouse to move or change jobs are much more problematic than is the case for traditional breadwinner-homemaker families, who follow the (male) breadwinner's career opportunities.[2] In the 1960s and 1970s, even among two-earner households, such decisions were overwhelmingly based on the husband's career advancement, with little consideration given to the wife's employment or options.[3] However, evidence on which spouse's career has priority (much of it from the 1980s or earlier) may be out of date. At the beginning of the twenty-first century, we can no longer assume that the majority of couples treat wives' careers as secondary.

In this chapter, we address the following questions: To what extent do patterns of favoring husbands' careers over those of their wives persist among contemporary dual-earner couples? Are couples' assessments of career hierarchy—that is, whose career is prioritized in decision making—consistent with the career decisions they report? And what factors predict husbands' and wives' perceptions of whose career has been favored?

We draw on the key life-course themes throughout this volume, particularly the notion of linked lives (the ways in which spouses' work trajectories intersect with each other) and couple-level adaptive strategies in the prioritization of their careers. The notion of deliberate strategies is especially relevant because now couples can consciously choose among diverse approaches to negotiating two careers and each spouse's family responsibilities. In the past, at least for middle-class couples, there was only one viable option: prioritizing the husband's career.

Couples' Intersecting Careers

Theoretical Models

There are many ways in which the strategy of favoring one spouse's career can affect the other's career. Major decisions about whether to move for one spouse's career advancement arguably have the greatest impact on husbands' and wives' work lives. One spouse may be a tied mover, following the other spouse's career move to a new location, or a tied stayer, staying in the location of the other spouse's job, although the opposite might be better for his or her own career. Even when moving is not at issue, demands at home can lead couples to decide that one spouse should quit or scale back at his or (more typically) her job while the other spouse increases or maintains the same level of work involvement.[4] How couples prioritize their careers is likely to influence decisions about whose career is advanced and whose is put on the back burner.

Social scientists have approached couples' decisions about their two careers from many directions; here we offer the three most common explanations. Economic models, using human capital theory, focus on how disparities between husbands' and wives' education and skills (sometimes represented by current earnings) influence the relative profitability of available options. Summarizing this perspective, Gary Becker theorizes that in order to maximize household utility, decisions should consistently favor the career advancement of the partner who has the comparative advantage in market labor, or the higher earnings potential, at the outset.[5] His model is explicitly gender-neutral but implicitly gender-specific—as long as only women can bear children, they will have a comparative advantage in the home domain, giving their husbands a comparative advantage in the work domain by default. Economic models need not invoke gender to elicit gender-specific outcomes. For instance, in Jacob Mincer's family migration model couples calculate the income gain or loss for each partner for each option and choose the option that maximizes the net family gain, even though it may entail a great personal loss for one partner.[6] The partner with the higher earnings is likely to be prioritized in relocation decisions, regardless of gender. But, because men typically earn more than women, this model usually predicts favoring the husband's career.

In the family power approach, the relative resources that each partner controls influence the ability of each to sway the decision in his or her favor, and the results do not necessarily maximize the joint outcome.[7] That is, relative resources impact decisions by affecting the nature of the spouses' exchange. Furthermore, the interaction between husband and wife is a social exchange, in which the terms are deliberately left unspecified (rather than an explicit economic exchange). As such, the value of each partner's sacrifices and contributions is subject to interpretation and, as Richard Curtis points out, the partners' relative access to power and authority can sway the balance of that interpretation.[8]

Role and social constructionist theoretical models focus on how men and women are socialized toward gender-specific behavior and how institutionalized structures repeatedly reconstruct gendered divisions and inequalities.[9] In these models, couples enact, to a greater or lesser extent, cultural patterns of behaviors and attitudes predicated on the male breadwinner model, including the tradition of giving priority to husbands' careers rather than those of wives. Although scholars debate about whether early socialization or current circumstances influence individuals' gendered behaviors more strongly, the implications for career hierarchy are the same: couples' career-prioritizing decisions should be affected by the gender of the spouse whose career is favored (or sacrificed), above and beyond any economic or practical factors.

It is important to note that the economic and family power models include many of the same predictors of couples' decisions. The husband's and wife's relative resources (e.g., education, income, and occupational status) figure prominently in both approaches and predict similar outcomes, although through different processes. Role and social constructionist theories can be seen as complementing, rather than competing with, models based on relative resources—gender-role attitudes and structural options and constraints influence decisions about mate selection and early investments in career advancement that result in differences in resources between spouses. Later, gender-specific attitudes and behaviors can influence career-prioritizing decisions, net of purely economic considerations.

Empirical Research

Existing evidence about couples' career-prioritizing decisions focuses on migration.[10] The traditional assumption that husbands' jobs are more important than their wives' jobs is reflected in attitudes about family migration in previous decades. In the 1977 Quality of Employment Survey, men and women were asked about their willingness to relocate for a hypothetical promotion opportunity. Although income was positively related to both men's and women's (hypothetical) willingness to move for their own careers, employed wives expressed much greater reluctance to move for their own career advancement than did husbands.[11] Furthermore, more than one-half of married women (56%) said they were reluctant to move because of family considerations (including their husbands' jobs), a reason seldom given by men (16%). Although women expressing nontraditional gender-role attitudes were somewhat more willing to move, the substantial gender difference persisted. Similarly, when polled in the early 1980s, more than two-thirds of Americans said that a wife should quit a "good and interesting" job if her husband is offered a very good job elsewhere, but only one in five thought a husband should do the same if the positions are reversed.[12]

Much of the research on concrete decisions uses one of two approaches. Some researchers start with patterns of observed migration in large data sets and infer the individual decisions that led to those behaviors. Others analyze specific decisions couples have made, typically using small, in-depth studies or focusing on groups unusually likely to face career-prioritizing decisions. Research of the first type indicates that wives' labor-force involvement has traditionally had little to no influence on relocating[13] and that wives' incomes tend to decline directly after moving, largely due to subsequent unemployment or underemployment.[14] Based on a study of married women in the National Longitudinal Surveys, Daniel Lichter concludes, "differentials in female migration may largely be a function of factors external to their own employment experiences."[15] At the same time, dual-earner couples have typically been less likely to relocate than single-earner couples, in theory because the wife's employment means that fewer distal opportunities for the husband would result in a net family gain.[16] Nevertheless, wives are more often tied stayers than are husbands; the gap between married men's and married women's incomes decreases with urban size, consistent with the premise that wives' options are limited by the location of their husbands' jobs.[17]

Many interpret this evidence as suggesting that husband-centered migration contributes to gender differences in earnings. Others offer a different perspective, arguing that migration does not reduce women's employment rates or women's proportion of household income after accounting for self-selection bias or that the negative effect of moving on women's incomes is short-lived.[18] The debate is essentially over whether these findings imply causality or selection—are wives' careers adversely affected by husband-centered migration, or do women and men make different human capital investments earlier in life in anticipation of favoring the husband's career? Our life-course interpretation is that both dynamics could operate at various points in the spouses' relationship, typically reinforcing one another but occasionally reversing in response to situational constraints and opportunities.[19]

Another line of research asks members of dual-earner couples about ongoing or recent career-prioritizing decisions. Husband-centered migration is also prevalent in these accounts. For instance, in Anne Green's case study of migration decisions among thirty dual-career couples living near London, the husband's career was favored in the decision in approximately two-thirds of couples, whereas the wife's career was favored in one-sixth of couples. These decisions were often described as favoring the career that was more highly paid, most secure, or most locationally constrained (e.g., specialized), which was usually the husband's career.[20]

In a similar vein, Leroy Gill and Donald Haurin asked whether husbands' decisions to remain in the military (which severely constrains wives' occupational choices) were influenced by their civilian wives' potential earnings. Using data on over 1,300 couples, Gill and Haurin find that the economic consequences for the wife did affect the husband's decision, but were not weighed as heavily as either the consequences for the husband or his preferences.[21]

Particular attention has been paid to couples in which both spouses are highly educated professionals in the same field. Here, the selection argument mentioned earlier makes little sense; wives in these couples have invested heavily in human capital, obtaining doctoral, medical, or other advanced degrees, presumably with the intention of pursuing highly paid careers. Because women pursuing advanced degrees are likely to delay marriage into their late twenties or early thirties, however, the men they are likely to meet—and later marry—in their school and work environments tend to also be highly educated professionals. As such, even women who are doctors or professors frequently have the same (or lower) education and income relative to their husbands. Given strong competition for specialized positions, the two-body problem of finding jobs for spouses in the same field can lead to a choice between living apart for years at a time or one spouse—typically the wife—accepting a position of lower status.[22] In one study of almost four hundred women physicians, those married to other physicians were found to be twice as likely to have made sacrifices in their own careers to accommodate their husband's careers than those married to nonphysicians.[23]

The overarching conclusion of these various studies is that couples' decisions to move have most often hinged on the husbands' careers. Major decisions that do not involve relocating but do require spouses to change jobs most likely followed a similar pattern.[24] Still, the evidence thus far has been unable to clearly distinguish which of the models discussed earlier most accurately describes couples' strategic decisions about relocating. Part of the problem is that studies providing the level of detailed data necessary to test one model typically do not have the level of detailed data required by the other models. Another part of the problem is the lack of variation on crucial measures during the decades for which the most information is available. Given the situations of most couples in the 1960s and 1970s, these models all predict the same behavior—that is, favoring the husband's career in major decisions.

But times have changed, and the career-prioritizing strategies of contemporary couples may have as well. In *The Cornell Couples and Careers Study*, we focus on a demographic group that may be more likely than most to break with traditional patterns: dual-earner couples who are, for the most part, in professional, managerial, and technical occupations. We anticipate that couples in this sample vary both in relative education and attainment levels (with some wives earning as much or more than their husbands) and in the degree to which their career-prioritizing strategies reflect the gender-specific patterns of the past. Also, because this study includes both members of each couple, we can compare husbands' and wives' perceptions as to whose career has had priority.

According to explanations based on relative resources, couples in which the wife has more labor-force experience or is better educated than her husband should be more likely to either treat the spouses' careers as equal or to favor the wife's career. According to gender-based explanations, couples with nontraditional attitudes should be least likely to favor the husband's career to the detriment of the wife's career. On the other hand, the more structural aspects of role theory, along with the social construction of gender approach, hold that institutions and policies central to couples' work and family strategies continue to favor the male breadwinner model. This structural lag may reinforce traditional patterns even in nontraditional dual-earner couples.[25]

Patterns of Career Hierarchy

We assess career hierarchy patterns (i.e., whether one spouse's career generally takes precedence) in three stages. First, which partners say their own careers have been prioritized in major decisions and which partners say their spouses' careers have been prioritized, and to what extent do spouses agree? Second, are reports of career priority in decision making corroborated by a concrete measure of career priority, the resolution of specific career-opportunity decisions? And third, how well do spouses' relative resources and gender-role attitudes predict the career hierarchy strategy they report?

One measure of career hierarchy is self-reported career priority, or spouses' perceptions of whose career has been prioritized in major decisions over the course of their relationship. A second measure, more directly related to behaviors, is available for men and women who report facing opportunities in their careers that, if taken would have required their spouse to make significant changes. Among these couples, the resolution of opportunity decisions is another indication of career hierarchy and can be compared to self-reported career priority.

Consistent with the social construction of gender perspective, persistent gender differences in occupational experiences and attainment, and the husband-centered migration patterns documented in prior studies, gender is likely to be a key factor in career hierarchy. We expect that for most dual-earner couples in *The Cornell Couple and Careers Study*, both measures of career hierarchy will indicate that husbands' careers take precedence over those of their wives. Specifically, more spouses will report prioritizing husbands' careers than wives' careers in major decisions, and men should be more likely than women to take advantage of career opportunities that require their spouses to make significant changes. In contrast to previous generations (in which husbands' careers almost always took precedence), we expect a substantial proportion of these couples to favor both spouses' careers equally or to favor wives' careers.

Second, it cannot be assumed that these indicators are related. When husbands and wives say that one spouse's career has been prioritized, is this reflected in actual decisions? We expect some couples to say that they prioritize their careers equally or that the wife's career is prioritized in major decisions, but we would hesitate to put very much weight on these claims if we discover that the wives in these couples are just as likely as other wives to turn down actual career opportunities or that their husbands are just as likely as other husbands to take advantage of opportunities that require their wives to make career changes. Even reporting that an individual faced an opportunity that required major changes on the part of his or her spouse, regardless of the outcome, could have implications for career hierarchy. Potential career moves may be sought by, offered to, or recognized as possibilities only by those who would consider asking their spouse to relocate for their career.

Ideally, the third stage of analysis would assess whether gender-role attitudes and resource differences between spouses immediately prior to any given decision predicts the resolution of that decision. But because important decisions could have occurred at any point since their relationship began, it is impossible to ascertain a couple's situation at the time of each decision, even though we know the spouses' educational and employment histories. Instead, we assess whether the reported career priority in decision making is related to characteristics assumed to precede couple-specific career opportunities: estimates of spouses' initial relative resources (age, education, and work hours at the beginning of their relationship) and current gender role attitudes (as rough proxies for longer-term patterns).

Consistent with a relative resources argument, we expect that when husbands are older than their wives and better educated at the beginning of their relationship, couples are likely to prioritize husbands' careers over wives' careers in subsequent major decisions. The reverse should be true if the wife is older or better educated. In this model, we see age difference as reflecting the additional time the older spouse has had to establish his or her career, net of differences in educational attainment (i.e., the older spouse could acquire work experience and skills while the younger spouse was still in school). Spouses' work hours at the beginning of the relationship are used as an indicator of initial labor-force involvement. To the extent that working longer hours implies a greater investment in or commitment to work, we hypothesize that the career of the spouse working more hours early in the relationship will have priority in the couple's later career decisions.

Because we cannot reliably obtain past attitudes in retrospective interviews, we use current gender-role attitudes to estimate spouses' general tendency to endorse or reject traditional ideas.[26] We expect that men and women who believe in traditional gender roles will be most likely to prioritize the husband's career and most unlikely to prioritize the wife's career. Couples who reject traditional gender roles may embrace a wide range of nontraditional ideals. Although we expect couples with nontraditional gender-role attitudes to be less likely than couples with traditional attitudes to prioritize the husband's career, we cannot predict whether they will be more likely to give greater priority to the wife's career or to give equal priority to both careers.

The Cornell Couples and Careers Study Measures

We use structured interview data from both members of 803 dual-earner couples in *The Cornell Couples and Careers Study*.[27] As outlined in the appendix, most of these couples are college-educated and in professional or managerial occupations.[28] We include both married and cohabiting couples, referring to members of all couples as "spouses" for ease of presentation.

Couples' Career Hierarchy   To measure career hierarchy, we asked respondents, "Think about all the major decisions that you and your spouse have made since you have been together, such as changing jobs, having children, going back to school or moving. Overall, whose career was given more priority in these decisions, yours or your spouse's?" Respondents could also report that neither career was prioritized or that spouses took turns prioritizing their careers.

Another survey item asked if respondents had ever had a "career or education opportunity that would have required your spouse to make significant changes, like moving to a different city or taking a different job." If yes, the follow-up question asked, "What happened—did you turn down the opportunity, took it but arranged things so your spouse wouldn't have to make any significant changes, or took it and your spouse made the changes?" The responses "both compromised" and "something else" were also accepted. We use two measures in the following analyses: whether the respondent faced an opportunity decision and, if so, its resolution.

Initial Relative Resources   Differences between spouses in age, education, and work hours at the beginning of their relationship indicate initial relative resource differences. Educational attainment is divided into three categories (based on empirical relationship to income): having less than a bachelor's degree, having a bachelor's degree or a master's degree (i.e., MA or MS), and having an advanced professional degree (e.g., MBA, PhD, MD, or JD).[29] One rough measure of initial relative resources used here is whether spouses were in the same educational category when they began living together or whether the husband or the wife had greater attainment. Two-thirds of the couples (65%) had the same level of educational attainment, the wife's education was higher in 13 percent, and the husband's was higher in 22 percent.

Net of difference in education, difference in age represents the relative time spouses had available to work on their career advancement. The wives in this sample are, on average, forty-three years old and the husbands forty-five years old.[30] Age differences in this sample range from the wife being fourteen years older to the husband being twenty years older. On average, husbands are about two years older than their wives (with a median difference of one year). Based on the distribution of age differences, couples are divided into three categories: wife is older (19%), husband is the same age or older by up to two years (46%), and husband is more than two years older (35%).

We use job history data to calculate each spouse's weekly work hours at the beginning of their (current) relationship.[31] Men and women who married or began cohabiting before starting their first major job (primarily those still in college when the relationship began) are coded as working zero hours, as are those who left their job when they married or moved in together or who for other reasons were not working when their relationship began.

For those who were working when their relationship began, weekly hours are grouped into reduced (1–38 hours), regular (39–45 hours) and long (more than 45 hours).[32] Most people were either not working (45% of women and 32% of men) or were working regular hours (39% of women and 42% of men) when their relationships began. On average, men were much more likely to be working long hours than women (22% versus 9%). For the 734 couples with complete data on their work status when their relationship began, in 140 (19%) neither spouse was working, in 190 (26%) only the husband was working, and in 100 (14%) only the wife was working. In the remainder, both spouses were working, including 136 (19%) couples in which both spouses were working regular hours and 105 (14%) couples in which the husband was working longer hours than the wife. The majority (92%) of the couples in *The Cornell Couples and Careers Study* sample are in one of these five groups.

To indicate spouses' relative initial work hours, we identify whether the husband and wife were working the same hours at the beginning of their relationship (e.g., both working regular hours or both not working) and, if not, which spouse's initial work hours fall into the higher category. The initial work-hour categories were the same for 42 percent of couples; in 40 percent the husband's category was higher and in 18 percent the wife's category was higher.

Traditional Gender-Role Attitudes   We asked respondents to indicate their level of agreement with the following statements (using a five-level Likert scale): "It is usually better for everyone if the man is the main provider and the woman takes care of the home and family;" "It is more important for a wife to help her husband's career than to have one herself;" "A preschool child is likely to suffer if his or her mother works;" and "A working mother can establish just as good a relationship with her children as a mother who does not work" (reverse-coded). We constructed a scale by averaging responses to these four items. Reliability is estimated at .80. The scale ranges from 1 to 5; higher scores indicate more traditional gender-role attitudes. The mean scores in this subsample are 2.1 (SD 0.9) for women and 2.4 (SD 0.8) for men.

How Couples Prioritize Their Careers

Self-Reports of Overall Career Priority

Even in this sample of contemporary middle-class couples, husbands' careers are more often given greater priority (see table 12.1). Just over one-half of respondents (54% of man and 53% of women) say that the husband's career had priority in major decisions. Almost one-third (31% of men and 30% of women) report that neither spouse's career was given priority or that they took turns. The remaining one-sixth prioritized the wife's career. Although husbands' and wives' reports are correlated (Pearson $r = .434$, $p < .0001$), in exactly two-fifths of couples, husbands and wives give different reports of whose career had priority. Such findings shed more light on couple-level dynamics than would be gained by typical surveys, which include reports from individuals and treat them as representatives of their households. For instance, if we obtained reports from only one spouse and one-half of men and one-half of women said their decisions prioritized the

Table 12.1   Spouses' Reports of Whose Career Was Prioritized in Major Decisions

	Husband's Report			
	His Had Priority	Neither/Took Turns	Hers Had Priority	Total
Wife's Report — His Had Priority	309 (38%)	99 (12%)	17 (2%)	425 (53%)
Neither/Took Turns	82 (10%)	112 (14%)	47 (6%)	241 (30%)
Hers Had Priority	44 (5%)	35 (4%)	58 (7%)	137 (17%)
Total	435 (54%)	246 (31%)	122 (15%)	803

Source: *Cornell Couples and Careers Study*, 1998–99.

husband, we might conclude that husbands' careers were prioritized in one-half of the couples studied. Yet in *The Cornell Couples and Careers Study*, in only 38 percent of couples do spouses agree that the husband's career has been prioritized. Similarly, although one-third of men and women report that their careers have been prioritized equally, fewer than one-half of them have a spouse who agrees, and the disagreement is even greater for those who report that the wife's career has been prioritized.

We expected this sample of primarily highly educated, professional dual-earner couples to report that they took turns or gave priority to wives' careers more often than other family types. We know that in the majority of single-earner couples, it is the wife rather than the husband who opts out of the labor force,[33] which offers some indication of career hierarchy. The broader sample of *The Cornell Couples and Careers Study* includes 104 couples in which only the husband is working, and, indeed, few of them report either of the nontraditional career priority patterns.[34] In these couples, fully 79 percent of wives and 88 percent of husbands (with 68% couples in agreement) report that the husband's career had priority. In fact, in only one couple did neither spouse say that they favored the husband's career in major decisions.

In table 12.1, spouses who disagree about whose career had priority fall either above or below the diagonal. In 20 percent of couples (represented by the top triangle of the table), both the husband and wife attribute a higher priority to their spouse's career than their spouse does. This includes couples in which both say the other spouse's career had greater priority, and those in which one spouse says the other's career had greater priority while the other spouse says neither had priority. We characterize these couples as disagreeing in the "both other" pattern. In another 20 percent of couples (in the bottom triangle), both the husband and wife attribute a higher priority to their own career than their spouse reports. We characterize these couples as disagreeing in the "both own" pattern. In both groups, the largest single report combination is one spouse saying the husband's career had priority and the other spouse saying that neither career has been prioritized.

Table 12.2   Career Opportunities by Couple-Level Career Priority[a]

		Wife Reports Opportunity	Husband Reports Opportunity
All couples	803	161 (20%)	340 (42%)
Agree: his career prioritized	309 (38%)	45 (15%)	156 (50%)
Agree: neither/took turns	112 (14%)	24 (21%)	39 (35%)
Agree: her career prioritized	58 (7%)	18 (31%)	16 (28%)
Disagree: both say own	161 (20%)	32 (20%)	73 (45%)
Disagree: both say other's	163 (20%)	42 (26%)	56 (34%)

[a]From *Cornell Couples and Careers Study*, 1998–99. Career priority is self-report of whose career has been favored in major decisions.

Self-Reports of Career Opportunity Decisions

Our second indicator of career hierarchy is the occurrence and resolution of career opportunities that require the other spouse to make significant changes (see table 12.2). As expected, husbands are more likely to report having had such opportunities than are wives (42% versus 20%). Spouses' chances of reporting an opportunity are significantly related: 24 percent of women whose husbands report opportunities report one themselves, compared to 18 percent of women whose husbands do not report an opportunity (results not shown). Similarly, 50 percent of men whose wives report opportunities report one themselves, compared to 40 percent of men whose wives do not report an opportunity.[35] This is consistent with assortive mating, in which people marry those who are similar in attributes such as education, social status, and occupation type, in part because they are exposed to similar others at school, work, and other social settings. So, spouses may share characteristics that influence how likely they are to face career opportunities that would require moving or other significant changes for the other spouse.

The chances of facing a major career opportunity differ by couples' ratings of career priority. Proportionally, men in couples in which both agree that his career has been prioritized are the most likely to report opportunities (50%), whereas men in couples in which both agree that the wife's career has been prioritized are the least likely (28%) to report such opportunities. Men in couples in which both agree that neither career had priority fall in the middle (35%) in terms of having a career opportunity. The same holds true for women. Among couples in which discrepant assessments of career priority are reported the proportions of wives and husbands reporting opportunities most closely resemble those of couples who agree that neither career was prioritized or that they took turns. The exception is the pattern of husbands' opportunity reports among couples in which spouses each say their own career has been prioritized, which more closely resembles that of couples who agree that the husband's career has been prioritized.

Table 12.3 Relationship between Couple-Level Career Priority Reports and Resolution of Opportunity Decisions among Those Who Faced a Career Opportunity[a]

	N	Wife's Resolution		
		Took It; Spouse Changed	Compromised/ Other	Turned It Down
All	157[b]	51 (32%)	18 (11%)	88 (56%)
Agree: his career prioritized	44	11 (25%)	4 (9%)	29 (66%)
Agree: neither/took turns	24	8 (33%)	2 (8%)	14 (58%)
Agree: her career prioritized	18	13 (72%)	1 (6%)	4 (22%)
Disagree: both say own	31	9 (29%)	7 (23%)	15 (48%)
Disagree: both say other's	40	10 (25%)	4 (10%)	26 (65%)

	N	Husband's Resolution		
		Took It; Spouse Changed	Compromised/ Other	Turned It Down
All	336[a]	159 (47%)	35 (10%)	142 (42%)
Agree: his career prioritized	153	95 (62%)	8 (5%)	50 (33%)
Agree: neither/took turns	39	9 (23%)	8 (21%)	22 (56%)
Agree: her career prioritized	16	3 (19%)	2 (13%)	11 (69%)
Disagree: both say own	72	37 (51%)	7 (10%)	28 (39%)
Disagree: both say other's	56	15 (27%)	- 10 (18%)	31 (55%)

[a]From *Cornell Couples and Careers Study*, 1998–99. N = 803.
[b]Four women and four men who reported career opportunities had missing values for career hierarchy rating and are not included here.

How were these opportunity decisions resolved? The results are shown in table 12.3. Wives are more likely to turn down opportunities than are husbands (56% versus 42%), whereas husbands are much more likely to take opportunities than are wives (47% versus 32%). A third group of respondents reports either taking opportunities but arranging it so that their spouses would not have to move or change jobs or compromising in some other way (11% women and 10% men).

If the proportion of opportunities turned down by both men and women seems surprisingly high, consider the types of decisions involved. Career moves that require the other spouse to move or change jobs are a particular (and presumably small) subset of advancement opportunities. Any career move that involves relocating entails practical and emotional costs that may outweigh the individual's own potential career gain, regardless of how it would affect his or her spouse. Considering the effects on the other spouse's career further complicates the equation in dual-earner couples, reducing the likelihood that the career move is taken.[36] As the two spouses' investments in their respective careers and returns on those investments become more similar, relocating for one spouse's career is less likely to garner a large enough gain to compensate for both moving costs and the other spouse's career losses.

Earlier we asked whether resolutions of opportunity decisions (in the subset of couples who reported career advancement opportunities) would corroborate spouses' reports of career priority in decision making. In general, they do (see table 12.3). Wives are most likely to report turning down opportunities when spouses agree that the husband's career has been prioritized (66%) and most likely to have taken advantage of opportunities when spouses agree that the wife's career has been prioritized (72%). Similarly, 62 percent of husbands in couples who agree that his career has been prioritized took advantage of their opportunity, whereas, in the small group who agree that the wife's career has been prioritized, 69 percent of husbands turned their opportunities down.

Looking at opportunity resolutions among couples with discrepant perceptions of career priority, we see that these proportions most closely resemble those of the couples who agree that neither spouse's career had greater priority or that they had taken turns. For either spouse, the perception that the husband's career has been prioritized (wives in the "both other" group and husbands in the "both own" group) has a stronger relationship to the individual's own opportunity resolution than the spouse's (different) perception. In these cases, resolutions most closely resemble those in couples who agree that the husband's career has been prioritized. Recall that among couples who disagree about career priority, the largest single group (of the three) in each category comprises one spouse saying that the husband's career had priority and the other saying that neither career had priority or they took turns (61% of those who disagree in the "both other" pattern and 51% of those in the "both own" group).

Predicting Career Priority

Up to this point, we have been looking at the extent to which reports of opportunity decisions corroborate spouses' reports of whose career has been prioritized in major decisions. Now we examine how factors of the couple's past—including the resolution of career opportunities faced by the wife or the husband—help to predict spouses' current perceptions of career priority. Do initial relative resources and gender-role attitudes affect the likelihood that couples will deviate from tradition and choose a strategy other than favoring the husband's career in major decisions?

We use categorical logistic regression[37] to assess predictors of obtaining each of the four less-common couple-level career priority categories—agreeing that neither career was given greater priority, agreeing that the wife's career has been prioritized, disagreeing in the "both own" pattern, and disagreeing in the "both other" pattern—compared to the omitted category—agreeing that the husband's career was given higher priority.[38] Regression results for the best-fit model are shown in table 12.4. Although measures of initial work-hour categories and spouses' relative initial work hours are significantly related to wives' individual

Table 12.4 Assessing Couple-Level Career Priority Ratings[a]

		Agree: "Neither Career Had Priority"			Agree: "Her Career Had Priority"			Disagree: "Both Own"			Disagree: "Both Other"		
		b	SE	OR[b]	b	SE	OR[b]	b	SE	OR[b]	b	SE	OR[b]
Intercept		3.0277**	0.5712	20.65	2.1062**	0.7365	8.22	1.0960*	0.4728	2.9922	2.2323**	0.4958	9.32
Differences at beginning of relationship													
His initial education higher	(a)	−0.6871**	0.2446	0.50	−1.0390***	0.3643	0.35	−0.5339**	0.1928	0.5863	−0.2459	0.1998	0.78
Her initial education higher	(a)	0.4782†	0.2642	1.61	0.9096***	0.3180	2.48	0.5450*	0.2188	1.7246	0.1637	0.2460	1.18
He is older by zero to 2 years	(b)	0.0549	0.1915	1.06	0.0175	0.2450	1.02	0.2602†	0.1554	1.2972	0.0223	0.1683	1.02
He is older by more than 2 years	(b)	−0.1053	0.1753	0.90	−0.6342**	0.2394	0.53	−0.4478**	0.1516	0.6390	−0.0733	0.1541	0.93
Current attitudes													
Her traditional attitudes		−0.8551**	0.1843	0.43	−0.9853**	0.2542	0.37	−0.4171**	0.1358	0.6590	−0.5535**	0.1473	0.57
His traditional attitudes		−0.8139**	0.1909	0.44	−0.5616*	0.2494	0.57	−0.1156	0.1494	0.8908	−0.5363**	0.1616	0.58
Resolution of past career decision													
She took opportunity	(c)	0.2086	0.4822	1.23	1.4764**	0.4990	4.38	0.1104	0.4153	1.1167	0.1199	0.4333	1.13
She compromised	(c)	0.2539	0.7419	1.29	0.2375	0.9355	1.27	0.8263	0.5223	2.2848	0.2734	0.6350	1.31
She turned down opportunity	(d)	−0.0695	0.3923	0.93	−0.9195†	0.5426	0.40	−0.4534	0.3335	0.6355	0.1784	0.3348	1.20
He took opportunity	(d)	−1.5407**	0.3299	0.21	−1.6401**	0.5214	0.19	−0.3580	0.2387	0.6991	−1.4401**	0.2893	0.24
He compromised	(d)	1.1984**	0.4287	3.31	0.8174	0.6668	2.26	0.1522	0.4776	1.1644	0.8329*	0.4089	2.30
He turned down opportunity	(d)	0.0919	0.2743	1.10	0.2317	0.3914	1.26	0.0307	0.2552	1.0312	0.2250	0.2444	1.25
−2LL (Intercept only)		2298.3											
−2LL (Full model, df = 662)		1862.3**											
Improvement (df = 48)		436.0**											
AIC (Intercept only)					2302.3								
AIC (Full model)					1966.3								
N					714								

[a] Categorical logistic regression. From *The Cornell Couples and Careers Study*, 1998–99.

See table 12.1 for illustration of "both own" (bottom triangle) and "both other" (top triangle) patterns of disagreement about career priority.

Reference groups for categorical independent variables: (a) same education category at beginning of relationship (less than bachelors; bachelors or masters; professional or doctorate); (b) wife older; (c/d) she/he reported no career opportunity. ** Indicates $p < 0.01$; * indicates $p < 0.05$; † indicates $p < 0.10$; b indicates unstandardized regression coefficient; SE indicates standard error.

[b] Odds ratios (OR) represent the difference compared to the reference group for the dependent variable: spouses agree husband's career was prioritized in major decisions.

reports of career priority as predicted (results available upon request), they do not improve the model fit for couple-level agreement of reports and are omitted. The predictors in the final model include the remaining indicators of spouses' initial relative resources (age difference and relative education at the beginning of the relationship) and current traditional gender-role attitudes (as proxies for longer-term patterns of same).[39] It could be argued that perceptions of career priority follow directly from the resolution of career prioritizing decisions for couples who faced such decisions. We include the resolution of career opportunities to assess whether other factors retain importance.[40]

We find, as expected, that an initial difference in education tends to lead to prioritizing the career of the more educated spouse. Compared to couples with equal education at the beginning of the relationship, those in which the husband had more education early on are more likely to agree that his career was priori-tized than to agree that the wife's career was prioritized or that neither career was prioritized, or to disagree in the "both own" pattern. Conversely, when the wife initially had more education, spouses are more likely to agree that her career was given priority. Neither the husband's age nor the wife's age alone influence assessments of career priority; rather, it is the difference in spouses' ages that matters. When husbands are more than two years older than their wives, couples are less likely to agree that the wife's career had priority or to disagree in the "both own" pattern than to agree that his career had higher priority.

We expected that husbands and wives with more traditional gender-role attitudes would be more likely to give priority to husbands' than to wives' careers, and we found this to be the case. Husbands' and wives' traditional gender-role attitudes are positively related to couple-level agreement that the husband's career had greater priority (the interaction between spouses' attitudes was not significant).

Compared to men and women who never faced a career opportunity that would have required their spouse to move or change jobs, we expected that those who took advantage of such an opportunity would be more likely to say that their own career had priority. Similarly, we expected that workers who turned down such an opportunity would be more likely to say that their spouse's career had prior-ity. This relationship, shown in table 12.3, does not disappear once other factors are considered. When wives took advantage of a career opportunity, spouses are more likely to agree that her career was prioritized. When husbands took advan-tage of a career opportunity, spouses are more likely to agree that the husband's career was given greater priority in decisions. When husbands compromise—neither turning down the opportunity nor taking it and requiring their wives to change jobs but instead finding some third option—spouses are also more likely agree that neither spouse's career had priority.

Because this sample is based on exempt employees of seven large organi-zations, it is prudent to ask whether the model being tested is influenced by organizational membership. Career hierarchy could be related to organizational membership in at least two ways. First, employees may face different demands in terms of remaining in one location or transferring to other locations, either due to the nature of the organization or to the occupations common to that organization. Second, "referent" spouses were selected based on their above-average occupational attainment (exempt or professional status), but their spouses are likely to have lower attainment levels more reflective of the population average.[41] In this sample, then, belonging to one of the participant organizations may be correlated with higher average attainment.

Here our dependent variable is a process that occurred over time—namely, whose career was given priority over the course of the couple's relationship. Conceptually, career hierarchy thus temporally precedes, and might predict, organizational membership in this sample.[42] We conducted supplemental analyses to test whether this is true in our sample. After accounting for differences in initial work experience and education, neither of the career hierarchy measures (reported career priority or the occurrence or outcome of career opportunity decisions) differentiate between membership in the seven organizations for men and women who are employed by one of them. However, as we expected, career hierarchy does distinguish respondents who are employed at any of these large organizations from those who are employed elsewhere.[43] Husbands and wives who report that their own career was given priority in decisions are more likely to be the only spouse employed at one of our seven organizations. Those who report that neither career had greater priority are more likely to be in couples in which both are working for one of these organizations (rather than only the husband or only the wife).

Summing Up

When faced with decisions about prioritizing spouses' career opportunities, contemporary couples more often choose the strategy of favoring the husband's career than of favoring the wife's career. However, we find a significant shift away from traditional patterns in this sample of middle-class, dual-earner workers in upstate New York. Yes, gender differences in career hierarchy are still present, but they are much less pronounced than the almost-universal prioritization of husbands' careers seen in past generations. In almost two-thirds of couples, one or both spouses report that in major decisions, their two careers have been prioritized equally or the wife's career has been prioritized. Still, twice as many men as women report facing a career opportunity that would have required their spouse to move or change jobs, and almost one-half of these men (compared to one-third of the women) took advantage of that opportunity.

Although perceptions of egalitarianism do not necessarily denote egalitarian behaviors, we find that career opportunity decisions generally corroborate self-reports of career priority. Wives who see their careers (or neither career) as having had greater priority are more likely to have faced career opportunity decisions and to have taken advantage of them. Similarly, husbands who say that decisions prioritized either their wives' careers or neither spouse's career are less likely to have taken opportunities that required their wives to move or change jobs.

Two of the relative resources that we expected to predict career priority are, in fact, important. Couples in which husbands are older or had more education than their wives at the beginning of their relationship are less likely to prioritize her career over his, whereas those in which she had more education early on are less likely to have prioritized his career. Also, as we expected, couples in which either spouse's gender-role attitudes are more traditional are apt to favor the husband's career. Combined with gender differences in facing career opportunities and taking advantage of them, this suggests that gender has a dramatic impact on career hierarchy above and beyond the pragmatic considerations associated with women's generally lower relative resources.

Concrete decisions about specific career opportunities influenced perceptions of career priority, but still made up only one part of the story. Compared to couples in which spouses have not faced major career opportunities, taking advantage of an opportunity predicts favoring an individual's own career for both husbands and wives (although recall that many more men than women fit this description). And when husbands compromised on a career opportunity, spouses are more likely to agree that they took turns prioritizing their careers than that they favored his career.

In conclusion, this study offers evidence of links between early differences in spouses' relative resources, decisions that favor one spouse's career, and spouses' overall perceptions of career priority. Certain gaps remain in our knowledge of the related processes, as is often the case early on. Still, we have a greater understanding of which contemporary dual-earner couples adopt the strategies of prioritizing the wife's career or giving both partners' careers equal priority and which couples retain the traditional strategy of favoring the husband's career. These insights should be useful in our continuing attempts to comprehend how husbands' and wives' career pathways enable and constrain one another over the life course.

PART THREE

COMMUNITY, ORGANIZATIONAL, AND POLICY CONTEXTS

13

Sunday Morning Rush Hour

Heather Hofmeister and Penny Edgell

The U.S. family has changed since the 1950s. The family's relationship to religious institutions has also changed. As wives and mothers have entered and remained in the workforce, especially during the active child-raising years, the relationships among religion, family, and work can no longer be taken for granted. Here we focus on dual-earner families' lifestyles (specifically combining work, family, and religion) in upstate New York. We ask whether socioeconomic factors such as status, income, and hours spent at work combine with lifestyle factors such as life stage, gender enactments, and gender attitudes to explain religious involvement. Do those who attend religious services have a more family-centered lifestyle in general than those who do not attend? If so, then religious institutions may encourage members to seek or even demand family-friendly workplace policies or otherwise foster among members the use of work-family strategies that help to buffer family life from greedy work institutions.

Work and Family Influences on Religious Involvement

Religious involvement is a very broad concept that encompasses layers of meaning and a broad set of behaviors from private devotions to the affirmation of a religious identity and organizational participation. Previous studies have viewed religious involvement, especially the choice to affirm a religious identity or the choice to attend a church or synagogue, as an individual choice. Such choices may be shaped by personal beliefs but also, in part, by time constraints on involvement due to long work hours. Social status also plays a role because religious involvement can be a way to signal establishment in a local community. Forms of religious involvement are also shaped by life stage, especially family formation, because religious institutions provide a context for socializing children through moral and ethical codes. Religious institutions also provide particular lifestyles and sets of cultural practices associated with gender ideology, social class, or ethnicity. Religious involvement can also signal a desire for traditionalism in family life.

We see religious involvement as a couple-level choice that is a kind of family strategy.[1] We ask, "How does religious involvement express and facilitate various work-family lifestyles?" In so doing, we shift the focus from predictors of individual's religious involvement to an analysis of the reciprocal causal nature of religious involvement, family formation, work constraints, and lifestyles rooted in gender ideology and social class. Following the lead of earlier studies,[2] we use church attendance as a general proxy for other forms of religious involvement; however, realizing that involvement is more complex, we also explore how church attendance is related to other forms of religious involvement.

Choice and Constraint: Time Scarcity

In explaining individual-level religious involvement, one focus has been the time constraints on involvement. Bradley Hertel notes that the rapid movement of women into the paid labor force in the 1970s instigated the workforce hypothesis, which says that increasing labor force participation leads to reduced religious participation.[3] The underlying reasons for this are sometimes left unspecified, although a simple economic analysis seems to underpin this work— time is a scarce resource, and spending more time on work leads to less discretionary time for voluntary activity such as church attendance. Dual-earner families with long work hours must necessarily have a time scarcity; thus families with two earners must reduce their church attendance.

Indeed, husbands and wives work more hours combined than they did in the 1970s.[4] Time invested in work reduces the availability of hours for other domains of life. The extent to which this extra work time comes out of time spent in religious involvement is not known. On the other hand, couples who work long hours also tend to have the most resources with which to buy services that may ameliorate the effects of the time squeeze.[5]

Although working long hours has become the norm in some occupations and professions, we know that some individuals make choices to scale back on work investment to spend more time with their families.[6] To some extent, the choice to be more involved in religious institutions may have more to do with a total lifestyle picture than with specific means-ends calculations or time available.[7]

Modernizing Tendencies of the Workplace

Other researchers assume that workforce participation exposes people to modernizing tendencies that erode commitment to traditional institutions.[8] Evelyn Lehrer's review of the literature on religion and female labor force participation points to Timothy Heaton and Marie Cornwall's work, which concludes that men's and women's employment patterns are the most similar by gender among those who do not participate in religion and the most different by gender for those in exclusivist Protestant groups. Ecumenical Protestants and Catholics are in the middle.[9] Lehrer's earlier work shows that religion is an important determinant of women's labor-force participation when children under age six are in the household, with evangelical and fundamentalist Protestant women least likely to be in the labor force.[10]

Context: Social Class

Work may have an entirely different relationship to religion, one that has nothing to do with time availability or the secularizing tendencies of the workplace. Religious involvement may still express social status and economic security, as found in early work on the subject.[11] The social class hypothesis says that higher occupational status leads to more religious participation and that those in the labor force, and especially those with higher status, ought to participate more in organized religion.[12] Hertel argues that the social class hypothesis is mostly about the experiences of men, taking for granted that men's social class determines their wives' social class.[13] But Wade Roof and William McKinney argue that social class is decreasing in significance for U.S. religious participation. Poll and General Social Survey (GSS) data show that nonaffiliation is no longer clearly associated with low levels of status and education.[14] Theodore Caplow and colleagues confirm this declining relevance of religion to social class, observing that in Middletown in the 1920s, religious involvement was largely a middle-class phenomenon, but by the 1970s it was much more evenly distributed among middle- and working-class people.[15] Well-off couples, on the one hand, are more likely to attend than the poor, in part because attendance has traditionally been part of a package of socially required norms and conventions for the middle class. On the other hand, the lifestyle of well-off couples is more secularized and less traditional—women who are in the labor force tend to be more egalitarian in their gender attitudes than women who are out of the labor force.[16]

Linked Lives: Marriage and Parenthood

As for the effects of marriage in general, not including employment effects, Hertel finds that involvement in organized religion is lowest for single men, higher for married men, higher yet (slightly) for single women, and highest for married women. Couples tend to be more involved in religious institutions than singles and to have stronger religious identities. Parenthood increases couples' involvement, especially when parenting multiple children.[17] For married men, participation is lowest for those without children and increases gradually with the arrival and aging of children. Married women join religious institutions when children are born but tend to become more active members when children reach school age.

The chance to spend time together as a family used to be part of the appeal of religious attendance, in addition to the socialization benefits provided by religious services to children. But families may place less priority on spending time together in these conventional ways. Other avenues for spending quality time with children, such as children's athletic events, may replace religious attendance, especially if they take place on Sunday morning. Either alternative could reduce the influence of children on their parents' religious participation compared to previous findings.[18]

Role Conflicts and Strains: Gender Ideology

Attendance may be less a function of an individual's structural location (being married, having children, and type of work) and more a function of an individual's attitudes about family roles and lifestyles.[19] These attitudes may moderate both religious participation and structural location, including employment and the choice to marry and/or have children. Lyn Gesch finds, using GSS data, that women with traditional attitudes are far more conventionally religious than women with egalitarian ideals. She shows that women with traditionalist ideals are less likely to be in the labor force, more likely to be in local conservative congregations, and tend to be older and less educated. Gesch suggests that these underlying differences in attitudes, not workforce participation per se, drive religious participation for boomer and postboomer women.[20]

Charles Hall takes a similar approach, using path analysis of data from questionnaires from over three hundred women readers of *Christianity Today*. Instead of viewing religious involvement as a dependent variable influenced by labor-force participation, he examines how religious beliefs (those held by individuals and those endorsed by a church) are directly related to women's labor-force participation. The strongest predictor of labor-force participation for women is their own idealized view of their preferred family and work roles. Egalitarian religious beliefs have a positive effect on workforce participation mediated through this idealized role preference. He also finds a negative direct effect between belonging to a more traditional church and labor-force participation.[21] Darren Sherkat shows the effects of fundamentalism (defined as the view that the Bible is the literal word of God) on women's choice of both long-term continuous housewifery and on leaving the workforce at least when children are young.[22]

Evidence of These Tensions

Hertel finds evidence in the GSS from 1972 to 1990 that the patterns of religious involvement for single women and older cohorts of men (pre–World War II births) consistently support the social class hypothesis—full-time employment is linked with religious involvement. This link is reversed for married women and men born since World War II, suggesting that the workforce hypothesis applies—those employed full-time are less involved in religion than those employed part-time. He finds one exception: for the subset of post–World War II cohort married men who work full-time, religiosity is increased by full-time employment.[23]

Hertel's work is important because he takes into account simultaneously the effects of employment and family formation on religious involvement in a way that is sensitive to the fact that religious involvement is largely a voluntary and expressive activity. Choosing religious involvement (or not choosing such involvement) can express agreement (or disagreement) with more traditional gender ideology, the social status that comes with full-time employment, and a more general maturity and social establishment or the rejection of religious identity as a status marker. Without measures of the meaning of religious involvement in men's and women's lives, Hertel's analysis nevertheless points to the importance of understanding the fit between religious involvement and multiple dimensions of an individual's life—gender and gender ideology, employment, and social status.[24]

We build on Hertel's analysis by incorporating the same focus on the fit between religious involvement and multiple life dimensions, but we extend it by seeing religious involvement among couples as a couple-level choice, shaped and constrained by couple-level dynamics.

Do Husbands and Wives Attend in Different Ways?

The literature reviewed thus far examines gender differences in attendance, but it does not consider the differences between members of the same couple. Are wives who attend a lot married to husbands who are attending with them? That is, do spouses attend at the same rate, or does one attend more than the other? What influences couples' likelihood of attending together? And how does couple-level attendance correlate with the factors discussed, particularly gender ideology, family formation, social class, and time constraints on involvement? Is religious involvement something that is still largely in the woman's sphere of social life?[25] Based on the gender differences in attendance patterns in samples of married people who are not married to one another, it seems likely that husbands' attendence is based on one set of factors, whereas wives' attendence is based on another set of factors. No research has examined couples' attendence together based on responses from both partners.

How Does Religious Involvement Serve as a Mechanism for Generating Family Social Capital?

An individual's community involvement, including religious involvement, is an important source of the network ties that give access to social capital. In the best review of the social capital literature, Alejandro Portes draws on Pierre Bourdieu to argue that social capital can be decomposed into two elements: social relationships, which allow people to claim access to their associates' resources, and the amount and quality of the resources themselves.[26] Couples who do not attend local congregations may be reducing their access to one set of local networks that confer social capital.

Declines in religious participation come with an additional cost. Religious institutions are important for making sense of life transitions. Births, marriages, illness, and death are inevitable aspects of life. These themes of life and loss are organized, explained, and given a medium for personal emotional expression and public acknowledgement through formal religious institutions. When families do not link themselves with a religious home, they lose this forum for processing some of life's most profound and difficult questions and challenges.

Religious Involvement: *The Cornell Couples and Careers Study*

In previous work we investigate the relationship between the amount of time a person spends at work and the amount of time spent in community involvement.[27] With a randomly sampled population of one thousand upstate New York adults (one-half of them in dual-earner couples), we found that, contrary to popular rhetoric and intuitive assumption, busy dual-earner couples were not unlike breadwinner-homemaker couples in their levels of community involvement. Instead, families' community involvement is related to their social class standing and life stage.

Although linked, religious involvement is different from other types of community involvement in a number of ways, which is why we choose to analyze them separately. Religious involvement tends to be associated with personal expression. As such, religious participation may not be as influenced by social class and life stage as are other kinds of community involvement. Dual-earner families may think of religious involvement as one more time demand that is less and less relevant in light of all the competing conflicts of modern life. Alternatively, religion may be an important grounding mechanism in family life, a priority that is maintained even when time and energy are scarce.

To investigate these questions about the links among work, family, and religion in dual-earner couples, we use a module of questions specifically on religious and community involvement, asked of a random one-third of the couples in *The Cornell Couples and Careers Study*. We test predictors of couples' religious attendance using measures shown to be relevant for individuals' attendance. We then predict couples' attendance using nominal logistic regression.

What We Mean by Religious Attendance

We asked the standard seven-response-item GSS attendance question with a transition, "Next, we'd like to ask a few questions about your community. How often do you attend religious services?" Responses were never, hardly ever except for holidays, less than once a month, about once a month, two to three times a month, once a week, and more than once a week. Our two-level attendance variable identifies those attending never or hardly ever (nonattenders) and those attending less than once a month or more (attenders). This binary measure alleviates concerns that many survey respondents overreport weekly service attendance.[28] We create a four-category couple attendance variable: whether both attend more than just holidays, called dual-attenders (50.9%); whether the husband attends and wife does not (6.9%); whether the wife attends and husband does not (13.8%); and whether neither attends (28.4%).

Church attendance, although not a perfect proxy for all forms of religious involvement, is highly correlated with the salience of religion, traditional views of religious authority, religious homogeneity, and a strong identification with a particular religious group.[29] Church attendance, then, is a good, but not perfect, indicator of other forms of religious involvement. In our sample, whether couples share the same faith[30] predicts couples' attendance pattern; an average of 70 percent of couples in which spouses share the same faith both attend church compared with only 18 percent of couples in which spouses have different religious identities and none of the couples in which both spouses are not religious. Unlike

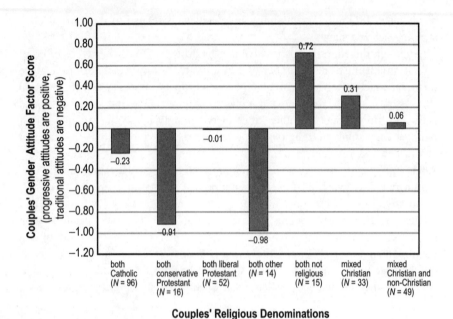

Figure 13.1 Couple-level gender factor by couples' religious similarity. *The Cornell Couples and Careers Study*, 1998–99. Subset $N = 272$. $p < .001$.

religious salience and religious identity, church attendance is an activity that requires an investment of time; it is therefore a good measure to use to examine the effect of time spent at work on religious involvement.

Couples' religious identity is also related to other aspects of religious and family life. Examine the differences in gender attitudes according to couples' faith shown in figure 13.1. Conservative Protestants and Catholics are more traditional than the average for the sample; couples who are not religious or who have mixed-faith marriages are more progressive in their gender attitudes.

When we say both spouses attend church, they may or may not be attending together. Although the majority of couples in which both attend do attend together (82% of wives and 86% of husbands in "both attend" couples admit to attending with their spouses),[31] others do not—both may attend, but they visit different congregations. In addition, sometimes spouses have different perspectives of whether they attend together. In some cases, one spouse attends frequently and the other may join him or her much less often. The one who attends less often is correct in saying "I attend with my spouse," whereas the more frequent attender is equally correct in saying "I attend alone." We do not mean to imply that couples are in the pew together when we say they both attend, although that is often the case.

Social Class and Religious Attendance

Independent variables used to predict couples' religious attendance include predictors from the social class hypothesis, the workforce hypothesis, and the lifestyle hypothesis. (See list at the end of this chapter.)

Social class is not a strong predictor of couples' religious attendance in this middle-class sample. We find slight differences by wives' income—wives earning less money are more likely to attend, whether or not their husbands attend. Similarly, wives who earn a lower proportion of the household income are more likely to attend, especially with their husbands. For example, wives earn 44 percent of the household income in couples who do not attend, but only one-third of the household income in families in which both partners attend ($p < .001$). Husbands' income and the total household income do not help to predict attendance.

Husbands' job prestige, on the other hand, may help predict couples' attendance (although wives' prestige is not significant). Husbands with the lowest job prestige are concentrated in couples in which neither spouse attends ($p < .10$). Whether one or both spouses have college degrees or are managers, does not aid in predicting attendance patterns in bivariate analyses.

Time in the Workplace and Religious Attendance

Husbands' work hours and commuting time, alone, do not predict attendance patterns, but wives' do. Wives who work fewer hours a week and commute shorter distances tend to be in couples in which both spouses attend, whereas wives who work longer hours tend to be nonattenders or to attend alone. Wives who work farther from home may have lives more separate from their husbands' in other ways; in this case, they more often attend alone.

Further, wives who work more than forty-five hours a week and are married to husbands who work less than forty-five hours a week are more likely to attend alone than other wives (22.5% of wives who attend alone fit this work-hour pattern, compared with 14% of wives who are in couples in which neither attends and 8.6% of wives in couples in which both attend). Couples with traditional work patterns (i.e., he works longer hours than she does) are more likely to attend together. When members of couples both work the same number of hours, especially long hours, they are less likely to attend services and these husbands are also likely to attend alone.

Work-hour patterns, then, do help predict attendance patterns ($p < .01$), but not according to a simple time-scarcity model.[32] The relationship of work hours to attendance has more to do with what those work hours represent, either more egalitarian earnings structures in the family or a separation of spouses' activities.

In some couples both members have college degrees or more, in other couples only one member has a college degree, and in still others neither has a college degree. These patterns of education are not statistically significant for attendance patterns when considered in isolation, but education does predict attendance patterns when considered in the context of other elements of couples' lives.

Indicators of a Family-Centered Lifestyle

Lifestyle factors have especially strong predictive power for couples' joint attendance patterns, with the presence of children or the age of the youngest child in the home an important predictor. More than one-half of couples without children at home do not attend, but the percentage of nonattenders drops to only 22 percent for those couples with preschoolers and to 20 percent for those with grade-school-age children. Families with children of any age are more likely to have both parents attend, followed by mothers attending alone. Parents of elementary-school-age children are the most likely to both attend ($p < .001$).

Gender attitudes are another indicator of a family-centered lifestyle. Among couples with traditional gender attitudes, husbands tend to attend alone or both attend. The women and men with the most progressive gender attitudes are in couples in which wives attend alone[33] (see figure 13.2).

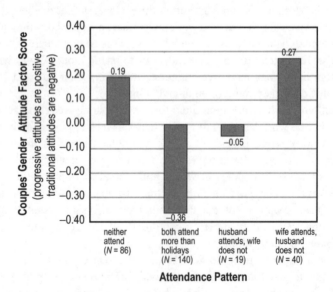

Figure 13.2 Couple-level gender attitude factor score by attendance pattern. *The Cornell Couples and Careers Study*, 1998–99. $N = 287$. $p < .001$.

Other measures of family-centered or traditionally oriented lifestyles do not predict attendance; whether the spouses both agree that the husbands' career takes priority or whether they agree that the wife takes care of child-related emergencies during the workday are both unrelated to church attendance.

Predicting Couples' Attendance

Nominal logistic regression predicts the likelihood of couples being in one attendance category over another, considering couples' social class, workforce status, and family-centeredness. Our nominal logistic regression uses 273 couples in the survey who were included in the religious involvement module and answered all the questions in full. We test the following variables for their predictive power for couples' attendance patterns: husbands' job prestige, wives' salary, wives' work hours, whether both have a college degree, couples' gender ideology, whether the household has a child age twelve or younger, whether the spouses identify with different faiths, and whether the wife is a conservative Protestant (see Table 13.1).

Couples Who Both Attend

Whether the members of the couple have different faiths is the primary predictor of attending alone versus both spouses attending. Interfaith couples are twenty-one times more likely to have only one spouse attend than they are to both attend. One striking result is that the presence of children does not affect the likelihood of spouses attending together versus one parent going alone, controlling for other aspects of family and work life.

Four lifestyle elements—college degrees, traditional gender attitudes, children, and the same faith—are the strongest predictors of whether both spouses attend religious services or neither attends. Couples who both have college degrees are twice as likely to both attend, and those who have children under twelve are almost three times more likely to both attend compared with couples in which neither attends (see table 13.1).

Couples with egalitarian gender attitudes are 78 percent more likely to not attend than to both attend. Those in interfaith marriages are nineteen times more likely to not attend than to both attend.

We see these results as indicators of different family lifestyles, with attenders being more family-centered and more traditional—with children, a shared faith, and traditional gender attitudes. Education as a predictor of attendance suggests that church attendance and education have a cohesive fit as part of a socially

Table 13.1 Nominal Logistic Regression of Couple Attendance Patterns[a]

	One Spouse Attending vs. Both Attending (N = 56/135)			Neither Spouse Attending vs. Both Attending (N = 82/135)			One Spouse Attending vs. Neither Spouse Attending (N = 56/82)		
	Coef	StDev	Odds Ratio	Coef	StDev	Odds Ratio	Coef	StDev	Odds Ratio
Constant	-0.83	1.32		-0.05	1.20		-0.79	1.22	
Husband's prestige score	-0.01	0.02	0.99	-0.02	0.02	0.98	0.01	0.02	1.01
Wife's salary	0.00	0.00	1.00	0.00	0.00	1.00	0.00	0.00	1.00
Wife's work hours	0.00	0.02	1.00	0.02	0.01	1.02	-0.02	0.02	0.98
Both have college degrees	-0.47	0.42	0.62	-0.90*	0.39	0.41	0.43	0.40	1.53
Couple's gender attitude	0.51	0.22	1.66	0.57***	0.20	1.78	-0.07	0.22	0.94
Child under 12 at home	-0.23	0.39	0.79	-1.03**	0.37	0.36	0.80*	0.38	2.23
Interfaith marriage	3.08***	0.46	21.77	2.96***	0.44	19.26	0.12	0.38	1.13
Wife is conservative Protestant	-0.26	0.60	0.77	-0.98	0.62	0.38	0.72	0.61	2.06

[a]Subset N = 273. *indicates p < 0.05; **indicates p < 0.01; ***indicates p < 0.001. Coef, coefficient; StDev, standard deviation. From *Cornell Couples and Careers Study*, 1998–99.

established way of life; it also suggests that community institutions such as churches more easily facilitate a more educated, professional or managerial lifestyle.

Couples in Which One Spouse Attends Alone

Recall that being in an interfaith marriage is the primary difference between couples in which only one member attends and both attend.[34] The presence of elementary-school-age children predicts whether one spouse attends alone compared to couples in which neither attends. Couples with a child under age twelve are more than twice as likely to have one spouse attending than to not attend at all. The presence of children under twelve is the primary predictor of wives attending alone, whereas husbands are more likely to attend alone than not to attend at all when they and their wives have college degrees.

Those Who Do Not Attend

We asked all our nonattenders (110 wives and 129 husbands) five possible reasons why they do not attend more often (they could agree with as many as they wanted). One-quarter (25%) of wives and 16 percent of husbands who do not attend agreed that services interfered with time spent with family. And one-quarter (25%) of wives, but only 14 percent of husbands, agreed that they were too tired on the weekends. Only approximately 8 percent of wives and husbands agreed that services interfered with their work schedule. A large percentage of wives (44%) agreed that their husbands' lack of enthusiasm for attending was a reason they did not attend more often, but only 15 percent of husbands said the same of their wives. Few wives (8%) agreed that they did not attend more because their area congregations were unwelcoming, but a few more husbands (14%) agreed.

One-quarter of wives agreed that they were either too tired on the weekends or that services interfered with time spent with their families (some selected both), which suggests that time availability is a factor in church attendance for some. But by far most wives did not attend because of their husbands' lack of enthusiasm, which suggests that family lifestyles and attitudes play a stronger role in nonattendance than time availability.

Summing Up

We ask whether social class, work-related issues, or family-related issues are the strongest predictors of religious attendance for middle-class dual-earner couples. We find that spouses who both attend regularly tend to have traditional gender attitudes, elementary-school-age children, college degrees, and the same faith, all of which are family attributes. Individual job prestige, salary, and work hours do not play a strong role in predicting couples' attendance when we consider the context of family circumstances and attitudes.

Spouses are more likely to attend alone when they have a child at home under age twelve. This finding is particularly true for women, who traditionally have been responsible for moral instruction in the home. Husbands with more education (in couples in which both have college degrees) attend alone rather than not attending at all, perhaps signifying that church attendance is part of a package of social establishment for these husbands, whether or not their families join them.

Nonattenders are more likely to be childless; having a child under twelve at home means one or both spouses are likely to attend. Nonattenders' egalitarian gender attitudes also set them apart. In general, the choice not to attend church may reflect a less traditional lifestyle on a number of dimensions.

Families make time for the things they value.[35] Couples who choose to attend together may already be more traditional in their gender attitudes and family lifestyle, or the process of attending may influence their lifestyle choices so that they become more traditional or more family-oriented.

Is it the secularization of attitudes and not increased time spent at work that leads to lower religious participation? Secularization and time spent at work are linked to the same set of phenomena: to succeed at work may require secularized attitudes and time commitment. We certainly find little evidence that work hours impede religious attendance; rather, work hours reflect a lifestyle that prioritizes paid labor over family formation. Then again, these data are focused on couples at one point in time, and we may be seeing a life stage phenomenon that these data cannot address. Often couples cycle in and out of religious participation over their life course, depending on their own spiritual needs, the needs of their children, and their social standing. We only know about their religious attendance at this one point in time, when their attendance may reflect where they are in life (especially their children's lives) rather than their own deeply held values and priorities about faith and family.

It seems clear that local congregations provide an environment that supports family-centered lifestyles. Some congregations provide day care; activities focused around children; parenting support; and counseling in personal, family, and work-family matters. Through their activities and discourse, they also discourage the careerism and materialism that hinder family and community life.[36] Religious leaders can offer particularly authoritative and often effective moral critiques of social and political issues because congregants legitimate their leaders as moral authorities.[37] The mobilization of clergy in favor of family-friendly workplace policies might provide not only the encouragement some need to take advantage of such policies, but might also help to create a broader public base of support for reforms that make work institutions more adaptive to the needs of families.

Too often, religious involvement is examined as an isolated choice made by individuals, with only a few indications of social context. But involvement is a social activity fostered by social connections, among the most important of which are family ties. The current trend in family research toward treating couples and families as a distinct level of analysis can shed new light on religious-involvement dynamics by emphasizing the joint nature of decisions to allocate time but also to express a religious identity for the whole family.

Description of variables used

Income: Household income is the sum of both individual incomes. The ratio of wives' income to the total household income is the wives' income divided by the sum of both spouses' incomes.

Education: The measure of the education level of the couple indicates whether both have a college degree or more, neither have a college degree, or only one has a college degree or more.

Job prestige: Prestige scores, calculated from the two-digit census occupational code list, measure the relative prestige of husbands' careers versus their wives' careers through a ratio variable.

Professional status of couples: Couples are identified by whether both members are professionals or managers, one of them is a professional or manager and the other is not, or neither holds a professional or managerial job.

Work-hour patterns: The couple-level measure of work hours is calculated on a weekly basis in five categories.[38] These categories indicate whether one member of a couple works fewer than thirty-nine hours and the other works forty-five hours or fewer, both work 39–45 hours, the wife works more than the husband does (she is working more than forty-five hours while he is working forty-five or fewer), the husband works more than the wife does (he works more than forty-five hours and she works forty-five or fewer), or both work more than forty-five hours a week.

Life stage/children: Life stage indicates the set of responsibilities for dependents and spouses that often coincide with, but can also transcend, cohort differences. The life stages used in this chapter are based on the age of the youngest child in the home, specifically whether there is a child at home under age twelve.

Gender attitudes: Gender attitudes are beliefs about what had been traditionally gender-appropriate behaviors of men and women in relation to one another and of women in relation to their children. Typically, traditional gender attitudes are beliefs that men should have precedence in leadership and job decisions and that women's first priorities should be as mothers. In this study, gender attitudes are operationalized using a scale of four questions on which people ranked their agreement. We created a factor scale of the four gender-attitude questions. Factor scales are superior to simple summed scales if we suspect the questions are not equally direct measures of the underlying phenomenon under study or if data are skewed; gender-attitude questions are just such a case. Using factor analysis, factors result that are normalized at zero with a standard deviation of 1 for each factor, that is, the measure that takes into account the relative value of each individual question in contributing to the conceptual picture formed by the questions taken together. Wives' and husbands' gender attitudes were created first for each spouse using his or her own responses to the four items. Then all responses from both spouses, a total of eight responses, formed a couple-level gender ideology measure. This couple-level measure yielded three principle components, two of which are described in this chapter. The first factor measures the progressive or traditional gender attitudes of the couple, with positive measures indicating more progressive attitudes and negative measures indicating more traditional attitudes than the sample mean of zero. The second factor reflects the divergence within the couple. Zero indicates absolute agreement between spouses on the eight measures. Positive scores indicate that husbands are more progressive than their wives, and negative scores indicate that wives are more progressive than their husbands.

Housework division: We measure time spent on housework on workdays for each spouse, and each spouses' degree of satisfaction with the contribution of the other. For couple-level measures of the division of household labor, we create a ratio of the wives' minutes on chores to the total number of minutes spent on chores of both spouses (wives' minutes divided by the sum of wives and husbands' minutes). We also create a variable of couple-level satisfaction with the time each spends. The indicators are whether both want less or the same amount of time from their spouses; husbands want their wives to spend more time, but wives want less or the same from husbands; wives want more time from husbands, but husbands are satisfied; and both want more time from the other spent on chores and responsibilities. Who takes time off work for children's needs is likely to be an indicator of family lifestyle. Parents only were asked whether the respondent or the partner is more likely to respond to needs of children during the workday or whether it depends. Couples did not always agree on who was most likely to respond; a couple-level variable indicates whether both said the wife responds, both said the husband responds, both said it depends, or they gave different answers. Couples in which both agree that the wife takes time off are considered more traditionally oriented in their lifestyle. Couples were also asked whether they favored the husbands' career, the wife's career, or neither's career in past decisions. Couples who agreed that the husbands' career was favored in household decision making are following a more traditional model of career priority.

14

The New Technology Climate

Noelle Chesley, Phyllis Moen, and Richard P. Shore

Innovations in information technology (IT) are reconfiguring physical space and time. This ability to connect in new ways suggests that boundaries between work and family may be more permeable than they used to be. In this chapter we investigate the ways information and communication technology (especially computers and cellular phones/pagers) are reshaping the work-family interface. Does this technology constitute a set of new tools that can help workers better coordinate and manage their work and personal lives? Are patterns of IT use similar or different for men and women in two-earner couples overall or at different life stages? Is IT use part of a process of shifting or weakening of the boundaries between work and home, and, if so, are these changing boundaries good or bad for families?

There is little doubt that computers, email, the Internet, cellular phones and pagers, fax machines, electronic calendars, and similar devices are becoming firmly entrenched in daily life. Just fifteen years ago, approximately 8 percent of households had a computer; by 2000, more than one-half of American households did.[1] Internet access at home has also increased rapidly with just over 40 percent of households having access in 2000 (up from 18 percent in 1997).[2] In addition, cell phone subscriptions skyrocketed in the 1990s. In 1990, just over 5 million people were subscribers to a cellular phone service; by 1999 that figure had risen to 86 million.[3]

Scholars are beginning to recognize the potential import of IT for the work-family interface. David Watt and James White call for research investigating the role that computer use might play in changing family life. They ask whether there are such things as "computer widows/widowers" or "computer orphans" and whether computers are part of family adaptive strategies used to manage complex lifestyles.[4] Susan Lewis and Cary Cooper suggest that advances in IT and communication technology may be blurring the boundaries between paid work and home life.[5]

Although a growing body of research examines IT use in the workplace, few studies assess its impact in the home.[6] Furthermore, although scholars speculate about the ways in which IT may be influencing the quality of both work and family life, empirical studies are scarce. According to the National Science Foundation "[r]esearch on the actual impacts of IT on home, family, and individual household members is *extremely limited in scale and scope*."[7]

In this chapter, we draw on qualitative and quantitative data collected from dual-earner couples in *The Cornell Couples and Careers Study* to examine IT use, as well as its implications. We focus both on who uses these technologies and whether such use is helping to resolve conflicts between their work and family careers. IT use, in this study, refers to the use of a computer at home for work, email at home or work, the Internet, cellular phones and pagers, and home fax machines. In our survey we asked both members of couples whether they used each of these devices to manage their work and home responsibilities on a regular basis. These technologies allow workers to do their jobs while at home (or anywhere) or to maintain contact with family members while at work, suggesting that the traditional demarcation between the two activities may be less relevant for families using the tools of the Information Age.[8]

Technology and the Work/Family Interface

The rise of telework or telecommuting, made possible by the proliferation of IT and communication technologies, represents a direct and growing influence on the work-family interface. Although estimates vary, the consensus is that approximately 10 percent of the workforce teleworked in 2000, and most experts believe such work arrangements are bound to continue to increase in the future.[9] A report by the U.S. Department of Labor suggests that telework arrangements "particularly benefit workers facing childcare or eldercare responsibilities," although they also open up the possibility of worker exploitation if employers require homework that exceeds normal working hours.[10] Studies that assess the influence of telework programs on work outcomes such as absenteeism and productivity suggest that an individual's doing some or all of his or her work remotely is negatively linked to absenteeism and can result in greater productivity.[11]

Research assessing the influence of teleworking on home life is more limited. Early studies suggest that teleworkers without primary-care responsibilities experience improved family relations and high levels of family-related life satisfaction. Yet such positive connections may be more difficult to establish for workers with caregiving responsibilities.[12]

Ellen Galinsky and Stacy Kim compare parents who said they "usually worked at home or usually worked at home and another location" to parents who reported "usually working at a location other than the home." The researchers also compare the reports of children whose parent or parents do some work at home to children of parents whose work takes place outside of the home. They find that the effects of working at home on family and work outcomes are mixed. Both groups of parents were equally likely to report that they found it difficult to manage work and family life, and teleworking mothers were more likely than nonteleworking mothers to say that their job interfered with their ability to be a good parent. In addition, children whose fathers work from home were more likely to say that their father had difficulty "focusing" on them and was "not in a good mood when they were together" than the children of nonteleworking fathers.[13] Although the ability to do at least some work from home may make it easier to meet the refrigerator repairperson, such work arrangements may also make it more difficult to leave work behind.[14]

Investigating Family Strategies within a Life Course Framework

A life-course theoretical framework seeks to connect changes in individual lives with ongoing changes in society.[15] Life-course models point to the adaptive strategies of individuals and families in the face of shifting opportunities and constraints associated with social, cultural, or technological dislocations.[16] We view IT use as a form of strategic action, with families actively modifying their behavior through the use of these new tools to react to changing circumstances.[17] The use of IT and communication technologies may well be an adaptive strategy, allowing workers to better coordinate and manage the time demands of their individual work and family lives.

Spillover theory is a useful framework for elaborating the processes that may underlie the influence of IT use on the work-family interface. In broad terms, this theory suggests that moods and behavior can transfer directly from one setting to another.[18] Scholars usually distinguish between direct and indirect spillover effects. The direct effects of spillover occur when specific conditions in one setting directly affect another. For example, an employee may be required to stay late at work to meet a last-minute deadline, and, as a consequence, be unable to pick up a child from the day-care center at the expected time. In this case, a direct spillover effect is observed because the late pickup from day care is a direct consequence of the last-minute work deadline. Indirect effects occur when conditions in one setting produce psychological consequences that influence how individuals feel or behave in another setting. Thus, a great day at work might influence individuals' feelings or interactions with a spouse or child once they are home, or an argument in the morning can affect interactions with colleagues throughout the workday. As these examples illustrate, spillover effects may be positive or negative and do not necessarily flow in one direction (see Roehling, Moen, and Batt, chap. 7 in this volume).

IT use can make individuals more accessible. Parents can use cell phones to reach older children in school, perhaps facilitating communication and coordination among family members. The use of pagers, home computers, fax machines, and email can enable certain kinds of paid work to be accomplished outside the office. The opportunities for better integrating employment and personal responsibilities through IT use are there, but concerns about use and work-life boundaries exist. When portable technologies are used to facilitate work, is overwork a problem?[19] As people use email and cellular phones to communicate, do they see one another less?

Barry Wellman describes research evidence concerning the Internet's influence on community life. He notes that findings about the Internet's effect on community have been mixed, although most studies seem to find that the Internet enhances rather than detracts from community.[20] Norman Nie describes contradictory findings from research on Internet use and sociability; he reports that some studies demonstrate that Internet users are more social than nonusers, whereas others indicate that Internet use, particularly heavy use, is associated with fewer social interactions.[21] However, the only truly longitudinal study of Internet use (conducted by Robert Kraut and colleagues) has shown that some new users become more depressed, alienated, and isolated during the first six months of Internet use (although a follow-up study found that these negative consequences of use dissipated over time).[22] Research that examines how IT use influences a number of dimensions of life quality for individuals and families is required if we want to know when such use is an effective way to manage the work-life interface.

Asking and Answering Questions about Technology Use

In this chapter, we outline three broad questions concerning the influence of IT use on the work-family interface. First, we focus on the distribution of IT and communication technology use among dual-earner couples. Based on the characteristics of computer and Internet use for individuals in the United States we anticipate that:

- IT use will differ by gender, age, education, and income level, with those who are male, younger, and more affluent and educated showing higher levels of use.
- Patterns of IT use will differ across couples, with couples at different life stages exhibiting different patterns of use.

Next, we examine whether IT use is associated with a blurring of boundaries between work and home. Because IT appears to facilitate connectedness between home and work, we theorize that greater use will result in weakening boundaries between work and home activities through a spillover process. Common assumptions are that IT use facilitates the performance of work at home or attention to family tasks in the workplace. A number of studies, however, indicate that employment often has more of a negative impact on family life than family life has on work life. And, as reported in Roehling, Maen, and Batt (chap. 7 in this volume), positive spillover from home to work is often greater than positive spillover from work to home. We expect, then, that IT use will be related to both negative spillover from work to home and positive spillover from home to work. These spillover experiences may, in turn, affect psychological well-being, depending on the relative mix of negative or positive spillover effects. Gender may also be an important consideration given that women traditionally bear the brunt of domestic responsibilities, and, in our sample of dual-earner couples, are also involved in paid work. We expect that:

- Greater IT use will be associated with negative work-to-family spillover for both women and men.
- Greater IT use will be associated with positive family-to-work spillover for both women and men but with negative family-to-work spillover for women only.

Finally, we examine the connection between IT use and psychological well-being to offer suggestive evidence of whether IT use enhances the life quality of dual-earner couples. Given prior evidence showing that early Internet adopters may be more susceptible to loneliness and depression,[23] we hypothesize that:

- IT use will be associated with lower levels of psychological well-being, net of other factors.

Technology Use and Dual-Earner Couples

The Cornell Couples and Careers Study provides a unique opportunity to examine the relationship between technology use, spillover, and psychological well-being. We know of no other existing data set that contains measures of so broad a range of information about communication technologies as well as measures of spillover, work and family characteristics, psychological outcomes, and other relevant attitudinal variables. Placing all these elements within a family context (through information about the spouses and the life stage of each couple) is an additional strength if we are to better understand the implications of technology use for life quality. (See app. for descriptions of measures and the sample.)

We asked a subset of respondents who participated in in-depth interviews or focus groups whether any technologies help them better manage their home and work responsibilities and, if so, which ones. Similarly, we asked which technologies are not helpful. We draw on this qualitative information to help gain insight into couples' IT use as an adaptive strategy.

Technology Use as an Adaptive Strategy

Respondents in the in-depth interviews and focus groups spoke very specifically about the types of technologies they use and why, thus indicating active and conscious decisions about their use. Most cited concrete circumstances that prompted them to use particular technologies to resolve problems or to improve existing family or work conditions. For example, a manager at Vantech, who is also a mother of two and whose husband spends the workweek in another city, explained:

> My husband also has an 800 number pager, so when he's in [city name], I can leave the usual "call this number back," but I can also leave a text message with that 800 number service, so he doesn't always call me back, but I can be sure to [remind him to] call your father today because it's his birthday. Just little things like that, I know he's only a phone call away, and mentally if you think of it that way, that's just like thinking that he's here in [city name], I know that I can always get in touch with him. . . .

This example illustrates a situation in which IT facilitates the management of the work-family interface; other respondents describe decisions and actions aimed at limiting the influence of IT in their lives. A forty-something employee of a health-care organization and mother of two teenage girls declared, ". . . my vacation time, for instance, is my vacation time. So I've been known to—and don't tell anybody this—you know, purposefully not have the answering machine on if I'm not around, or something. The only [time] somebody's going to get me is if they catch me, and I'm right there. . . ."

The point of these two examples is not to speculate about whether IT is a positive or negative force in peoples' lives but, rather, to illustrate the concrete ways members of dual-earner couples describe their IT use. Our interviewees emphasized the importance of information and communication technologies in their lives. Respondents typically reported using information technology to bridge geographic distances, to catch up on work while at home, or to gather information more easily and efficiently. They focused their discussions on cellular phones, pagers, computers, and the Internet as helpful in managing work and family needs. "I can work at home. I mean, typically, I don't work a lot of overtime here, because I really don't want to, but I will go home after my kids go to bed, like 8 o'clock, work a couple of hours at night. I do that a lot. But I can do it because I have a computer there and a lot of my job I do right on the computer, so . . ." (senior analyst employed part-time at Upstate U and mother of two young children). Or ". . . we get on the Internet, and we look around, and, as a matter of fact, it even helps us with shopping, whatever . . ." (forty-eight-year-old male supervisor who works at Utilco with one child). Or "I think some of this stuff is very important. Because without the technology of being able to bring my PC home with me in a shoulder bag, I wouldn't be able to squeeze in those extra few minutes that I need to wrap up projects. Without being able to have a cordless phone, it would be real difficult to be able to watch and play with my daughter and talk at the same time . . ." (twenty-something marketing manager who works for a small high-tech company[24] and is the mother of two children).

How individuals come to use specific technologies is another important theme emerging from the interviews and focus groups. Sometimes employers require employees to use a particular device (computer, cellular phone, pager, etc.) both inside and outside of the office. In this case, the people we talked with were typically wary of the role of technology in their lives and were much more likely to focus on its negative aspects. "They've [the employer] given us a cell phone, and that's exactly what it's for, I mean, to do my job. If you are on the road to go to your appointment, I mean, you have to call and make appointments or check your voicemail, or do whatever—and long-term is they do want us to have a laptop . . . not yet, thank God, but it's supposedly coming" (account manager employed in a health-care organization and mother of two children). Or "I remember when cell phones first came out, my [business] partner said 'you know, should we get car phones?' and I said 'I think I'm working hard enough, already. When I'm driving from one client to another, I need to think about what's happening. I don't need this car phone.' He said 'yeah, you're right. We should just get them for the staff'" (private-sector businessman turned college instructor, now working at Upstate U, father of five adult children).

These quotations illustrate the flavor of many responses, highlighting issues about relative control and power over time and availability. At the same time that families use technology strategies to better meet their work and family responsibilities, employers use these same tools to manage or restructure work. As the quotations suggest, the goals of workers and employers regarding technological strategies may not only be quite different, they may even be in conflict.

Who Uses IT to Manage Work and Family Life?

We expected to find, and did find, that men, younger respondents, and the more highly educated and affluent are more apt to use each technology strategy (see table 14.1). Descriptive statistics show that more men regularly use each of the technologies we asked about than do women, with the exception of cell phones and pagers to communicate with family members; about the same proportion of men and women use cell phones and pagers to stay in touch with family members (see figure 14.1).

With the exception of email, those ages 55–64 are less apt to use most of the technologies than are younger respondents.[25] There are also differences by family life stage. Fewer respondents with children of various ages use email; parents are more likely to use a cell phone or pager and less likely to use email for family communication. This pattern is consistent with our in-depth interviews, in which a number of childless respondents mentioned that although they did not use a cellular phone now, they probably would use one if they had kids. Finally, husbands and wives under forty without children use the Internet regularly much more than their counterparts in other life stages.

In general, more highly educated people regularly use IT for managing work and family life.[26] However, this pattern is not evident for cell phone/pager use. Men with some college or a bachelor's degree use these tools more (either for work or family reasons) than men with graduate-level education. Fifty-two percent of husbands with some college and 47 percent of husbands with a bachelor's degree use a cellular phone or pager for work compared to only 34 percent of men with graduate education. However, the differences are not as large for men who use cellular phones or pagers for family reasons. Here, approximately 54 percent of men with some college or a college degree use these tools to communicate regularly with family, compared with 44 percent of men with a graduate degree. These findings may be linked to a trend toward cellular phone and pager rejection. In an article by the Gannett news service, a journalist offers anecdotal evidence that the cell phone is "increasingly becoming the tool of the proletariat,"[27] an observation that may be consistent with the lower proportions of most highly educated cell phone/pager users in our sample.

Table 14.1 Information Technology Use[a]

Characteristics	Total Number	Email		Pager/Cellular		Computer for Work at Home	Fax for Work at Home	Internet for Information
		Home to work	Work to home	Phone for Work	Phone for Family			
Total	1,606	42.3	37.5	35.3	49.1	67.1	14.1	65.4
Gender								
Men	803	47.8	39.7	43.1	50.1	71.1	17.4	70.9
Women	803	36.7	35.4	27.5	48.2	63.1	10.7	59.9
Significantly different?		***	*	***		***	***	***
Age								
24–34 years old	166	42.2	47.0	36.1	53.0	63.3	15.7	69.3
35–44 years old	736	45.2	35.5	38.9	51.9	69.4	14.7	65.1
45–54 years old	569	39.9	36.6	32.9	48.2	68.0	14.4	67.1
55–64 years old	135	36.3	41.5	25.2	33.3	55.6	7.4	54.8
Significantly different?		*	*	**	***	**	***	*
Life stage								
Nonparents, wife under 40	82	45.1	53.7	30.5	35.4	67.1	13.4	84.1
Launching (kids ages < 6)	396	47.7	38.9	39.1	54.8	67.7	16.4	63.1
Early establishment (kids ages 6–12)	452	42.3	29.2	35.8	52.0	69.2	14.2	65.3
Late establishment (kids ages 13–18)	268	35.4	30.2	35.8	49.6	70.1	12.7	65.7
Nonparents, wife ages 40 and above	110	39.1	42.7	34.5	33.6	63.6	13.6	69.1
Adult children in home (ages 19+)	92	40.2	47.8	31.5	55.4	58.7	13.0	64.1
Empty nest	206	42.2	49.0	30.1	42.2	63.1	12.1	60.7
Significantly different?		*	***		***			*
Educational attainment								
Some college	460	24.3	25.9	34.1	49.3	47.0	9.1	49.8
Bachelor's degree	574	43.2	37.1	39.5	51.6	68.6	15.2	69.3

Graduate education	572	55.8	47.4	32.0	46.5	81.8	17.0	74.0
Significantly different?		***	***	***	***	***	**	***
Household income								
$0–74,999	382	30.4	29.6	25.4	36.4	53.1	9.7	55.0
$75,000–99,999	520	37.1	39.0	32.3	49.6	63.7	11.5	64.4
$100,000 and over	704	52.6	40.8	42.9	55.7	77.3	18.3	71.7
Significantly different?		***	***	***	***	***	***	***
Organizational affiliation[b]								
Other[c]	663	26.1	27.1	31.7	49.8	57.5	13.4	56.4
Transco	76	55.3	55.3	56.6	67.1	80.3	13.2	63.2
Utilco	76	40.8	42.1	73.7	71.1	80.3	17.1	80.3
Valley View Medical	62	3.2	4.8	27.4	32.3	21.0	1.6	43.5
Citizens Health	32	40.6	28.1	43.8	50.0	65.6	21.9	71.9
Upstate U	198	61.1	64.1	19.7	40.9	74.2	14.1	73.7
Lake U	86	60.5	62.8	15.1	29.1	77.9	14.0	69.8
Vantech	406	59.6	37.4	41.9	51.2	79.1	16.3	75.1
Significantly different?	***	***	***	***	***	***	***	***
Occupation type[b]								
Manager	449	53.9	41.6	44.8	52.1	77.3	15.4	71.7
Professional	634	44.8	40.9	30.3	47.8	72.2	13.6	69.1
Tech, sales, administrative support	358	30.7	32.4	33.2	52.0	54.7	14.5	56.4
Other	147	24.5	23.1	36.1	41.5	46.9	10.9	53.7
Significantly different?		***	***	***	†	***	***	***

[†] indicates $p < 0.10$; [*] indicates $p < 0.05$; [**] indicates $p < 0.01$; [***] indicates $p < 0.001$. From *Cornell Couples and Careers Study*, 1998–99.
[b] Denominators for Organizational Affiliation and Occupation type are 1,599 and 1,588 respondents, respectively. This does not substantially alter the overall percentages by type of technology.
[c] Spouses of respondents most often worked for organizations other than those highlighted in this study. In addition, a small number of respondents left their jobs to work for other firms in the time period between recruitment and interview.

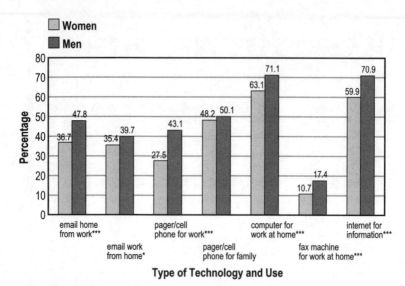

Figure 14.1 Technology use of women and men in dual-earner households. Source: *The Cornell Couples and Careers Study*, 1998–99. $N = 803$. *** $= p < .001$; ** $= p < .01$; * $= p < .05$; $+ = p < .10$.

Consistent with our expectation and findings from studies of nationally representative samples, higher proportions of IT users tend to be higher earners. We also observe variations in use by employer and occupational group. Managers and professionals are more apt to use each of the technology strategies (with the exception of fax use at home for work and cell phone/pager use for family communication), suggesting that people in certain occupations or workplaces may have greater access to and options to use IT to manage the work-family interface than others.

In sum, our descriptive evidence suggests a number of contextual factors (gender, life stage, education, income, and occupation) underlie the use of IT. To see which of these are most central, we analyze two basic types of IT use: computer use (email, home computer, or Internet) and cellular phone/pager use (for work, family, or both), using multivariate statistical techniques (see table 14.2).[28]

Computer Technology   Education matters most in the use of computer-related technologies to manage work and home, for both women and men. Respondents with a graduate degree are more than twice as likely as those with only some college to use computer strategies. By contrast, life stage does not predict the use of computer strategies for either women or men. Our models indicate that work characteristics are more important than family characteristics in

Table 14.2 Predictors of Womens' and Mens' Technology Use[a]

| | Computer Strategies[b] | | | | Cell Phones/Pagers[c] | | | |
| | Women (model 1) | | Men (model 1) | | Women (model 2) | | Men (model 2) | |
	Odds Ratio	p-value	Odds Ratio	p-value	Odds Ratio	p-value	Odds Ratio	p-value
Individual characteristics								
Education (omitted, some college)								
Graduate degree	**2.68**	**0.01**	**2.44**	**0.03**	0.97	0.90	**0.36**	**0.00**
Bachelor's degree	1.32	0.32	1.38	0.29	1.43	0.11	**0.58**	**0.03**
Family characteristics								
Life stage (omitted, empty nest)								
Nonparents, wife under 40	2.77	0.22	2.00	0.28	0.58	0.25	1.85	0.17
Launching (kids ages <6)	1.29	0.53	1.09	0.84	1.49	0.21	**1.90**	**0.03**
Early establishment (Kids ages 6–12)	1.23	0.56	1.30	0.53	1.43	0.22	1.57	0.12
Late establishment (Kids ages 13–18)	2.08	0.07	1.37	0.51	1.09	0.78	1.81	0.06
Nonparents, wife age 40 and above	1.07	0.91	2.01	0.25	0.59	0.20	1.11	0.79
Adult children in home (ages 19+)	1.56	0.40	1.12	0.85	1.73	0.19	2.08	0.09
Log of household income	0.74	0.43	2.09	0.08	1.31	0.35	**2.43**	**0.00**
Work characteristics								
Organizational affiliation (omitted, Vantech)								
Other organizations	**0.31**	**0.01**	**0.31**	**0.00**	0.79	0.41	1.44	0.11
Transco	1.05	0.96	0.50	0.24	1.39	0.51	**3.54**	**0.00**
Utilco[d]	238.61	0.64	2.94	0.19	1.88	0.32	**5.24**	**0.00**
Valley View Medical	**0.25**	**0.01**	0.43	0.36	0.66	0.33	2.39	0.26
Citizens Health	1.76	0.63	0.26	0.14	1.17	0.79	2.73	0.18
Upstate U	3.19	0.13	0.75	0.61	**0.49**	**0.03**	0.71	0.28
Lake U	1.54	0.63	1.12	0.88	**0.27**	**0.00**	0.49	0.10

Table 14.2 Predictors of Womens' and Mens' Technology Use[a]

	Computer Strategies[b]				Cell Phones/Pagers[c]			
	Women (model 1)		Men (model 1)		Women (model 2)		Men (model 2)	
	Odds Ratio	p-value	Odds Ratio	p-value	Odds Ratio	p-value	Odds Ratio	p-value
Occupation type (omitted, other)								
Manager	2.01	0.16	1.72	0.21	1.30	0.50	0.96	0.91
Professional	2.28	0.06	1.45	0.37	1.03	0.93	1.24	0.53
Administrative/technical	1.14	0.75	0.92	0.83	1.25	0.54	1.48	0.24
Respondent's work hours	**1.03**	**0.00**	1.00	0.84	**1.03**	**0.00**	**1.04**	**0.00**
Respondent's commute (min.; only included in model 2)	N/A	N/A	N/A	N/A	**2.84**	**0.01**	1.11	0.77
Respondent's perceived work control[e]	**1.86**	**0.00**	**2.12**	**0.00**	1.13	0.23	**1.64**	**0.00**
Spouse's work hours and technology use								
Spouse work hours	**0.97**	**0.04**	**0.98**	**0.02**	1.00	0.72	**0.98**	**0.00**
Spouse uses computer technology[f]	**4.97**	**0.00**	**3.57**	**0.00**	0.87	0.60	0.96	0.88
Spouse uses cell phone or pager[f]	1.31	0.26	1.06	0.82	**5.96**	**0.00**	**5.59**	**0.00**
Constant	3.69	0.76	**0.00**	0.05	**0.00**	0.06	**0.00**	**0.00**
Sample Size[g]	786		791		787		792	
−2 log likelihood	530.40		619.46		885.33		834.45	

[a]Binary logistic regression results. N/A, not applicable. Bold figures represent significant results discussed in text. From *Cornell Couples and Careers Study*, 1998–99.

[b]Outcome variable is 0/1 and measures whether a respondent used one (or more) of four computer strategies to manage work and family life on a regular basis: (1) email to communicate with work while at home, (2) email to communicate with family while at work, (3) a computer at home for work, (4) the Internet for shopping, banking, and information.

[c]Outcome variable is 0/1 and measures whether a respondent used a cell phone or pager for work or for family reasons (or both).

[d]All of the women at this organization used computer-related technology, which may account for the large odds ratio.

[e]Two cases had missing work control scores. The two missing cells were replaced with the mean score for wives with the same organizational affiliation, occupation type, and work hours.

[f]1 indicates use; 0 indicates no use.

[g]Sample size is out of a possible 803 couples. Most missing cases occurred because of missing occupation type (see table 14.1).

predicting the use of computer technology. The patterns are quite similar for men and women, contrary to our expectation.

Even after taking into account a number of personal and work-related factors, the employing organization makes a difference in predicting computer use. Compared to those working at Vantech, a large, established manufacturing firm, respondents working at other organizations are considerably less likely to use computer-based technology to manage their work and domestic life. Women working more hours tend to be somewhat more likely to use this technology, and, for both men and women, having a spouse who puts in more hours on the job is related to a somewhat lower likelihood of use. Finally, having a spouse who uses one or more of these computer strategies predicts whether the respondent uses them. This is an important finding because it suggests that couple dynamics may shape IT use to manage work and family life.[29]

Cellular Phones and Pagers   One of the more striking differences in the models predicting use of cell phones and pagers are the pattern differences by gender (women's and men's model 2 in table 14.2). For example, men with more education are less likely to use a cell phone or pager for work or family reasons, whereas men with young children at home and those with higher incomes are more likely to use them. But neither of these factors predict women's use of cell phones or pagers. Note that education is positively related to use of computer-based technology strategies, but negatively related (for men) to cell phone/pager use.

The place of employment makes a difference in whether workers are more or less likely to use cell phones/pagers. For example, women working at the two universities in our sample are less likely than women employed at Vantech (a large manufacturing firm) to regularly use cell phones/pagers in their work and/or family life. In contrast, men employed at Transco and Utilco are much more likely (over three and five times, respectively) to use these tools to manage work and family life on a regular basis. This again points to the potential role of organizations as promoters (or possibly inhibitors) of IT use.

Other important characteristics include work hours, the length of the work commute, and autonomy in the scheduling and timing of work. Both men and women who work more hours each week are more apt to use cell phones and/or pagers; but men married to women who work more hours are slightly less likely to use these tools. In addition, women with a longer commute between home and work are more likely to use these communication technologies, but this is not the case for men. What matters for men is control over time spent on the job. Men who report a high level of autonomy in scheduling their work are about one and one-half times more likely to use a cell phone or pager than those with more rigid work arrangements. Having a spouse who uses a cell phone or pager makes it five times more likely that an individual also uses a cell phone or pager. This again underscores the importance of couple-level dynamics in shaping the use of IT to manage the work-life interface.

Is IT Use Associated with Blurred Boundaries between Work and Home?

Earlier we suggested a possible connection between IT use and the blurring of boundaries between work and home. One way to measure the blurring boundaries between two domains is to capture the extent to which behavior and moods associated with one domain transfer to the other. This is exactly the sort of phenomenon that spillover questions are designed to measure, permitting some assessment of the role of technology use in blurring the boundaries between home and work. We analyze technology use in two ways. First, we examine the overall level of technology use by both wives and husbands. This variable measures how many IT strategies couple members use on a regular basis to manage work and home life.[30] Because our findings in table 14.2 point to IT use as a couple-level as well as an individual strategy, we also look at a couples' joint use of computer technology and cellular phones/pagers, examining whether couples' patterns of technology use are important predictors of spillover.

We expected that IT use would mean higher levels of negative work-to-family spillover for both women and men,[31] and we do find a positive relationship between the number of IT strategies used and the level of negative work-to-family spillover for the individuals in our dual-earner sample (see model 1 for men and women in table 14.3). We also compare couples with different patterns of use (each spouse uses the technology, the husband uses it but the wife does not, and the wife uses it but the husband does not) to couples in which neither uses the technology to see if certain use patterns matter for negative work-to-family spillover (see model 2 in table 14.3). We find that men's use of computer technology is related to significantly higher levels of negative work-to-family spillover for men, regardless of whether their wives use computer technology (this is not the case for women). Furthermore, husbands in couples in which the wife uses a cell phone or pager but the husband does not, report higher levels of negative work-to-family spillover than husbands in couples in which neither couple member reported using cell phones or pagers.

Higher levels of IT use are associated with greater positive work-to-family spillover for women, although our results suggest that a husband's increased use of technology may detract from this relationship.[32] In spite of this potentially more complicated relationship, IT use is generally associated with higher levels of positive work-to-family spillover for the women in our dual-earner sample. There is little connection between negative family-to-work spillover and technology use, contrary to our expectation, with one exception: husbands who use a cellular phone or pager, but whose wives do not, report less negative family-to-work spillover than husbands in couples in which neither member uses a cell phone or pager.

By contrast, IT use predicts positive family-to-work spillover for both men and women. Women in couples in which both spouses use cellular phones or pagers report more positive family-to-work spillover than do women in couples in which neither spouse uses these devices. Husbands who do not regularly use cellular phones or pagers, but whose wives do, report less positive family-to-work spillover than do husbands in couples in which neither spouse uses a cellular phone or pager. These results suggest that it is not only the individual's own technology use, but the combined use by both spouses that matters when it comes to spillover experiences.

IT Use and Psychological Well-Being

Thus far, we have shown how the use of IT varies across our sample of dual-earner couples and that this use is related to both positive and negative spillover. But is IT use related to life quality? To answer that question, we examine the connection between technology use and four aspects of psychological well-being—negative affect, perceived constraints, mastery, and growth—to assess whether IT strategies are good or bad for members of dual-earner couples.

In terms of affect, we find a similar pattern for the men and women in our dual-earner sample, with one key exception. Women's negative affect (depressive mood) is predicted by their husbands' use of technology rather than the women's own use, with women whose husbands use IT to manage work and family reporting slightly less negative affect (see table 14.4, women's model 1). Spillover experiences may help explain this effect (see table 14.4, women's model 2) with men's technology use possibly promoting positive family-to-work spillover. For men, however, IT use is associated with slightly higher negative affect (see table 14.4, men's model 1). This may be explained by a link between IT use and negative spillover (both work-to-family and family-to-work).

We find an association between technology use and a sense of personal mastery for women, but not for men, and this association persists even after we account for the presence of spillover, suggesting that there is something about IT use that may foster a sense of mastery in women that is not captured by spillover. We also find a positive relationship between increased IT use and personal growth for both men and women. IT use continues to be a significant predictor of personal growth even after we account for spillover experiences, suggesting that the use of IT may foster new learning.

Table 14.3 Relationship between IT Use and Spillover[a]

Type of Spillover and Technology Use	Work-to-Family Spillover								Family-to-Work Spillover							
	Women				Men				Women				Men			
	Model 1		Model 2		Model 1		Model 2		Model 1		Model 2		Model 1		Model 2	
	b[b]	p-value	b	p-value	b	p-value	b	p-value	b	p-value	b	p-value	b	p-value	b	p-value
NEGATIVE SPILLOVER																
Technology use																
Number of IT strategies used																
Wife (7 strategies possible)	**0.03**	**0.02**			−0.05	0.67			0.02	0.09			0.01	0.65		
Husband (7 strategies possible)	−0.02	0.37			**0.03**	**0.01**			−0.01	0.66			0.00	0.81		
Couple's use of computer-related techs (omitted, neither use)																
Both use			0.14	0.15			**0.23**	**0.03**			−0.09	0.40			0.09	0.39
Husband uses/wife does not			0.01	0.96			**0.28**	**0.02**			−0.16	0.19			0.05	0.68
Wife uses/husband does not			0.01	0.90			0.16	0.17			−0.18	0.16			0.10	0.42
Couple's use of cellular phone/pager (omitted, neither use)																
Both use			−0.02	0.65			0.10	0.07			0.07	0.22			−0.08	0.16
Husband uses/wife does not			0.00	0.96			**0.20**	**0.00**			0.04	0.49			**−0.14**	**0.04**
Wife uses/husband does not			0.07	0.32			0.02	0.73			−0.02	0.80			−0.01	0.84
Sample size	785		785		790		790		785		785		790		790	
Adjusted R^2	27.8%		27.9%		24.9%		25.6%		19.1%		18.9%		14.4%		14.6%	

POSITIVE SPILLOVER

Technology use

	Model 1 (b)	Model 1	Model 2 (b)	Model 2	Model 3 (b)	Model 3	Model 4 (b)	Model 4	Model 5 (b)	Model 5	Model 6 (b)	Model 6	Model 7 (b)	Model 7
Number of technology strategies used														
Wife (7 strategies possible)	0.05	**0.00**			0.00	0.87			**0.04**	**0.01**			−0.02	0.23
Husband (7 strategies possible)	−0.03	0.08			0.03	0.12			0.02	0.10			**0.04**	**0.02**
Couple's use of computer-related techs (omitted, neither use)														
Both use			−0.14	0.33			0.01	0.97			0.02	0.85	0.19	0.17
Husband uses/wife does not			−0.28	0.07			0.00	0.99			−0.06	0.70	0.25	0.09
Wife uses/husband does not			0.01	0.95			0.08	0.61			0.00	0.99	0.17	0.28
Couple's use of cellular phone/pager (omitted, neither use)														
Both use			0.07	0.33			0.05	0.50			**0.22**	**0.00**	−0.02	0.83
Husband uses/wife does not			0.04	0.64			−0.05	0.53			0.06	0.46	−0.08	0.33
Wife Uses/Husband does not			−0.04	0.66			−0.09	0.32			−0.07	0.42	**−0.26**	**0.01**
Sample size	785		785		791		791		785		785		791	
Adjusted R^2	3.7%		3.0%		4.9%		4.6%		4.4%		4.7%		2.8%	

[a] Ordinary least squares (OLS) results. Models controlled for education, negative affect (in negative models only), life stage, log of household income, organizational affiliation, occupation type, work hours, commute to work, and perceived work control. See the appendix for further documentation of these measures. From *Cornell Couples and Careers Study*, 1998–99.

[b] b indicates unstandardized regression coefficient.

Table 14.4 IT Use, Spillover, and Psychological Well-Being[a]

	Negative Affect								Perceived Constraints							
	Women				Men				Women				Men			
	Model 1		Model 2		Model 1		Model 2		Model 1		Model 2		Model 1		Model 2	
Technology Use and Spillover	b[b]	p-value	b	p-value	b	p-value	b	p-value	b	p-value	b	p-value	b	p-value	b	p-value
Technology Use																
Number of IT strategies used																
Wife (7 strategies possible)	0.02	0.13	0.01	0.41	0.01	0.55	0.00	0.62	0.00	0.84	-0.01	0.56	0.00	0.85	0.00	0.95
Husband (7 strategies possible)	-0.02	0.03	-0.01	0.13	0.02	0.04	0.01	0.21	-0.01	0.55	0.00	0.89	-0.01	0.23	-0.01	0.19
Spillover																
Positive work-to-family			-0.04	0.07			-0.01	0.74			-0.05	0.01			-0.02	0.45
Negative work-to-family			0.26	0.00			0.27	0.00			0.15	0.00			0.13	0.00
Positive family-to-work			-0.08	0.00			-0.05	0.03			-0.06	0.01			-0.12	0.00
Negative family-to-work			0.15	0.00			0.15	0.00			0.14	0.00			0.04	0.13
Sample size	785		785		790		790		783		783		790		790	
Adjusted R^2	5.8%		23.4%		2.8%		21.7%		3.7%		13.8%		3.8%		11.6%	

	Personal Mastery								Personal Growth							
	Women				Men				Women				Men			
	Model 1		Model 2		Model 1		Model 2		Model 1		Model 2		Model 1		Model 2	
Technology Use and Spillover	b	p-value	b	p-value	b	p-value	b	p-value	b	p-value	b	p-value	b	p-value	b	p-value
Technology Use																
Number of IT strategies used																
Wife (7 strategies possible)	**0.03**	**0.00**	**0.03**	**0.00**	0.00	0.71	0.00	0.90	**0.03**	**0.00**	**0.02**	**0.01**	0.00	0.64	0.00	0.79
Husband (7 strategies possible)	-0.01	0.23	-0.01	0.13	0.01	0.29	0.01	0.43	-0.01	0.40	-0.01	0.35	**0.02**	**0.02**	0.02	0.07
Spillover																
Positive work-to-family			0.06	**0.00**			0.02	0.32			**0.11**	**0.00**			**0.06**	**0.00**
Negative work-to-family			-0.15	**0.00**			**-0.07**	**0.01**			**-0.07**	**0.01**			-0.03	0.22
Positive family-to-work			0.02	0.19			**0.13**	**0.00**			**0.07**	**0.00**			**0.10**	**0.00**
Negative family-to-work			-0.04	0.14			0.01	0.68			-0.02	0.35			0.02	0.44
Sample size	784		784		790		790		785		785		791		791	
Adjusted R^2	5.6%		11.3%		8.4%		14.0%		8.1%		15.0%		4.7%		9.1%	

[a]From *Cornell Couples and Careers Study*, 1998–99. Ordinary least squares (OLS) regression results. Models controlled for education, negative affect (in negative models only), life stage, log of household income, organizational affiliation, occupation type, work hours, commute to work, and perceived work control. See the appendix for further documentation of these measures.

[b]b indicates unstandardized regression coefficient.

Summing Up

A focus on the experiences of middle-class couples is particularly important in examining strategies of IT use, given that people with higher income and more education are the early adopters of such technologies. Thus, our sample is part of the population most likely to actively use IT in their daily life. Our evidence demonstrates that various types of IT are clearly in the repertoire of most dual-earner couples' adaptive strategies as they attempt to manage and better coordinate their work and personal lives. But we show that this depends in part on where people work. Not only are some organizations more likely to foster (or impede) some types of technology use, but our qualitative analysis suggests that employers, too, use technology to better manage and adapt to a changing work environment. However, not everyone can afford this technology or works for an employer that provides it; whatever benefits or constraints we observe are probably specific to well-educated, relatively well-off, dual-earner families.

We examine not only individuals' IT use, but also their spouses' to better understand how couples use these technologies as a strategy for managing work and family life. We also investigate a phenomenon highlighted as a potential consequence of IT use—the blurring of boundaries between work and home. Although we find evidence that IT use weakens the boundaries between home and work (via spillover), this blurring may have both positive and negative implications for dual-earner families. IT use does predict more negative work-to-family spillover, but it also predicts positive spillover from both work-to-family and family-to-work for women. Our models examining couple-level use of computer and cell phone/pager technology demonstrate that one spouse's IT use may shape the other spouse's experiences of spillover. Unfortunately, our cross-sectional models do not allow us to untangle cause and effect. We cannot say definitively that more technology use results in spillover. It may be that couples who already experience more spillover generally turn to technological tools to control it.

We find that the broad category of IT and communication technology may help empower couples to manage their multiple work and family time obligations. Moreover, we show a connection between the use of these tools and a sense of mastery for women, as well as a positive relationship between IT use and personal growth for both women and men. Although technology use is related to men's negative affect, this link disappears once negative spillover effects are accounted for. This suggests that technology might operate on men's moods precisely because of work-to-family and family-to-work spillover.

Clearly, IT and communication technology will become even more embedded in twenty-first-century homes and workplaces. What we see is the promise of staying connected with loved ones; but these technologies also keep workers connected to their jobs 24-7. Our study shows that individuals—and couples—

actively strategize to use these technologies to their advantage while simultane-ously dealing with negative spillover experiences. How to promote the positive impacts of technology use and minimize the negative influences on work and family life will be the challenge, not only for families but for human resource policy and practices.

15

Alternative Employment Arrangements

Janet H. Marler, Pamela S. Tolbert,
and George T. Milkovich

Part-time work, temporary work, independent contracting, and self-employment have experienced unprecedented increases in the last several decades. These employment arrangements characterize approximately 25–30 percent of the workforce, and they are growing fast.[1] The rate of growth in part-time workers is 30 percent greater than in the overall work force, the rate of temporary agency workers is more than five times greater, and the growth in self-employment now equals the growth in civilian employment. These changes coincide with the increasing participation of married women in the labor force, the prevalence of dual-earner households, and the restructuring of the traditional employment relationship within many organizations.[2] How have these simultaneous changes in employment arrangements and the demography of the workforce affected families' strategies for managing work and family responsibilities? In this chapter we describe five couple-level employment strategies and examine their relationship to husbands' and wives' demographic and work characteristics, life stage, and objective and subjective measures of work and family success.

Gender Roles and Nonstandard
Work Arrangements

The term "nonstandard work arrangement" (NSWA) refers to a number of different work and employment arrangements including part-time work, self-employment, independent contracting, and temporary and on-call work. The latter three categories are also called alternative employment arrangements.[3] As of 1997, approximately 9 percent of the U.S. workforce was self-employed (nearly one-half of these are independent contractors), approximately 3 percent were in temporary or on-call work arrangements, and approximately 18 percent worked in part-time jobs.[4] These various arrangements contrast with standard work arrangements along one or both of two main dimensions: reduced time commitment to work activities and reduced dependence (at least in principle) on a single employer.

Part-time work is clearly identified with a reduction in normal work hours, and temporary and on-call arrangements often involve reduced work hours as well. Reducing the time spent on work activities by one or both members of a couple is one strategy for managing work and family demands when both are part of the workforce. Because working less than full-time conflicts with the traditional male provider role,[5] however, it is less likely to be used by men. Researchers have found that married women often choose part-time jobs[6] because they feel such jobs permit them to better combine both work and family roles. Men who work part-time, on the other hand, are more likely to be doing so involuntarily.[7]

Temporary and on-call work and independent contracting also often involve reduced dependence on a single employer. It is common for workers in such arrangements to move from employer to employer, working on a short-term, project basis. These semientrepreneurial employment arrangements have the potential to provide workers with more flexibility than traditional full-time arrangements and thus to enable them to better manage work-family commitments. In principle, workers can turn down work occasionally as their schedules demand, and they may have more latitude in adapting work schedules to fit with their personal and family life. There are limits to this, of course, because turning down employment opportunities may affect future opportunities and economic security. Indeed, research on the impact of temporary work arrangements on flexibility reaches conflicting conclusions. Several studies suggest that married women choose temporary work arrangements because these arrangements allow better balancing of work and family demands, but the evidence is weak.[8] Other researchers argue that temporary agency work is quite inflexible and that the only reason married women accept it is because they are secondary wage earners.[9] Both views suggest, however, the impact of gendered templates on the use of such NSWAs. The male breadwinner role limits men's propensity to trade potential work autonomy (and concomitant potential financial insecurity) for a greater ability to meet family demands.

Research evidence suggests similar conclusions about self-employment. In theory, self-employment can provide individuals with greater flexibility in allocating time to work insofar as they are less constrained by organizational scheduling and by the expectations and demands of hierarchical superiors. Research on self-employment indicates that women are more likely to take advantage of this potential flexibility than men, however. Using qualitative research methodology, Karyn Losocco studied the influence of gender ideology on the behavior of self-employed men and women. She found that self-employed men tend to work long hours, consistent with the male breadwinner role, whereas women structure their work hours flexibly to coincide with family demands.[10]

Two key studies by Arne Kalleberg and colleagues, using the 1995 Current Population Survey data, compare work and family variables for men and women involved in several types of nonstandard work arrangements, including temporary, and on-call work, self-employment, independent contracting, and part-time work. They offer two general conclusions. First, men are much more likely than women to cite economic reasons for having NSWAs. Second, there are significant gender differences in the quality of jobs within and across the different types of NSWAs. For example, self-employed professional men are more likely to be in quality jobs (which the investigators define by above-average wages and attitude toward work). Temporaries working as secretaries are much more likely to be in low-quality jobs.[11]

These large-scale studies are the first to provide a broad perspective on NSWAs by examining gender, occupational, family, and other demographic differences. There are no studies, however, of how these work arrangements are affected by couple-level, rather than individual, choices. Thus, we do not know whether or how couple characteristics are related to individual members' use of standard or nonstandard work arrangements or how such linked choices affect individual and couple-level career outcomes.

Gender and Career Outcomes

Much of the existing research on career success reflects a bias toward both traditional employment arrangements and the male-provider career template of success (see also Moen, Waismel-Manor, and Sweet, chap. 9 in this volume). Most studies conceptualize careers in terms of upward mobility in a single company and increasing income attainment which, as Sonya Williams and Shin-Kap Han (chap. 6 in this volume) point out is characteristic of only one subset of employees. In this model, career success is often measured using financial indicators, such as hourly wages[12] and salaries, or occupational attainment measures, such as number of promotions.[13] Predictors of such objective success typically include educational attainment, hours worked, and work involvement. Particularly in early studies, variables such as gender, number of children, and marital status are used simply as controls; the neglect of family characteristics most likely reflects the fact that most samples were predominately male.

In contrast to objective career success, subjective career success represents perceptions or feelings of success.[14] Individuals may meet objective success criteria, but, nevertheless, not perceive themselves successful, and vice versa.[15] The predictors of objective success are not the same as for subjective success (see Moen, Waismel-Manor, and Sweet, chap. 9 in this volume), but, still, most studies examining subjective career success treat gender as a control variable and do not systematically explore gender differences. One of the few studies to address such differences, by Saroj Parasuraman and colleagues of 111 male and female entrepreneurs, found that gender is not directly related to perceptions of career success and family satisfaction. Rather, its effect on perceived career success and family satisfaction is mediated by workers' allocation of time between work and family, perceptions of work and family conflict, and the nature of the work demands.[16]

Overall, however, the literature on careers has neglected gender-linked influences on both objective and subjective indicators of success, and little is known about the impact of NSWAs on career outcomes for couples, on couple-level choices, or on individual perceptions of career success.

Nonstandard Work Arrangements as a Couple-Level Strategy

We use *The Cornell Couples and Careers Study* data to examine both the use of NSWAs as a couple-level strategy for managing work and family responsibilities and the impact of such arrangements on career outcomes.[17] Our classification of individuals' employment arrangements is based on a series of self-report questions. Respondents indicated whether in their main job they were self-employed, temporary, contract, seasonal, or an on-call employee, if they were employed full-time or part-time, and the number of hours that they worked officially. We coded workers as part-time if they defined their work as part-time and worked fewer than thirty-five hours a week.[18] The distribution of NSWAs in our data roughly approximates that found in national U.S. studies. Approximately 3 percent of workers in both our data and national data are employed in temporary work arrangements, and nearly 10 percent are self-employed (including independent contractors). A somewhat larger proportion of the national workforce holds part-time positions (17.6%) than our sample (11.3%). Women in our data set are more heavily represented in NSWAs than they are at the national level. A little more than two-thirds of those holding temporary or on-call positions in the

Cornell Study data are women; approximately one-half of such workers are women in the national data. In our data, one-half of the independent contractors and self-employed are women, whereas only little more than one-third of the workers in this category in the national data are women. And almost all employees holding part-time time positions in our sample are female (94%); women are also overrepresented among part-time workers in the national data, but approximately one-third of such workers are male.

We use the two dimensions of NSWAs, reduced work time and reduced dependence on an employer, to create four categories of work arrangements at the individual level: working full-time in alternative employment (i.e., temporary or on-call workers, independent contractors, or self-employed); working part-time in alternative employment; working full-time in traditional jobs (i.e., employed on a regular basis by a single employer); and working part-time in traditional jobs. There are striking differences in the representation of men and women in these categories.

The predominant category for both men and women in this sample of dual-earner couples is full-time traditional employment, although a much higher proportion of men than women (87% versus 65%) fall into this category. Ten percent of the men hold full-time nontraditional jobs, as do 6 percent of the women. Consistent with traditional gender expectations, almost none of the men work in part-time arrangements, either traditional or nontraditional, but nearly one-third of the women in the sample do.

Combining husbands' and wives' employment arrangements produces sixteen possible configurations of couple-level employment arrangements. As in the case of work hours (see Moen and Sweet, chap. 2 in this volume), husbands' and wives' employment arrangements are clearly related. A little over 60 percent of the husbands who are employed full-time in traditional jobs have wives that are also employed in such jobs. When one spouse has a NSWA, however, the other spouse is much more likely to hold a traditional full-time position. Although the small number of men who work part-time (total $N = 25$) makes it hard to draw firm conclusions about couples in this group, couple-level arrangements follow a pattern similar to those in which the husband has a full-time nontraditional job.

Overall, five couple-level strategies predominate.[19] Far and away the largest category contains couples in which both husbands and wives work full-time traditional jobs (type 1). The second most common configuration is one in which wives work part-time and husbands work full-time, both in traditional employment (type 4). Three-quarters of the couples in the Cornell Study fall into one of these two configurations. Only three other configurations contain at least forty couples. One, representing approximately 8 percent of our couples, is that in which wives work full-time traditional jobs while their husbands work full-time nontraditional jobs (type 2). Another, approximately 6 percent of the couples, reverses this—wives work full-time nontraditional jobs while husbands work full-time traditional jobs (type 3). And, finally, in approximately 7 percent of the couples, husbands work full-time traditional jobs while their wives work part-time nontraditional jobs. Because of the small number of couples represented by other cells, our remaining analyses focus on these five couple strategies.

Analysis of Couple-Level Employment Strategies

We examine a number of characteristics that might be expected to differentiate couples that use different strategies, including life stage, age, education, gender ideology, and work characteristics.

Life Course Factors: Life Stage and Age

The likelihood of couples' using the various strategies appears to be strongly influenced by the wives' life stage, as shown in figure 15.1. Type 1 couples (in which both hold full-time traditional jobs) are most likely to be nonparents or couples whose children have left home. Seventy-five percent of nonparents under forty, 65 percent of the nonparents over forty, and 73 percent of the empty nesters fall into this category. A relatively high percent of nonparents are also type 2 couples (in which wives hold full-time traditional jobs and husbands hold full-time nontraditional jobs). Fifteen percent of the nonparents under forty and almost one-fifth of nonparents over forty are type 2. The absence of children in the household may weaken breadwinner pressures on husbands, allowing them to move into more entrepreneurial (and potentially higher-risk) work arrangements. For women, not having children at home seems to facilitate the adoption of employment arrangements conventionally identified with men—full-time traditional jobs.

Having children, and particularly young children, at home is associated with type 4 arrangements (in which husbands work in full-time traditional jobs and wives work in part-time traditional jobs). Thirty-four percent of the couples in the launching (preschooler) stage fall into this category, and 28 percent in the early establishment (grade-school-age children) stage do so. However, it is important to note that, even in these stages, the predominant couple employment configuration remains type 1. The percentage of couples classified as type 4 and type 5 decline at later life stages. Overall, these results suggest that departures in couple-level employment strategies from type 1 are conditioned by the life stages of couples, but that type 1 (both working full-time traditional jobs) remains the preferred (or most feasible) arrangement.

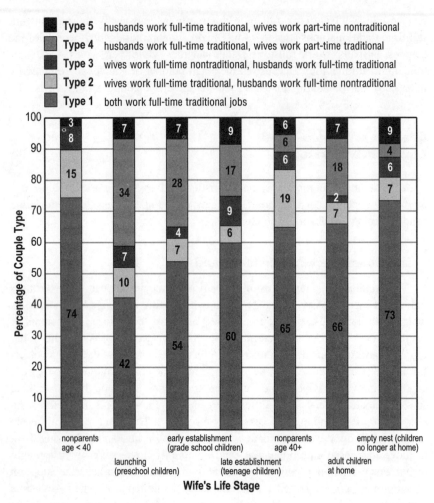

Figure 15.1 Couple-level strategies by wife's life stage. Source: *Cornell Couples and Careers Study*, 1998–99.

Human Capital, Gender Ideology, and Work Characteristics

Table 15.1 shows the average scores for characteristics of wives and husbands of each couple configuration—age, education, number of children, gender ideology, and work characteristics.[20]

Couple strategies do not appear to be distinguished by age differences, per se. Couples in which wives hold full-time non-traditional jobs (type 3) tend to be relatively young, but this is also true of couples in which wives work in part-time traditional jobs (type 4). A number of interesting differences among the couples do emerge, however. Spouses (both male and female) who hold full-time non-traditional jobs (types 2 and 3) have comparatively low levels of educational attainment, as do wives who work in part-time jobs (types 4 and 5). In four of the five couple types, husbands have higher levels of educational attainments than their wives do, but in type 2 couples (in which wives work full-time traditional jobs and husbands hold full-time nontraditional jobs) this is reversed. In these couples, wives have slightly higher levels of education than their husbands. Couples in which wives hold full-time traditional jobs (types 1 and 2) tend to have fewer children overall, especially compared to couples in which wives hold part-time positions (types 4 and 5). Wives in types 1 and 2 also score the highest on the measure of egalitarian gender ideology; both spouses in types 4 and 5 score significantly lower on this scale.

Work Characteristics

Table 15.1 also compares members of different couple types on several work characteristics, including the number of hours respondents report actually working each week (versus the number they officially work), the prestige of their occupations (coded using the two-digit 1990 standard occupational classification system; see app.), whether their jobs require the supervision of other workers, and the amount of control they perceive having in their work (see app.).

Wives who hold traditional full-time jobs (types 1 and 2) report working longer hours, on average, than do other wives. Interestingly, husbands of wives who work part-time (types 4 and 5) report working relatively fewer hours than other husbands. Patterns of occupational prestige closely follow patterns of educational attainment. Husbands whose wives work part-time (types 4 and 5) are in more prestigious occupations than other husbands, whereas wives in type 1 and 2 couples are in more prestigious occupations than other wives. In consequence, the gap in occupational prestige for husbands and wives is greatest in couples in which wives hold part-time positions. As in the case of education, only in type 2 couples (in which wives work full-time traditional jobs and husbands work nontraditional jobs) does the prestige of wives' occupation exceed that of their husbands, on average. In these couples, wives are also more likely to hold supervisory positions than are their husbands; the reverse is true for other couple types. On the other hand, there do not appear to be any substantial differences by couple strategy in members' perceived control of work.

In sum, couples in which wives work full-time traditional jobs, and especially those in which their husbands work nontraditional jobs, are likely to have fewer children, to hold more egalitarian gender ideologies, and to have both spouses work longer hours. Wives in such couples tend to have more education, be in

Table 15.1 Means of Human Capital, Family, Work Characteristics, and Objective and Subjective Success by Couple Type and Gender[a]

	Type 1		Type 2		Type 3		Type 4		Type 5	
	Wife FT/Trad	Husband FT/Trad	Wife FT/Trad	Husband FT/Nontrad	Wife FT/Nontrad	Husband FT/Trad	Wife PT/Trad	Husband FT/Trad	Wife PT/Nontrad	Husband FT/Trad
Age	43.2	45.3	41.9	43.7	42.1	44.0	41.5	43.2	44.5	45.8
	(7.3)	(7.8)	(7.6)	(9.6)	(7.6)	(7.6)	(6.6)	(7.0)	(6.7)	(6.9)
Years of education	4.2	4.6	4.5	3.4	3.8	5.5	3.3	4.9	3.9	5.4
	(2.7)	(2.9)	(2.3)	(2.8)	(2.6)	(2.8)	(2.5)	(2.4)	(2.4)	(2.4)
Total children	1.9	1.9	1.8	1.8	2.0	2.0	2.4	2.4	2.4	2.4
	(1.3)	(1.3)	(1.6)	(1.6)	(1.1)	(1.1)	(1.1)	(1.1)	(1.1)	(1.1)
Gender role ideology	4.0	3.6	4.1	3.7	3.8	3.7	3.4	3.3	3.3	3.1
	(.8)	(.7)	(3.7)	(.9)	(.8)	(.7)	(.9)	(.8)	(.9)	(.9)
Average work hours/ week	46.7	50.0	47.2	53.0	42.7	51.9	27.9	49.2	23.9	49.8
	(8.2)	(8.5)	(7.7)	(13.4)	(16.1)	(9.8)	(9.9)	(6.6)	(13.2)	(6.1)
Occupational prestige	53.1	54.9	54.4	48.5	51.2	54.8	51.8	56.6	51.7	57.8
	(10.2)	(11.3)	(9.2)	(11.0)	(11.0)	(8.8)	(11.7)	(8.8)	(11.1)	(8.8)
Supervisory status	39%	48%	46%	44%	34%	53%	21%	43%	11%	57%
	(49)	(50)	(50)	(50)	(48)	(50)	(41)	(50)	(31)	(50)
Perceived control of work	3.3	3.6	3.4	3.7	3.4	3.7	3.3	3.5	3.5	3.7
	(.8)	(.8)	(.8)	(.9)	(1.1)	(.7)	(1.0)	(.8)	(1.0)	(.6)
Salary	47,159	65,196	48,376	54,172	36,040	66,782	25,155	68,932	16,588	78,083
	(24,481)	(26,158)	(17,757)	(36,787)	(32,324)	(25,173)	(17,411)	(23,466)	(17,392)	(21,162)
Combined salary	111,070	111,070	100,740	100,740	94,023	99,022	92,709	92,709	93,702	93,702
	(38,628)	(38,628)	(46,322)	(46,322)	(38,691)	(35,772)	(28,052)	(28,052)	(31,239)	(31,239)
Hourly wage	20	26	20	20	19	26	18	28	15	32
	(8.8)	(10.3)	(6.4)	(11.4)	(12.2)	(8.1)	(11.5)	(9.1)	(13.5)	(8.5)
Perceived success in work life	80.4	77.8	81.8	79.6	80.9	81.1	79.7	79.2	81.5	77.8
	(12.9)	(14.0)	(13.5)	(13.7)	(19.1)	(11.5)	(14.4)	(12.3)	(14.6)	(11.5)
Perceived success in personal/family life	84.6	82.8	82.9	84.5	88.3	85.4	86.4	85.0	88.6	83.8
	(13.4)	(15.5)	(12.9)	(12.3)	(12.2)	(10.8)	(13.8)	(12.2)	(10.0)	(12.6)
Perceived success balancing work/family	75.0	74.1	74.2	71.4	82.1	66.7	79.9	75.7	82.3	73.5
	(16.8)	(17.3)	(13.6)	(20.7)	(12.5)	(24.9)	(15.6)	(14.6)	(16.2)	(15.8)

[a]FT, full-time; Nontrad, nontraditional; PT, part-time; Trad, traditional. Values in parentheses are standard deviations. Source: *Cornell Couples and Careers Study*, 1998–99.

more prestigious occupations, and hold positions involving supervisory status. On the other hand, husbands whose wives work part-time (either traditional or nontraditional) jobs are likely to be in more prestigious occupations than are other husbands. How do these differences relate to career outcomes for each spouse and for the couple as a unit?

Career Outcomes

Following traditional career research, we examine individuals' annual salary as a measure of career success.[21] In addition, we examine the combined salaries for each couple as an alternative indicator of career outcome, along with subjective indicators of how successful individuals feel in both their work and family lives. The averages (means) of these measures are also shown by couple type and by gender in table 15.1.

In couples in which wives work part-time (types 4 and 5), husbands tend to earn higher annual salaries than other husbands. Wives in such couples, not surprisingly, earn markedly less than other wives. In fact, there appears to be a moderate inverse relationship between the relative earnings of wives and husbands in different couple types—the higher the relative earnings of husbands, the lower the relative earnings of wives. When the couple is taken as the unit of analysis, however, a rather different picture emerges. Couples in which husbands and wives both work full-time traditional jobs (type 1) earn the highest combined salaried income. Those in which wives work full-time traditional jobs and husbands work nontraditional jobs (type 2) have the second-highest level of combined income, despite the comparatively low earnings of husbands. These objective indicators of career success, however, may or may not be related to individuals' more subjective assessments of their work success. They also provide no obvious insights into other aspects of life success, such as an individual's feeling successful in his or her personal life or in balancing work and family life.

We use three measures of perceived success: success in work, success in personal or family life, and success in balancing work and family/personal life. (See Moen, Waismel-Manor, and Sweet, chap. 2; app.). There is very little variance in how successful wives perceive themselves to be at work across the various couple configurations. Similarly, no clear pattern emerges among husbands for the various types. However, notable differences occur among the types of couples in perceptions of personal success and in balancing. Wives who work nonstandard jobs, full-time nontraditional or part-time jobs (types 3, 4, and 5), rate themselves as more successful in family life than do wives who work traditional jobs; wives who work full time and whose husbands hold full-time nontraditional jobs (type 2) feel least successful on this dimension. Husbands in the various couple types vary less in their perceptions of success in family life. In general, wives'

perceptions of success in family life are related to both their own work arrangements and those of their husbands. In contrast, these strategies have much less
influence on husbands' perceptions of personal success.

A similar pattern emerges among wives in perceptions of success in balancing work and family. Wives in nontraditional jobs (types 3 and 5) are especially
likely to feel successful at balancing family and work compared to women
working in traditional jobs, even compared to those who work part-time traditional jobs (types 1, 2, and 4). But the opposite holds true for husbands: husbands
of wives who work nontraditional jobs (types 3 and 5) rate themselves as less
successful in balancing work and family than do other husbands.

Couple-Level-Strategy Effects on Objective Career Outcomes

To examine the impact of couple-level strategies on career outcomes more
closely, we have regressed the different career outcomes on couple types (constructed as dummy variables), controlling for the effects of individual and spousal
human capital and work characteristics. Table 15.2 presents the results of the first
of these regressions, examining the impact of couple types, along with individual human capital and work characteristics, on the individual salaries of husbands
and wives.

The effects of the individual and work characteristics on earnings are very
similar for husbands and wives. As is commonly found in studies of earnings
determinants, age has a positive curvilinear relation to salary for women, and the
results suggest similar curvilinearity for men, although the squared term does not
attain significance. Increasing education, greater autonomy and supervisory
responsibility, higher-prestige occupations, and longer work hours are all positively related to the salaries of men and women. Net of couple type, work hours,
and other factors, the number of children in a family has no effect on the
earnings of either husbands or wives.

The reference category for the couple type dummies is type 1 (in which both
husband and wife work in full-time traditional jobs). Women in type 3, 4, and 5
couples have significantly lower salaries than those in type 1 couples. In each
case, the women have NSWAs, either working nontraditional full-time jobs (type
3) or part-time jobs (types 4 and 5). Thus, it appears that, net of other factors
(including number of hours worked, supervisory status, and other work characteristics), women are penalized for alternative employment status.

A more complex picture emerges for husbands. Similar to the findings for
women in full-time nontraditional work, men in type 2 couples (in which
husbands hold full-time nontraditional jobs and wives hold full-time traditional
jobs) earn less than those in type 1 couples. Husbands in type 3 couples (in which

Table 15.2 Regression of Wives' and Husbands' Salaries and Couples' Combined Salaries on Couple Type[a]

	Wives		Husbands		Couples	
	b	SE	b	SE	b	SE
Wife's age	3,344	863***			4,830	2,129*
Wife's age squared	(42)	10***			(57)	24**
Wife's education	2,172	284***			2,127	513***
Wife's control of work	3,636	744***			5,541	1,275***
Wife: supervisor	6,644	1,392***			5,429	2,376*
Wife's occupational prestige	274	67***			274	113**
Wife's hours worked/week	765	75***			719	129***
Husband's age			2,326	924**	806	1,923
Husband's age squared			(19)	10	(3)	21
Husband's education			2,095	326***	2,296	483***
Husband's control of work			4,879	1,041***	5,331	1,464***
Husband: supervisor			10,178	1,598***	8,772	2,245***
Husband's occupational prestige			322	84***	366	119**
Husband's hours worked/week			697	84***	596	120***
Number of children	(1,052)	652	(162)	770	(725)	1,133
Couple type 2[b]	(1,703)	2,380	(7,582)	3,038**	(9,045)	4,246*
Couple type 3[b]	(13,043)	2,867***	(2,183)	3,517	(15,411)	4,987**
Couple type 4[b]	(4,671)	2,195*	6,433	2,084**	415	3,734
Couple type 5[b]	(9,428)	3,324**	9,662	3,233**	(1,955)	5,651
Intercept	(89,254)	18,551***	(85,026)	20,908***	(176,381)	34,775***
R^2	0.48***		0.34***		0.35***	

[a] *indicates $p < .05$; **indicates $p < .01$; ***indicates $p < .001$; b, unstandardized regression coefficient; SE, standard error.
[b] Couple type 1 is the reference category.
Source: *Cornell Couples and Careers Study*, 1998–99.

husbands work full-time traditional jobs and wives work full-time nontraditional jobs) do not differ significantly in their earnings from those in type 1. However, husbands in type 4 and 5 couples (in which husbands work full-time traditional jobs and wives work part-time) earn significantly more. The causality is difficult to ascertain here: Do such men earn more because their wives work less, or do their wives work less because their husbands earn more? These are intriguing questions, but, unfortunately, given the cross-sectional nature of the data, we cannot address them here.

We can, however, examine the effects of couple types on combined family income. Economists have long argued that the family is the economic unit of decision making, so it is rather surprising how little research on economic attainment has focused on family earnings. In the last two columns of table 15.2, we present the results of the regression of combined earnings on the characteristics of each member of the couple and on couple type. As suggested by the previous analysis, both husbands' and wives' characteristics exert significant independent effects on the couples' level of earnings. The hours worked by both members are the strongest determinants of earnings, followed by the husbands' level of education and the wives' job autonomy and education. Net of individual characteristics, there are significant differences in the joint earnings of the types of couples. Type 2 couples (in which husbands hold full-time nontraditional jobs and wives hold full-time traditional jobs) earn significantly less than the reference set (type 1 couples), as do type 3 couples (in which husbands hold full-time traditional jobs and wives hold full-time nontraditional jobs). This suggests that nontraditional jobs carry economic penalties for families. However, type 4 and type 5 couples, which are characterized by wives working part-time, do not have significantly different earnings from type 1 couples. It may be that although there are economic penalties associated with part-time work, the reduction in the number of hours spent at work by wives allows their husbands to focus their energies more on work and thus to earn more, all else being equal. Nontraditional arrangements in which individuals work full-time may not provide their spouses with the same ability to concentrate their energies on their work. Conversely, wives of high earners may feel they can afford to work part-time.

Couple-Level-Strategy Effects on Subjective Career Outcomes

Couples are likely to choose nontraditional work arrangements with an eye to maximizing work and family outcomes that are not purely economic. Thus, in evaluating their success as a strategy, it is important to consider the impact of such arrangements on subjective perceptions as well as objective indicators of success (such as earnings). Accordingly, we have regressed the three measures of perceived success—success in work, success in personal life, and success in balancing work and family—on couples' individual characteristics, family measures, and work arrangements. The results of these analyses are presented in tables 15.3 for wives and husbands.

We draw two main conclusions about wives from table 15.3 (the first six columns). One is that couple employment configurations have no significant effect on wives' perceptions of success in work or in personal and family life, net of other factors in the model. The second is that only wives in type 3 couples (in which wives work in full-time nontraditional jobs) feel they are significantly better able to balance work and family roles compared to those in the reference group (type 1, both spouses working full-time traditional jobs). Surprisingly,

Table 15.3 Regression of Wives' and Husbands' Subjective Success on Couple Type[a]

	Wives' Perceived Success						Husbands' Perceived Success					
	Work		Life		Balance		Work		Life		Balance	
	b	SE	b	SE	b	SE	b	SE	b	SE	b	SE
Salary	0.001	0.00	0.00	0.00	0.00	0.00	0.00	0.00**	0.00	0.00	0.00	0.00
Age	0.259	0.96	−1.41	0.92	−0.58	1.10	−1.04	0.84	0.21	0.89	−1.794	1.31†
Age squared	0.003	0.01	0.02	0.01	0.01	0.02	0.01	0.01	−0.00	0.01	0.022	0.011*
Education	0.142	0.24	−0.54	0.23†	−0.51	0.27†	−0.31	0.21	0.19	0.23	0.333	0.267
Number of children	1.153	0.51*	0.39	0.49	1.53	0.67*	−0.34	0.49	1.44	0.53	−0.732	0.615
Control of work	0.514	0.58	0.17	0.56	−3.24	1.24***	2.60	0.64***	0.03	0.69*	3.780	0.804***
Supervisor	1.537	1.07	−0.57	1.03	0.02	0.06	0.68	1.00	−0.15	1.07	−0.839	1.25
Occupational prestige	0.141	0.05**	0.00	0.05	−0.28	0.07***	0.00	0.05	−0.03	0.06**	−0.163	0.065***
Hours worked/week	0.086	0.06	−0.17	0.06**	0.00	0.00	0.08	0.05	0.00	0.06	−0.46	0.068***
Spouse's salary	−0.017	0.02	0.00	0.00*	0.00	0.00	0.00	0.00	0.01	0.00	0.00	0.00
Spouse's age	−0.269	0.86	−0.06	0.83	1.65	0.99†	0.30	0.93	−0.31	0.00	0.856	1.16
Spouse's age squared	0.001	0.01	0.00	0.01	−0.02	0.01†	0.01	0.01	−0.25	0.01	−0.01	0.013
Spouse's education	−0.213	0.22	−0.17	0.21	−0.05	0.25	−0.06	0.23	−1.21	0.24	−0.324	0.286
Spouse's control of work	0.217	0.66	0.52	0.64	0.16	0.76	0.01	0.56	0.05	0.60	0.169	0.702
Spouse's supervisor	−1.185	1.03	0.12	0.99	0.79	1.19	0.11	0.10	0.05	1.11	−1.799	1.31
Spouse's occupational prestige	−0.111	0.05*	0.03	0.05	−0.10	0.06	0.03	0.05	−0.09	0.05	0.019	0.062
Spouse's hours worked/week	0.113	0.06*	0.03	0.05	0.04	0.06	−0.10	0.06		0.06	0.005	0.074
Couple type 2[b]	−0.202	1.90	−1.27	1.83	−0.30	2.19	0.90	1.85	0.59	1.97	−2.796	2.32
Couple type 3[b]	0.437	2.25	2.86	2.16	6.32	2.59***	2.31	2.19	2.08	2.34	−5.098	2.74†
Couple type 4[b]	1.569	1.68	−1.77	1.61	−0.45	1.93	−0.39	1.63	0.76	1.74	3.197	2.04
Couple type 5[b]	3.986	2.54	−0.87	2.44	−2.06	2.92	−4.86	2.47*	−1.32	2.64	0.19	3.09
Intercept	60.471	15.77	15.33	1.52	5.90	1.82	8.25	1.53	11.30	1.63	10.44	1.92
Adjusted R^2	0.040		0.03		0.10		0.05		0.01		0.12	

[a] *Indicates $p < .05$; **indicates $p < .01$; ***indicates $p < .001$; †indicates $p < .10$; b, unstandardized regression coefficient; SE, standard error.

[b] Couple type 1 is the reference category.

Source: *Cornell Couples and Careers Study*, 1998–99.

neither having a husband in a nontraditional job nor working reduced hours in a part-time job significantly increases perceived success in balancing.

The last six columns in table 15.3 show the regressions for husbands. Two interesting effects of couple type are suggested in this table. First, husbands in type 5 couples (in which wives work in a part-time nontraditional job) feel significantly less successful at work than those in the comparison group (type 1). This is hard to interpret because the wives in such couples could be expected to absorb the most responsibility for domestic chores. This couple-level strategy does not seem to have any effect on perceived success in personal life or in balancing work and family. However, husbands in type 3 couples (in which wives also work in nontraditional jobs, but full-time) also appear to feel less successful in balancing work and family than those in type 1 couples. It may be that the nontraditional jobs that many women hold are, in fact, less flexible (e.g., by being more unpredictable) than traditional jobs, and they affect the work and family lives of spouses.

Discussion

It is clear from this analysis that couples' employment arrangements reflect well-defined gender-based work and family roles, even at the beginning of the twenty-first century among educated middle-class couples. Departures from traditional full-time employment arrangements occur primarily among wives; a large minority of women adapt their work over their life course to accommodate increasing caretaking responsibilities at home. Husbands' employment arrangements reflect men's traditional good-provider role, which declines once the children leave home. At that time, both husbands and wives have greater role flexibility and fewer constraints by gender, and this appears to also be reflected in an increasing proportion of men in NSWAs and women in traditional employment.

Our results also indicate that there are some costs, especially for men, when couples' employment strategies diverge from a traditional male breadwinner–female homemaker template. Men in nontraditional work arrangements earn significantly less as individuals than those who work full-time in traditional arrangements. Type 2 couples (in which the husband hold a full-time nontraditional job and the wife holds a traditional full-time job) have significantly lower combined earnings than type 1 couples (in which both spouses have full-time traditional jobs). In comparison, husbands appear to achieve greater objective career success when their wives have part-time work arrangements (or else wives of successful husbands can afford to work part-time). Men in type 4 and 5 couples earn significantly more, individually, than men whose wives work full-time. The difference in the combined earnings of type 1 couples compared to those in types 4 and 5 (in which the wives works part-time) is not significant once we control for the number of hours worked, but in absolute terms, type 1 couples' earnings are higher. Hence, men may pay a price as individuals for couple-level strategies that depart from traditional gendered roles—but as part of a family unit, they may benefit. Similarly, women in NSWAs earn significantly less, all else equal, than those who work full-time traditional jobs, but, as part of a couple, they do not pay a price overall.

The effects of couple-level career strategies on subjective career outcomes are also complex. Although women in NSWAs earn less as individuals, they do not perceive themselves to be less successful at work than those who hold full-time traditional jobs. In couples in which wives work a nontraditional job (type 3), women report feeling significantly more successful at balancing work and family, compared to those in type 1 couples. We do not find the same effect for men in type 2 couples (in which the husband works a nontraditional job and the wife works a traditional job), nor do wives who work part-time feel more successful than their counterparts in type 1 couples. Moreover, we find that although wives in type 3 couples feel more successful at balancing work and family, their husbands feel less successful than those type 1 couples. Overall, however, perhaps the most notable result is the absence of strong effects of couple-level employment strategies on individuals' perceptions of success in work life, in personal life, or in balancing work and family life. This could be either because couples adopt those strategies that are best suited to their circumstances or because couples simply psychologically adapt to the arrangements in place. In either case, although use of NSWAs may entail some objective career costs for individuals, they do not necessarily entail any sort of dissatisfaction with work and family arrangements or other psychic costs.

Summing Up

The unprecedented growth of NSWAs in the last half of the twentieth century represents significant change in the workplace. Our analyses examine both the determinants and consequences of couple-level alternative arrangements, including human capital, number of children, gender attitudes, life stage, work characteristics, objective success, and subjective success of wives and husbands in the most prevalent couple-level employment arrangements. NSWAs, which offer the possibility of greater flexibility, are used primarily by women who hold more conservative gender attitudes and by men with the less conservative attitudes. Couples with the wife in part-time employment and the husband in full-time traditional employment show significantly more conservative gender-role attitudes than do couples for which this configuration is reversed. In addition, over the life course, wives show a very noticeable pattern that involves moving out of traditional full-time employment into a NSWA once children are born. The proportion of men in full-time traditional employment, on the other hand, increases as they become fathers and only diminishes once the children leave home.

We also investigate whether the use of NSWAs is related to husbands', wives', and couples' success. We find that the effect of NSWAs as an adaptive strategy for working husbands and wives can be a mixed blessing. On one hand, couples in which the husband or wife works a full-time nontraditional job earn significantly less than couples in which both spouses in work full-time traditional jobs. On the other hand, for wives, this appears to result in a greater likelihood of feeling more successful in balancing work and family responsibilities, but husbands in such couples feel less successful in their family lives. Hence, we conclude that NSWAs cannot simply be categorized as effective or ineffective strategies for managing the demands of work and family in couples in which both spouses wish to remain in the workforce. They represent an important option for working couples, but one that has both costs and benefits relative to more traditional work options. The growth in such arrangements, however, suggests that more and more couples are willing to make the trade-offs involved in choosing NSWAs as an option and that this may be an increasingly important issue for organizational recruitment in the future.

16

Moving toward Retirement

Robert M. Hutchens and Emma Dentinger

Older workers often express an interest in reducing their work hours as they approach retirement. For example, a recent national survey of working men and women between the ages of fifty-one and sixty-one found "that 73 percent would have liked to continue working part time, after retiring from full-time positions."[1] This is, of course, not entirely surprising. We might expect that a rewarding retirement would include some time devoted to paid work. Employment not only provides income, but it also permits interaction with others and opportunities to reenact work roles with skill and competence.

Perhaps more surprising than this interest in continued work is our lack of knowledge about what types of late-midlife workers want to reduce their work hours and why so few actually do. Although surveys often give summary statistics indicating that older workers would like to reduce hours, they do not investigate whether this interest varies by gender, occupation, education, or industry.[2] We know little about the role that family and work play in this expressed interest in reduced work hours. Moreover, the number of older workers who actually move from full-time to part-time work is quite small. Approximately one-fifth of older wage and salary employees move from full-time to part-time work before completely retiring from the labor force, and those who do usually change employers.[3] This is apparently because of employment constraints; employers discourage gradual retirements, whereby the worker reduces hours without changing employers. Why would an employer not offer older full-time employees the option of working part-time with a corresponding cut in pay?

We tackle these issues in this chapter, beginning with a description of the types of older workers interested in reducing their work hours as they near retirement. Although the analysis begins with individuals, it also considers interest in reducing hours within the context of couple-level data. We then examine the gradual retirement policies and practices in the seven organizations participating in *The Cornell Couples and Careers Study*. Using interviews with human resource managers in these organizations, we briefly assess why some organizations permit gradual retirement, whereas others do not.

Older Employees and Their Interest in Work-Hour Reductions

The choices workers make as they near retirement are influenced by their roles as employees and as family members and by past choices (such as educational attainment or the development of a retirement plan). The ongoing tensions between choice and constraints at this shifting gears life stage are therefore salient in this chapter, as are the themes of structural lag and adaptive strategies to help explain the various patterns in workers' interest in work-hour reduction before retirement. Constraints include the requirements of a particular job (e.g., managers usually work full-time); current choices operate chiefly through the relative assessments of work and family roles. Before turning to our own analysis, we first discuss existing theory and evidence regarding patterns of work-hour-reduction behavior among older workers.

Theories about Work-Hour-Reduction Behavior among Older Workers

Most of what we know about work-hour reductions in the United States, including the hypotheses that we discuss here, draws on empirical data in the form of interviews with workers and observed behavior. Several national surveys have followed older workers as they moved from full-time work to full-time retirement.[4] These surveys provide valuable information on when and how older workers in earlier cohorts actually reduced hours.

A major goal of this existing research has been to measure how often older workers reduce their hours in anticipation of retirement. The usual conclusion is that, for workers retiring in the 1970s, the great majority of full-time workers moved to full-time retirement without an intervening part-time job. Those few who moved to part-time work tended to change employers.[5] The self-employed provide an interesting exception to this; they are much more likely to become part-time workers in their career jobs. Scholars explain this behavior with two hypotheses. The first is that career jobs often have a minimum hours constraint,[6] meaning that for workers to retain their jobs they must work a minimum number of hours. Although this affects workers of all ages (see also Clarkberg and Moen 2001; Clarkberg and Merola, chap. 3 in this volume), it may be of particular importance to older workers who wish to devote less time to work, perhaps due to health concerns or a desire to spend more time with friends and family. A minimum hours constraint, however, prevents this; workers who want to reduce their hours must either move to a new job or take full retirement. This also explains why self-employed men behave so differently from their wage and salary counterparts. The self-employed do not face a minimum hours constraint; they are free to choose the amount of time they spend on the job.[7]

The second explanation for these results focuses on pensions.[8] Private pensions can be structured so as to discourage part-time work in the career job. For example, some private pensions base a retired person's pension benefits on earnings during the final year or years prior to retirement. A person who chooses to work half-time at half-pay before retiring, therefore, loses as much as one-half of all future pension benefits. In such a system, a 10 percent decrease in earning can translate into a lifetime loss of approximately 150 percent of annual earnings.[9] Also, some pensions are structured in ways that encourage workers to retire at specific ages or tenure.[10] In such plans, full-time workers who delay retirement past the specified point (e.g., thirty years of job tenure) will actually have lower lifetime pension benefits. This could cause people to retire from their career jobs, take their pensions, and either drop out of the labor force or go to work for a different employer. The self-employed, again, do not behave this way because they are not subject to the types of pension plans that cover wage and salary workers.

Of course, both hypotheses could be correct. Employers with minimum hours constraints could also offer pensions that discourage part-time work. Alternatively, some jobs may have minimum hours constraints and others may have pensions that discourage part-time work. For the present, we simply view both as interesting alternative hypotheses about older workers' behavior.

Interest in Hour Reductions among Older Workers: *The Cornell Couples and Careers Study*

Several surveys have asked older workers about their work-hour preferences. The respondents often indicate an interest in moving to less stressful jobs. For example, a 1989 Harris poll found that "more than half of all workers age 50 to 64 would continue working if their employer were willing to retrain them for a new job, continue making pension contributions after age 65, or transfer them to a job with less responsibility, fewer hours, and less pay as a transition to full retirement."[11] To examine this issue, *The Cornell Couples and Careers Study* not only looks at who among married, middle-class, full-time workers is interested in a reduced schedule, but also examines relevant employer policies and practices.

There are several reasons to study such data. As people live longer, more will want or need to work longer, and employers will have to respond to this trend. In fact, the absence of such opportunities may be an example of structural lag, whereby institutions do not adjust to changing demands. To anticipate and respond to such changing demands, the institutions must know what is causing the change. Moreover, knowledge about employees' interest in work-hour reduction could help employers implement programs that are more appropriately tailored to worker needs.

Therefore, our analysis focuses on full-time workers (working thirty-five hours or more) who are expecting to retire within the next ten years from each of the seven organizations in the Cornell study. We ask three questions: How much interest is there in working reduced hours before retirement? Who is interested in working reduced hours before retirement? What predicts interest in working reduced hours before retirement?

The dependent variable in our analysis comes from the question "On a scale of 0 to 100 where 0 equals no interest and 100 equals maximum interest, how interested are you in working a reduced schedule before you retire?" We restrict our sample to respondents expecting to retire in the next decade who currently work for one of the seven companies, as well as the small number (thirty-five) of spouses also working for them. After eliminating self-employed and part-time workers, we have data for 264 respondents, 181 men and 83 women in middle-class two-earner households, 94 percent of whom are white.

Compared to the total 1998–99 Cornell study sample, our sample is older. It includes the World War II generation (born between 1923 and 1945) and the baby boom generation (born between 1946 and 1964) and excludes younger respondents. The women in our subsample, all full-time workers, put in slightly more hours on the job (on average) than do women in the total sample, some of whom work part-time (thirty-nine official hours versus thirty-six, and forty-eight actual hours versus forty-two). Otherwise, our sample is comparable to the larger one. We answer our first two research questions with simple descriptive statistics and contingency tables.

How Much Interest Is There in Working Reduced Hours before Retirement? One reason why older workers may not reduce hours is that they have little interest in doing so. Overall, we find that over one-half (52%) of our sample express more than passing interest (defined as 50–100 on a 0–100 scale) and 48 percent express little or no interest (less than 50 on a 0–100 scale). Thirty percent express absolutely no interest (0) and 16% express highest interest (100). The average level of interest is 39 for men and 56 for women (44 combined).

This is comparable to the 1989 Harris poll and somewhat lower than the 73 percent cited at the beginning of the chapter. Note, however, that our sample is slightly younger than in prior surveys and that our sample was given the opportunity to gauge their level of interest on a 0–100 scale.[12]

Who Is Interested in Working Reduced Hours before Retirement? In table 16.1, we divide interest in working a reduced schedule into three categories.[12] The Medium category represents the average amount of interest, by gender; the Low and High categories represent lower and higher than average interest, based on reports 1 standard deviation or more away from the average.

Overall, more women than men are interested in reducing their paid work hours before retirement. Almost one-half of the women but only one in five men

Table 16.1 Older Workers' Interest in Reduced Hours before Retirement[a]

	Women				Men			
	Low	Medium	High	Total N	Low	Medium	High	Total N
Children at home	22.2%	50.0%	27.8%	18	34.4%	42.6%	23.0%	61
Adult children left	34.4%	37.5%	28.1%	32	35.4%	46.2%	18.5%	65
Adult children home	36.4%	36.4%	27.3%	11	35.9%	43.6%	20.5%	39
No children	27.3%	45.5%	27.3%	22	18.8%	56.3%	25.0%	16
High school, less	50.0%	20.0%	30.0%	20	55.0%	40.0%	5.0%	20
Associate's degree	27.3%	45.5%	27.3%	11	40.0%	46.7%	13.3%	30
Bachelor's degree	19.0%	38.1%	42.9%	21	32.3%	38.7%	29.0%	62
Master's Degree	21.7%	65.2%	13.0%	23	30.8%	51.3%	17.9%	39
Professional degree	37.5%	37.5%	25.0%	8	20.0%	53.3%	26.7%	30
Retired spouse	46.2%	46.2%	7.7%	13	40.0%	40.0%	20.0%	5
Managers	36.7%	40.0%	23.3%	30	45.3%*	37.5%*	17.2%*	64
Professionals	27.6%	44.8%	27.6%	29	22.1%*	48.1%*	29.9%*	77
Tech., Sales, Administration	18.8%	37.5%	43.8%	16	29.2%	54.2%	16.7%	24
All others	37.5%	50.0%	12.5%	8	50.0%*	50.0%*	00.0%	16
Vantech	31.6%	47.4%	21.1%	19	35.4%	41.6%	23.0%	113
Transco	—	—	—	2[b]	36.4%	45.5%	18.2%	11
Utilco	33.3%	16.7%	50.0%	6	50.0%	40.0%	10.0%	20
Valley View	87.5%**	12.5%**	00.0%	8	—	—	—	3[b]
Citizen's Health	—	—	—	1[b]	—	—	—	2[b]
Upstate U	20.0%	48.6%	31.4%	35	13.0%[†]	65.2%[†]	21.7%[†]	23
Lake U	25.0%	50.0%	25.0%	12	22.2%	55.6%	22.2%	9
Overall Interest	26.5%	31.3%	42.2%	83	33.7%	45.3%	21.0%	181

[a]Subsample from the *Cornell Couples and Careers Study*, 1998–99. Low, medium, and high categories were created from the mean ± 1 standard deviation, separately by gender. Rows sum to 100%. Sample includes married/partnered full-time workers from seven companies expecting to retire in the next ten years. Chi square tests within gender: [†]indicates $p \leq .10$; *indicates $p \leq .05$; **indicates $p \leq .01$.

[b]Low numbers.

report higher than average interest.[13] Conversely, approximately one-quarter of the women and one-third of the men report lower than average interest. This difference is substantial enough that throughout the chapter, we report results separately for women and men; this illustrates the complexity of the issue.

Simple percentages by parenting stage, spouse retirement status, professional degree, company, and occupational status highlight differences in this sample of respondents who expect to retire over the next ten years. Particularly noteworthy is that women with young children and men without children appear to be most interested in work-hour reduction. Also, having a retired spouse matters for women but not for men,[14] and professional status relates to lower interest among women and higher interest among men. Consistent across gender, managers and Other occupations report less interest; workers at Valley View Medical are less interested, whereas workers at Upstate Utility are more interested.

What Predicts Interest in Working Reduced Hours before Retirement?
To answer this question, we develop linear regression models predicting interest in working a reduced schedule prior to retirement among workers (as a 0–100 scale). Models are estimated with and without James Heckman's corrections for selection into the sample.[15] Men and women are modeled separately because our initial analyses suggest rather substantial gender differences. We use a multilevel approach, beginning with individual-level factors and then sequentially adding in job-level variables, organization-level variables, and variables that indicate perceived success in balancing work and family.

Both the sociological and economic literatures emphasize that labor supply depends on the characteristics of individuals, and that should apply to the present problem. We expect the situation at home to matter. For example, having a child at home may influence an individual's preference for reduced hours, although the direction of influence is not clear.[16] Education should also play a role. We know that more educated workers tend to retire at later ages. It is reasonable to hypothesize that they will also tend to prefer a retirement that mixes work with leisure. Workers with pensions are often discouraged from reducing their hours before retirement because their pension might lose or lower its value. This may therefore reduce their interest in reduced hours when questioned.[17] Finally, because our dependent variable is attitudinal, we include a measure of negative affect at the time of the survey-data collection; subjective attitudes and preferences may be affected at a particular time by depressive feelings, which we want to control for.[18]

Note that a worker's age is not used to explain interest in reduced hours. Because respondents were only asked about their interest in reduced hours if they intended to retire within ten years, age plays a fundamental role in sample selection. For statistical reasons, age is used to test for selection bias, but is not used to explain a respondent's interest in reduced hours.[19]

Table 16.2 Married Women's Interest in Working Reduced Hours before Retirement[a]

Independent Variables	Model 1[b]	Model 2	Model 3	Model 4	Model 5
Worker characteristics					
Young kids	−7.09	−12.25	−19.73	−23.19[†]	−24.48[†]
Adult kids left	−11.80	−11.68	−11.63	−15.07	−16.13
Adult kids home	−8.38	−11.90	−20.46	−28.79[†]	−29.39*
No children	(ref)	(ref)	(ref)	(ref)	(ref)
Profesional degree	−15.64	−8.09	−4.23	−8.96	−8.78
Pension plan	11.29	9.59	11.79	14.65	16.25
log (household income)	32.97**	24.95[†]	25.85[†]	28.76*	30.80*
Negative affect	24.06[†]	18.64	20.66	18.82	22.35[†]
Spouse characteristics					
Intends to retire soon		−17.04*	−21.43*	−17.51*	−21.37[†]
Retired		−36.51**	−40.64**	−36.07**	−39.41**
Profesional or manager		19.72*	18.82	14.91	16.54
Pension plan		4.49	5.23	2.45	1.91
Job constraints					
Job tenure			−0.99[†]	−1.37**	−1.36*
Managers			−15.15	−8.84	−13.51
Company constraint					
"No"				(ref)	(ref)
"Maybe"				20.06*	18.17*
"Yes"				60.35*	58.55*
Work/family assessments					
Work success					0.43
Family success					−0.15
Balancing success					0.08
Adjusted R^2	0.049	0.113	0.159	0.235	0.212
Model significance (df)	0.147 (7)	0.047 (11)	0.019 (13)	0.003 (15)	0.010 (18)

[a] Subsample from the *Cornell Couples and Careers Study*, 1998–99. Of those expecting to retire in the next ten years, $N = 83$. [†] indicates $p \leq .10$; * indicates $p \leq .05$; ** indicates $p \leq .01$. Numbers in table are b, the unstandardized regression coefficient.

[b] Model not significant at $p = .10$ level.

Model 1 in tables 16.2 and 16.3 examines these relationships for women and men in our sample. In general, worker characteristics influence men's interest in working a reduced schedule before retirement, whereas household factors are more of an influence on women's interest.[20] The ages and circumstances of children do not influence interest in work-hour reduction before retirement in model 1, but we can look ahead to models 4 and 5 in table 16.2 and see the effect of dependent children: young children and adult children still living at home have a strong negative effect on women's interest compared to childless women. For men, the added education of a professional degree (PhD, MBA,

Table 16.3   Married Men's Interest in Working Reduced Hours before Retirement[a]

Independent Variables	Model 1	Model 2[b]	Model 3	Model 4[b]	Model 5
Worker characteristics					
Young kids	−2.96	−0.12	2.85	2.82	1.11
Adult kids left	−6.63	−5.15	−2.92	−2.84	−1.74
Adult kids home	−9.51	−9.44	−4.97	−4.95	−6.00
No children	(ref)	(ref)	(ref)	(ref)	(ref)
Profesional degree	16.57*	16.17*	17.32*	17.64*	19.54*
Pension plan	−9.93	−10.24	−11.63	−11.62	−10.95
log (household income)	2.98	4.01	8.90	8.62	8.67
Negative affect	15.39*	16.40*	17.53*	17.87*	13.38
Spouse characteristics					
Intends to retire soon		6.88	6.86	6.88	6.35
Retired		−6.92	−9.07	−9.30	−9.55
Not employed		6.04	5.62	5.31	3.72
Profesional or manager		1.30	0.09	0.24	−0.14
Pension plan		−2.54	−1.30	−1.40	−2.40
Job constraints					
Job tenure			0.37	0.37	0.51
Managers			−13.30*	−13.20*	−13.00*
Company constraint					
"No"				(ref)	(ref)
"Maybe"				−1.14	−0.11
"Yes"				0.84	−2.49
Work/family integration					
Work success					−0.09
Family success					0.23
Balancing success					−0.48*
Adjusted R^2	0.034	0.019	0.050	0.039	0.056
Model significance (df)	0.072 (7)	0.228 (12)	0.065 (14)	0.124 (16)	0.073 (19)

[a] Subsample from the *Cornell Couples and Careers Study* 1998–99. Of those expecting to retire in the next ten years, $N = 181$. * Indicates $p \leq .05$.
[b] Model not significant at $p = .10$ level.

etc.) is associated with greater interest in working a reduced schedule before retirement.

These differences between men and women are quite striking. They are consistent with the claim that men and women approach time allocation between work and home in very different ways. They are also consistent with a broader literature that finds distinct differences in the determinants of retirement behavior for men and women.[21] Note, however, that for both men and women, depressive feelings at the time of the survey appear also to be positively related to saying that reducing hours before retirement would be a good idea—a change of circumstance would be welcome.

Model 2 in tables 16.2 and 16.3 takes into account spousal characteristics, with equally significant gendered results. Here we measure whether spouses intend to retire within ten years, whether they are already retired, their occupational status, and whether they have and use a company-sponsored pension plan. None of these spousal characteristics affect men's interest in reduced work hours. Retirement intentions, behavior, and occupational status of spouses and partners, however, are significantly related to women's interest. Specifically, having a retired husband or a husband who intends to retire within ten years reduces wives' interest in working part-time before retirement.[22] Conversely, having a working professional or managerial husband increase wives' interest in moving into part-time work. Whether their wives have pension plans, which would contribute to the retirement well-being of both members of couples, has a small negative effect on interest for men and a small positive effect for women, but is not statistically significant in either case.

Jobs can impose concrete constraints that influence a worker's interest in reduced hours. Managerial status and years of job tenure are likely to be associated with such constraints. Employers may require full-time managers and may be more likely to offer part-time work to more senior workers. Such employer policies could influence a worker's interest in reduced hours. Model 3 in tables 16.2 and 16.3 examines the effects of employer-imposed job constraints. Job tenure here represents years on the job and therefore a positive coefficient indicates that the longer the time spent on the job, the more interest there is in reduced work hours due to employer-sanctioned autonomy of choice. This is indeed the case for men, although not statistically significant; for women, the longer the time on the job, the less interest there is in reduced work hours. Male managers are less likely to express interest in reduced work hours; results for female managers are statistically insignificant.

In models 4 and 5, we test two unique hypotheses whose examination is possible due to the nature of the design of *The Cornell Couples and Careers Study*. Because we have corresponding data on specific employers, model 4 addresses whether there are direct company effects due to employer flexibility in granting gradual retirements to employees. The categories "No" (no gradual retirements), "Maybe" (varying flexibility), and "Yes" (allows gradual retirements) are derived from analyzing the human resource manager interviews in the 1998–99 Cornell study. We see that these distinctions matter for women but not for men, after controlling for worker and job-related factors. Women working at companies that offer greater flexibility are more likely than women at inflexible companies to express interest in reducing their preretirement hours.

Model 5 takes into account subjective assessments of work and family roles. According to the literature on work-family issues,[23] how workers evaluate their current work and family-life domains individually and collectively can influence future work behavior. Work Success is an attitudinal assessment of feelings of work success; Family Success is an attitudinal assessment of feelings of family or personal-life success. Balancing Success refers to feelings of success in work and family role integration. We expect that when respondents feel successful in a role, they will want to spend more time in that role; for example, high work-role success will lead to less of an interest in reduced hours. We also expect that success in balancing work and family roles will lead to a desire to keep the current situation as it is, implying less interest in reduced work hours. Surprisingly, these measures are not significant for women in our sample. The balance of work and family is, however, significant for men; feelings of joint work and family success discourage men in our sample from reducing work hours.

Couple Interest in Work-Hour Reductions for Older Workers

In line with this volume's focus on linked lives, we now turn our attention to examining these same workers as members of couples to clarify some of what we learned from the regression models. A couple-level analysis can inform our understanding of the future retirement timing some couples will face and the joint adaptive strategies[24] that they may employ regarding reduced hours. To do so, we employ descriptive statistics based on typologies we create of couples' interest in reduced work hours. The typologies are: both spouses have higher interest and both spouses have lower interest (the congruent-interest couples); husband has higher interest but wife has lower interest and wife has higher interest but husband has lower interest (the discongruent couples; see table 16.4).[25] Approximately two-thirds of the spouses (104) reported that they also intend to retire within ten years and were then asked about their level of interest in working a reduced schedule before retirement. The one-third of spouses who did not report an intention to retire within ten years despite their partners' interest in doing so tended to be younger wives.[26]

Complete information is available for the 104 couples who both intend to retire within the next ten years, which we examine here. Overall, we find similar-size groups of couples except that fewer couples fall into the group in which the husband has higher interest but the wife has lower interest. Looking at the data in table 16.4, we can confirm that wives are more interested in reduced hours than are their husbands.

Couples in which both spouses report higher interest in working reduced hours also report the greatest age difference between spouses; in contrast, couples with both spouses reporting lower interest also report the smallest age difference. This suggests that the similar-age couples in this subsample, who will be eligible for Social Security and pension benefits roughly at the same time, wish to retire completely, whereas the couples who differ in age may prefer to reduce their work

Table 16.4 Couple Typologies for Interest in Working Reduced Hours before Retirement Selected Characteristics[a]

	Congruent Interests		Discongruent Interests	
	Both Higher Interest	Both Lower Interest	Husband Higher/ Wife Lower	Wife Higher/ Husband Lower
Number of couples	31	29	15	29
Average age difference (years)	3.97	2.10	2.47	3.41
Average joint work success	88	90	90	84
Average joint family success	82	82	85	81
Average joint balancing success	78	82	82	82
Median household income	$125,000	$90,000	$95,250	$105,000

[a] Subsample from the *Cornell Couples and Careers Study*, 1998–99. Of those expecting to retire in the next ten years, $N = 104$. Lower Interest equals 0–49 on a 0–100 scale; Higher Interest equals 50–100 on a 0–100 scale. Success scores are based on a 0–100 scale.

hours as a strategy to experience leisure together because they otherwise would not be able to collect full retirement benefits together. When the wife reports a higher interest in reduced hours, she and her husband are likely to be further apart in age than when the husband is the one who reports higher interest in reduced hours. This finding suggests that wives consider a future reduction in work hours as a strategy to spend time with their retired (older) husbands before their own full retirement. It is important to keep in mind that we only know this occurs when wives report that they intend to retire within ten years.

As noted earlier, taking a reduced work-hour schedule before retirement is possible only if the (presumably) accompanying reduction in salary and possibly benefits will not be a hardship to the couple. We see, looking at the median household incomes for each couple typology, that this is in fact represented in our data: couples that both report higher interest in working a reduced schedule also report the highest household income, and couples that both report lower interest in working a reduced schedule also report the lowest household incomes.[27]

Among the couples with congruent interests in working reduced hours before retirement, couples in which both members report higher interest also report slightly less joint perceptions of success in their work roles (see our regression models, as well as concept measurement in app.) than the couples in which both spouses report lower interest, although both reports are high in general. This finding is not surprising; couples who feel relatively successful at work do not want to reduce their work hours. In terms of work-family integration, couples who report higher interest also report lower perceived success levels in integrating work and family roles, suggesting that only those who are unsatisfied with their current work-family integration want to change things by reducing their work hours before retirement. We speculate, given our regression results in the previous section of this chapter, that husbands are fueling these couple findings.

Employer Policies toward Work Hour Reductions by Older Workers

Whereas several national studies mirror our findings that older workers are often interested in reduced hours, only a handful of studies examine employer responses.[28] To some extent, these studies compound the puzzle of why gradual retirement is so rare. For example, Kathleen Christensen reports that 90 percent of 521 large companies offered regular part-time work and 22 percent offered job sharing. Yet gradual retirement was only available in 9 percent of the firms. In most cases gradual retirement took the form of an informal arrangement offered to professional and managerial workers.[29] Why is that? Are the arrangements kept informal so that employers can be selective about who takes gradual retirement and who does not? Why does the policy tend to be focused on professionals and managers as opposed to, say, clericals and salesworkers?

Gradual Retirement in the Seven Organizations

The Cornell Couples and Careers Study permits a new assessment of how employers react to older worker interest in reduced hours. In a study of gradual retirement in our seven organizations, we address two questions. First, does the organization permit some form of work-hour reduction for older workers? Second, do organizations with family-friendly human resource policies tend to permit work-hour reductions by older workers?

In each of the seven organizations, a trained interviewer went through a questionnaire with a benefits manager (a manager in charge of administering employee benefits).[30]

The Questionnaire

At the beginning of the interview, the interviewer asked the manager to list the first names of three full-time employees who were age fifty-four or above.[31] The interviewer then selected one of the three, and the subsequent interview focused on that person. For example, the interviewer asked about the person's job title, how long the person had worked for the organization, and the manager's assessment of the person's job performance. The interviewer then posed the following question: "Suppose that on his/her next birthday, (NAME) came to you and said he/she was thinking about retiring, but would like to try retirement by working two days a week for the next two years. After two years he/she would fully retire. Could this be worked out in a way that would be acceptable to you and your organization?" If the answer was "Yes," further questions probed salary, benefits, and whether employees had actually done something like this in the past two years.

We also asked about the possibility of "retire and rehire." In informal conversations with managers and older workers—conversations that preceded the development of the questionnaire—we learned of people who had formally retired from the organization and then returned to work part-time (retire-rehire option). These part-timers often received their preretirement wage rate, collected pension benefits, and were covered by the retiree health plan. Of course, this is quite close to gradual retirement. The only real difference is that the worker is classified as a "retiree" and no longer has the rights and obligations of a "regular" employee.

Results

Of the seven organizations in the interviews, two were quite clear in prohibiting gradual retirement, two were equally clear in allowing gradual retirement, and the other three stood in between. The major surprise was that all seven permitted the retire-rehire option and that, in several of the organizations, older employees were taking advantage of that option. Summaries for two of the organizations give the flavor of the interviews.

Vantech: An Unambiguous "No" Vantech is a large manufacturing firm that is in the midst of reducing its labor force by at least 20 percent. It is currently using financial incentives to encourage early retirement. The firm's formal policies prohibit gradual retirement. A full-time worker is expected to either remain full-time or take full retirement. Although employees can retire and then return to the firm as a contract worker, the organization places a major restriction on this—the rehire option is only permitted when a retiree has been away from the firm at least one year.

Our questions about gradual retirement uncovered no informal mechanism for getting around these restrictions. The interview focused on Sandy, a fifty-five-year-old college-educated human resource generalist who has been with the organization for more than twenty years. In general, the manager has high regard for Sandy's work. Moreover, one-third of the people in Sandy's job title are employed as part-time workers. As such, this would appear to be an ideal situation for gradual retirement; there are already part-timers in this job classification, and Sandy is a valued worker.

Yet, when we asked about the possibility of Sandy taking gradual retirement, the answer was a clear and unambiguous "No." The manager we interviewed said that the firm does not offer gradual retirement because of legal issues that could arise with respect to benefits under the firm's defined benefit pension plan.[32]

Citizen's Health: An Unambiguous "Yes"   Citizen's Health is a health-care organization that is neither expanding nor contracting. Workers are covered by a defined benefit pension, but can also choose to participate in a defined contribution plan. Not only do its formal policies explicitly permit preretirement reductions in hours, but some older full-time employees have recently shifted to part-time.

Our interview focused on Jean, a fifty-five-year-old training assistant who has worked for more than ten years with the firm and earns less than $20,000 per year. Although Jean works full-time, 25 percent of others with her job title work part time. The manager we interviewed was only "somewhat satisfied" with Jean's performance compared to that of other employees with the same job title. Moreover, the manager indicated that if Jean were to leave this job, it would not be at all difficult to find a qualified replacement. Thus, although Jean is in a job in which partial retirement should be quite feasible, she may not be the kind of worker that the employer wishes to retain.

However, when we asked whether Jean could take a partial retirement and work two days per week, the answer was an unambiguous "Yes." She would receive 40 percent of her current salary, pay more for health insurance, and her vacation time would be reduced to four days per year. Moreover, the firm would cease making pension contributions because "she would not be eligible. The pension requires 1,000 hours within a calendar year."

An Assessment of Gradual Retirement in the Seven Organizations   The interviews with the seven organizations provide tentative answers to our initial two questions. Although we cannot generalize from seven observations, they provide interesting insights into the ways that employers approach work-hour reductions by older workers.

Does the organization permit some form of work hour reduction for older workers? Each organization has a different answer to this question. Some organizations strictly enforce formal policies against gradual retirement; others have similar formal policies, but permit informal ways around them; and still others embrace gradual retirement and currently employ partially retired workers.

One of the most intriguing findings concerned the retire-rehire option. All seven organizations permit some form of this. Again, however, policies differ across the organizations. Vantech only allows a rehire after one year of retirement. The other six organizations permit a rehire immediately after retirement, but are evidently quite selective about it. For example, although Transco would rehire a retiree for two days per week, the manager noted that the "rehiring of retired employees is very limited. It's only done if the person has a unique skill, say the design of a new product." We asked whether this has actually occurred in the last two years, the response was "It's been very limited—about a half dozen. They tend to be the technical, the engineer-type person."

Do organizations with family-friendly human resource policies tend to permit work-hour reductions by older workers? In our small sample, the answer is "No." Vantech is the most family-friendly in its human resource policies, but the least flexible about work-hour reductions by older workers. Citizen's Health is the least family-friendly, but appears to be quite comfortable with workers of any age shifting from full-time to part-time. The remaining organizations have a few family-friendly policies, but fewer than Vantech. These same organizations usually responded with a "Maybe" to our questions about work-hour reductions by older workers.

Summing Up

National data indicate that many older workers are interested in reducing their hours of work as they approach retirement. Data from the 1998–99 Cornell study are consistent with this: more than one-half of the people who plan to retire in the next ten years are interested in reducing their hours of work before retirement. We wanted to know if workers are influenced by their employers' policies (we know they are generally because of different-employer "bridge" jobs and retire-rehire option behavior) or by their own work and family circumstances. Our analyses support both explanations. Workers' interest in reducing hours prior to retirement appears to reflect choices and constraints set by their employers as well as their own work and family-role experiences.

Perhaps our most important finding is that perceived work-family integration predicts men's interest in reduced work hours. Men who feel relatively unsuccessful in integrating their work and family roles are more likely to want to reduce their work hours before retirement. Interestingly, that is not the case for women. One possible explanation is that women who feel unsuccessful in integrating work and family are less likely, in our sample, to be full-time workers. Those who feel that way are already working part time or not working at all.

Such considerations make us cautious about our second main finding: full-time male and female workers nearing retirement are very different when it comes to interest in reduced work hours. Not only are women more interested in reduced work hours, but several variables that influence women's interest have little effect on men, such as job tenure, family members at home, family income, and company policies toward gradual retirement. These gender differences may be due to differences in the ways that men and women think about and manage work and family. At this point, however, that is speculation; we do not have a coherent and convincing story to explain why the male and female results are so different.

We might expect organizations to offer opportunities for gradual retirement in response to workers' expressed interest in reduced work hours. National data indicate that this is not the case; gradual retirement is rare in the United States. This is reflected in the seven organizations examined here. Although two of the organizations embrace gradual retirement, the others either prohibit it or only permit it under restricted conditions. Although we cannot draw strong conclusions on the basis of seven observations, it appears that this inflexibility has little to do with family-friendly policies.

This inflexibility regarding gradual retirement stands in sharp contrast to the retire-rehire option. All seven organizations permit selected workers to retire and then come back as rehires. Although this changes workers' benefits, workers may be able to renegotiate wages to compensate for the lost benefits. There is an air of "anything goes" in the retire-rehire option.

Why would employers be open to negotiated retire-rehires and reticent about similar gradual retirements? After all, both situations involve an older worker shifting from full-time to part-time work. What is the advantage of retire-rehire? Although we can only speculate, two explanations seem especially plausible. First, perhaps because of minimum hours constraints, some employers may be selective in offering part-time work to older workers. A large number of part-time older workers may not easily fit into an organization that is built on full-time employees who have made long-term commitments to the firm. Rather, the organization may prefer to select specific older workers under a policy of retire-rehire.

Second, some employers may use the retire-rehire option to avoid costly ambiguity. In retire-rehire, the worker has officially retired, pension benefits are clearly established, and the duration of the rehire is quite possibly limited. In contrast, because it is a modification of an existing employment arrangement, gradual retirement could lead to questions (and even lawsuits) over pensions and terminations. We are left with the impression that the retire-rehire option offers the employer all the benefits of gradual retirement with few of the difficulties.

As the baby boom generation approaches retirement and more older valued employees express an interest in reduced work hours, it is likely that employers will respond with more flexible work opportunities. Some firms may have little problem with this. They make heavy use of part-time workers and can accommodate older workers who wish to move from full-time to part-time work. Others may wish to maintain workforces that are built around full-time workers. Their response could quite possibly take the form of increased use of retire-rehire.

17

The Case of Same-Sex Couples

Steven E. Mock and Steve W. Cornelius

Regardless of sexual orientation, couples share many common experiences; yet same-sex couples often forge new roles and strategies for family and careers without well-established systems of social support or well-defined social norms. Same-sex relationships are enduring despite a cultural climate of hostility or ambivalence toward them and a lack of legislation or public policies that legitimize them within existing social structures.

Studying same-sex couples is important to understand diversity among couples and families as they face the challenges of family and work in modern life. Despite the growing visibility of same-sex couples in contemporary society, we know little about their family and work experiences. For example, a 1995 review[1] of the major family research journals found only twelve of the 8,000 articles (0.15%) published between 1980 and 1993 directly related to gay or lesbian issues, and few of these addressed family or work. National probability survey data suggest that between 7 and 15 million Americans have exclusive same-sex attractions. With typical extended families, at least 50 million Americans are probably either same-sex attracted or have a family member who is.[2] This estimate underscores the serious inadequacy of our knowledge at this time.

The Cornell Couples and Careers Study provides a unique opportunity to explore same-sex couples, their relationships, and their work lives. Our study includes same-sex-attracted participants who were recruited through their work-

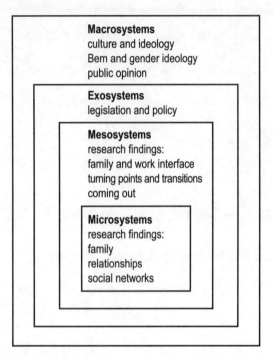

Figure 17.1 Bioecological model: the planes of proximal processes.

place, unlike many other studies which use samples of convenience (e.g., participants recruited through support groups of gay and lesbian community groups)
and therefore have many limitations. Moreover, in contrast to much research that
examines individuals with same-sex preferences, we interviewed both members
of same-sex couples.

We use the bioecological model of human development proposed by Urie
Bronfenbrenner[3] (see Moen, chap. 1 in this volume) as a conceptual framework
to guide our analyses and organize our results. The bioecological model provides
a framework to analyze the interdependent and dynamic interface among the individual, family, career, and sociocultural environment on the micro-, meso-, and
macrolevels. The preliminary findings presented in this chapter are organized in
the structure of this model, in what Bronfenbrenner describes as research in the
discovery mode[4]—the stage of research that develops hypotheses that warrant
further empirical testing. Macrosystems and exosystems are discussed in terms
of culture, public opinion and legislation (see figure 17.1). We present our results
from the Cornell study as mesosystems and microsystems, along with a discussion of relevant previous research.

Macrosystems

Adults in same-sex partnerships face several challenges at the interpersonal, institutional, legislative, and policy levels in the face of pervasive cultural and ideological messages. Stigmatization, intolerance, and lack of recognition are some of the macrolevel themes that affect same-sex-attracted adults, as does legislation at the state and federal levels.

Culture and Ideology

What is the basis of our culture's aversion to same-sex relationships? According to noted gender researcher Sandra Bem, as members of Western culture we acquire through socialization three lenses that shape our view of men and women: androcentrism, gender polarization, and biological essentialism.[5] Androcentrism is the assumption that the male experience is the norm of human experience. Gender polarization manifests itself in rigid and opposing gender roles and includes a devaluation of the female or feminine and anything that is a threat to masculinity and gender norms. Biological essentialism is the argument that supports androcentrism and gender polarization; it is the belief that the differences between men and women, including social and cultural differences, are biologically based and are thus natural and undeniable. Homosexuality represents a threat to all three ideologies in a culture that enforces compulsory heterosexuality. Bem says that Sigmund Freud believed that homosexuality and heterosexuality were essentially two variations stemming from the same original instinct and that he never viewed homosexuality as a form of mental illness or neurosis. However, several psychoanalysts after Freud pathologized homosexuality, although in 1973 it was finally removed from the *Diagnostic and Statistical Manual* of the American Psychiatric Association as a form of mental disease. The discord within the psychoanalytic community regarding homosexuality parallels that found among the general public.

Public Opinion

Although public support for the equal rights of gays and lesbians grows, public disapproval of homosexuality on moral and ideological grounds abounds. Alan Yang, a political scientist at Columbia University, integrates several major national public opinion surveys to present a picture of the historical changes and continuities in attitudes toward gays and lesbians.[6] Support for equal rights in employment rose from 56 percent in 1977 to 83 percent in 1999. Public opinion regarding gays in the military has grown from 51 percent in 1977 to 70 percent in 1999. However, public attitudes about the acceptability of homosexuality on moral or ideological grounds remains stable and evenly divided. Whether in 1977 or 1999, roughly 50 percent of survey respondents say that homosexuality is morally wrong. Disapproval of sexual relations between adults was measured at 70 percent in 1977 and rose to a high of 75 percent in 1985; it has dropped during the 1990s to 58 percent saying that sexual relations between two adults are "always wrong."

Public opinion regarding spousal benefits and marriage is less clear. In 1999, roughly 55 believe that same-sex spouses should be entitled to Social Security benefits and inheritance rights. However, in survey results from 1998, only 30 percent believed that marriages between same-sex adults should be legally sanctioned. Yet these polls show that Americans increasingly believe that same-sex-attracted adults are entitled to equal rights and fairness in policy, legislation, and the workplace. Same-sex couples have to balance moral censure with intellectual acceptance. This cultural climate might predict both sameness and differences between same-sex and opposite-sex couples—ideological messages that same-sex relationships are wrong, yet a growing body of policy and legislation that supports same-sex partners.

Exosystems

In the exosystem, an individual has no direct influence, but the system exerts influence on that individual's life. Examples of exosystems are workplace policies and local and higher-level laws that affect individuals and couples.

Public Policy and Legislation

According to a review of state and municipal laws of the United States,[7] only eleven states and the District of Columbia prohibit by law discrimination on the basis of sexual orientation in private business; eighteen states and the District of Columbia protect public employees from discrimination based on sexual orientation; and nine states and the District of Columbia protect citizens against discrimination in public housing on the basis of sexual orientation. At the time of the publication of the review, New York state was one of those states, with legislation protecting only public employees. Thus, for the same-sex dual-income couples in *The Cornell Couples and Careers Study*, only state employees are protected by state law; the rest rely on the policies of their individual workplaces for protection from discrimination at work. New York state is one of seven American states that offers domestic-partner benefits to state employees along with a growing number of private companies. Vermont stands alone as the only state with legislation that fully recognizes the domestic partnerships of same-sex couples, although it stops short of the word marriage and uses the term "civil union" instead. This lack of universal equality for same-sex couples at the state and national level has both practical and symbolic implications. The lack of domestic-partner benefits, adoption rights, child custody, protection from employment discrimination, and surviving partner Social Security benefits puts same-sex couples and their families at a significant disadvantage when compared with married couples. Symbolically, it tells same-sex-attracted adults that their relationships are less valid than opposite-sex relationships.

Public Opinion, Policy, and the Lives of Same-Sex-Attracted Adults

Public opinion surveys reveal two qualitatively different aspects of the cultural climate that same-sex couples live in. On the one hand, a growing percentage of the public endorses equal rights for gays and lesbians, but the more moral or emotional the issue in question is, the more contentious it is. For example, regarding partner benefits, employment protection, and protection from housing discrimination, approximately 70 percent of Americans support the rights of same-sex attracted people. However, when asked about the morality of homosexuality, 50 percent believe homosexuality is wrong, only 36 percent support gays and lesbians being able to adopt, and approval rates drop to approximately 30 percent for same-sex marriage. These results indicate a cultural climate that endorses equality and fairness on a sliding scale for same-sex couples; the more the issue is linked to morality, personal values, or ideology, the less people endorse equality for same-sex-attracted adults. Thus, the general societal stigmatization of same-sex-attracted adults is modified by the moral investment of the issue.

Same-Sex Couples at the Meso- and Microlevels

We have seen how the same-sex couples in our study fit into the context of their culture, with its challenges, stigmatization, and inconsistent policy and legislation. Following a description of the couples, we now examine how they balance family and career, reach decisions at career turning points, come out, and plan for the future.

Description of the Couples

Thirty-two women and seven men make up the same-sex couples in *The Cornell Couples and Careers Study*; all are in relationships. In addition to the results obtained from telephone surveys, two dual-career, female same-sex couples participated in in-depth face-to-face interviews. Thus, a little over 1

Table 17.1 Descriptive Characteristics of Same-Sex Couples and Matched Opposite-Sex Couples[a]

	N	Mean Age	Mean Income ($)
Same-Sex			
Women	32	38	48,000
Men	7	48	50,500
Opposite-Sex			
Cohabiting	30	42	50,000
Married	30	41	50,500

[a] From the *Cornell Couples and Careers Study*, 1998–99. N = 99.

Table 17.2 Number of Children in the Home[a]

Number of Children in Home	Female Same-Sex Homes	Male Same-Sex Homes	Cohabiting Homes	Married Homes
1	2			5
2	2		4	2
3				1
4			1	
5			1	

[a] From the *Cornell Couples and Careers Study*, 1998–99. Number of homes = 49.

percent of couples in the Cornell study are same-sex couples. U.S. Census data indicate that 1.1 percent of couples are in same-sex relationships, although this is considered an underestimation.[8]

The average age of the women is thirty-eight (SD = 6, range = 26–57), and forty-eight for the men (SD = 6, range = 42–59). The average individual income for women is $48,000 (SD = $20,000, min = $11,000, max = $95,000) and for the men is $50,000 (SD = $22,512, min = $12,000, max = $67,000).

Twenty-eight of the women are European-American/White (non-Hispanic), one is African American, one is Hispanic, and one is multiethnic. All the men are European-American/White (non-Hispanic). Among the female same-sex couples, two couples have two children and two couples have one child. In one family, their two children are grown and have left home; in another family, there is one child currently living in the home and another child not living there (reason unspecified). None of the male same-sex couples reports having children. For the purposes of comparison in certain analyses, fifteen cohabiting opposite-sex couples and fifteen married couples have been selected from the study and matched as closely as possible on age, household income, educational level, and number of children (see tables 17.1 and 17.2).

Mesosystem

Decision Making

In past research on career priority and how it relates to family and relationship dynamics, one study shows that female same-sex couples aimed for egalitarianism, but in male same-sex couples, the partner with the higher income had more influence.[9] In looking at whose career receives priority in the Cornell study, no significant differences emerged between the types of couples and decision-making strategies. However, a closer examination shows these trends. 33 percent of married women say their partner's career receives priority, compared with 11 percent for same-sex female couples and 15 percent for cohabiting couples. Among the same-sex couples, 35 percent of respondents report that their careers takes priority, compared with 23 percent of the cohabiting women.

Another study found that conflict and discord in decision making is detrimental to relationship satisfaction for both opposite-sex and same-sex couples.[10] In our study, decision-making congruence is similar across couples.[11] Couples moderately disagree in decision making across couple type despite satisfaction with the relationship being high among our sample overall.

Retirement Planning

Retirement is an important life transition that requires planning and multiple decisions that are likely to affect an individual's partner. In our study, retirement planning is assessed with the following question: "On a scale of 0 to 100 where 0 is none and 100 is a lot, how much planning have you done in each of the following areas to prepare for retirement—financial preparation, learning about retirement or health insurance options, considering housing arrangements, planning for health care needs, thought about 2nd or 3rd career, and thinking about volunteer work?"

The same-sex and opposite-sex couples share many patterns in retirement planning. For example, they plan to retire at similar ages, begin the planning process at similar times in their lives, and are planning for health-care and housing needs to a similar degree. However, married couples differ from the other couples in postretirement volunteering to a degree approaching significance (see table 17.3). Furthermore, female same-sex couples have a mean self-rating of degree of financial preparation lower than the other three groups and significantly lower than the married couples (see figure 17.2).

Because postretirement work and volunteering are associated with greater well-being,[12] these results imply that opposite-sex cohabiting couples and male and female same-sex couples may be at a disadvantage compared to married couples. Perhaps more important is the low rating of the degree of financial prepa-

Table 17.3 Retirement Plans[a]

	Age Expect to Retire	Age Began Planning	Degree of Postretirement Volunteering (%)	Degree of Financial Preparation (%)
Same-Sex				
Women	59	30	48	54
Men	60	35	47	60
Opposite-Sex				
Cohabiting	59	34	46	62
Married	60	32	63[b]	75[c]

[a] From the *Cornell Couples and Careers Study*, 1998–99. $N = 99$.
[b] Trend, greater than other three groups to a degree approaching significance $p = .055$.
[c] Significantly greater than female same-sex couples, $p < .05$.

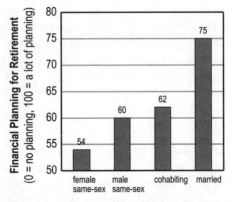

Figure 17.2 Self-rating of degree of financial planning for retirement. Source: *The Cornell Couples and Careers Study*, 1998, $N = 99$.

ration by female same-sex couples. Although previous literature suggests that women plan less for retirement than men, this study shows no effect for gender on the rating of financial preparation, although this is probably due to women in opposite-sex relationships reporting a higher degree of financial preparation and balancing the lower rating by the female same-sex couples. This result may point to a need for greater financial planning, particularly for female same-sex couples.

Coming Out

Coming out, or an individual's disclosing his or her nonheterosexual orientation, is often a critical turning point for people who are same-sex attracted. This experience can lead to individuals' redefining themselves, not only in terms of relationships and romantic attraction, but also in other spheres of identity such as education and career. Changes in career may stem from a reevaluation of values, the workplace climate for gay and lesbian employees, or the need to be economically self-sufficient. Studies of women's sexual attraction and self-identification regarding sexual orientation suggest that most women remain consistent over time regarding which gender they are attracted to, but for some women this is a more dynamic process.[13]

Coming out in adulthood has implications for relationships, work, and family. Although our study does not address coming out directly, we look at relationship history along with other variables, such as job change or a return to education. In a study that looks at the influence of coming out on the career trajectories of lesbians, evidence suggests that coming out in adulthood can have a moratorium effect on educational goals or career development (depending on which stage of career an individual is in), accompanied by a recycling of adolescent issues, such as experimenting with sexuality and a new identity.[14] Coming out, which could be a disruption in an individual's pattern of life, might also yield opportunities that reshape career and identity.

For six of the women in this study, their first significant relationship was with a man. We find that when these women made the transition from a male to female relationship there was a corresponding change in some other area of their lives. Three of the women changed their career or job, two returned to school, and one returned to work after not working during a twelve-year marriage. One of the men had his first significant relationship with a woman. When he changed from an opposite-sex relationship to a same-sex relationship, he also shifted from being a customer service representative to self-employment. The exact details of the interplay between job change or return to school and the meeting of the new partner are difficult to know. Which came first? Were these turning points the results of greater self-awareness or disclosure to others? Did the change of job or return to school provide the new relationship opportunity? In any event, coming out is accompanied by changes in multiple levels in an individual's life.

An excerpt from the Cornell study interviews illustrates the experience of two women who came out in adulthood and made the transition to a same-sex relationship. Mary (an alias), a 29-year-old multiethnic nanny, is in a relationship with Lilly, a 28-year-old white researcher. Here Mary talks about how she met Lilly: "We met in 1990 [eight years prior to the interview], I think. We were very close friends, we got to become very close friends. And that's how we actually got together. We were both considered heterosexuals before that—it just happened. Because we were such good friends, and then we got involved intimately, we kind of fell in love with one another." Lilly says they both had previous relationships with men, but then, ". . . we became closer than I think you are supposed to get, I guess, as friends."

Microsystems: Relationships, Children, Social Networks, and Division of Labor

The definition of family is becoming increasingly complex.[15] For example, a single same-sex-attracted parent with children and relatives living in the home and close friends might choose these to be family. In this chapter, and in keeping with the nature of the Cornell study, the families discussed here are dual-income couples, same-sex- and opposite-sex-attracted, with or without children in the home.

Relationships   Approximately 40–60 percent of gay men and 45–80 percent of lesbian women are in romantic relationships.[16] In an eighteen-month followup of their original survey, one study finds that same-sex couples had a similar level of relationship stability as opposite-sex cohabiting couples.[17] Of married couples who had been together for two to ten years, 6 percent had broken up, and, of those who had been together over ten years, 4 percent had broken up. Of cohabiting same-sex couples who had been together two to ten years, 12 percent had broken up (few couples in this sample were together for more than ten years). Of the male same-sex couples together for two to ten years, 16 percent had broken up, and, of those together over 10 years, 4 percent had broken up. Of the female same-sex couples who had been together two to ten years, 20 percent had broken up, and of those together over ten years, 6 percent had broken up. Clearly, married couples at the eighteen-month followup had a higher level of relationship stability, and, as states begin to enact legislation recognizing same-sex union, it will be interesting to see if this pattern extends to the same-sex couples.

Same-sex and opposite-sex couples also report similar levels of intimacy and relationship satisfaction.[18] In a longitudinal study of predictors of relationship outcomes, lesbian couples report higher levels of intimacy than opposite-sex couples, and both lesbian couples and gay male couples report a higher level of autonomy than heterosexual couples.[19] The relationship satisfaction levels reported in our study are consistent with previous findings. All couples report similarly high levels of relationship satisfaction (approximately 89%) and do not differ significantly between groups.[20]

In the Cornell study, twenty-seven is the average age for the first significant relationship for women in same-sex relationships and approximately 30 for men in same-sex relationships. For opposite-sex couples, it is approximately age twenty-six. None of the groups differed significantly in this respect.[21] However, couples did differ significantly in terms of average number of relationships;[22] cohabiting couples have the highest mean number of relationships (1.90) and married couples the lowest mean number of relationships (1.37). Both male and female same-sex couples report an average of 1.71 relationships.

Children and Child Care   Twenty-five percent (four) of the female same-sex couples in our study have children in the home. In the comparison groups, six cohabiting couples and eight married couples have children living with them (see table 17.2). Of those with children, no significant overall difference emerged between couple type or gender in the amount of time spent with children per day. These results contrast with a previous study[23] that finds that female same-sex couples shared child-care tasks more equally than opposite-sex couples.

Social Support   A social worker experienced at counseling lesbian couples reports that, due perhaps to stigmatization of their relationships, female same-sex couples sometimes tend to form a strong bond with their partners.[24] When compared with opposite-sex couples, same-sex couples tend to have bigger joint friendship networks ("joint" referring to friends the couple has in common), although both couple types have a similar number of kin included in their support networks.[25]

In our study, social support networks are measured by assessing the degree to which an individual turns to his or her partner, friends, neighbors, and relatives. Female same-sex couples turn to their partners to a greater degree than the other couple types and significantly more than the cohabiting couples. These results indicate that women in same-sex relationships may rely on their partners more. Both the female and male same-sex couples and the cohabiting opposite-sex couples turned to neighbors significantly less than did married couples.[26] Female same-sex couples and married couples tended to rely more on friends than did male same-sex and cohabiting couples.[27] Although previous research suggests that gay men also turn to friends, our small sample size limits our analysis of the male same-sex couples to descriptive statistics. We find, however, that couple types do not differ in the degree to which they turn to parents, coworkers, siblings, and other relatives for support.

Division of Labor in the Home   Although researchers have consistently reported that same-sex relationships are egalitarian in division of labor,[28] one later study shows on closer examination that only 25 percent are egalitarian in the division of domestic work.[29] In our study, an analysis of time spent on household chores shows no significant overall differences for either couple type or gender.

Lilly, the 28-year-old researcher who lives with her partner Mary, sheds some light on the issue of division of labor in the home:

> It's an issue that just came up the other night. Ah, I guess . . . I would say that we split things down the middle. I think that Mary felt like I wasn't doing my share . . . but, ah, we do split things, the trick is that we do very different—oh, the way we tend to divide, in general, is that there are certain tasks I hate, and certain tasks she hates, and then I don't do those and she . . . do you know what I mean? . . . I

think because I don't do the big things, I do all the little things, and I think they are things that sometimes she doesn't notice, you know? Um, I mean, you really notice it when you vacuum the floor, or when you do the laundry. . . . I try to do the daily things, which are kind of little, and, maybe less important . . . so that does make a difference.

Lilly seems to promote the concept of an egalitarian relationship, although her tone suggests that she might be unsure that her own actually is. She states that housework was a recent topic of discussion. It is possible that overall, their division of labor is fairly equal. Lilly's point about doing the "little things" relates to the microanalysis of housework by itemizing all the smaller component parts that constitute housework, such as the daily "straightening up" that Lilly does.

Summing Up

In using the bioecological model, the present chapter illuminates the importance of some of the key themes of this book, namely choice and constraint, adaptive strategies, and structural lag. Despite cultural stigmatization and persistent legislative inequality, same-sex couples form lasting relationships and successfully balance career and family. On the meso- and microlevels, we see both similarities and differences between same-sex and opposite-sex couples. For example, all couples in our sample report high relationship satisfaction, a similar division of labor at home, and similar time spent on child care across couple type.

The findings are more complex for social support and retirement planning. Female same-sex couples rely on their partners more than do the other couples, whereas both married couples and female same-sex couples turn to friends more than cohabiting couples and male same-sex couples. Two possible explanations for why the female same-sex couples turn to their partners are that their relationships may be refuges in a challenging social environment and that gender socialization encourages women to focus on relationships. Similarly, cultural and socialization processes can explain why married couples and female same-sex couples rely more on their friends and why male same-sex couples and cohabiting couples may rely on friends less. Our culture endorses marriage as the ideal relationship, and it could be that the male couples and cohabiting couples have developed more independence, rather than interdependence, due to this bias. The results for the female same-sex couples might be explained, again, in terms of gender socialization that encourages women to focus on relationships, including friendships.

The differences for retirement planning can probably be explained as gender socialization—with women being less exposed to financial-planning information than men. Also, our culture and legislation are centered on the notion that retired couples are married couples, and so the needs of cohabiting and same-sex couples are often ignored. We see here a complex interaction of the macro-, exo-, and mesolevels of development, resulting in differentiated experiences depending on gender, sexual orientation, and marital status.

The theme that emerges by placing the study of same-sex couples within the bioecological model is resilience. Despite stigmatization of same-sex relationships at the macro- and exolevel, findings at the meso- and microlevel suggest that these couples persevere and succeed. These findings are consistent with research that finds little evidence that sexual orientation is related to quality of life or health indicators.[30] Future research should examine possible sources of resilience such as the social networks, attitudes, and coping strategies that same-sex couples use to balance their work and family lives in a sometimes difficult environment.

The study of same-sex couples is an excellent example of how policy can inform research and, conversely, research can inform policy. By using Bronfenbrenner's bioecological model, it is possible to develop hypotheses about what makes the lives of same-sex couples unique and where the gaps and inadequacies are, both in legislation and research. *The Cornell Couples and Careers Study* stands as an example of an elegant method for including same-sex couples in career and family research.

18

Institutionalizing
Family-Friendly Policies

Mary C. Still and David Strang

Are companies that appear to be family-friendly places where more people take advantage of programs designed to help balance work and family? What is the relationship between an organization's construction of formal work-life programs, employee awareness of program availability, and employee use? This chapter describes the work-life policies and programs established by the seven organizations participating in *The Cornell Couples and Career Study* and discusses how these programs relate to the larger work-life movement as well as to the industrial and organizational environments of the specific companies. We then focus on what benefits the respondents in the study believe are available, an analysis that underscores the disjuncture between formal programs and employee perceptions. Finally, we address the impact of personal characteristics, work roles, and organizational context on work-life program use.

Students of organizations have long observed the gap between an organization's formal structure and the informal but structured patterns of behavior that arise within its walls.[1] What an organization claims it does and its day-to-day activities can diverge substantially. Special caution must be observed when considering new or innovative management practices because these are particularly susceptible to rhetorical excess and faddish adoption.[2] For example, George Easton and Sherry Jarrell find that only 59 of 274 firms that formally embraced Total Quality Management (TQM; the leading management change program of the early 1990s) went on to actually develop a systematic program. The authors note that "Many firms claim to be implementing TQM when, in fact, they have made essentially no changes (other than in their public rhetoric)."[3]

What sort of relationship exists between an employer's official adoption of work-life policies and employee perceptions and use? Although little research has asked this question directly, close observers of the field suggest the two are loosely coupled at best. "To many companies," writes Sue Shellenbarger, a *Wall Street Journal* columnist, "fashioning a family-friendly image is nothing more than that—an issue of image, not substance."[4] Genevieve Capowski claims that companies report offering family-friendly programs when only one or two employees in the organization work flextime or use some other form of alternative scheduling.[5] Many family-friendly policies may not be officially available to all employees, and those that are formally available may be informally discouraged, making work-life programs virtually useless to employees.[6] This disconnect has been acknowledged by work-life scholars, but we have just begun to explore its causes and consequences. Here, we respond to calls by scholars such as Shelley MacDermid, Leon Litchfield, and Marcie Pitt-Catsouphes for new research examining both employer and employee perceptions.[7]

The Origins of Work-Life Programs

Discussions began in the business press in the 1980s about how organizations help employees manage work and home as a response to the rising number of women of childbearing age in the workforce. Many companies with sufficient resources set up on-site or near-site day care[8]; firms that could not afford the expense or that wished to signal their responsiveness without spending too much money contracted for child-care referral services.[9] Reported success stories offered decreased absenteeism among users of child care as proof of efficacy.[10]

Increasing attention to work-family issues, along with institutional pressures, prompted a broader discussion of the social responsibility of companies. In the 1980s, government efforts to privatize human services led to tax incentives for corporations to provide child-care assistance, and federal agencies and business consultants pressed corporations to adopt child-care initiatives.[11] Media publicity facilitated the mimicry of exemplary programs, with human resource professionals playing the joint role of internal advocates and issue interpreters.[12] Later, elder care emerged as a related set of problems and solutions.

During the 1990s, discussions of family-friendly programs broadened into a more general discourse on how companies could facilitate their employees' abilities to meet work and family demands on their own time. As attention shifted to time management, a variety of strategies—part-time work, flextime, compressed workweeks, job-sharing, and time off for volunteer work—emerged as a new set of solutions. Although much about these programs continued to be motivated by the needs of families, the programs were available to all sorts of employees and not only those concerned with child care.

The shift from work-family to work-life[13] in the 1990s and 2000s has been facilitated by links to a more widespread and influential managerial movement, the quality movement.[14] As quality programs moved from Japan to the United States, they shifted from an emphasis on the cultivation of managerial and technical knowledge to a greater focus on employee participation and human relations.[15] Employee participation meant that employees had a voice in the way work was designed and executed, would be held responsible for group output, and, above all, were invested in the company's performance and well-being. Such investment and commitment are evidenced by volunteerism, in which workers are willing to go beyond the job requirements, to initiate change, and to actively solve organizational problems. Quality approaches define employees as internal customers whose needs must be met and argue that continuous improvement requires employee development and empowerment.

Flextime and other family-friendly benefits can also be seen as vehicles for inspiring commitment.[16] In many companies, active quality programs have helped put work-life issues on the table. In a multinational bank we are studying, a corporate quality program helped give rise to greater attention to the relationship between corporate culture and business performance, which in turn led to an effort to construct a work-life agenda.[17] At Corning, linking the work-life agenda to TQM was what made family-friendly policies "stick," according to a director of Quality Management.[18] In other companies, such as Dow and Steelcase, quality and work-life programs have developed in tandem and are hard to separate (e.g., Dow uses TQM tools like Pareto bar charts and opportunity mapping to show the impact of work-life programs).[19] Most generally, as a 1993 report for corporate executives written by leaders in work-life innovation argued, "The growth of the quality movement offers an opportunity to expand work/family awareness since many of the tenets and principles of total quality management coincide with the organization change objectives of the work/family agenda."[20]

Given the diversity in approaches to work-life, we follow the qualitative typology offered by Dana Friedman and Arlene Johnson and the quantitative typology offered by Jael Cutcher-Gershenfeld, Ellen Kossek, and Heidi Sandling[21] to distinguish different sorts of programs. We differentiate (1) child-care innovations, which alleviate employees' concerns with child care and aim at allowing employees to follow conventional schedules or to provide care during unusual work hours, such as evening shift; (2) time-control innovations, which focus on alternative scheduling and allow employees more discretion over their time;[22] and (3) symbolic innovations, which require little or no financial capital to undertake or continue and require no significant changes in employees' work practices. Table 18.1 identifies specific policies and programs in these categories, noting the sorts of arguments most strongly associated with each type.[23]

Table 18.1 Work-Life Programs by Type

Program	Category	Benefits of Adoption[a]
Flextime[b]	Time-control	Helps employees manage work and home demands
Job-share		Attracts best and brightest to firm
Telecommute[b]		
Compressed workweek		
Part-time work		
Phaseback for mothers		
Job guaranteed time off for childbirth		
Time off for volunteering[b]		
On-site or near-site childcare center[b]	Child care	Fills gap in local day-care availability, allowing employees to work
In-home daycare provider network		Reliable child care over which company has control reduces absenteeism due to child-care problems
Pay (beyond FMLA) for mothers/paid parental leave		Increases employee loyalty to organization
Dependent care fund		
Before- and after-school care[b]		
Day-care subsidies		
Backup child care		
Sick-child care[b]		
Summer program for kids[b]		
Elder-care, day-care- and disabled-care referral service[b]		
Day-care consortium contributor		
Company task force	Symbolic	Fills gap in availability of information
Pretax set-asides		Helps employees deal with role conflict, making them better workers
Adoption aid		
Support groups[b]		
Seminars on family[b]		

[a] Arguments for adoption as discussed in the press and by experts (i.e., *Working Mother* magazine; Conference Board 1991).
[b] Benefits also used to compute the dependent variable in regression analyses.

Work-Life Programs at Participating Organizations

An organization's needs, resources, industrial location, and characteristics (such as size) shape important elements of its approach to work-life issues. For example, the work-life policies of Vantech are conditioned by the fact that it is a major Fortune 500 firm with great international visibility and a real need to signal its progressiveness to a wide audience. In the academic world, much the same could be said of Lake University. Utilco, by contrast, is a regional utility whose policies are negotiated with the union that represents the majority of its employees. Citizens' Health and Valley View are much smaller organizations operating in local markets.

Industrial and organizational context also affects the demand for work-life programs. The manufacturing firms in our survey, like manufacturers nationwide, are experiencing considerable downsizing (Vantech in particular). Their employees thus tend to be preoccupied with job security and may be correspondingly less likely to strongly demand new benefits.[24] The two medical facilities, like the rest of the health-care industry, experienced much concern about job stability and radical restructuring in the early 1990s due to attempts at health-care reform. Respondents working for the two institutions of higher education have probably experienced less of an external threat to job security.

Table 18.2 summarizes some features of family-friendly programs across the seven organizations in *The Cornell Couples and Careers Study*. To develop a stronger sense of the genuinely substantial differences among these programs, we provide here a brief description of how each organization came to address work-life issues. These descriptions are primarily drawn from interviews with the human resource managers most closely involved in administering family-friendly policies.

Vantech

Vantech's work-life program follows on the heels of a long-standing tradition of concern for the welfare of employees and their families, and in fact the company has been described as an exemplar of "welfare capitalism." In the 1980s, changing demographics of the workforce and competition for the best employees led senior management to establish a work-life task force.[25] Nevertheless, executives at Vantech felt uneasy about becoming too involved in employees' family lives. According to a Vantech senior manager, pressure to expand work-life programs grew when company recruiters noticed an increase in questions about such benefits.[26] Vantech's extensive raft of formal policies are characteristic of large, successful organizations in tune with contemporary discussions of

Table 18.2 Formal Work-Life Programs, Participating Corporations[a]

Company	Type	Origin of Work-Life Program	Responsibility for Work-Life Program	Total Number of Benefits
Vantech	Manufacturing	Began in 1980s; company is nationally recognized for work-life program	Director of Diversity and Work-Life, HR[b]	16
Transco	Manufacturing	Company adopted template program from parent company in late-1990s; parent company has been recognized for work-life program	Work-Life Manager, HR	12
Utilco	Utility	Program adopted in late 1990s, has emphasis on employee wellness	Labor Relations Manager, HR	7
Citizens' Health	Health care	No formal program exists; employee needs are negotiated individually	No specific designee; HR	4
Valley View	Health care	No formal program exists; employee needs are negotiated individually	No specific designee; HR	3
Upstate University	Higher education	Company began using flextime in 1970s as a way of voluntarily reducing labor costs; responds now to individual employee needs	No specific designee; HR	9
Lake University	Higher education	Company conducted formal process to find best practices	Director of Work-Life	12

[a]From the *Cornell Couples and Careers Study*, 1998–99.
[b]HR, human resources.

corporate responsibility and performance. We suspect that Vantech's continuing efforts are not only the source of, but also a product of, its national reputation for family-friendliness (an important predictor of adoption).[27]

Utilco

Utilco's work-life program began in a very different way. "I got called into my boss's office and he said, 'Congratulations. You've just been made the wellness coordinator for the company,'" recalls a human resources (HR) manager. "And work/life got hitched on. [My boss] said, 'You don't have much of a budget.'" When asked to describe what wellness/work-life is at Utilco, she said: "Monthly meetings of an established committee. Yearly health fairs, brown bag seminars with a raffle. Lots of balloons." She calls the company's motivation for work-life policies "p.r.," and says that getting financial support has been difficult.

Because the union opposes benefits such as part-time work and flextime at Utilco (reasoning that such work replaces full-time jobs), meeting the needs of workers with families has been difficult, according to the HR manager. Although in the past salaried employees were allowed flextime, that situation changed due to the case of a union employee who came to work one-half hour early and left early to meet her disabled child at the bus. When the union found out about the case, it fought Utilco on the grounds that such benefits erode the standard eight-hour workday. "We ended up yanking flextime for everyone," the HR manager said. But she suspects informal flex time arrangements are still being made between some supervisors and employees.

Citizens' Health

Citizens' Health has no formal program and offers few work-family benefits. "We lump it in EAP [the Employee Assistance Program]," a HR manager explains. She describes the EAP: "It's a toll-free number, where [employees] can talk to a Masters degree social worker about all kinds of problems—home, work, marital." The company has few formal policies and responds to individual problems in informal ways.

Valley View

Like Citizens' Health, Valley View's work-life program, as such, is largely informal, although a formal child-care center is located on-site. Although there is no formal policy on flextime, the vice president of HR said both that it is difficult for employees in the business of patient care to work flexible hours and that flexible hours are privately negotiated with managers. He was unsure of the exact beginning of the hospital's on-site day-care center, but said it has existed since at least the early 1990s. Despite the appearance of a relatively comprehensive set of initiatives aimed at caregiving—on-site day care and sick care, as well as respite care for the elderly—the HR vice president qualified both the on-site day care and the elder care. The day-care center, which is locally contracted by another association, is used only by a handful of families because its hours (6 A.M. to 6 P.M.) are not adequate for many health-care workers, and the respite care is not a company initiative but a community service.

Transco

Transco, also a Fortune 500 manufacturer, had twin motives for developing work-life programs. Its parent company previously adopted numerous work-life policies and was publicly recognized by being awarded a spot on *Working Mothers'* "Best Companies for Working Mothers" list. Transco's development of work-life programs was thus encouraged by corporate headquarters. In addition, the company manager we interviewed noted that flextime was in demand well before a formal policy was put in place. Employees voiced their opinions through the company ombudsman, employee satisfaction surveys, and suggestion boxes around the plant. Transco's work-life program is now formalized as an official responsibility of a HR manager in the diversity office (as at Vantech).

Upstate University

Upstate University's work-life program is informal and inconsistent across the organization. Flextime and alternative scheduling were originally promoted within the university as a way of saving money. Employees banked hours and could take time off or were allowed to work fewer hours without pay. In large part, these policies were established to avoid layoffs. Work-life has become an employee-initiated program and is used primarily by clerical and administrative staff, according to a HR manager.

Lake University

Lake University's program resembles the planned approaches of the large manufacturers in our study, Vantech and Transco. It began when an internal advisory council investigated the needs of women on campus and determined that work-family balance was an issue of concern. As a result, the university developed policies for alternative scheduling, created a summer camp for employees' children (which supplemented preexisting on-site day care) and began a seminar on work-family issues. As at Vantech and at Transco's parent company, the process of developing a work-life program involved a systematic evaluation of

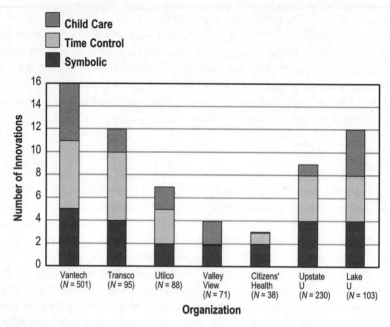

Figure 18.1 Number and type of work-life innovations, by participating organization. Source: *Cornell Couples and Careers Study*, 1998–99.

practices that other organizations had undertaken—a scanning of the environment for successful models to emulate.

Figure 18.1 shows the composition of work-life programs (as depicted by HR reports) across the seven organizations. Vantech, Transco, and Lake University show the largest breadth of initiatives; Valley View and Citizens' Health have few policies or programs formally in place. Valley View's and Lake University's benefits are nearly equally distributed among child-care, time-control, and symbolic initiatives. Transco's program offers few child-care benefits but as many time-control benefits as Vantech. Both Citizens' Health and Upstate University offer few child-care benefits, and both programs center on symbolic initiatives (nearly one-half of all initiatives at Upstate University and two-thirds at Citizens' Health). Formal work-life programs at Valley View consist of child-care and symbolic innovations (a configuration that makes sense in terms of the work that employees do—direct patient care requires the employees' physical presence, making time-control programs difficult at best).

Awareness of Work-Life Programs

Table 18.3 examines the relationship between the formal provision of benefits by organizations and employees' awareness of whether benefits are available to

Table 18.3 Employee Awareness and Use of Work-Life Policies, by Company and Benefit[a]

Company	Formally Available?	Respondents Wrong about Formal Availability (%)	Respondents Using Program That Does Not Formally Exist (%)
VANTECH			
Flextime	Yes	25.6	—
Child care	No	15.9	2
Telecommuting	Yes	57.9	—
Referral (child and elder care)	Yes	27.2	—
Parental support	Yes	26.0	—
TRANSCO			
Flextime	Yes	39.3	—
Child care	No	34.6	6.3
Telecommuting	Yes	51.8	—
Referral (child and elder care)	Yes	40.5	—
Parental support	Yes	53.0	—
UTILCO			
Flextime	No	52.5	39.8
Child care	No	13.3	1.1
Telecommuting	No	34.1	6.2
Referral (child and elder care)	Yes	65.4	—
Parental support	Yes	56.0	—
VALLEY VIEW			
Flextime	No	66.6	49.3
Child care	Yes	57.9	—
Telecommuting	No	33.2	3.8
Referral (child and elder care)	No	40.0	2.5
Parental support	Yes	49.0	—
CITIZENS' HEALTH			
Flextime	No	65.9	31.6
Child care	No	72.2	15.8
Telecommuting	No	52.8	4.1
Referral (child and elder care)	No	38.0	3.4
Parental support	No	61.0	15.8
UPSTATE UNIVERSITY			
Flextime	Yes	39.5	—
Child care	Yes	49.5	—
Telecommuting	No	44.6	20.7
Referral (child and elder care)	No	26.0	7.6
Parental support	Yes	37.0	—
LAKE UNIVERSITY			
Flextime	Yes	24.2	—
Child care	Yes	64.6	—
Telecommuting	Yes	35.8	—
Referral (child and elder care)	Yes	36.0	—
Parental support	Yes	18.0	—

[a] Comparison of five initiatives in which both human resource and employee accounts are available.
Source: *Cornell Couples and Careers Study*, 1998–99.

them. Although the overlap between the two sources of data is not perfect, employees were asked much the same questions about work-life benefits as the HR professionals. We focus here on comparable information for five major programs: flextime, telecommuting, day care, parental support (support groups and seminars) and child/elder-care referral.[28] Note that in this chapter we cannot focus on couples because we use company-level data in our analyses and comparable data are not available for most of the spouses, who work in a variety of firms other than the companies where we solicited respondents and interviewed HR administrators. Moreover, some of the spouses are self-employed or work in small businesses with no HR departments. Our sample size, thus, consists of the 1,082 respondents employed by one of the seven participating organizations in *The Cornell Couples and Careers Study* (462 women and 620 men).

Seventy-one percent of this sample of employees is unaware of or mistaken about at least one work-life policy or practice. That is, more than two-thirds claim that a policy is in operation that is not or that a policy that does formally exist does not. The frequency of errors varies substantially by organization. Ninety-two percent of Valley View employees are wrong about at least one of the five benefits about which we asked their HR department. Utilco (89%), Citizens' Health (87%), and Upstate University (87%) have similarly high numbers of misinformed employees. Employees at Vantech (57%) and Lake University (67%) appear to be better informed.

One in five employees is mistaken about the existence of the average policy or program, with telecommuting producing the most "wrong" answers and child care the most "right" answers. Percentages of misinformed employees range from 13 percent of Utilco respondents, who wrongly believe that child care is available to them, to the 72 percent of Citizens' Health respondents, who labor under the same misconception about their employer.

No particular policy shows systematically few or many errors across organizations, and in fact each of the five has the highest error rate in at least one of the seven companies. For example, employees at Vantech are particularly likely to think that telecommuting is not available, whereas employees at Lake University are more likely to be wrong about child care. The rate at which employees report that formally established programs are unavailable is somewhat greater than the rate at which they report that nonexistent programs are in operation, but the difference is not large. In other words, employees are almost as likely to claim the organization offers a benefit that in reality is not available as they are to say that it does not offer a benefit that is actually available. Error rates at Citizens' Health, where none of the five programs is formally established, are very high.

Employee perceptions of program availability might diverge from the organization's formal policies for a number of reasons, some of which come under the heading of perceptual errors or miscommunication. Some employees might define programs in idiosyncratic ways, mistaking telecommuting for occasional work from home. Organizations might not do a good job communicating about possible benefits; for example, the HR manager at Lake University notes that its flextime policy has not been widely advertised. Or employees might guess about the existence of a program based on their personal experience and that of coworkers.[29] Childless employees might not know that their organization offers child-care referrals or near-site child care. And as other scholars have pointed out, policies are only as good as the company's culture.[30] Organizations with corporate cultures that encourage overwork and heroic acts of overtime either blatantly or subtly discourage the use of many family-friendly programs. Some companies leaders view the programs as frivolous. In our sample of organizations, one work-life director recalls senior management's review of her $10,000 budget request for contracted child-care referral services: "You would've thought that I was taking their First Communion money. I'm sitting there in a meeting with a guy with four kids whose wife stays home, who says, 'What the hell is *this*?'"

But how do we account for employees who not only think a benefit is available when it is not, but actually say they use it? As table 18.3 shows, a large number of employees say that they use programs that do not formally exist. For example, almost one-half of the surveyed employees at Valley View say they are on flextime, although Valley View officially claims it has no flextime program. Approximately 20 percent of those surveyed at Upstate University say they telecommute and 15 percent at Citizens' Health say they receive on- or near-site child care, again in the absence of a formal program.[31] So many respondents cannot be deluded about their own situation. For example, although Utilco is very clear that it does not formally provide for flextime (recall our earlier discussion of union opposition), the HR manager we interviewed said, "Managers work it out with employees and I don't want to know about it."

We make no effort to judge whether, on balance, employees or HR administrators are better positioned to know what benefits are actually available. It is clear, however, that formal programs and employee perceptions of them are not well aligned. This suggests that researchers should not use employee perceptions as proxies for formal organizational policies or use formal policies as proxies for use.

Use of Work-Life Programs

Overview by Company and Type

Figure 18.2 examines use of work-life programs by company and program type; we again distinguish between child-care, time-control, and symbolic innovations. No organization offers widely subscribed on-site or near-site child care, and child-care referral is also little used on the whole. Of course, such programs

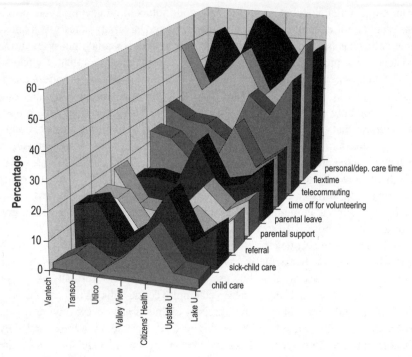

Figure 18.2 Percentage using at least one work-life initiative, by participating company and type. Source: *Cornell Couples and Careers Study*, 1998–99.

are largely restricted to employees with small children (about one-quarter of our sample). Citizens' Health shows the most active child-care and sick-child-care programs, consistent with the general popularity of these initiatives in the health-care sector.[32] Employees at Vantech, Transco, and Lake University are also rela-tively high users of child-care benefits.

Initiatives related to control over time involve more employees. Personal/ dependent-care time and flextime are the most commonly used programs across all organizations and are especially widely subscribed to at Vantech and Valley View. Valley View's case is particularly interesting because the HR office indi-cates that the organization does not offer flextime. Telecommuting is popular at Lake University, where professors as well as research and teaching assistants may be more likely to work at home because teaching loads (requiring physical pres-ence) tend to be lower than at Upstate. Telecommuting is also widely used at Citizens' Health, a medical facility with, in our sample, 90 percent professional employees. The other two time-control initiatives, parental leave and time off for volunteering, are more rarely used.

Table 18.4 shows the weak relationship between the formal availability of work-life benefits and use. In the overall sample, only the use of referral services

Table 18.4 Simple Correlations between Program Availability and Use, by Gender^a

	Flextime	Child Care	Telecommuting	Referral Service	Parental Support
Women N = 462	−0.014	0.022	0.009	0.028	−0.125***
Men N = 620	0.097**	−0.020	0.043	0.134**	0.057†
Entire sample N = 1,082	0.039	0.018	0.029	0.073**	−0.038

^{a†} Indicates $p < 0.1$; ** Indicates $p < 0.01$; *** Indicates $p < 0.001$. Source: *Cornell Couples and Careers Study*, 1998–99.

(child care or elder care) is significantly correlated with formal availability. Among women, the use of parental assistance or support initiatives is significantly but negatively correlated with formal availability, so female employees are less likely to use parental support programs when they are formally available and organized by their employer. Men's use of initiatives is more closely tied to formal availability, although not overwhelmingly so—the strongest correlation is a modest relationship ($r = .13$) between formal availability and use of referral services.

Who Uses Work-Life Programs?

Dependent and Explanatory Variables To model work-life program use by employees in *The Cornell Couples and Careers Study*, we construct a summary score across multiple programs.[33] For each respondent we count how many of the following eight programs are used: child-care referral, on- or near-site child-care, sick-child care, personal/dependent-care leave, parental leave with pay, flextime, telecommuting, and time off for volunteering. We exclude pretax set-asides and other symbolic initiatives, (although some researchers do include these benefits in global measures of work-life programming).[34] Our concern is with programs that explicitly or implicitly involve an organizational cost, whether through a financial outlay or the opportunity cost of an employee's time.

Individual Characteristics

Demand for family-friendly benefits. Program use should be greater among those who have a greater need for program benefits. We examine differences between women and men because in most families women are primarily responsible for child care, elder care, and the home. We also examine the impact of parenting a child under the age of six in the home because this should increase demand for child-care and for time-control programs.

Employee bargaining power. Workers with more skills and training should be in a stronger position to negotiate for benefits than are employees whose skills are less scarce or less critical to the organization. Past researchers have argued that skilled women in particular are more likely to receive family-friendly benefits.[35] We examine the effects of education, salary, and professional status on benefit use.

Awareness of work-life programs. We examine the impact of awareness of program availability by counting the number of programs in which the respondent correctly identifies whether a formal program exists. (This count is thus incremented when the respondent describes a formally adopted program as available and when the respondent describes a program that has not been adopted by the organization as unavailable.)

Control over work. Workers with a great amount of control over their work should be better positioned to use flexible benefits, especially those that allow them to work at home or during off-hours. We measure control via a scale developed by Linda Thiede Thomas and Daniel Ganster that combines respondents' perceptions of control over (1) the start and end times of each workday, (2) the number of hours worked each week, (3) working at home instead of at the workplace, (4) work that must be done at home to meet job demands, (5) when to take vacations or days off, (6) when to take a few hours off, (7) making or receiving personal phone calls, and (8) making or receiving personal email.[36]

Organizational Characteristics

Formal availability. We treat the number of family-friendly benefits officially offered by the company as a measure of the breadth of its work-life program. A larger number of benefits should lead to greater use. The absence of such a relationship suggests that formal policies may be irrelevant or may be used to signal concern in settings where active programs are costly or undesirable.

Organizational size. Size is perhaps the most consistent organizational correlate of employee rewards and innovativeness in general, and this relationship holds for work-life benefits.[37] Larger organizations tend to pay more and to provide more fringe benefits for a variety of reasons, including their strong market positions, skilled workforces, and propensity to develop strong internal labor markets.[38] Because we control for the number of formal work-life benefits, however, the impact of organizational size on use is not clear-cut. It is plausible that larger organizations would show a greater use net of program adoption (because factors such as an internal labor market should encourage program participation as well as organizational adoption of benefits) or less use (because large size often diminishes organizational flexibility). We measure size as the logged number of

employees because firm sizes in our sample vary substantially, with Vantech
being particularly large.

Percentage female. Organizations with many women employees are more
likely to adopt family-friendly benefits.[39] We anticipate that they also experience greater pressure to make work-life benefits real—that is, readily
available without strong barriers to use. Organizations with many women
employees should be more motivated to solve work-family conflicts, and
may develop progressive cultures that view family roles and responsibilities as legitimate within the workplace.

Table 18.5 gives the means and standard deviations for the explanatory variables and benefit use across organizations and gender. Substantial variation
appears on both dimensions. For example, the average salary at the Fortune 500
manufacturing firm Vantech is almost double that of the average salary at the
local hospital ($35,976 a year). Citizens' Health and Upstate University employ
the greatest proportions of professionals; the smallest percentage are at Valley
View and Vantech.[40] Many respondents have preschool-age children, with women
more likely than men to have young children in the home. Recall that the respondents we study in this chapter all work at one of the seven participating companies. All are married, but not to one another. Employees at Vantech, Transco, and
Lake University report having the highest levels of control over their work.

The seven organizations differ greatly in size. Vantech has the most employees (>30,000), followed by Utilco (>5,000) and Lake University (>5,000). The
health-care organizations are the smallest, with fewer than one thousand employees each. The percentage of women in the organizations also varies considerably,
from 18 percent at the manufacturer Transco to 84 percent at Citizens' Health.
The universities are the most gender-balanced (at 53% and 60%). Awareness of
work-family benefits is highest at Vantech and Lake University.

Average use of work-life programs ranges between one and two benefits for
almost all subgroups defined by employer and gender. Family-friendly initiatives
are used more extensively by women than men (only at Transco are men heavier
users, due to an extensive telecommuting program). Use is highest at Lake University, Valley View, and Citizens' Health. Use is moderate at Vantech (despite
the fact that its formal programs are the most extensive) and is especially low
among men at Valley View and Utilco and among women at Transco.

Regression Results   Table 18.6 shows the results from multiple regression
analyses of work-life program use. We examine the sample as a whole and also
develop separate models for women and men.

Most individual characteristics bear a weak relation to program use. The
effects of measures of employee bargaining power such as education, salary, and

Table 18.5 Descriptive Statistics, by Participating Organizations and Gender[a]

Organization	Gender	Age	School beyond high school (years)	Annual Salary	Professional	Child <6 at Home	Control over Work Scale	Awareness	Number of full-time employees	% female	Mean no benefits used
Vantech	Male N = 353	45.12 (6.63)	4.98 (2.33)	77,176 (22,323)	0.65 (0.48)	0.20 (0.40)	3.72 (0.57)	3.80 (1.31)	>10,000	36	1.58 (1.29)
	Female N = 148	40.70 (4.85)	4.88 (2.14)	64,114 (25,025)	0.68 (0.47)	0.34 (0.48)	3.74 (0.59)	3.79 (1.31)	>10,000	36	1.57 (1.29)
Transco	Male N = 57	42.86 (7.73)	5.44 (1.92)	74,980 (30,604)	0.79 (0.41)	0.26 (0.44)	3.68 (0.52)	3.33 (1.35)	>2,500	18	1.96 (1.44)
	Female N = 38	35.87 (7.10)	4.11 (2.18)	48,610 (29,678)	0.76 (0.43)	0.42 (0.50)	3.75 (0.64)	2.95 (1.63)	>2,500	18	1.16 (1.5)
Utilco	Male N = 61	45.20 (6.42)	3.67 (2.26)	76,100 (19,250)	0.75 (0.43)	0.25 (0.43)	3.40 (0.80)	3.03 (1.09)	>5,000	21	1.31 (1.30)
	Female N = 77	40.96 (6.09)	4.30 (2.13)	62,046 (18,744)	0.70 (0.47)	0.41 (0.50)	3.50 (0.70)	2.93 (1.14)	>5,000	21	1.37 (1.25)
Valley View	Male N = 11	42.36 (10.17)	2.73 (2.05)	47,363 (22,415)	0.55 (0.52)	0.18 (0.40)	2.60 (0.80)	3.36 (1.21)	<1,000	80	1.27 (0.79)
	Female N = 60	40.37 (7.57)	2.50 (2.00)	33,888 (12,530)	0.68 (0.47)	0.28 (0.45)	2.51 (0.79)	2.95 (0.999)	<1,000	80	1.9 (1.4)

Citizens' Health	Male	N = 17	43.41	6.82	85,470	0.88	0.53	3.33	2.71	<1,000	84	1.88
			(6.55)	(3.17)	(35,845)	(0.33)	(0.51)	(0.77)	(1.57)	—	—	(1.32)
	Female	N = 21	38.57	4.48	39,382	0.90	0.24	3.24	2.62	<1,000	84	1.88
			(8.69)	(1.99)	(16,321)	(0.30)	(0.44)	(0.93)	(1.43)	—	—	(1.3)
Upstate University	Male	N = 98	48.40	7.10	65,674	0.85	0.18	3.74	3.16	>1,000	53	1.44
			(10.37)	(2.62)	(22,868)	(0.36)	(0.39)	(0.62)	(1.17)	—	—	(1.24)
	Female	N = 132	43.46	5.21	42,599	0.90	0.21	3.65	3.14	>1,000	53	1.48
			(8.25)	(2.29)	(15,718)	(0.30)	(0.41)	(0.67)	(1.12)	—	—	(1.20)
Lake University	Male	N = 53	46.68	6.57	62,464	0.81	0.25	4.0	3.60	>5,000	60	1.8
			(10.45)	(2.87)	(34,297)	(0.39)	(0.43)	(0.71)	(1.26)	—	—	(1.27)
	Female	N = 50	44.88	4.92	45,471	0.78	0.32	3.78	3.80	>5,000	60	2.24
			(8.20)	(2.59)	(34,298)	(0.42)	(0.47)	(0.64)	(1.34)	—	—	(1.38)
Total			43.74	5.02	63,509	0.74	0.25	3.00	3.45	26,464.85	43.40	1.61
			(7.96)	(2.54)	(27,820)	(0.44)	(0.44)	(0.71)	(1.31)	(25,161.33)	(17.35)	(1.51)
			1,126	1,126	1,070	1,126	1,126	1,126	1,126	1,124	1,124	1,126

[a]Values (other than N) are means. Values in parentheses are standard deviations. Source: *Cornell Couples and Carers Study*, 1998–99.

Table 18.6 Regression Models Analyzing Work-Life Benefit Use[a]

	Entire Sample		Women		Men	
	b[b] (SE)	Significance	B (SE)	Significance	b (SE)	Significance
Individual characteristics						
Female	0.057 (0.091)	0.627	—	—	—	—
Child < 6 at home	0.000 (0.102)	0.000	0.134 (0.049)[†]	0.105	-0.107 (0.142)	0.449
Age	0.006 (0.006)	0.350	0.005 (0.009)	0.580	0.004 (0.008)	0.626
Education	-0.000 (0.017)	-0.001	-0.01 (0.028)	0.719	0.013 (0.022)	0.559
Salary	-0.000 (0.000)	-0.319	0.000 (0.000)	0.823	-0.000 (0.000)	0.856
Professional	0.004 (0.094)	0.969	-0.020 (0.153)	0.894	0.021 (0.120)	0.863
Awareness of work-life programs	0.106 (0.031)**	0.001	0.080 (0.049)[†]	0.105	0.121 (0.041)**	0.003
Control	0.193 (0.060)**	0.001	0.252 (0.087)**	0.004	0.171 (0.084)*	0.042
Organizational environment						
Size (LN)	-0.01 (0.067)	0.875	0.123 (0.107)	0.251	-0.114 (0.087)	0.190
Women (%)	0.007 (0.003)*	0.015	0.017 (0.005)***	0.000	-0.003 (0.004)	0.523
Number of benefits formally available	0.002 (0.025)	0.924	-0.029 (0.041)	0.487	0.034 (0.031)	0.276
Constant	0.08 (0.562)	0.887	-1.27 (0.824)	0.126	1.09 (0.753)	0.148
N	1,082	1,082	461		620	
R^2	0.030	0.087	0.058		0.033	

[a] [†] Indicates $p < 0.10$; * Indicates $p < 0.05$; ** Indicates $p < 0.01$; *** Indicates $p < 0.001$; [b] b, unstandardized regression coefficient; SE, standard error. Source: *Cornell Couples and Careers Study*, 1998–99.

professional status differs by gender, with mostly negative effects for women and positive effects for men, but coefficients are modest and not statistically significant. It is even more surprising that the same pattern of weak effects arises for gender and having very young children in the home. Women and women with preschool children are not much greater users of work-life programs than are men and women with no or older children, although a more fine-grained analysis of the use of specific programs might tell a different story.

We see consistent effects of awareness of work-life initiatives and control over individuals' work on program use. With both of these variables, however, it is difficult to be confident about causal direction. Are people who are better informed about formal programs then more likely to use them (because they know about them), or do people who need the benefits become aware of them when searching for ways to solve their problems? Does control over work lead to a greater ability to negotiate for work-life benefits, or does the use of programs such as telecommuting or on-site child care enhance individuals' control over work?

Organizational context influences program use in several important ways, although here (as is not the case for individual characteristics) differences between what influences men and what influences women arise. The larger the percentage of women in the organization, the more likely women are to use work-life benefits. Women may feel more comfortable or supported when they work in organizations with many female employees to develop alternative schedules that meet family demands.[41] By contrast, women who work in organizations with few women (such as Transco and Utilco) may feel pressure to behave "like men."[42] Bringing the children to work through on-site or sick-child care advertises a woman's maternal life, perhaps to the detriment of her identity as a worker. On the organizational side, companies with many women employees may do more to ensure that family-friendly programs are readily usable.

Although we have little direct evidence arbitrating between these two mechanisms, the regression results appear to support the latter. If organizations with many women construct a pro-family work environment, we expect men in those types of companies to use more work-family initiatives as well. Our data, however, show no such relationship ($p = .548$). It appears more likely that companies dependent on female labor find ways to accommodate demands for family-friendliness, although it is notable that they do not tailor programs to the needs of women so strongly that men become less likely to use them. In fact, working in an organization with many women has a slightly (nonsignificant) negative effect on men's use of work-life programs. We suspect that men in companies in which many women are using work-life programs—in particular those who use alternative scheduling programs that necessarily complicate coordination of work—may feel more pressure to work conventional hours so as not to further complicate matters. After all, in most modern organizations, it is still expected that someone is available to represent the department in meetings, to be called on for questions and emergencies, and to supervise staff.

We might think that the formal availability of benefits is a straightforward predictor of use; if a benefit does not exist, it cannot be used. But the story is not nearly so simple. Many formally unavailable benefits are available (at least to some employees) in practice, and formal programs may play largely symbolic roles. It is interesting to note that an important predictor of men's use is their awareness of formal work-life offerings, whereas for women being right about whether the company formally offered an initiative does not predict use. We believe this occurs because women negotiate exceptions to help them meet their work and family obligations and are less concerned with the formal availability of programs in their organization. Men, on the other hand, may feel more comfortable pursuing such programs when the organization has made them formally available, which results in, at the minimum, a tacit endorsement.

Summing Up

Four core findings emerge from our analysis of work-life benefits across the seven organizations and 1,062 workers in dual-career couples examined in *The Cornell Couples and Careers Study*. First, the formal work-life programs established by the organizations differ in substantial and largely predictable ways. The Fortune 500 manufacturer Vantech offers many more formal programs than any of the other organizations, in line with common understandings of the impact of organizational size and reputation. Other organizations follow in a way roughly correlated with size and are also linked to unionization (at Utilco), corporate sponsorship (at Transco), and industry.

The picture becomes much muddier when we turn to employee perceptions of which programs are formally available. The great majority of employees are wrong about the availability of work-life programs, at least some of the time. The larger and more formalized work-life programs (as at Vantech and Lake University) appear to have been better communicated to employees, but even here the disjuncture is startling. And although some of the difference between employee perceptions and HR reports may lie in employee misperceptions, it is also clear that formally established programs may not be readily available and that nonexistent benefits may be individually negotiated. A large number of employees not only believe that nonexistent programs are in operation, but actually use them.

Third, in developing regression analyses of who uses work-life benefits, we are struck by the modest effects of individual characteristics. Women are not significantly greater users of work-life programs than are men, and mothers with small children are not significantly greater users than women without children or with older children. Professionals are not significantly greater users than nonprofessionals. The modest level of these effects may have to do with our focus on a summary score of use or on limited variation within the sample we study. Or it may indicate that benefit programs have in fact been generalized from work-*family* to work-*life*.

Fourth, organizational level variables play a larger role in influencing program participation, but the pattern of these effects varies by gender. For women, the use of programs increases with the proportion of women in the organization. This makes good sense, given the fact that women are historically the key driving force behind work-life benefits and are its core constituency. In combination with the weak direct effect of gender on use, it suggests that the effective demand for work-life integration is more a question of political influence within the corporation than individual preferences and choices. For men, program use appears to hinge on the formal status of work-life programs. Unlike women, men are sensitive to whether programs have been formally established. And, unlike women, men's use of benefits is linked to their awareness of the program's formal existence. Both effects point to men's sensitivity to the way family-friendly policies are defined within their organization and to their reluctance to negotiate individual benefits in the absence of strong organizational signals that these benefits are legitimate.

It is important for job-seekers, the media, and researchers to critically evaluate accounts linking a company's formal work-life program to its desirability as a place to work. Increasingly, work-life experts are asking companies to track the use of benefits as an indicator of how well they allow employees to manage work and home demands. Our evidence of the (dis)connection between formal use and availability underscores the importance of this distinction. And our analysis of program use suggests an important irony: companies that innovate in the area of work-life by adopting many programs do not show particularly high levels of benefit use among their employees. In fact, among the core group they were originally targeted to serve—women—there is a small negative relationship between the formal establishment of family-friendly programs and benefit use.

19

Work-Life Integration: Challenges and Organizational Responses

P. Monique Valcour and Rosemary Batt

> I wish there were more flexibility, especially in our production environment. I've worked all my life around the rotating-work schedule, but this year alone I lost three excellent employees. They had each become single parents for one reason or another, and there's no way you can get child care in off hours and weekends. It just breaks my heart. Traditionally production has been a male-oriented thing, where one partner stays at home with the children and the other one works crazy schedules. . . . the world is changing, but the schedule is not.
>
> > —Manufacturing production supervisor married to part-time educational coordinator and father of two children ages 8 and 14

This chapter focuses on organizational responses to the challenges dual-earner couples face in integrating their work and family lives. We examine the effectiveness of various workplace characteristics and organizational initiatives for supporting work-life integration. We then develop a comprehensive model of organizational family responsiveness that incorporates work-life policies, traditional human resource incentives, and work redesign in the context of a workplace culture that facilitates the full implementation of these policies. We then test some of the components of this model as predictors of outcomes of interest to both workers and employers. Specifically, we assess the effects of formal policies and supervisor support for flexible work arrangements, traditional human resource incentives, and work-design measures on work-family conflict, perceived control, and turnover intentions. We do this within the context of dual-earner couples in *The Cornell Couples and Careers Study*, which enables us to take into account the characteristics of both spouses' jobs and workplaces.[1]

The Challenges of Work-Life Integration

Employees have traditionally faced the challenge of meeting the competing demands of work and family life with the assumption that they were solely responsible for managing their own balancing acts and could not expect significant assistance from their employers in this regard.[2] Both employers and employees often treated work and family domains as separate spheres of existence.[3] Typical of this presumption is a statement by an executive in the early 1990s: "Competent workers can handle work-family problems and there is nothing a company can really do to help the incompetent workers."[4] Similarly, in Arlie Hochschild's study of a supposedly family-friendly workplace, female executives avoid placing family photographs in their offices, and the norm of long work hours as a display of organizational commitment is dominant.[5]

Employees tend to experience work-family conflict when demands from work and family are both high and difficult to satisfy. Work-family conflict is a form of interrole conflict in which incompatible demands emanating from work and family domains make it difficult or impossible to satisfy both sets.[6] Employees from dual-earner families (the subjects of our study) are particularly likely to experience conflict between work and family.[7] Whereas most research has focused on individuals and the work-family conflict they personally report, a growing number of studies suggest that work-life issues must be understood in the context of both spouses' employment conditions. One study, for example, documents crossover effects from husbands' and wives' work schedules to family life,[8] and a 1988 study finds that husbands and wives in dual-earner couples restructured their work lives to accommodate family partly based on the job characteristics of their spouses.[9] A 1991 study finds relationships among employees' job security, income, and weekly work hours and their spouses' job involvement and satisfaction.[10] A 1999 study using data from *The Cornell Couples and Careers Study* reports that couples devise joint strategies for managing the demands of two careers, often by scaling back the demands of one spouse's job.[11] Hence, in our analysis, we assess the effects of spouses' employment conditions on one another's reported work-family outcomes.

Evidence for the deleterious effects of work-family conflict on individuals, families, and organizations has been building (see Roehling, Moen, and Batt, chap. 7 in this volume). Research suggests that dual-career couples are very concerned about work-life integration and committed to preserving time with their family.[12] Both quantitative and qualitative research suggests that many workers feel their employers could be—and should be—much more family responsive.[13] Some companies have responded to employee demands for better work-life integration as a critical component of recruitment and retention strategies.[14] A few firms are beginning to link family responsiveness to overall corporate strategy, particularly as a component of work quality and productivity improvements.[15]

Research has begun to document the positive outcomes of corporate work-life initiatives.[16] Through such programs as flexible work arrangements, reduced work time, dependent care, financial benefits, and culture-change initiatives, companies can reduce employees' work-family conflict,[17] improve their job satisfaction,[18] and improve elements of corporate performance including absenteeism[19] and retention.[20] But the research documents more positive outcomes for employees[21] than for employers, for whom findings are more mixed.[22] In our quantitative analysis in this chapter, therefore, we examine outcomes of interest to employees (work-family conflict and employee control over work-family integration) as well as employers (employee-turnover intentions).

The Dimensions of Organizational Family-Responsiveness

Early studies of work and family focus on programmatic initiatives for dependent care, flexible scheduling, and the like. Over time, researchers have increasingly recognized the limitations of programmatic initiatives for responding to nonwork demands and have focused on a wider range of workplace conditions, including work design and workplace culture. There is, however, no general consensus on what, in fact, constitutes a family-responsive work environment. In this paper, we develop a comprehensive model of organizational strategies for work-life integration. We use the term "family" as shorthand to signify the demands employees face from the nonwork arena. Thus, we recognize that all employees, not only those with spouses and children living at home, experience the demands that result from personal relationships and involvements outside of the workplace. In our view, a family-responsive employer recognizes, legitimates, and responds to the challenges of integrating work and nonwork demands for employees at all stages of their family life cycle. A family-responsive employer provides:

- A broad range of work-life programs that provide employees with control over their working time and support in meeting their family and personal needs

- Adequate pay, benefits, and employment security
- Work designed to provide employees with discretion and control in meeting work and life demands
- A workplace culture, transmitted formally by organizational policies and informally by supervisors and coworkers, that values and supports the work-life integration of all employees

With respect to formal work-life policies, we include dependent-care policies as well as those designed to create greater flexibility in working time. Inflexible schedules and excessive work hours consistently produce conflict between work and family.[23] Working time policies constitute a range of approaches to flexible schedules as well as those designed to reduce total work hours. Specific policies include flextime, family leaves, dependent-care time, time off for volunteering, compressed workweeks, job sharing, part-time work, and telecommuting.[24] Employees from dual-earner families value flexibility highly;[25] some are even willing to switch jobs to have more.[26]

The role of supervisors is particularly important in implementing formal flexible scheduling and work time policies as well as informal working arrangements and schedules. Supervisors are responsible for staffing levels, allocation of work assignments, and unit output. Although supportive supervisors often can allow more flexibility than exists in the written policies of the organization, unsupportive supervisors can subvert employers' family-friendly policies.[27] Thus, companies must train supervisors and create a workplace culture that facilitates consistent policy implementation.

The second dimension of a family-responsive workplace is adequate employment and income security. Historically, employers used pay, benefits, and promotion opportunities to reduce turnover and induce long-term commitment to the firm. These policies, or internal labor-market rules, protected (mostly male) breadwinners (and their families) from the vicissitudes of competitive labor markets.[28] Such policies provided the kind of employment security and income growth that create family stability.[29] Thus, high pay and benefits, employment security, and career development opportunities should create an environment in which employees view their employers as supportive of family needs and demands. Ironically, however, at a time when employers have begun to initiate family-friendly policies, many have simultaneously undertaken policies of downsizing, outsourcing, and contingent staffing in order to reduce pay, benefits, and a commitment to long-term employment relations.

The third dimension of a family-responsive workplace comprises work designed to allow employees to meet their work and nonwork demands on a daily basis. Flexible scheduling policies have proven insufficient to meet these needs. For example, a nationally representative survey of nearly three thousand employees found that working parents experience less work-family conflict when they have jobs with greater autonomy, more schedule control, and fewer demands.[30] By contrast, formal family-friendly policies had no effect on reported levels of work-family conflict for these employees. Autonomous work design not only leads to higher levels of motivation and satisfaction,[31] but also signals to employees that they are trusted to get their work done and manage their time effectively.[32] Employees who report greater control over managing work and family demands also report lower work-family conflict, more job satisfaction, and fewer physiological stress–related symptoms.[33]

Employers often worry, however, that greater individual autonomy simply undermines productivity. Some research by Lotte Bailyn and others, however, suggests otherwise.[34] Bailyn's research group undertook intervention projects at three corporations in the early 1990s. In one case, a team of product-development engineers at Xerox worked in an environment that emphasized long hours and "face time" as a sign of commitment to the employer. Long meetings, documentation requirements, and the interference of supervisors in the day-to-day work of the engineers meant that the real work of product development took place before or after daytime work hours, thereby creating a vicious circle of longer hours, high stress, and low productivity. The intervention team examined time use and redesigned the work so that supervisors were severely restricted in the time they could interact with the engineers. As a result, the engineers increased their autonomy and control over work routines and schedules, substantially increased their productivity, and decreased their total work hours.

The relationship between work-life integration and other dimensions of work design is more ambiguous. For example, firms have increasingly adopted more collaborative or team-based forms of work organization to improve workplace quality, efficiency, and coordination. Although there is considerable support for the idea that team collaboration and coordination improve organizational performance,[35] there is little research on how these forms of work organization affect employees' ability to manage work and family. On the one hand, the ability to collaborate or coordinate work with other colleagues may increase flexibility if coworkers are able to substitute for one another or establish norms of reciprocity in which they agree to help one another meet work and nonwork demands. Some studies have found positive effects of team-based systems on work-life outcomes.[36] On the other hand, the demands of collaboration and group coordination may increase work hours or the rigidity of work if they lead to time-consuming meetings or heightened peer-group pressure.[37]

The use of information technology is another area of work design that is rapidly changing, and the nature of its impact on work-life integration is also unclear. Portable computers, faxes, voice mail and email allow workers to bring work into the home more easily, but may have effects that are similar to those of telecommuting. Researchers have found very mixed outcomes for telecommuting because, although it increases flexibility, it also allows work to invade or spill over into home life more. As Noelle Chesley, Phyllis Moen, and Richard Shore (chap. 14 in this volume) describe, the little research on this aspect of work design has produced ambiguous findings on the effects of technology on the work-life interface.[38] Accordingly, we include a measure of information technology use in our analyses.

Finally, the workplace culture in general must support and legitimate employees' nonwork role demands. This environment shapes the attitudes of managerial as well as nonmanagerial employees. For example, Susan Eaton, in her 2000 study of five hundred technical and professional employees in biotechnology firms, found that formal and informal family-friendly policies and benefits increased organizational commitment and satisfaction only to the extent that employees felt free to use the policies without detriment to their workplace relations or career success.[39]

The organization must also create an environment that recognizes variation in the work-life interface of employees over their life course. Parents experience more work-family conflict than nonparents,[40] and thus need to be given special attention. However, to the extent that employers view work-life policy as focused on parents (particularly women) and privilege them over other employees who are single or whose children are grown, employers risk creating divisiveness at work.[41] Accordingly, in this chapter we frequently use the term "work-life" rather than "work-family" to signify that employees, both male and female, of all family structures and life stages have legitimate demands on their time, energy, and psychological involvement from domains outside of their jobs.

Qualitative Evidence from *The Cornell Couples and Careers Study*

Our field research includes a series of focus groups involving 114 employees in our seven participating organizations. The demographic profiles of the focus-group participants mirrors those of the survey respondents. Employees' supervisors were not present at the discussions, which were structured to cover the following three broad open-ended questions. First, what are the challenges you face and the strategies you use in combining work and family? Second, what arrangements (e.g., formal policies or informal arrangements) does your employer offer to help you combine work and family? Also, what arrangements have you used, what have you not used and why, and what has been helpful? Third, what would be ideal for you in terms of combining work and family?

Our results are based on a textual analysis of the focus-group transcripts, which involved coding passages relating to work-life support offered by the organizations. Table 19.1 provides frequencies for the thematic codes we have identified. The statements from the focus groups highlight the importance of flexible working time arrangements. They emphasize the utility of such policies as the

Table 19.1 Frequency of Themes in Focus Group Transcripts

Themes Related to Work-Life Policy	Frequency
Access to Flexible Working Time	
No company policy on flextime; up to supervisor discretion; varies by department/supervisor	52
My department/supervisor is flexible	46
In my department, flexibility is handled informally (e.g., leave if you need to, make the time up later)	31
My department/supervisor is not flexible	16
Flextime can make it difficult to coordinate work and manage the department	11
Flexibility is difficult because of lack of coworker support	9
Family leave policy helpful	7
Higher-level employees have more flexibility	9
Being able to use vacation time in small chunks for family needs is helpful	5
Lack of flexible work policies signals lack of investment in employees	5
Total Work Hours and Workload	
The company has work-life policies, but the reality is it is hard to use them because of work demands	22
The main problem is that we are asked to do too much work (due to downsizing and being understaffed)	16
Ability to work part-time is a helpful work-life policy	11
Ability to job-share is a helpful work-life policy	6
Wages	
Organization should pay us more; that would be a family-friendly policy	9
Unpaid leave is not helpful because people cannot afford the loss of wages and benefits	4
Dependent Care	
Dependent care time is a helpful policy	3
Culture	
The culture does not support use of work-life policies	17

ability to leave in case of emergencies to attend to family needs, to arrange work schedules to accommodate family demands, and to do part of their work at home. School holidays, children's illnesses, or breakdowns in child-care arrangements are particularly problematic for the dual-career families in this study if neither parent has access to flexible scheduling. The comments also reveal the resentment felt by employees due to unequal access to flexible working time. A second related theme concerns the negative effects of long work hours and overly demanding workloads, which undermine the benefits of flexible work arrangements or other work-life policies. A third thematic area is the need for adequate pay and benefits. In sum, although many employees report being able to make individual flexibility arrangements with their supervisors, a wide range of critical comments from employees indicates dissatisfaction with overall organizational support for work-life integration.

Access to Flexible Scheduling

A dominant theme in the focus groups is that the companies either have no formal policies for flexible scheduling or make the implementation of formal policies contingent on supervisor approval and that, as a result, access to such scheduling is unequal, arbitrary, and often insufficient. Unequal access derives from several sources, including variation in departmental tasks, the nature of work and technology, occupational differences, and supervisor attitudes. Interdepartmental variability is a persistent theme running through the focus-group discussions. For example, a professor with two grown children describes the extent of variation among departments at Upstate University:

> There's a lot of variation from one area to another. I didn't realize just how much variation until I ended up on a committee last year that was looking at some of the things like flex time. Well, we were informed that there is no flex time. There is no comp time. However, in reality, I've been very fortunate to work for a department all these years that is very flexible and very humane, and kind of just does its own thing. It's sort of a "don't ask, don't tell" kind of thing. And what happens as a result is that people are fiercely loyal and grateful to their supervisor.

Other focus-group participants emphasize technological and occupational sources of variation. One Transco manager explains that he feels caught between company rhetoric emphasizing family supportiveness and manufacturing technology that has to be run on a rigid schedule:

> To a certain extent I think it's lip service. These family-friendly policies are nice on paper, but a lot of them are hard to implement. I as a supervisor can't always implement what the company has set up, so I think we are setting people up with unrealistic expectations, and then sometimes we can't follow through on them. Like I had a guy in my group who wanted to do flex time and flex to the second shift, but it would've been very difficult to do. I really made an effort, but we needed two people in the department doing what he did on first shift.

Another Upstate University professor in her mid-forties (the mother of four school-age children, married to a computer programmer) observes, "I think a lot of it has to do with whether you're faculty or staff. As a faculty member, I've always felt a great deal of freedom. But there are a lot of people who are strictly hourly wage people who don't have near the flexibility in trying to do the kinds of things that we can do. So it's really two different worlds in the same office." These statements are consistent with past research showing that workers with higher wages and occupational status have a wider range of flexible benefits than their lower-wage counterparts.[42]

Variation in access, however, can also occur among people in the same department or occupational group, based largely on the arbitrary discretion of supervisors. For example, a forty-year-old female part-time marketing specialist at Utilco with a preschool child reports, "My manager allows me to work part of my time at home, whereas some others don't. My situation hasn't gone through Human Resources and probably shouldn't, because it probably wouldn't get approved."

Although many employees rate their own supervisor favorably, they go on to cite other examples of inequitable treatment. Also, although employees are grateful for the flexibility that they have personally negotiated, informal deals come at a price—employees feel beholden to supervisors, who expect a return for their favors. As one mother of two in her late thirties employed by Lake University states:

> We've talked about flexibility, but it's all based on what your supervisor is willing to allow you to do. And that puts you in a mode of groveling, begging, feeling anxious about whether it's going to be okay. You worry about how you might end up paying for it later. At some point down the road somebody is going to say, "you know, we gave you all the breaks." Since it's not a formal policy, it's seen as a privilege rather than as a right, and there's a big difference there.

These informal deals can create hard feelings or resentment from other employees who do not receive such special treatment, leading to divisiveness at work. Informal approaches to flexibility also lack the symbolic stamp of programs developed and supported by the organization. If employees and their supervisors believe that the only way they can accommodate work and family demands is by circumventing employers' rules and regulations, then it is likely that a breakdown of respect and trust will occur between employer and employee. This erosion of trust could, in turn, undermine morale and commitment to the organization. A 48-year-old man working for Utilco as a systems engineer notes, "A real flextime policy would be a part of a covenant in that it would be a formal recognition by management that we are professionals who do our work. When things need to be done, we're here, regardless of the time. Yet all the company has is the paternal system where your boss is the one who decides whether you'll have this flexibility."

All in all, the lack of formal policies for flexible working time not only limits access but leads to the development of informal deal-making between employees and their supervisors and to divisions and perceptions of inequality among employees who do and do not gain access to privileged schedules.

Access to Reduced Work Hours and Workloads

Excessive work demands also make for a family-unfriendly work experience, even when employers have work-life policies on the books. Although flexible schedules help solve work-life integration when total work hours are reasonable, excessive work hours, no matter how flexibly allocated, are likely to interfere with family and personal life.[43] Employees in companies that have downsized or that emphasize "face time" and prioritize work above all else typically have more complaints about workplace inflexibility and heightened work-family conflict. A Transco production planner with a schoolteacher wife and grown daughter explains, "You've got the workload of two people, but it's all on you. All these programs are coming in, but forget the programs, just think about what's a realistic expectation without causing me to leave this job."

A colleague from the planning department (a father of three, married to a medical transcriptionist, with a live-in parent) seconds this opinion, "We don't need an employee assistance program, we need more employees!" Similarly, a forty-eight-year-old Vantech software engineer, married to a CPA and mother to one middle school and one college student, explains that she officially works part-time with a lower salary and reduced benefits so she can, in fact, limit herself to a regular full-time (forty-hour) workweek: "The hours we are expected to work just seem to grow and grow. I'm part-time, 32 hours a week. Now that my kids are older, I would be more ready to go to 40, but once you officially work 40, then they expect you to work 60. So if I say I'm working 32, most of the time I end up working 40, but at least it stops at 40."

Focus-group participants feel that a family-responsive employer would guard against the tendency for work time to expand without limit. Although employers alone do not determine how much time employees spend at work,[44] they set staffing levels, expectations, and demands. A female engineer with two teenage children and twenty-four years of service to Vantech comments, "It used to be you were working really hard if you worked 50 hours a week. Now this is just adequate, and the new buzz word is to say you work 60 hours a week. I think there is something wrong with that, and businesses should stop promoting it. I think that this company can do something about changing the perception that you're not a professional unless you work 60 hours a week."

Past research shows that employers' efforts to set limits on the workday can reduce employees' work-family conflict and even improve corporate productivity.[45] In some focus groups, employees identify these types of efforts as important organizational strategies to support work-life integration. A Vantech production supervisor in his late thirties with two school-age children says, "I think the company should step up to the plate and address the issue of how many hours a week people actually work. We should not allow the demands of work to creep beyond 50 to 60 hours—where does it stop? The company needs to step in and put some limits in effect, because otherwise it will continue to creep."

Other solutions include job-sharing or part-time arrangements, but these options are not widely available to employees at the seven participating organizations in *The Cornell Couples and Careers Study*. Individual employee initiative is the common catalyst for these types of arrangements, and some professionals are able to reduce hours through negotiations with their supervisors. One Upstate University administrator with two children (ages three and six) explains her situation: "I job share with another professional. It works great, but I had to write up a proposal for it and work it out with my boss. We worked together to go forward on it."

Another Transco planning specialist, a mother of a nine-year-old and four-year-old twins and married for fifteen years to a business administrator, describes her efforts to set up a job-sharing situation and her feeling that she is lucky to have succeeded:

> I was lucky to work out a job sharing arrangement because there was another woman in my department who did the same thing as me and was also struggling after she had her second baby. So we went to the human resources person and she was supportive but said the company doesn't have this in place. So we did the research and went to the president of the division and we went through a couple of struggles, but eventually they accepted it. I'm so glad it worked out, because it's been great for me and my family.

However, as in the case of flexible schedules discussed previously, individually negotiated deals to reduce work hours create divisions among employees and perceived inequality at work. Some employees are not successful in their negotiations. For example, a Citizen's Health senior account executive with two children describes her experience: "I had a job-sharing arrangement when my first child was little, but I now have a two-year-old and the company won't allow me to do this. I think that when the company was smaller, they were willing to work with us, but now that we've grown to be a bigger organization, they just don't do that. And they're really strict with the hours. I asked if I could work 8–4:30, but they weren't willing to do that."

Similarly, a forty-five-year-old Vantech information systems manager, married to a lab technician and with two grown children, expresses his frustration with the lack of organizational consistency regarding reduced working time arrangements:

> With job sharing and part time, it's not consistent throughout the company. There are some areas where if you say you want to go part time, they'll say either work full-time or you have no job. They don't give you the flexibility even though if you look at the structure of your job and what is required for the position, you could easily do that on a part time basis, or by taking part of the work home if need be.

In sum, focus-group participants highlight the need for reduced work hours as part of an overall flexible working time policy. In the absence of such policies, workers push for individual exceptions to rules, leading to perceptions of inequality between the haves and have-nots.

Beyond Work-Life Policies and Informal Supports

Thus, increasing the apparent flexibility of a job or career while still expecting workers to commit boundless time and energy to work does little or nothing to advance the cause of work-life integration.[46] Note that the professionals in our study tend to enjoy job autonomy and control over their work, but also experience conflict between work and nonwork life.

Formal and informal work-life policies alone do not address the full range of challenges that working families face in trying to successfully integrate work and the rest of life. Job security, pay, career-development prospects, benefits, and other job features that are important to employees and their family stability are also components of organizational family responsiveness.[47] Several focus-group participants frame the issue of compensation in terms of its impact on the work-life interface. A forty-six-year-old Utilco engineer, father of two teenagers and married to a nurse, says:

> I haven't had a pay raise in three years, and that may appear to be a personal "bitch," but it has a tremendous impact on the family and the strain. I honestly feel that it falls very closely in line with the theme of what we're talking about here. And also, every year for benefits, we get a smorgasbord of options, but they're all reduced. They've gone down for the last five years now. We've been forced into an HMO-type medical benefit, and our cost has increased. That impacts on your family life because it impacts on your budget. And also on the quality of medical care you and your family get.

Repeated comments among focus-group members also emphasize the importance of embedding work-life policies in an overall organizational culture that validates and respects employees' needs to reserve time and energy for nonwork activities. Themes of respect, trust, and employee empowerment were recurrent, as in the statement of a Vantech chemical engineer in her thirties with an elementary school child: "I think there needs to be an environmental shift for people to say that we really do embrace people who have families that are important to them, that they can still be very good workers and excellent contributors, and we will work with them so they can manage well with work and with family. And I don't know how you do that in a policy; it's more of a complete shift in thinking."

The overall conclusion that we draw from our review of the qualitative data is that formal work-life policies alone do not make a family-responsive employer.

The design of human resource practices, the organization of work, and the overall culture regarding the relative importance of employees' work and nonwork lives form the backbone of an integrated approach to work-life balance.

Quantitative Results from *The Cornell Couples and Careers Study*

We now turn to survey data of a subsample of couples from *The Cornell Couples and Careers Study* and use regression analysis to investigate the predictors of work-family conflict, control over work circumstances, and individuals' intention to leave their present employer. We report results from 264 married or cohabiting opposite-sex couples in which both members are employed. This subsample, approximately one-third of the overall Cornell study, represents participants who were randomly administered the module of survey questions containing the measures of job and workplace characteristics. (For a description of the overall sample, please see app.)

Measures

Dependent Variables   We have three dependent variables: work-family conflict (negative spillover from work to family), employee control over work, and intention to quit one's job. The first two measures capture individuals' day-to-day ability to manage time and commitments to work and family.

> **Work-family conflict.** This is a two-item scale of negative spillover from work to family (see Roehling, Moen, and Batt, chap. 7 in this volume, for source and wording of items).
>
> **Employee control over work.** To measure this, we asked employees how much choice they have over their daily work schedule, weekly work schedule, their use of vacation and personal time, their ability to receive personal phone calls and email at work, the amount and timing of work that must be done at home in order to meet work demands, and the place at which they work (home versus regular workplace). The scale (alpha = .76) is adapted from Linda Thomas and Daniel Ganster. Responses are measured on a scale of 1–5.[48]
>
> **Intention to turn over.** This is measured by a scale score comprising five items that ask whether respondents plan to stay with their present employers until retirement, how many more years they expect to stay, whether they have recently talked to colleagues or friends about looking for another job,

whether they are actively looking for another job, and whether they are seriously considering quitting.

Independent Variables   Independent variables include three measures of traditional human resource incentives, two measures of formal and informal work-life support, and five work-design measures.

Human Resource Incentives

Salary. This is measured with a single item based on the question: "What is your annual salary from paid employment, including any bonuses, overtime, and/or commissions, before taxes and other deductions?"[49]

Job security. This is based on respondents' answer to: "Think of a scale of 0 to 100, where 0 means you are certain you will lose your present job and 100 means you are certain you will be able to keep it. How certain is it that in the next couple of years you will be able to keep your job?"

Career development benefits. This is measured by an additive index of three types of career support: education and training, tuition reimbursement, and career-development services.

Formal and Informal Work-Life Support

Flexible scheduling policies. This is an index measuring whether employees are granted five types of benefits relating to the flexible use of work time: paid family leave, personal/dependent-care time (small increments of time off during work hours to attend to personal or family needs), flextime, telecommuting, and time off for volunteering. Note that we measure availability, not use, of flexible scheduling policies.[50] The variable takes on values ranging from 0 (have none) to 5 (have all five).

Supervisor support. This is a four-item scale based on the following items: how frequently in the past three months employees' supervisors have switched schedules to accommodate their family responsibilities, have listened to their problems, have juggled tasks or duties to accommodate their family responsibilities, and have shared ideas or advice. Responses range from 1 (never) to 5 (very often). The alpha reliability coefficient is .68.[51]

Work-Design Measures

Decision-making autonomy. This is a scale based on the following three items: "I determine what I need to do in order to complete my assignments," "I am able to influence what procedures, tools, and material I use in doing my work," and "I am able to influence which specific tasks I am assigned to do."[52] The response format was a scale of 1–5, where 1 = strongly disagree and 5 = strongly agree. The alpha reliability coefficient for this scale is .68.

Coordination. This is a three-item additive scale that measures how frequently employees coordinate with colleagues in their own departments, colleagues outside of their departments, and managers or supervisors in their departments in order to accomplish their work tasks.[53]

Flexible technology use. This is an additive index of six items that measure employees' use of email, beepers, cellular phones, or fax machines to communicate with work while at home or with home while at work and the use of a portable computer or home computer to do work.

Work hours. This is a single-item measure that asks employees, "On average, how many hours a week do you actually work, including any paid or unpaid extra hours that you put in beyond your official work week?"

Travel. This is a dummy variable that measures whether the respondent is required to do overnight travel as a regular part of the job.

Control Variables

Children. This is the number of children living in the home. It is likely that having children will be positively related to work-family conflict and negatively related to perceptions of control over managing work and family matters.

Affect. This is a five-item scale used to control for negative disposition or affect.[54] Employees rated how frequently in the past month they have felt in good spirits (reverse scored), so sad that nothing could cheer them up, restless or fidgety, nervous, or that everything was an effort. Coefficient alpha for this measure is .61.

Age. This is self-reported and should be negatively related to turnover intentions.

Job tenure. This measures the number of years that employees have been in their jobs.

Results

Mean Levels of Work-Family Conflict, Employee Control over Work, and Turnover Intentions Most of our husbands and wives report experiencing work interference with family at least some of the time; the mean for both groups is approximately 2.7 on a scale of 1 to 5, with 1 representing "never" and 5 representing "all of the time." Eighty-one percent of wives and 72 percent of husbands report that their jobs make them feel too tired to do the things that need attention at home at least some of the time. Fifty-seven percent of wives and 67 percent of husbands report that job worries distract them while they are at home at least some of the time. Both wives and husbands report having a fair amount of control over their work circumstances, with husbands reporting slightly higher levels—a mean score of 3.6 on a scale of 1 to 5 versus 3.2 for wives. Approximately two-thirds of the employees in our sample have no plans to leave their current employers. Slightly more husbands than wives do intend to change employers before they reach retirement.

Results from Regression Analysis   Table 19.2 presents the results (coefficients and overall model fit) of the regression analyses of work-family conflict, employee control over work, and turnover intentions for wives and husbands, respectively. For ease of interpretation, we present standardized beta coefficients for the models of work-family conflict and control over work, which were estimated using ordinary least squares (OLS) regression. The figures in the columns under Turnover Intentions are coefficients from ordered probit models. The predictors, which are grouped into sets, include three of the four dimensions of organizational family responsiveness identified in the introduction to this chapter (formal and informal policies for work-life support, traditional human resource incentives, and work design), spouse's work characteristics, and control variables. We discuss the findings for each set of predictors for all three dependent variables. We present results for wives and husbands separately because in models using the full sample, the coefficient for an indicator variable for gender was significant in regressions of all three outcomes. Gender is a key consideration, not only because past research has documented differences in the level and nature of work-family conflict experienced by women and men, but also because some research reports that women have higher levels of turnover than men.

Concerning policies for work-life support, access to flexible scheduling has surprisingly little impact on the work-family outcomes tested. It has no effect on the work-family conflict or the reported control over work of either wives or husbands. It is negatively related to turnover intentions, but this relationship holds only for husbands. By contrast, supervisor supportiveness has a strong negative effect on wives' work-family conflict and is negatively related to both wives' and husbands' turnover intentions. Thus, women whose supervisors support their efforts to integrate work and the rest of life experience lower levels of work-family conflict, and both women and men who enjoy supervisor support are less likely to quit their employers.

Traditional human resource incentives (salary, job security, and career-development benefits) affect all three outcomes. Salary is positively related to both work-family conflict and control over work for husbands; this seemingly paradoxical effect may signify that highly paid jobs are likely to both impose extensive demands on their incumbents and also grant them a high level of control

Table 19.2 Regressions of Work-Family Conflict, Control over Work, and Turnover Intentions[a]

	Work-Family Conflict		Control over Work		Turnover Intentions	
	Wives	Husbands	Wives	Husbands	Wives	Husbands
Work-Life Support						
Flexible scheduling	−0.08	0.04	−0.04	0.02	−0.20	−0.32*
Supervisor support	−0.27***	0.03	0.05	0.02	−0.62*	−0.75*
HR Incentives						
Salary (log)	0.05	0.16*	−0.02	0.27**	−0.53	−0.63
Career development	0.04	0.07	−0.04	0.04	0.35	0.36
Job security	−0.14*	−0.15*	0.04	0.00	−0.02*	−0.04***
Work Design						
Decision autonomy	−0.01	−0.05	0.26***	0.17**	0.27	0.00
Coordination	0.07	0.13*	−0.07	−0.11[†]	0.07	0.05
Flexible technology	0.12[†]	0.05	0.35***	0.36***	0.19	0.25[†]
Work hours	0.15[†]	0.05	−0.17*	−0.19**	−0.02	−0.02
Travel	0.04	−0.06	0.20**	0.18**	0.74[†]	0.13
Control over Work[b]					−0.40	−0.81**
Spouse Variables						
Work hours	−0.02	−0.08	0.08	0.05	0.03	−0.01
Salary (log)	−0.03	0.01	−0.04	0.03	−1.18*	0.37
Job security	0.00	0.02	0.05	0.01	0.00	0.00
Flexible technology	0.00	−0.03	−0.08	−0.14*	0.12	0.14
Flexible scheduling	0.00	−0.02	−0.05	−0.04	0.06	−0.24[†]
Control Variables						
Children	−0.08	0.02	−0.13*	−0.18**	0.12	−0.02
Negative affect	0.31***	0.47***	0.07	−0.02	0.14	−0.29
Age	0.02	−0.04	0.08	0.02	−0.07*	−0.13***
Job tenure	−0.01	−0.11[†]	−0.06	0.01	−0.20***	−0.11**
N (couples)	234	218	234	218	205	198
F	5.6***	6.72***	5.99***	6.61***	65.23***	83.02***
R^{2c}	0.33	0.39	0.35	0.39	0.15	0.18
Adjusted R^2	0.27	0.33	0.29	0.33		

[a] Figures in columns under Work-Family Conflict and Control over Work are standardized beta coefficients; figures under Turnover Intentions are coefficients from ordered probit model. [†] Indicates $p < 0.10$; * Indicates $p < 0.05$; ** Indicates $p < 0.01$; *** Indicates $p < 0.001$; HR, human resource.

[b] The control variable was only included in the turnover equations.

[c] This figure is a "pseudo R^2" in the turnover equations, which were estimated using ordered probit models.

Source: *Cornell Couples and Careers Study*, 1998–99.

over their working conditions. There is no relationship between salary and any of the three outcomes for wives. The availability of career-development benefits has no impact on any of the outcomes for either husbands or wives. Job security is negatively related to both work-family conflict and turnover intentions for both wives and husbands, however. This result indicates that women and men who feel secure in their jobs experience lower levels of work interference with family and are less likely to leave their employers.

The work design block of predictors affects work-family conflict and turnover intentions to a modest degree and has a very strong impact on employee control over work. Decision-making autonomy, flexible technology use, and travel are all strongly and positively related—and work hours is strongly and negatively related—to control for both wives and husbands. In addition, the coefficient for coordination with others is negative and marginally significant, but only for husbands' reported control over work. These results suggest that both men and women who have a high level of autonomy in their jobs, who use technology to stay connected between work and home, and who travel as part of their jobs enjoy high levels of control, whereas those who work long hours report lower levels of control. With respect to work-family conflict, husbands who must coordinate extensively with others in the course of their work report higher levels of work interference with family. For wives, using flexible technology and working longer hours are both associated with more work-family conflict, albeit the coefficients for these variables are only marginally significant. Two variables reach marginal levels of significance in the models predicting turnover intentions: wives whose jobs involve travel and husbands who use technology to stay connected between work and home both tend to report increased plans to leave their employer.

There are very few significant effects of spouse variables in our models. None of the variables measuring spouses' work hours, salary, job security, flexible technology use, or access to flexible scheduling has any effect on the reported work-family conflict of either wives or husbands. One coefficient is significant in the models predicting control over work—wives' use of technology to stay connected between work and home is negatively related to husbands' reported control. In the turnover models, husbands' salary is negatively related to wives' turnover intentions, whereas the coefficient for wives' access to flexible scheduling is marginally significant and negatively related to husbands' turnover intentions.

Summing Up

This chapter extends previous research on work-life integration by identifying challenges that employees from dual-earner couples face in integrating their work and nonwork lives and by developing a comprehensive model of organizational family responsiveness involving formal and informal policies and practices for work-life support, traditional human resource incentives, and work redesign, all within the context of an organizational culture that values and supports the work-life integration of all employees. We use both qualitative and quantitative data to examine the model.

The respondents in *The Cornell Couples and Careers Study* are a group of middle- and upper middle-class employees. For the most part, they are well paid, are well educated, work primarily in professional or managerial occupations, and enjoy a relatively high level of control over their work. Despite these advantages, however, they report a considerable amount of work-family conflict. Analyses of focus-group discussions indicate that many of the work-nonwork conflicts experienced by our couples are time-based. Lack of flexibility in the timing and place of work and excessive time demands hamper the effective integration of work with the rest of life, and the simple availability of benefits and policies designed to provide temporal flexibility does not represent an adequate organizational response to the work-life challenges employees face. In the regression analyses, flexible scheduling policies have no effect on work-family conflict or control over work, but are associated with lower turnover intentions for husbands. Focus-group results do, however, suggest that employees value flexible scheduling policies and find them useful. Yet although many focus-group participants report having worked out useful flexible scheduling arrangements on an individual basis, the fact that such arrangements are not available across the board constitutes a shortcoming in organizational responsiveness to the challenges of work-life integration. Our qualitative data suggest that employees' access to flexible scheduling is uneven and may depend on the type of work they do, the hierarchical level they occupy in their organizations, and/or the idiosyncratic attitudes of their supervisors.

With respect to informal work-life policies, the importance of supervisor support is quite evident both in the regression and qualitative analyses. Supervisor support is associated with less frequent work-family conflict, with higher levels of control over work for wives, and with decreased turnover intentions for both wives and husbands. Focus-group analyses suggest that supervisors who are helpful and supportive of their employees' family demands tend to engender more gratitude, loyalty, and respect from workers. Yet although supervisor support, like formal policies, is clearly important, it is no magic bullet for dual-earner couples struggling to integrate work and life demands. Informal workplace support from supervisors and formal work-life policies should represent two complementary elements of a family-responsive organization. Although some of the employees in the Cornell study appear to enjoy both types of work-life support, our focus-group data suggest that in some organizations formal and informal elements function in a compensatory rather than complementary manner. For example, the focus groups at the two large manufacturing organizations (Vantech and Transco) indicate that, although these firms have work-life policies on the books, the overall organizational culture is not particularly supportive of work-life integration. By contrast, some of the health-care and educational employers have few formal policies in effect, yet most employees indicate that supportive supervisors grant them the flexibility they need to manage their family and personal responsibilities.

The qualitative data shed light on the symbolic importance of formal work-life initiatives. Employers who develop, implement, and publicize work-life policies send a signal throughout the organization that work-life issues are important. This signal serves to legitimate employees' desires and efforts to integrate work and nonwork roles and to demand reasonable accommodations from their employers to help them be successful at work and beyond. If the bulk of organizational family responsiveness occurs informally at the level of supervisor discretion, employees may perceive a lack of trust and respect from their employer. This understanding, in turn, may undermine job satisfaction and organizational commitment while creating resentment toward the employer.

Both qualitative and quantitative results provide support for our contention that the difficulties of work-life integration cannot be addressed solely through programs designed to provide flexibility and limit overall work demands. Traditional human resource incentives also play a part. Focus-group results demonstrate that adequate pay and benefits are important components of organizational family responsiveness. For instance, employees identified salary freezes and unsatisfactory health insurance as stressors. Although regression analyses show that salary is positively related to work-family conflict for husbands, we suspect that this may be picking up the fact that highly paid jobs often have a higher overall level of work demands. Salary is also positively related to control over work for husbands, and husbands who report high levels of control over work have significantly lower turnover intentions. The regression analyses also reveal the importance of job security; this variable is associated with less work-family conflict and lower turnover intentions for both wives and husbands. Among dual-earner couples, worries about losing a job constitute a work-domain stressor that negatively affects family and personal life. Because two careers must be considered in any episode of job change, our employees may be less mobile than employees without working spouses and therefore place a high value on job security. This suggests that organizations can enhance their employees' work-life integration by emphasizing job security in their human resource practices.

Work design constitutes another dimension of our model of organizational family responsiveness. Both quantitative and qualitative data demonstrate the impact that job demands and work design elements have on the work-life interface. Regression analyses show that long work hours are linked to increased work-family conflict and lower levels of work control, whereas job autonomy increases control over work. Work that requires frequent coordination with other people is associated with more work-family conflict and less control over work for husbands. The use of communication technologies, including cellular phones, faxes, email, and portable computers, gives wives and husbands more control over their work, but is also associated with more work-family conflict for wives. This may be due to the fact that the use of these technologies allows the demands and pressures from the work domain to intrude into the home itself. Focus-group results also highlight some of the ways in which work design affects work-life integration. Frequent meetings and inflexible work schedules both impair employees' ability to mesh work and life harmoniously. For instance, some employees describe how rigid manufacturing work processes prevent them from being able to modify their work schedules in order to meet family demands. Others report having coworkers who expect them to be continuously available for meetings, even early in the morning or in the evening, thereby reinforcing workplace cultures of overwork.

Organizations must be vigilant and responsive to the problem of overwork. Our qualitative data show that crushing workloads (often resulting from organizational downsizing and the redistribution of tasks to fewer employees) and workplace norms that demand long work hours constitute serious barriers to satisfactory work-life integration. Although several of the organizations in the Cornell study have a number of flexible scheduling and other work-life policies on the books, these employers have made little progress in institutionalizing reasonable limits on work time demands. Workplace norms that demand extensive "face time" undermine and limit the effectiveness of formal work-life policies. One employee in the focus groups even reported electing a part-time work schedule, with reduced pay and benefits, in order to limit herself to a regular full-time workweek. Such individualized solutions to the challenges of work-life integration clearly indicate that organizations are failing to systematically meet employees' work-life needs.

All in all, the results of the study reported in this chapter provide support for the argument that organizational family responsiveness involves multiple elements. Formal work-life policies, informal work-life support from supervisors and other organizational members, favorable human resource incentives, and work designed to provide employees with a reasonable level of work demands and a high level of control over the conditions of their work are all important for supporting employee work-life integration. Our qualitative data suggest that a workplace culture of family responsiveness is also a critical element and that barriers to effective work-life integration derive in part from organizational cultures that fail to appreciate the importance of employees' family and personal lives. Unequal access to flexible scheduling, unreasonable work demands, inadequate compensation and benefits, job insecurity, and employees' often having to take on primary responsibility for presenting a convincing case to their employers that they should be granted flexibility all signal a lack of systematic respect for employees' personal and family needs. In order to fully address the challenges of work-life integration, there must be support from all levels of the organization, from the CEO on down through the ranks. Only when employers truly believe that systematic work-life integration constitutes a win-win situation for themselves and their employees and back this belief up with policies and programs to give employees flexibility, limit work demands, and provide adequate human resource incentives will the promise of work-life integration be realized.

This chapter has implications for future research on work-life integration. Rather than focusing on a limited set of work-life policies, we have advanced and tested a broader, more integrated model of factors that affect employees' work-life integration. We urge future researchers to continue in this vein by measuring multiple elements of formal and informal work-life supports, traditional human resource incentives, work design, and organizational culture. Our regression analyses also reveal some interesting gender differences in the prediction of work-family conflict, control over work, and turnover intentions that are deserving of further research. Finally, although we do not find many significant effects of spouses' work characteristics and work-life supports on husbands' or wives' outcomes, we encourage future scholars to take a couple-level approach to the study of work-life integration in dual-earner couples. It is possible, for instance, that the work-life supports that husbands and wives enjoy in their workplaces could have either an additive or multiplicative effect on work-life integration at the couple level. To the extent that future research can identify the combination of workplace characteristics and work-life supports that best enhance work-life integration for dual-earner couples, employers, employees and their families all stand to benefit.

Epilogue: Toward a Policy Agenda

Phyllis Moen

We began this book with the case of Karen Hughes, a woman in her forties in a dual-earner family with a teenage son still at home who left her powerful and high-status, desirable job as White House counselor for "family reasons." Such events may indeed become metaphors for our times. Members of the first workforce (launched with industrialization and fully institutionalized by World War II) knew where their priorities lay, as classic studies of the organization man show. But in the twenty-first century, most workers in the new workforce are, like Karen Hughes, living in two cultures, at work and at home, each with distinctive modalities, values, and demands. Is it the case, as Sylvia Ann Hewlett claims, that women like Hughes will always have to choose to prioritize either their family careers or their occupational careers, but not both? Where in this equation are their husbands? Where in this equation are the growing numbers of older workers or workers without children in the new workforce who may also want a reduced-hour work schedule? Where are forward-thinking corporations seeking to design their work and working environments to be more flexible and worker friendly? And where is the nation's fundamental commitment to equality of opportunity across gender and age divides (even absent a consensus as to equality of outcome)?

We have shown that many dual-earner, middle-class couples *are* managing well, despite the mismatch between their personal goals and obligations and the outdated rules of the occupational career-retirement game. But for many, if not most, at some point in their life course the only alternative is for one or both spouses to scale back—at work, at home, or both. And at another point the only alternative is remaining in their demanding, long-hour primary career jobs or else take total retirement. We believe people *can* do it all, have it all, but not necessarily at the same time or in any conventional order. What is required is a rethinking of the culture and structure of both work and careers. Assisting a toddler or a teenager move toward greater independence may seem like a lifetime project, but, in truth, those of us who have been there know the time flies by. Unfortunately, as currently configured, occupational career building and family career building occur simultaneously, and the hidden infrastructure of time in the form of work hours and occupational career paths wreaks a severe toll (in benefits, in salary, in future prospects) to any deviations from the lockstep path of continuous, full-time (or more) work. Accordingly, many middle-class two-earner couples have opted to reduce the family side of the work-family equation by having no or fewer children, delaying marriage or parenthood, or leaving one marriage for another. Many also find that one partner (disproportionately women) must scale back in their career goals and work hours. And the vast numbers of workers moving toward retirement find they have but two options: full time (or more) work in their career occupations or full-time retirement, with few phased retirement options in between.

The findings throughout this book suggest that simple assumptions about work-family balance portray a very limited picture of a much more complicated, variegated phenomenon. *The Cornell Couples and Careers Study* portrays the life course challenge to work-family research and policy as dealing with more than issues related to working mothers or child care. We have shown the contingent nature of life paths and life quality: how work and home circumstances and behavior patterns affect work and family investments, conflicts, successes, personal growth, and emotional well-being; how couple as well as individual choices and constraints alter men's and women's resources, power, roles, career patterns, preferences, and expectations. We need theoretical and policy analysis models that move beyond static snapshots of individuals to focus on couples' conjoint trajectories of work, family, and well-being across the life course. These trajectories (or careers) play out in a world undergoing profound societal changes in the workforce, the economy, families, communities, and gender norms but few corresponding changes in labor force or work-place policy and practice related to the lockstep career template.

What are the necessary policy ingredients that prime movers—corporations, unions, governments as regulators as well as employers, nonprofit organizations, and other change agents—can place on the national agenda? Our evidence suggests concrete policy innovations that can broaden the array of options available to working families. An easy first step would be for employers to clarify, enforce, and further develop existing rules and regulations already on the books regarding time and career path flexibilities and to foster a culture supporting alternative work-hour and career options. Many of the people in our study do not even know what opportunities are already available to them. Many are afraid to take advantage of existing options because doing so might signal a less-than-full commitment to their jobs, exacting costs in future promotions, salary increases, and even job security. For example, people working in downsizing corporations are especially reluctant to try to reduce their hours, even to a more "sane" forty-hour workweek, fearing the outcome might be layoffs. And many of the people in our study say they work long hours and do not take advantage of flextime arrangements because, realistically, their job requires such hours. Clearly needed is a reassessment by managers of rising expectations in this twenty-four-hour global economy about workload, deadlines, and what is called low-value work (attending unnecessary meetings, filling out unnecessary forms).

Second, this points to the need for employers and governments to keep track of the variations in work-hour and career path arrangements among their own workforces and in the nation at large, as well as tracking their implications for occupational, salary, pension, and benefit attainment. We were surprised to find how few human resource people we interviewed even know how many of their employees were working part time or part year or even how many were on some form of flextime. Some human resource people do not even know what their firm's policies are regarding, for example, phased retirement. Keeping and reporting such statistics might serve to legitimate alternative work hours and career paths and possibilities, especially if they show that workers opting for them do not pay a price for doing so. Related to this, several magazines and professional organizations give family-friendly and similar awards to companies who adopt particular policies; a better gauge of the worker friendliness of corporations might be the proportion of their workforces actually using them. Corporate leaders, along with those handing out rewards, need to recognize that job security is also a key component of friendliness or work-life quality. Several of the people we interviewed believe that their employers offered more family-friendly benefits even as they undertake massive downsizing, as if to shift the focus from the layoffs and forced early retirements.

Third, visionary employers might recognize that the growth in the workforce has slowed, that this is a new workforce, more heterogeneous in every way from the first workforce of the first half of the twentieth century, and that, a skilled, invested, flexible, and energized workforce is the secret to productivity gains. To attract, retain, and gain the commitment and loyalty of employees they need to change the old rules of the game: the outdated assumptions of linear, full-time, lockstep career paths. Offering a menu of career path and work-hour options would better fit the needs and values of contemporary workers, enabling, for example, preretirees to shift down to reduced hours rather than retiring completely, or mothers and fathers of infants to cut back on hours for a year without sacrificing either their benefits or their long-term career options. Moving to a focus on occupational career and family career pathways reframes and broadens the work-life issue (mostly aimed at working mothers) to work-hour and career path issues of all workers, men and women, at different ages and stages.

This brings up a fourth policy innovation: viewing risks and transitions as key human resource, workforce, and labor issues. Today's climate of downsizing, mergers, and bankruptcies fosters a sense of uncertainty and ambiguity about work and career paths, with few viable safety nets. Many people expect to and will change jobs, but health insurance and other benefits remain tied to employers, even as employers cut back on their benefit packages and eligibility options. Workers also experience other life course exigencies and uncertainties as they marry someone with occupational goals of their own, move to a new locale, become parents, divorce, adopt, get sick, remarry, have a car accident, have a parent who develops Alzheimer's disease, or begin to think about retirement. All these real-life experiences strain an already strained workforce, pointing to the need for policies around the life course risks and vulnerabilities of workers.

Finally, and most important, the United States as a society must recognize the need to reshape the lockstep social organization of careers and the life course. Clearly, the traditional occupational career script (based on the obsolete breadwinner-homemaker template and the disappearing social contract between workers and employers equating seniority with security) is eroding. But workforce policy innovation, whether at community, corporate, state, or federal levels, is a long-term and complicated project. It requires far more than small changes around the edges of existing arrangements. Rather, we need bold inventions that reconfigure prevailing assumptions and policies undergirding work hours, career paths, worker control, work design, family strategies, reward structures, and benefits. This brings us to a fifth recommendation: the need for a comprehensive reassessment of the hidden and outdated assumptions embedded in the Fair Labor Standards Act, Unemployment Insurance, Social Security, payroll taxes, and welfare. We recognize such institutional-level change as actually updating existing policies occurs at a glacial pace. But the costs of doing nothing are outweighing the costs of change, and now is the time to begin. An important start would be to identify and modify specific rules and regulations embedded in federal policies and programs that currently constrain workers' options. Meanwhile, as we have shown, working families manage their jobs at work and at home and their relationships at home and at work as best they can. But policymakers in both the public and private sectors and in organized labor can increase the menu of work-hour and career path options available to this new workforce. Karen Hughes is not really a symbol of women who scale back. Her employer, President Bush, will have her as a consultant long-distance, and, I expect, we will see her very much in the political game. Making a range of such flexibilities available to all workers makes sense at all stages of the life course. In that way this nation can continue to invest in and use the talents of its people and continue to have a responsive and committed workforce and responsive and committed families.

Appendix

Methodological Notes on *The Cornell Couples and Careers Study*

Phyllis Moen, Patricia V. Roehling, Stephen Sweet,
Bickley Townsend, Shinok Lee,
Deborah Harris-Abbott, Liane O'Brien,
and Kristin Campbell

Most research on spillover and work-family issues has been with either a select sample (nonrandom) of employees in one specific company or with a nationally representative sample of employees. These samples have included a heterogeneous group of workers of various occupations and socioeconomic backgrounds. Our unique sample, by contrast, consists of middle-class (defined as at least one member of the couple having attended college), primarily professional, dual-earner couples, a particularly hard-working upwardly mobile segment of society. Both the men and women in our sample, for example, work longer hours and make more money than similar couples in the 1997 National Study of the Changing Workforce (see table A.5 later in this appendix).

The goal of *The Cornell Couples and Careers Study* (funded by the Alfred P. Sloan Foundation as part of the Cornell Employment and Family Careers Institute, a Sloan Center for the study of working families) is to examine working families in context. This context includes a variety of circumstances, including the participating couples' life stage and each spouse's employment situation and workplace environment. This study extends the analysis of occupational careers by locating plans and experiences as operating in tandem, with the linkages between partners being a central focus in the research design. The data were collected primarily to facilitate the study of middle-class dual-earner couples.

The findings reported in this book draw on three primary data sources: a series of focus-group interviews and one-on-one in-depth interviews, a telephone survey of working couples, and interviews with human resource personnel at the participating companies. In our sample of dual-earner couples at least one spouse works at one of seven strategically selected organizations. Here, we first detail our methods and sampling strategies, then discuss some inherent limitations to the study, and conclude with directions for future research efforts.

Organizations: Sampling Strategy and Characteristics

The principal investigator (Phyllis Moen) made inquiries to a variety of company representatives in an effort to create an organizational sample that would reflect the diversity of employment experiences of middle-class working couples within the restructured and restructuring economy of the late 1990s in upstate New York. The final selection of companies hinged, to a great extent, on the willingness of company gatekeepers to advance the research project and provide lists of employees to the research team. Seven organizations participated in the study: two manufacturing companies, one utility company, two health-care organizations, and two universities. We use pseudonyms for all participating organizations.

Manufacturing and Utility Sectors

All three participating organizations in the manufacturing and utility sectors are large U.S.-owned corporations that are publicly traded on the New York Stock Exchange. Each participating company was undergoing a significant period of restructuring and downsizing during the time of the data collection (1998–99).

Vantech, the largest organization and the organization employing the largest percentage of our respondents, is a multinational manufacturing corporation. Due to a highly competitive business environment, Vantech began downsizing in the late 1980s, with the goal of cutting approximately 20 percent of the workforce. Layoffs were underway at the time we interviewed workers and their spouses in 1998.

Transco, a subsidiary of a large multinational conglomerate, is in the manufacturing sector. As part of a cost-cutting effort by its parent company, Transco began downsizing in the mid-1980s. The first round of layoffs reduced the workforce substantially; other layoffs followed. These layoffs were ongoing at the time data were being collected for *The Cornell Couples and Careers Study.*

Utilco is a large utility company in upstate New York. Following deregulation of the utility industry, increased competition forced it to institute restructuring and downsizing. At the time of the data collection, Utilco was undergoing a series of layoffs aimed at both hourly and professional employees.

Health-Care Sector

Valley View Medical is a nonprofit community health-care organization. In contrast to the participating companies in the manufacturing and utility sectors, Valley View Medical has never had to lay off an employee. In fact, over the past ten years this facility has expanded and added services. Most employees at Valley View Medical are skilled (e.g., nurses and physical therapists), technical (e.g., x-ray technicians and medical technologists) or clerical workers. Although a medical facility, physicians are not employed by Valley View Medical.

Citizen's Health is a nonprofit health-service company serving central New York residents. At the time of the data collection, Citizen's Health was concluding a friendly merger with another health-service company. No layoffs had occurred or were expected to occur as a result of the merger. The majority of Citizen's Health employees are administrative, technical, and support staff.

Higher Education Sector

Upstate University offers associate's, undergraduate, master's, and doctoral degrees. In the past ten years, enrollment at Upstate University has steadily increased and the university is currently on a sound financial footing. In the 1990s, a program of managed attrition was implemented to decrease staff size. A negligible number of staff (less than 1 percent) were laid off.

Lake University is a nationally recognized institution of higher education offering undergraduate, master's, doctoral, and professional degrees. The university has managed most of its recent needs to decrease staff size through attrition, laying off approximately 2 percent of its workforce from 1996–99.

Organizational Data Collection Methods

We obtained information about each organization from its human resources department, using two methods for collecting the data. First, members of the human resources departments in the participating organizations were asked to complete a questionnaire that addressed easily quantifiable information about the organization and its employees (e.g., number of employees, available benefits, and turnover). Second, we conducted a one- to two-hour, face-to-face, structured interview with a human resource manager. The interview focused on the human resource policies and practices of the organization, particularly employees' use (and any obstacles to use) of work-life and family-friendly policies (such as flexible work arrangements, dependent-care programs, and phased-retirement options).

Differences among Organizations

We chose to sample workers in organizations rather than using a sample frame based on individual residences because of a desire to assess how the context of work environments influences the plans, expectations, and experiences of working couples. Work environments vary in a number of ways, including job security (especially as influenced by downsizing histories), company policies, company size, organizational goals, and the demographic characteristics of the employees. The organizations also differ in the proportion of their employees who are in professional or managerial (exempt) positions and in the proportion of women both in their total workforce and among exempt employees. Women are underrepresented in the manufacturing and utility sectors and overrepresented in the health-care sector. This reflects similar gender divisions in these sectors in the nation at large (see table A.1).

Worker and Spouse Interviews: Sampling Strategy and Methods

Selecting the Sample

From each of the participating organizations we identified a sample of workers in two-earner families and surveyed this sample along with their spouses or partners. Once an organization agreed to participate in *The Cornell Couples and Careers Study*, the employer sent a letter to its exempt (salaried) employees in upstate New York describing the study. Most of the organizations (Vantech, Transco, Utilco, Lake University, Citizen's Health, and Upstate University) sent letters to a random sample of their exempt workforce. Valley View Medical sent letters to all employees (exempt and nonexempt) who were enrolled in the company's family medical plan. Enclosed in the mailing was a response card. Those returning the card to the Cornell Employment and Family Careers Institute were then entered into a respondent pool.

We randomly selected participants from the respondent pool for the focus groups and one-on-one in-depth telephone interviews. All respondents in the pool were contacted to participate in the telephone survey, including those who had already participated in a focus-group or in-depth interview.

Table A.1 Organizations Participating in the *Cornell Couples and Careers Study*[a]

Sector	Code	Full-Time Employees in Upstate NY	Women in Participating[a] Organization's Workforce (%)	Employees Who Are Exempt (%)[b]	Exempt Employees in Organization Who Are Women (%)	Women in National Workforce in 1997 (%)[c]
Manufacturing	Vantech	10,000+	36	30	26	32
	Transco	2,000–4,999	21	45	19	
Utility	Utilco	5,000–9,999	21.3	26	not available	29[d]
Health care	Valley View Medical	less than 2,000	80	18	68	76[e]
	Citizen's Health	less than 2,000	84	30	63	79[f]
Higher education	Upstate University	2,000–4,999	53	69	44	52[g]
	Lake University	5,000–9,999	60	Not available	30	

[a] "Participating" refers to employers permitting the recruitment of their employees for *The Cornell Couples and Careers Study.*
[b] Employees classified as exempt are salaried and not eligible for overtime pay. We use exempt employees as a proxy for professional/managers.
[c] From Statistical Abstract of the United States 1998.
[d] Includes transportation and communication as well as public utilities.
[e] Employees in hospital industry.
[f] Employees in health services, except hospitals.
[g] Employees in colleges and universities.

Response Rate

It is difficult to estimate a response rate in the manner customarily desired, due the to the logistical constraints of generating organizational interest and participation. Unfortunately there was no possibility of participating organizations' agreeing to track the responses of employees solicited for the study.

In the initial letter to exempt employees (sent by the participating employers), potential respondents were alerted to the fact that we were studying dual-earner couples. Those who returned response cards were those interested in participating who believed they were eligible for the study (members of dual-earner couples). Due to employer concerns about confidentiality, the participating organizations did not provide access to information about those respondents who did not return response cards or even the number of letters sent out. Therefore, we are unable to distinguish between potential respondents who did not want to participate in the study and those who did not respond because they deemed themselves ineligible.

Qualitative Data

Focus Groups   We conducted fourteen focus groups, involving the participation of a total of 112 workers. Two focus groups took place at each of the seven participating organizations. All focus groups lasted from 12:00 noon until 1:00 PM at the employees' workplace and were led by Cornell Employment and Family Careers Institute faculty or staff. Prior to each focus group, we assured all participants that any information discussed would remain confidential. We taped and later transcribed each session. On average, each focus group consisted of approximately ten participants, but ranged from five to twelve. These were mixed-gender groups and, depending on the gender composition of the employing organizations participating in the study, the number of male and female participants varied for each group. A total of forty-one men and seventy-one women took part in the focus groups. The focus groups addressed a range of topics, including employee benefits (which benefits were and were not helpful and which were missing), employer policies, use of time, the use of technology to manage work-family roles, and the best practices used to manage work-family responsibilities. All participants received a complimentary Cornell Employment and Family Careers Institute mug and were provided with a catered lunch.

In-Depth Interviews   We also conducted 150 in-depth telephone interviews (eighty-five women and sixty-five men). Most were with workers in the seven participating organizations, but some of their spouses were interviewed as well (in a separately scheduled interview at a different time). We have in-depth interview information on thirty-seven married (or cohabitating) couples. An additional set of interviews were conducted on coworking couples (fourteen), couples in which both partners work for the same organization.

Prior to the interview, we assured participants that any information discussed would remain confidential. We taped the interviews with the participants' permission and later transcribed them. The interviews averaged approximately one hour in length, although there was considerable variation depending on the detail of answers given, other time constraints, and/or the amount of interviewer probing. The in-depth interview consisted of open-ended, semistructured questions addressing a broad range of experiences and cognitive assessments, including work and family history, the nature and timing of career and family decisions, and the strategies/practices used to manage work-family responsibilities (see the section Variable Definitions for a list of questions). Respondents received a thank-you note and a complimentary mug for their participation.

Quantitative Data

Telephone Survey All the workers in the respondent pool from the participating employer organizations were informed by a letter that they would be receiving a telephone call from the Cornell Employment and Family Careers Institute to schedule the survey. Prior to each interview, potential respondents were screened to assess their eligibility for the survey. The goal of the present study is to understand dual-earner couples. Therefore, to be eligible for the survey, all workers[1] over age thirty were required to be married or cohabiting. Additional requirements for inclusion in the study were:

- both the workers and their spouse/partners had to be employed (we included couples in which one member was retired but have not used them in the analyses)
- both the workers and their spouses/partners had to agree to participate

The only inclusion requirement for workers under the age of thirty was that they be employed.

There are six sections to the survey instrument: life history, work life, home life, the work-family interface, psychological well-being, and demographics. In addition, each respondent was randomly assigned to be interviewed using one of three modules: (1) strategies, policies, and practices of individuals and companies, (2) communities, networks, and religion, or (3) life transitions and expectations. Thus, we administered each module to one-third of the sample. Both workers and their spouses/partners received the same module. The modules allow for an efficient and effective way to both broaden the question base and obtain more detailed information on issues of interest. This approach, however, precluded the possibility of analyzing relationships of variables between modules.

We conducted a vast majority of surveys (98%) using a computer-assisted telephone interview. However, thirty-six surveys (2%) were administered in a written format to respondents who either were hearing-impaired or who had initially declined participation. The average length of the survey was approximately one hour.

As an incentive to participate in the survey, each worker and spouse/partner received $25 upon completion of the telephone survey ($50 per couple). A survey was not considered complete until both workers and their spouses/partners (if applicable) had finished their separate surveys.

Telephone Survey Respondents

Demographics and Education

Our telephone survey sample consists of 1,236[2] employees (respondents) from one of the seven organizations and 980 spouses/partners. In 170 cases, the spouses/partners were also employed in one of the seven participating organizations. Most of the sample consisted of dual-earner couples (979) in which both the respondents from the seven participating organizations and their spouses/partners were interviewed separately. Of the 979 couples, 918 are married and 61 are cohabiting. Eighteen of the sixty-one cohabiting couples are same-sex couples. In fifteen of the same-sex couples, both partners are women, and in three both partners are men. We also interviewed fourteen respondents who are under thirty and neither married or partnered.

The average age of the workers interviewed from our respondent pool in the seven participating organizations is forty-four years old (SD = 8.16, N = 1,236, range 22–73). Men are on average forty-six years old (SD = 8.06) and women are somewhat younger, on average 42 years old (SD = 7.8). On average, the spouses are also forty-four years old (SD = 8.08, N = 980), regardless of gender. Almost all (93.6%, N = 2,074) of the workers and spouses interviewed are white non-Hispanic. Of the remaining workers and spouses, 1.8 percent (N = 40) are African American, 1.8 percent (N = 32) are Asian, and 2.8 percent (N = 70) are other ethnic groups.

In line with the professional and managerial composition of the sample, among the workers in the seven participating organizations, 94.2 percent of the men and 90.5 percent of the women have obtained additional education beyond high school (see table A.2). Many have at most a bachelor's degree (36.7% men and 37.9% women) and approximately one-third of the sample (31.6% men and 34.4% women) have a graduate or professional degree. The main gender difference is at the doctoral level, with 12.5 percent of the men and only 3.5 percent of the women holding a doctoral degree. There is also a gender difference in per-

Table A.2   Demographic Information of Couples in the *Cornell Couples and Careers Study*[a]

	Referent Respondents in Participating Organizations		Spouses	
	Men	Women	Men	Women
High school graduates	5.8%[b]	9.5%[b]	17.8%	18.2%
Some college	11.7%[b]	17.3%[b]	19.3%	22.9%
College degree	36.7%[b]	37.9%[b]	32.2%	33.3%
At least some post graduate education	45.5%[b]	35.5%[b]	29.6%	25.4%
Personal income[b,c] (mean)	$74,398	$48,135	$53,577	$28,448
Standard deviation	($25,808)	($24,473)	($29,193)	($28,080)
Household income (mean)	$103,300	$95,190		
Standard deviation	($55,755)	($39,785)	—	—
N	532	388	388	532

[a]From the *Cornell Couples and Careers Study*, 1998–99. $N = 1,715$, except for missing or inappropriate cases; excludes singles and same-sex couples.
[b]Significant difference between worker and spouse $p < 0.01$.
[c]Significant difference for gender $p < 0.01$.

sonal income among workers in the seven participating organizations, with men averaging approximately $74,398 and women averaging approximately $48,135.

Note that the average number of years of education and the average income is higher for the workers in the seven participating organizations than for their spouses (see table A.2). The men tend to have more years of education and higher incomes than the women. On average, the couples have had 1.24 (SD = 0.52) committed relationships (16% are in their second or subsequent marriage). Most (88.5%) have had children; on average they have 2.34 (SD = 1.08) children.

The majority of the workers we interviewed from the participating organizations work at least full-time hours (98.9% of men and 85% of women). Thirty-five percent of the married/cohabiting workers from the participating organizations are managers, and 43.5 percent of the workers are in professional occupations. The remaining respondents are in technical, sales, administrative support, service, or production occupations. Table A.3 shows the occupational status of workers[3] within each type of participating organization. As table A.3 illustrates, the majority of the workers (50.2%) are employed in the manufacturing sector.

Life Stage

We operationalize life stage based on the wife's age, marital status, and family status.[4] Workers of different ages are at different stages, both in their occupational

Table A.3 Occupational Status of Respondents by Employment Sector[a]

Type of Organization	Distribution (%)	Manager (%)	Professional (%)	Other (%)
Manufacturing	50.2	34.2	46.4	19.4
Utility	7.7	38.5	30.8	30.8
Health care	10.6	27.1	36.8	36.1
Higher education	31.5	32.2	41.8	26.1

[a]Includes referent respondents and spouses who work at participating organizations. $N = 1,170$. Occupational status significant by sector at $p < 0.01$. From the *Cornell Couples and Careers Study*, 1998–99.

careers and their family careers. Because a couple's fertility potentials are determined, in large part, by the wife's age, we use this to construct the dividing point among younger and older childless couples, at age forty. Although our focus is on couples, we do include in our study workers in their twenties (but not discussed in this volume) who are not yet married or partnered but who can give us a sense of younger workers' expectations and experiences regarding the work-family interface. There are two types of nonparents based on the wife's age (see table A.4). The nonparents, wife-under-age-forty group consists of both young workers who are single (anticipatory stage) and those who are married or partnered but do not have children. The other group of nonparents consists of couples in which the wife is age forty or above, representing couples who are less likely to ever have children. Respondents with preschool-age children (under 6) living in the home are typically launching both their occupational careers and their families. Similarly, parents with school-age children living in the home are in the early or late establishment stages, depending on the age of their youngest child (6–12 versus 13–18). Parents with adult children (nineteen or older) living in the home are in the adult children stages. Respondents who are parents but whose adult children have left the home are in the empty nest stage.

Context: Upstate New York

A detailed analysis of the economic context of upstate New York and its relationship to the findings of *The Cornell Couples and Careers Study* is provided in the report *How Family Friendly Is Upstate New York?*[5] available through the Cornell Careers Institute. This report documents some key aspects of the context of upstate New York at the turn of the twenty-first century. In contrast to the robust national economy in the late 1990s, New York state—and upstate New York in particular—was experiencing below-average growth on several measures.

Table A.4 Description of Life Stages

Groups	Stage	Parental Status	Age	Age of Youngest Child in the Home[a]	Distribution[b]
Nonparents	Wife under age 40	Nonparents	20–39	N/A	143 (6.5%)
	Wife ages 40 and above	Nonparents	40+	N/A	199 (9.0%)
Total nonparents					342 (15.5%)
Parents of preschool-age children	Launching	Parents	21–62	under 6	513 (23.1%)
Parents of school-age children	Early establishment	Parents	27–59	6–12	555 (25.0%)
	Late establishment	Parents	26–69	13–18	337 (15.2%)
Total parents of school-age children					892 (40.2%)
Parents of adult children at home	Adult children	Parents	37–64	19+	148 (6.7%)
Empty nest	Empty nest	Parents	36–73	Adult children no longer at home	321 (14.5%)

[a]N/A, not applicable.
[b]N = 2,216.
Source: *Cornell Couples and Careers Study,* 1998–99.

These included declines in manufacturing employment, stagnant population growth, and an aging population.

Strengths and Limitations of the Sample

The goal of *The Cornell Couples and Careers Study* is to understand the complex interface between work and family among middle-class dual-earner couples. A unique strength of this study is that we are able to locate the respondents within the organizational and community contexts in which they work and live. As a product of the sample design, greater information was obtained than typically revealed in large national surveys of randomly selected households. The sample is not representative of the diversity of the United States as a whole but offers one of the most comprehensive appraisals of the experiences, strategies, and life histories of middle-class couples available.

This being said, critical readers will be concerned about the generalizability of the findings. One concern is the geographic locale of upstate New York and whether the experiences of middle-class couples in this area are typical of the larger U.S. population of middle-class couples. Although perhaps to a greater extent than most other states, New York experienced the types of downsizing and corporate restructuring typical of the economy as a whole. As such, we think that our sample captures couples in the context of moderate job insecurity in situations in which other employment opportunities are available. Such a case typifies the U.S. economy at the turn of the twenty-first century.

In order to determine how comparable our sample is to the broader sample of U.S. middle-class dual-earner couples, we compared our respondents to respondents in the 1997 National Study of the Changing Workforce, a nationally representative sample of employed American adults. To ensure that we were comparing similar subgroups of the population, we selected for our analysis only those respondents (from both data sets) who were exempt (not eligible for overtime pay) and who had an employed partner/spouse.

Our sample does differ somewhat from the subset of the National Study of the Changing Workforce (see tables A.5 and A.6). Workers in our seven employing organizations and their spouses, on average, are older, have a higher annual salary and household income, have more education, are more likely to be classified as professionals or managers (78% versus 67%), and report a lower workload than the national sample of dual-earner exempt employees. The workers in our sample, but not their spouses, report having less free time than the national sample. There are no differences between the groups in the number of hours worked per week. Overall, our sample represents a slightly older, more educated, and financially successful segment of exempt workers than found in the national sample.

Table A.5 Comparison of exempt dual-earner employees from the 1997 *National Study of the Changing Workforce* with exempt employees from the *Cornell Couples and Careers Study*[a]

| Variable | 1997 National Study of the Changing Workforce | | | Cornell Couples and Careers Study | | | | | |
| | | | | Referent Workers in Participating Organizations | | | Spouses of Referent Referent Workers in Participating Organizations | | |
	Mean	SD	N	Mean	SD	N	Mean	SD	N
Age	41.33	10.0	488	44.38**	8.07	1,084	44.13**	8.11	486
Annual salary	$43,485	$40,955	435	$64,308***	$26,500	1,068	$53,298***	$27,864	480
Household income	$82,174	$64,447	451	$97,579**	$49,341	1,024			
Work hours per week	47.42	11.07	489	45.32	9.32	1,068	43.87	10.15	458
Free time during workday (min)	86.7	82	493	81.82**	70.57	1,073	80.06	61.97	469
Workload	3.17	0.74	492	2.92*	0.53	1,074	2.90**	0.54	470

[a]From the *Cornell Couples and Career Study*, 1998–99. *Indicates significantly different from NSCW respondents at 0.05 level; **Indicates significantly different from NSCW respondents at 0.01 level; SD, standard deviation.

Table A.6 Comparison of Educational Levels of Exempt, Dual-Earner Employees

Data Source	High School Degree or Less (%)	Some Postsecondary Education (%)	Bachelor's Degree or Higher (%)
National Study of the Changing Workforce	16	26	58
Cornell Couples and Careers Study			
Workers	7	11	82
Spouses	9	11	79

[a] From the 1997 *National Study of the Changing Workforce* with exempt employees from the *Cornell Couples and Careers Study*.

The generalizability of the study also hinges on the types of organizations represented. Our sample includes two manufacturing companies, one utility company, two health-care organizations, and two universities. The difficulties of creating organizationally based samples should not be underestimated. We consider ourselves fortunate to have created a data set representing some of the diversity in the organizational context of work careers. Although it would be desirable to have other industries represented, we leave this to other researchers and to our own ongoing research.

Our findings reflect the experiences of middle-class dual-earner couples and the linkages between partners' careers, not those of unmarried (or at least unpartnered) individuals, unemployed couples, or single-earner families. Additional studies should analyze as well the experience of couples in lower-income families and minority ethnic groups.

In sum, *The Cornell Couples and Careers Study* uses a multimethodological approach to study middle-class dual-earner workers and their spouses. The sampling methods enable the linking of workers with the organizational context of their employment situation. The surveys of human resource professionals, focus groups, and in-depth interviews, along with extensive life history data, create a contextual understanding of the nexus of work and family roles and how employees and organizations respond to these often competing demands. Telephone interviews provide a means of statistically analyzing these same concerns. By studying couples in context, this study provides direction for future initiatives in work, family, and life course research.

Variable Definitions

Demographic Information

Birth cohort. Each respondent's birth cohort assignment was based on his or her self-reported year of birth. The birth cohorts represented in this sample include: the World War II generation (born 1923–45); the leading-edge baby boomer generation (born 1946–56); the trailing-edge baby boomer generation (born 1957–64); and the post–baby boomer generation (born 1965–78).

Date of first marriage. "In what month and year did you first marry or live with someone in a marriage-like relationship?"

Marital dissolution. Marital dissolution was measured using a series of questions beginning with, "Are you still with [name of spouse]?" If no, then, "How did this end?" Response options included separated/moved out, divorced, spouse/partner died, and other (specify). The questions continued with, "In what month and year did this happen?"

Number of partnerships. Respondents were asked a series of questions concerning the start and end dates of all marriage and marriage-like relationships. After being asked for the beginning date (and ending date, if applicable) of the first partnership, respondents were asked, "Have you had any other marriages or periods of living with someone in a committed relationship?" The beginning and ending dates of all subsequent relationships were then collected.

Dates of birth of children. This is based on the respondent's report of the dates of birth of all children with whom the respondent ever resided for six months or more or with whom the respondent lived at the time of the survey.

Couples' life stages. Couples were categorized into life stages based on the life stage of the female partner in each couple. The rationale for this system of categorization is the notion that a couple's experiences are influenced by the woman's location within the life course with respect to childbearing and its attending responsibilities. The couples' life stages are (1) nonparents under age forty, (2) launching (with kids under age six), (3) early establishment (with kids 6–12 years of age), (4) late establishment (with kids 13–18 years of age), (5) nonparents ages forty and over, (6) individuals with adult children (kids 19 or older in the home), and (7) empty nest (kids no longer at home).

Education

Have college degree. After responding to questions about high school attendance, respondents were asked a series of questions concerning their spells of education. These questions began with, "Did you have any education after that?," and continued with, "What type of schooling was that?," followed by "What degree, if any did you earn?" The response options for the final question were: (1) high school diploma, (2) GED, (3) associate's degree, (4) bachelor's degree, (5) certificate (teaching credential, certification, etc.), (6) master's degree, (7) professional degree (JD, or MBA), (8) medical degree (MD, DDS, or DVM), (9) doctoral degree (PhD), (11) no degree earned, (99) don't know. The questions were repeated until no additional spells of education were reported.

Job Variables

Work status. Each respondent's work status was measured using several questions. First, "Are you currently working now for pay, looking for work, retired, or something else?" The response options for this question were (1) working for pay, (2) looking for work (and not laid off), (3) retired from paid employment (currently working for pay), (4) retired from paid employment (not currently working), (5) on family leave, (6) homemaker/student, (7) disabled, (8) not working and not laid off, and (9) laid off.

Employment schedule and terms. These questions inquired about the schedule and terms of the respondent's work, including (1) full-time versus part-time employment, (2) regular salaried employment, (3) regular hourly employment, (4) temporary employment, (5) contract work, (6) seasonal employment, and (7) on-call work.

Occupation. Each respondent's occupational level was derived from his or her description of current duties and was based on census codes. The question that inquired about current duties was, "Would you tell me again what kind of work you do (did)? What are (were) your main duties and activities?"

Job prestige. Job prestige scores were calculated according to the method described by Keiko Nakao and Judith Treas[6] through the use of three Bureau of Labor Statistics diGit job classifications, which in the Cornell study dataset range from a low score of 25.73 to a high score of 73.51.[7]

Type of employer. "At your (main) job (thinking about the job you retired from/were laid-off from), are (were) you self-employed, a private employee, or a government employee?" Response options were (1) self-employed, (2) family business, (3) private employee, (4) government employee, (5) non-profit organization/university employee, (8) refused, and (9) don't know.[8]

Industry sector. The sample is divided into four sectors: manufacturing (701 respondents), health care (143 respondents), higher education (445 respondents), and utility (112 respondents).

Multiple employment. "How many jobs do you hold currently?" Response options were (1) one, (2) two, (3) more than 2, (8) refused, (9) don't know.

Age at first employment. "How old were you when you began your first major job?"

Number of employers during lifetime. The number of employers that a respondent had was determined from responses to a series of questions about all major jobs held by a respondent during his or her lifetime. These questions began with an inquiry into the start date of the respondent's first major job, "In what month and year did you begin your first major job?" and continued with "How old were you when you left this job?" The start and end dates for subsequent jobs were similarly requested. All questions into a respondent's job spells were repeated until the respondent reported that he or she still held the last job previously discussed.

Actual work hours. "On average, how many hours a week do (did) you actually work, including any paid or unpaid extra hours that you put in beyond your official work week?" (Note: If a respondent's answer was missing, his or her spouse's estimate of the respondent's work hours was inserted.)[9]

Preferred work hours. "If you could do (have done) what you wanted to, ideally how many hours would you like (have preferred) to work each week?"[10]

Reasons for difference between actual and preferred work hours. "What is the main reason you work (worked) the hours that you do (did) rather than working less/more?" Response options were (1) current number of hours is standard for this position, (2) couldn't find a full-time job, (3) attending school, (4) want less stress in my life, (5) want to pursue other interests, (6) not healthy enough/emotionally able to work full-time, (7) caring for child(ren), (8) caring for spouse/partner who is ill, (9) caring for an elderly person, (10) enjoy working, (11) need the money, (12) job requires it, (13) want to get ahead/get promoted, (14) other (specify).[11]

Interest in reducing hours. Respondents who reported that they planned to retire within the next ten years were asked, "On a scale of 0 to 100 where 0 equals no interest and 100 equals maximum interest, how interested are you in working a reduced schedule before you retire?"

Travel required for job. "Do you travel as part of your job? (do not include day trips)."

Commuting time. "Normally, how long does it take you to get from home to work (on your main job) including stops along the way for any reason? (one way)."[12]

Tenure at current company. Tenure is computed from life history data that chart job shifts.

Company size. "Thinking about the location where you work (worked), about how many people are employed there by (workplace name)?"[13]

Coordination at work. "Next, I am going to read you a list of people with whom you can potentially coordinate your efforts in your daily work in order to accomplish your work tasks. For each group of these people, please tell me if you coordinate with them: a) employees or colleagues in your work unit or department; b) employees or colleagues outside of your work unit or department; c) managers or supervisors in your work unit or department; d) customers or clients." The response options were (1) daily, (2) weekly, (3) monthly, (4) rarely, and (5) never.[14]

Attitudes about Work

Job security. "Think of a scale of 0 to 100, where 0 means you are certain you will lose your present job and 100 means you are certain you will be able to keep it. On this scale, how certain is it that during the next couple of years, you will be able to keep it?"[15]

Workload. The workload index measure is based on the mean response to three items about the respondent's main job: "My job requires(ed) working very fast," "My job requires(ed) working very hard," and "I am (was) asked to do excessive amounts of work." Response options were (1) strongly agree, (2) agree, (3) disagree, and (4) strongly disagree (alpha = 0.65).

Decision-making autonomy. This is an index measure based on the mean response to three items: "I determine what I need to do in order to complete my assignments," "I am able to influence what procedures, tools, material I use doing my work," and "I am able to influence which specific tasks I am assigned to do." Respondents were asked to indicate the extent to which they agreed with the items using a scale 1–5, where 1 is strongly disagree and 5 is strongly agree (alpha = 0.69).[16]

Control at work. The index measure for control is based on the mean response to eight items. These items were introduced with: "Think of a scale of 1 to 5, where 1 equals very little and 5 equals very much. On this scale, how much choice do (did) you have in each of the following: 1) In determining when you begin (began) and end (ended) each workday or each workweek; 2) In determining the number of hours you work(ed) each week; 3) In deciding to work at home instead of your usual place of employment; 4) In determining the amount and timing of work you must do (did) at home in order to meet your employment demands; 5) In deciding when you take (took) vacations or days off; 6) In deciding when you can take (took) a few hours off; 7) Whether or not you can (could) make or receive personal phone calls; 8) Whether or not you can (could) make or receive personal email while you work" (alpha = 0.75).[17]

Supervisor support. Supervisor support is an index measure based on the mean response to the following items: "How often in the last 3 months has your supervisor done each of the following? 1) switched schedules (hours, overtime hours, vacation) to accommodate my family responsibilities; 2) listened to my problems; *3) was critical of my efforts to combine work and family; 4) juggled tasks or duties to accommodate my family responsibilities; 5) shared ideas or advice; *6) held my family responsibilities against me." The responses were on a scale of 1–5 where 1 is never and 5 is very often. (* indicates these items were reverse-coded; alpha = 0.56.)[18]

Work performance. An index measure of self-rated work performance was created based on the mean response to four items. These items began "Thinking of your work over the last 3 months (job prior to retirement), how would you evaluate each of the following? 1) the quantity of work output; 2) the quality of your work output; 3) the accuracy of your work; 4) the service provided to customers or clients." The response options were (1) needs(ed) much improvement, (2) needs(ed) some improvement, (3) satisfactory, (4) good, and (5) excellent (alpha = 0.78).[19]

Success at work life. "How successful do you feel about your work life?" The responses were on a scale of 0 to 100, where 0 means "not successful at all" and 100 means "absolutely successful."[20]

Turning points at work. Respondents were asked about the occurrence of any recent turning points involving work or career. The question was "The next question is about a turning point you may have had in the recent past, involving your job or career. This would be a MAJOR change in the way you feel or think about your job or career, such as how IMPORTANT or MEANINGFUL it is to you, or how much COMMITMENT you give it. Have you had a turning point like this in the last three years?" If the response was yes, the follow-up question asked, "What was that turning point about? Was anything special happening in your family or personal life at that time?"[21]

Workplace Benefits

Fringe benefits. Questions concerning the prevalence and use of workplace benefits were introduced with the statement: "The next questions are about fringe benefits (you had) on your main job. Please tell me whether each fringe benefit is (was) available, to YOU through your employer and if you currently use it (used it)." The fringe benefits covered in this series of questions were: health insurance, sick leave, paid vacation days, parental/family leave with pay, personal time/dependent-care time, flextime, telecommuting, retirement plan, retirement planning services or classes, referral services for child care or elder care, information, services, or other assistance on parenting, information, seminars, or other assistance for the disabled caregiving, a child-care center at or near the work location, a sick-child-care center at or near the work location, time off for volunteering, tuition assistance for further education for the respondent or his/her family, education and training programs, career-development or -planning services, wellness program/workout facilities, 401(k) plan, dental coverage, life insurance, and employee-assistance program. The response options for these questions were (1) available, use it, (2) available, do not use it, (3) not available, and (9) don't know. Respondents who answered "available, do not use it" were then asked the follow-up question, "Do you think you will use it in the future?"

Social Psychological Orientation

Negative affect. This is an index measure based on the mean response to five items. The questions were introduced with the statement, "For each of the following, please tell me HOW MUCH of the time in the past month you felt this way: 1) all of the time; 2) most of the time; 3) some of the time; 4) a little of the time; 5) none of the time." The questions were (1) "First, how much of the past month did you feel in GOOD SPIRITS?", *(2) "What about feeling so SAD that nothing could cheer you up?" *(3) "What about feeling RESTLESS or fidgety?", *(4) "What about feeling NERVOUS?", (5) "How much of the time did you feel that EVERYTHING was an effort?" (* indicates these items were reverse-coded; alpha = 0.61.)[22]

Egalitarian gender-role attitude. Overall gender-role orientation was assessed using the mean response to four items that each used a five-point scale: (1) "It is usually better for everyone if the man is the main provider and the woman takes care of the home and family," (2) "It is more important for a wife to help her husband's career than to have one herself," (3) "A preschool child is likely to suffer if his or her mother works," and *(4) "A working mother can establish just as good a relationship with her children as a mother who does not work." The following coding system was used: (1) strongly agree, (2) agree, (3) unsure, (4) disagree, and (5) strongly disagree. (* indicates this item was reverse-coded; alpha = 0.80.)[23]

Personal growth. This index measure was based on the mean response to the following three items: *(1) "For me, life has been a continuous process of learning, changing, and growth," *(2) "I think it is important to have new experiences that challenge how I think about myself and the world," and (3) "I gave up trying to make personal improvements or changes in my life a long time ago." Response options were (1) strongly agree, (2) agree, (3) disagree, and (4) strongly disagree. (* indicates this item was reverse-coded; alpha = 0.70.)[24]

Personal mastery. This index measure was based on the mean response to the following four items: "I can do just about anything I really set my mind to," "When I really want to do something, I usually find a way to succeed at it," "Whether or not I am able to get what I want is in my own hands," and "What happens to me in the future mostly depends on me." Response options were (1) strongly agree, (2) agree, (3) disagree, and (4) strongly disagree. (All items were reverse-coded; alpha = 0.78.)[25]

Perceived constraints. This index measure was based on the mean response to the following four items: "I often feel helpless in dealing with the problems of life," "What happens in my life is often beyond my control," "I have little control over the things that happen to me," and "There is really no way I can solve all the problems I have." Response options were (1) strongly agree, (2) agree, (3) disagree, and (4) strongly disagree. (All items were reverse-coded; alpha = 0.78.)[26]

Marriage and Family Variables

Success at family life. "How successful do you feel about your family or personal life?" Responses were on a scale of 0 to 100, where 0 means "not successful at all" and 100 means "absolutely successful."[27]

Couples' disagreement. "Couples sometimes have different opinions about issues in life. How much does your opinion differ from your (spouse's/partner's) on the following issues? First, what about money matters, such as how much to spend, save, or invest? What about household tasks, such as what needs doing and who does it? What about leisure time activities, such as what to do and with whom?" Response options were (1) a lot, (2) some, (3) a little, and (4) not at all. (All items were reverse coded; alpha = 0.58.)[28]

Marital satisfaction. "On a scale of 0 to 100, where 0 means 'not satisfied at all' and 100 means 'absolutely satisfied,' what number indicates how satisfied you are with your relationship/marriage?"[29]

Family satisfaction. Overall satisfaction with family life was measured using the mean on five items, each of which consists of a five-point scale. "For each statement, please indicate how well the statement describes your family and in this case a family is defined as all individuals that live with you. 1) You are satisfied that you can turn to your family for help when something is troubling you. 2) You are satisfied with the way your family talks over things with you and shares problems with you. 3) You are satisfied that your family accepts and supports your wishes to take on new activities or directions. 4) You are satisfied with the way your family expresses affection, and responds to your emotion, such as anger, sorrow, or love. 5) You are satisfied with the way your family and you share time together." Response options were (1) never, (2) hardly ever, (3) some of the time, (4) almost always, and (5) always (alpha = 0.79).[30]

Work-Family Interface

Work and family spillover. For each of the four types of spillover, an index measure was created based on the mean response to the two individual items relating to the construct in question. This whole series of questions was introduced with, "These questions are about how your job may affect your family and personal life, and how your family and personal life may affect your job. How often have you experienced each of the following in the past year?" Response options were (1) all the time, (2) most of the time, (3) sometimes, (4) rarely, and (5) never. (All items are reverse coded.)[31]

Negative family-to-work spillover. "Personal or family worries and problems distract you when you are at work. Activities and chores at home prevent you from getting the amount of sleep you need to do your job well" (alpha = .37).

Positive family-to-work spillover. "Talking with someone at home helps you deal with problems at work. The love and respect you get at home makes you feel confident about yourself at work" (alpha = .56).

Negative work-to-family spillover. "Your job makes you feel too tired to do the things that need attention at home. Job worries or problems distract you when you are at home" ($r = .55$).

Positive work-to-family spillover. "The things you do at work make you a more interesting person at home. The things you do at work help you deal with personal and practical issues at home" ($r = .54$).

Balancing work and family. "How successful do you feel about balancing work and family life?" Responses were on a scale of 0 to 100, where 0 means "not successful at all" and 100 means "absolutely successful."[32]

Career hierarchy. "Think about all of the major decisions that you and your spouse/partner have made since you have been together, such as changing jobs, having children, going back to school or moving. Overall, whose career was given more priority in these decisions, yours or your spouse/partner's?" Response options were (1) your career, (2) spouse's/partner's career, (3) neither, (4) took turns, (8) N/A, (88) refused, and (99) don't know.

Whose career took priority. This construct was measured using questions that inquired whether the respondent had ever faced an opportunity decision and whether the spouse had ever faced an opportunity decision. The question was, "Have you (Has your spouse/partner) ever had a career or education opportunity that would have required your spouse/partner (you) to make significant changes, like moving to a different city or taking a different job?" If the response was yes, the follow-up question asked, "What happened: did you (he/she) turn down the opportunity, took it but arranged things so your spouse/partner (you) wouldn't have to make any significant changes, or took it and your spouse/partner (you) made the changes?" The response options were (1) turned down, (2) took it, but arranged so spouse wouldn't have to change, (3) took it and spouse changed, (4) both compromised (if volunteered), and (5) something else (specify).

Time and Technology

Time on chores (workday). "On average, on days when you're working, about how much time do YOU spend on home chores and things like cooking, cleaning, repairs, shopping, yard work, and keeping track of money and bills? Do not include child care in your estimate."[33]

Time spent on child care. "On average, on days when you're working, about how much time do you spend taking care of or doing things with children?"[34]

Free time (workdays). "On average, on days when you're working, about how much time do you spend on your own free-time activities?"[35]

Free Time (Nonworkdays). "About how much time do you spend on free-time activities on days when you are NOT working?"[36]

Managing tasks at home. An index scale of family management was created based on ten items. Respondents were asked to use a 1–5 scale where 1 means "does not describe you at all" and 5 means "exactly describes you," to indicate the degree to which they felt the following statements described them: *(1) "When there is a task to be done at home, you wait until the last minute to do it," (2) "You think about when to do a task at home, and not just how much time it will take," (3) "Each week you decide something specific you can do for your family," (4) "When planning a task at home, you think the plan through so that your goal is clear before you begin doing the task," (5) "Before you begin a task, you figure out how much of your time, money and energy you can devote to this particular task," (6) "Before starting a complex task, you have a firm idea about how to judge the outcome," (7) "As you work at home, you check whether things are going as you want them to," *(8) "You are pleased if the work just gets done; you do not spend time thinking about how effectively it was done," (9) "When things are not going well, you figure out another way to do it," and (10) "When a task is done, you think about how well you like the results." (* indicates that these items are reverse-coded; alpha = 0.69.)[37]

Technology use. Respondents were asked to indicate whether they used each of the following types of technological services and shortcuts: "Do you use any of the following services or technologies to manage work and home life on a regular basis?" (1) email to communicate with work while at home,

(2) email to communicate with family while at work, (3) beeper or cellular phone to keep in touch with work, (4) beeper or cellular phone to keep in touch with family, (5) portable computer or home computer to do work, (6) fax (machine) to communicate with work while at home, (7) automated banking (direct deposit or automatic bill payment), (8) shopping by catalog, (9) telephone for shopping, banking, or other services, (10) Internet for shopping, banking, or other services, (11) eating out more than once per week, (12) shortcuts for eating at home (take-home meals, etc.), and (13) drive-thru windows or pay-at-the-pump gas.

Retirement

Retire with current employer. "Do you expect to stay with your present employer until retirement?" Response options were (1) yes, (2) no, and (9) don't know.[38]

Retirement planning. "On a scale of 0 to 100, where 0 is none and 100 is a lot, how much planning have you done (did you do) in each of the following areas to prepare for retirement? 1) financial preparation; 2) learning about retirement or health insurance options; 3) developing hobbies or interests; 4) considering different housing arrangements; 5) planning for health care needs; 6) thought about a 2nd or 3rd career after retirement; 7) thinking about volunteer work in the community after retirement."

Age began retirement planning. "At what age did you start to plan for retirement?"[39]

Age of retirement. "At what age do you expect to retire?" (If already retired, "At what age did you retire?")

Religion

Religious affiliation. "What is your religious preference?" Response options were (1) Protestant (prompt for denominational preference), (2) Catholic, (3) Jewish (prompt for Reform, Conservative, or Orthodox), (4) other, (5) none, or (6) atheist or agnostic.[40]

Religious attendance. "Next we'd like to ask a few questions about your community. How often do you attend religious services?" Response options were (1) never, (2) hardly ever, except holidays, (3) less than once a month, (4) about once a month, (5) 2–3 times a month, (6) once a week, (7) more than once a week, and (9) don't know.[41]

With whom attend religious services. "Typically, with whom do you attend services?" Response options were (1) alone, (2) spouse/partner, (3) one or more of your children but not your spouse/partner, (4) everyone in your immediate family, (5) other (friends), and (9) don't know.[42]

Finances

Individual income. "What is your annual salary from paid employment, including any bonuses, overtime, and/or commissions, before taxes and other deductions? (If retired, "What is your individual annual retirement income, before taxes and other deductions?")[43]

Household income. "What is your total household income from all sources?"[44]

Income adequacy. "On a scale of 0 to 100, where 0 equals very inadequate and 100 equals much more than adequate, how well does your family's current household income meet your family's financial needs?" (PROMPT: By household income we mean any income coming from salary, child support, investments, pensions, and all other sources.)[45]

Health and Caregiving

Health. "Think of a scale from zero to ten where 0 is a person with serious health problems and 10 is a person in the very best health. On this scale of zero to ten, what number best indicates how your health has been lately?"[46]

Energy level. "Think of a scale from zero to ten where 0 is a person who never has any energy and 10 is a person who is always full of energy. On this scale of zero to ten, what number best indicates how much pep or energy you've had lately?"[47]

Caring for infirm relative. "Within the past year, have you provided regular special attention or care to any family members because they were elderly, disabled, have a chronic illness or are infirm in some way?" Response options were (1) yes, and (2) no.[48]

Other

Date of last geographic move. "When was your last move to a different community?"

Notes

1. Introduction

1. Many members of the new workforce (especially women) find it necessary to scale back at some point in their occupational careers, often in tandem with their family responsibilities or to better mesh with their husbands' careers (see Becker and Moen 1999, and chap. 2 of this book).

2. A more complete discussion of the trends in women's employment and their consequences can be found in Blau and Ehrenberg (1997); Blau, Ferber, and Winkler (1998); England and Farkas (1986); Ferber and O'Farrell (1991); Moen (1992); and Spain and Bianchi (1996). Tilly and Scott (1978); Degler (1980); and Cott and Pleck (1979) provide historical overviews.

3. See appendix as well as Moen et al. (1999).

4. Matilda White Riley has been the leading scholar in developing the concept of structural lag (see Riley, Kahn, and Foner 1994). For a discussion of structural leads see Moen (2001).

5. Arlie Hochschild (1997) is responsible for the phrase and the illumination of the realities embodied in the concept of "time squeeze."

6. See Elder (1998a); Giele and Elder (1998); Moen (1992); Moen, Dempster-McClain, and Williams (1992).

7. See Giele and Elder (1998).

8. See Pavalko and Smith (1998).

9. See Quick and Moen (1998).

10. See Quick and Moen (1998).

11. See discussion of three jobs by Christensen and Gomory (1999) and of three careers by Hertz and Marshall (2001) and Moen and Han (2000, 2001).

12. See Goode (1960).

13. The notion of strategic action encompasses both deliberate choices and normative, culturally prescribed ways of behaving. See Moen and Wethington (1992).

14. See Becker (1981).

15. See Becker and Moen (1999).

16. See Mayer (1986, 167).

17. See Bem (1994); Moen (1998, 2001).

18. See Elder (1978); Moen and Han (2000, 2001); Pavalko and Smith (1998); Aldous (1996).

19. See Menaghan (1989); Pearlin, Lieberman, Menaghan, and Mullan (1981); Thoits (1986).

20. See Crouter and Manke (1994); Greenhaus and Beutell (1985); Kanter (1977); Moen and Han (2000, 2001).

21. See Moen (1994, 2001); Riley and Riley (1994).

22. See Schor (1991); Galinsky and Bond (1998); Clarkberg and Moen (2001). For a discussion of contingent work see Christensen (1995) and Barker and Christensen (1998).

23. See Moen and Yu (1999).

2. Time Clocks: Work-Hour Strategies

1. Special thanks to Kristin Campbell for analysis and David McDermitt for help with producing the figures.

2. See Hochschild (1999).

3. See Williams (2000); Moen (1992). Moreover, their choices are constrained by the outmoded lockstep template of career paths as continuous full-time employment throughout adulthood, with workers viewed as having no family responsibilities or personal interests that might interfere with their investment in their jobs.

4. For a further discussion of effective strategies see Moen and Yu (1999, 2000); strategies around the retirement transition are discussed by Moen, Kim, and Hofmeister (2001).

5. See also the discussion of typologies in Moen and Yu (2000).

6. See Bolger et al. (1989); Repetti (1989); Repetti, Matthews, and Waldron (1989); Marks (1977); Moen, Dempster-McClain, and Williams (1989, 1992); Sieber (1974); Thoits (1983).

7. See Glaser and Strauss (1973).

8. See Schor (1991).

9. Both Moen and Yu (2000) and Clarkberg and Moen (2001) report similar findings, using different nationally representative data sets.

10. This is a statistical tool that enables us to assess the relative probabilities of a couple adopting a work-hour strategy, weighing how much influence particular factors have in predicting their response. Each regression is structured with a binomial dependent variable; for example, regressions predicting being in a high commitment work-hour strategy (1) are compared with all others in the sample (0). We have structured the analysis so that couples who are both managers, who are both in high-prestige jobs, and who are nonparents are the comparison groups. As already discussed, these couples theoretically have the greatest inclination to adopt the heavy work-hour commitment, which is rewarded and promoted in the twenty-first-century economy.

An added advantage of the logistic regression approach is that predictions are made while controlling for the influence of the other factors of interest. In other words, this model examines the impact of jobs, gender ideologies, and life stages, net of one another. In this way, we know that results are not confounded with one another (e.g., occupation configurations resulting from gender ideology orientations), and we also minimize the possibility of spurious results.

11. To study the impact of job prestige, we divide couples into four groups, similar to those identified in the manager/nonmanager configuration. In this case we divide job prestige, a variable identifying the relative status of occupations, at the median value. This creates four groups of couples, both high prestige, husband high/wife low, wife high/husband low, and both low prestige.

12. See Gerth and Mills (1946).

13. In *The Couples and Careers Study*, gender-role orientations are measured using a composite index based on four Likert-type questions. These questions assess whether respondents think it is better for the man to be a provider and the woman to stay home, it is more important for a wife to help her husband's career than to have one herself, a preschool child will suffer if his or her mother works, and a working mother can establish as good a relationship with her children as a nonworking mother.

14. For a discussion of scaling back, see Becker and Moen (1999).

15. The coefficients presented in table 2.2 show how these life stages correspond with the probabilities of couples' engaging in the various work-hour strategies compared to dual-manager high-prestige couples with no kids. Once children are born, couples are less likely to adopt a high commitment work-hour strategy. For instance, compared to nonparents, couples with preschool or school-age children are nearly twice as likely to adopt a neotraditional work-hour configuration than a high commitment strategy. Also, compared to nonparents, parents at the launching stage are over three times more likely (3.08) to adopt an alternative commitment strategy (with neither working long hours). Couples free from the responsibilities of raising preschool and school-age children have an increased likelihood of adopting a crossover commitment strategy.

16. See Becker and Moen (1999). Consistent with previous research, we find the tendency is for couples with children at home to scale back and reconfigure their work-hour arrangements.

17. To fully understand this dynamic, however, we require longitudinal data, tracing couples over time.

18. See Barnett and Rivers (1996).

19. See Goode (1960); Coser and Rokoff (1971).

20. See Hochschild (1989, 1997).

21. See Orrange (1999). Neglected in this "Ozzie and Harriet" world of the 1950s are the disadvantaged (by poverty and/or minority status) women and men who work for low wages as single or cobreadwinners. What this means is that employed women typically continue to shoulder domestic responsibilities (and even expect to do so).

22. Moen and Yu (2000); Barnett and Rivers (1996). Their evidence using a nationwide sample reinforces the findings reported in this chapter.

23. See also the gender differences found by Moen and Yu (1999, 2000).

24. But we cannot capture change over the life course using cross-sectional data.

25. Work-hour strategy significant at $p < .001$; life stage significant at $p < .001$.

26. See also the findings on gendered career paths reported in Han and Moen (1999a, 1999b) and the discussions in Moen and Han (2000, 2001).

27. See Riley and Riley (1994); Moen (1994); Moen and Han (2000, 2001); Han and Moen (2001).

3. Competing Clocks: Work and Leisure

1. See Robinson and Godbey (1997, chap. 16); Jacobs and Gerson (1998).

2. See Clarkberg and Moen (2001); Bluestone and Rose (1997); Clarkberg (2000); Robinson and Godbey (1997).

3. See Jacobs and Gerson (2001); Merola (2001).

4. See Jacobs and Gerson (1998); Hochschild (1989, 1997); Jacobs and Gerson (2001).

5. Schor (1991); Robinson and Godbey (1997).

6. See Bluestone and Rose (1997); Robinson and Godbey (1997); Schor (1991).

7. See Jacobs and Gerson (1998).

8. See Schor (1991); Sharp (1981); Lee and Lapkoff (1988); Gronau (1977).

9. Robinson and Godbey (1997).

10. Jacobs (1998).

11. See Drago et al. (1999).

12. Gronau (1977); Juster and Stafford (1985); Robinson and Godbey (1997).

13. See Becker and Moen (1999); Clarkberg and Moen (2001).

4. Family Clocks: Timing Parenthood

1. Gilman (1989, 270).

2. See Moen (1992).

3. See Becker (1981).

4. Milkie and Peltola (1999, 480).

5. Becker and Moen also find this pattern, although their research suggests that men do make adjustments. In some cases, the spouse who first finds success in a career "may be the one who subsequently has the primary career during a significant proportion of the life course" (1999, 1003).

6. See Drobnic, Blossfeld, and Rohwer (1999, 133).

7. Cramer (1980).

8. See Altucher (2000).

9. Willekens (1991).

10. See Chadwick and Heaton (1992).

11. See U.S. Census Bureau (2000a).

12. See Chen and Morgan (1991).

13. See Menken (1985, 469).

14. See Heck et al. (1997).

15. See Chen and Morgan (1991, 528).

16. All organization names have been changed to protect the privacy of respondents.

17. See Thomson (1997).

18. There is one case of twins, as well as a couple that chose to have a third child, hoping to have a girl.

19. See Menken (1985).

20. See Williams, Abma, and Piccinino (1999).

21. Because women's labor-force participation rate is increasing even for mothers with young children, however, the group that leaves the labor market represents a smaller and smaller portion of the total population.

5. Commuting Clocks: Journey to Work

1. See Rouwendal and Rietveld (1994).

2. See Fagnani (1993); Green (1997); Rose and Villeneuve (1998).

3. See van Ommeren, Rietveld, and Nijkamp (1997).

4. See Howell and Bronson (1996); Levinson and Kumar (1997); 2000 U.S. Census data.

5. See Fagnani (1993); Levinson and Kumar (1997).

6. See Assadian and Ondrich (1993); Blumen (1994); Camstra (1996); Johnston-Anumonwo (1992); Madden (1981); McLafferty and Preston (1997); Pratt and Hanson (1988).

7. But see Fagnani (1993).

8. See, for example, Becker and Moen (1999); Moen and Wethington (1992).

9. See Fulton (1983).

10. See Szinovacz and Ekerdt (1995); Hughes and Galinsky (1994).

11. There are many excellent studies of the ways in which role sets are bundled. See Brines (1994); Hochschild (1989); Komarovsky (1964); Potuchek (1997); Stanfield (1996); Ward (1993); Wilkie, Ferree, and Ratcliff (1998).

12. See Turner and Niemeier (1997).

13. Bielby and Bielby's 1977 study (Bielby and Bielby 1992) uses interviews with 162 wives and 197 husbands in dual-earner families taken from the Quality of Employment Survey (representative multistage probability sample of adults sixteen years or older, working twenty or more hours a week).

14. Fagnani uses a 1988 snowball study of forty early-middle-age wives (35–42 years old) with two to three children each, who had either moved within the previous four years (1984–88) or were about to move in the Île-de-France (greater Paris) region. The wives all had high levels of education and were employed. In one-half the households, husbands were also interviewed separately in the home (Fagnani 1993).

15. See Howell and Bronson (1996); Levinson and Kumar (1997).

16. Logit models are employed to explain proportion of minutes in each day spent in different domains: work, home, shopping, and other. Independent predictors are activity frequency, season, gender, age, household income, life stage, residential density, region, and metro population. "Travel

duration depends on activity duration as well as the more traditional measure of activity frequency" (Levinson 1999, 167). Activities are substituted for one another rather than being complementary to one another (the exception is that people who spend a lot of time at home also spend a lot of time shopping). But people who spend a long time at work spend less time at home.

17. For examples of studies that demonstrate the ways couples "do gender," see Bellah et al. (1985), Brines (1994), Hochschild (1989), and West and Fenstermaker (1993, 1995).

18. Nine of these wives are considered professional, eight are in sales or technical or administrative support. Six of the twenty-five wives are day-care providers, one teaches piano, one is a farmer, two are artists, five do some kind of multilevel marketing or vendor/sales from home, four do transcribing from home, one is a technical writer, and one does a combination of catering and computer billing.

19. Levinson (1999).

20. See Blumen (1994); Johnston-Anumonwo (1992); Madden (1981); Preston, McLafferty, and Hamilton (1993); Turner and Niemeier (1997).

21. See Blumen (1994); Camstra (1996); Fagnani (1993); Hanson and Pratt (1992); Johnston-Anumonwo (1992); Johnston-Anumonwo, McLafferty, and Preston (1995); Madden (1981); McLafferty and Preston (1997); Turner and Niemeier (1997); Veen and Evers (n.d.).

6. Career Clocks: Forked Roads

1. Pavese (1961, 76).

2. See Han and Moen (1999a, 2001); Moen (1998); Barley (1989).

3. See, for example, Han and Moen (1999a); Elder (1992, 1995); O'Rand and Henretta (1982); Rosenfeld (1980). We employ the term "career" neutrally with respect to orderliness and disorderliness of work history, as in Spillerman (1977).

4. See Elder (1992, 1995); O'Rand and Henretta (1982); cf. Hughes ([1937] 1994).

5. See Elder (1995).

6. See Breiger (1995); Rosenfeld (1992).

7. See Wilensky (1961).

8. See Spenner, Otto, and Call (1982).

9. See, for example, Rosenbaum (1984).

10. See Kalleberg, Knoke, and Marsden (1995); Osterman (1984); cf. Althauser (1989).

11. See Jacobs, Kohli, and Rein (1991); DeViney and O'Rand (1988); Pampel and Weise (1983); cf. DiPrete and Krecker (1991); Sørensen and Tuma (1981).

12. Of the 829 cases in the analysis sample, 658 are married to other members of the analysis subsample (i.e., there are 329 couples in the analysis subsample). The remaining 171 cases have spouses who were under age forty-four.

13. See Abbott and Hrycak (1990) for an extended introduction to this technique. See Han and Moen (1999a); Abbott and Barman (1997); Stovel, Savage, and Bearman (1996); Blair-Loy (1999); and Chan (1995) for its recent application in substantive areas.

14. See Abbott (1995).

15. See Pavalko (1997).

16. See Tuma and Hannan (1984).

17. See Pavalko, Elder, and Clipp (1993); Rindfuss, Swicegood, and Rosenfeld (1987); Rosenbaum (1984); Hogan (1978); Wilensky (1961).

18. The optimal matching algorithm produces measures of similarity and dissimilarity between the sequences, which were then used as inputs for a hierarchical cluster analysis to produce the career pathways typology. An adapted version of DISTANCE (Stovel 1996) written in SAS/IML was used to perform the optimum matching. The cluster analysis was performed on all five of the dimensions simultaneously to identify a set of typical pathways, using Ward's minimum variance method to group objects at each step of the solution. Further technical details of the procedures used in the analysis are available upon request.

19. Upward and downward mobility are not exclusive categories; some respondents experienced both types.

20. The survey item wording is "On a scale of 1 to 100, where 0 means 'not successful at all' and 100 means 'absolutely successful' how successful do you feel about your work life?"

21. The survey item wording is "On a scale of 1 to 100, where 0 means you are certain you will lose your job and 100 means you are certain you will be able to keep it, how certain is it that during the next couple of years you will be able to keep it (your present job)?"

22. The survey item used for this test is worded "On a scale of 1 to 100, where 0 means 'not successful at all' and 100 means 'absolutely successful' how successful do you feel about balancing work and family life?" The sample mean on this measure was 80 and the means, controlled by gender, ranged from 75 to 80.

23. Four of the couples in the analysis sample are same-sex couples and are not included in this analysis.

7. Spillover

1. See Almeida, Wethington, and Chandler (1999).
2. See Higgins, Duxbury, and Irving (1992).
3. See Allen et al. (2000); Boles, Howard, and Howard (2001); Higgins, Duxbury, and Irving (1992); Eagle et al. (1998); Goff, Mount, and Jamison (1990); Greenhaus, Parasuraman, and Collins (2001); Kossek and Ozeki (1998); Mauno and Kinnunen (1999); O'Driscoll, Illgen, and Hildreth (1992).
4. See Allen et al. (2000); Eagle et al. (1998); Fox and Dwyer (1999); Frone, Russell, and Barnes (1996); Grzywacz (2000); Grzywacz and Marks (2000); Higgins, Duxbury, and Irving (1992); Hughes, Galinsky, and Morris (1992); Kossek and Ozeki (1998); Near, Rice, and Hunt (1987); O'Driscoll, Illgen, and Hildreth (1992); Pisarski, Bohle, and Callan (1998); Tingey, Kiger, and Riley (1996).
5. See Meissner (1971); Rousseau (1978); Wilensky (1960).
6. See Lambert (1990).
7. See Lambert (1990).
8. See Lambert (1990); Near, Rice, and Hunt (1987); Rain, Laine, and Steiner (1991); Staines (1980).
9. See Judge and Watanabe (1994).
10. See Rain, Lane, and Steiner (1991); Tait, Padgett, and Baldwin (1989).
11. See Evans and Bartolome (1984b); Champoux (1980).
12. See Kahn et al. (1964, 19); see also Goode (1960).
13. See Eagle, Miles, and Icenogle (1997); Kinnunen and Mauno (1998); Williams and Alliger (1994); Gutek, Searle, and Klepa (1991).
14. See Thomas and Ganster (1995).
15. See Marks (1977).
16. See Beutell and Wittig-Berman (1999); Eagle et al. (1998); Frone, Russell, and Cooper (1992); Thompson and Blau (1993); Williams and Alliger (1994).
17. See Eagle et al. (1998); Guteck, Searle, and Klepa (1991); Hughes, Galinsky, and Morris (1992); O'Driscoll, Illgen, and Hildreth (1992); Wallace (1999).
18. See Eagle et al. (1998); Kirchmeyer (1992, 1993).
19. See Kirchmeyer (1992, 1993).
20. See Kirchmeyer (1992).
21. See Aryee and Luk (1996).
22. See Duxbury and Higgins (1994).
23. See Bolger et al. (1989).
24. See Eagle et al. (1998); Kirchmeyer (1993).
25. See Duxbury and Higgins (1994); Williams and Alliger (1994).
26. See Duxbury, Higgins, and Lee (1994); Eagle, Miles, and Icenogle (1997); Wallace (1999).
27. See Williams and Alliger (1994); Duxbury and Higgins (1994); Duxbury, Higgins, and Lee (1994); Gutek, Searle, and Klepa (1991).
28. See Eagle et al. (1998); Eagle, Miles, and Icenogle (1997); Wallace (1999).

29. See Duxbury et al. (1992); Jones and Fletcher (1993); Kirchmeyer (1993); Moen and Smith (1986); Parasuraman and Greenhaus (1993).
30. See Bowen (1998); Thomas and Ganster (1995); Goff, Mount, and Jamison (1990). Eagle et al. (1998) found a negative relationship.
31. See Bromet, Dew, and Parkinson (1990); Carlson and Perrewe (1999).
32. See Greenhaus et al. (1989); Maume and Houston (2001).
33. See Fox and Dwyer (1999).
34. See Pisarski, Bohle, and Callan (1998); Thomas and Ganster (1995).
35. See the review by Christensen and Staines (1990); see also Eagle et al. (1998).
36. See Fox and Dwyer (1999); Frone, Russell, and Cooper (1992); Higgins, Duxbury, and Irving (1992); Vinokur, Pierce, and Buck (1998).
37. See Fox and Dwyer (1999); Greenhaus et al. (1989); Rydstedt and Johansson (1998); Marshall and Barnett (1993); Mauno and Kinnunen (1999).
38. See Greenhaus et al. (1989).
39. See Crouter (1984); Duxbury, Higgins, and Lee (1994); Eagle et al. (1998).
40. See Fox and Dwyer (1999).
41. See Crouter (1984); Marshall and Barnett (1993).
42. See Kinnunen and Mauno (1998).
43. See Duxbury, Higgins, and Lee (1994). Eagle et al. (1998) found that divorced parents had the highest levels of family-to-work and work-to-family conflict, but the difference was statistically different from dual-earner couples with children.
44. See Marshall and Barnett (1993).
45. See Higgins and Duxbury (1992); Kirchmeyer (1993).
46. See Adams, King, and King (1996); Carlson and Perrewe (1999).
47. See Fox and Dwyer (1999); Marshall and Barnett (1993).
48. See Marshall and Barnett (1993).
49. See Repetti (1994); Repetti and Wood (1997).
50. See Bolger et al. (1989); Wethington (2001).
51. See Bolger et al. (1989).
52. See Jones and Fletcher (1993).
53. See Greenhaus et al. (1989).
54. See Greenhaus et al. (1989).
55. See Moen and Yu (1999).
56. See Duxbury and Higgins (1994) and Duxbury, Higgins, and Lee (1994), who further divide parenthood into those with children under the age of six and those with children over the age of six. Marshall and Barnett (1993) divide parenthood into those with children under the age of twelve and those with children twelve and older.
57. See the Appendix at www.lifecourse.cornell.edu/about_time.html for a breakdown of the number of respondents in each life stage.
58. See Thomas and Ganster (1995).
59. See Barnett et al. (1993); Tait, Padgett, and Baldwin (1989).
60. Table 7.1 at web address www.lifecourse.cornell.edu/about_time.html defines the predominant patterns of spillover that we have identified in our sample of middle class workers.
61. See, for example, Goode (1960).
62. See table 7.2 at www.lifecourse.cornell.edu/about_time.html for a summary of the regression equation for family-to-work spillover.
63. See Greenhaus et al. (1989).
64. See table 7.3 at www.lifecourse.cornell.edu/about_time.html for a summary of the regression equation for work-to-family spillover.

8. Well-Being

1. See, for example, Abel and Hayslip (1987); Kim and Moen (2001); Lachman (1986); Lachman and Weaver (1998); Moen (1996); Rodin, Timko, and Harris (1985); Rowe and Kahn (1998); Ryff and Keyes (1995); Carter and Cook (1995).

2. See the large body of research by Bosma, Stansfeld, and Marmot (1998); Ganster and Fusilier (1989); Karasek (1990); Kohn and Schooler (1973); Parker, Chmiel, and Wall (1997); Theorell and Karasek (1996); Thomas and Ganster (1995).

3. Thomas and Ganster (1995). Evidence also suggests that control has significant influences on psychological adjustment even after workers have left their career jobs. See, for example, Carter and Cook (1995); Fretz et al. (1989); Hendrick, Wells, and Faletti (1982); Mutran, Reitzes, and Fernandez (1997); Taylor and Shore (1995). In their survey of individuals ages 50–70, Herzog, House, and Morgan (1991) find that those who had stopped work and felt they had had little or no choice reported lower levels of health and psychological well-being compared to those who had voluntarily retired and those working the amount they liked.

4. See Kim and Moen (2001); Elder (1995).

5. For a discussion of the ecological perspective, see Bronfenbrenner (1995). Moen, Dempster-McClain, and Williams (1989); Musick, Herzog, and House (1999); and Spitze et al. (1994) all draw on a role context approach.

6. See the work by Cox and Bhak (1978); Hendrick, Wells, and Faletti (1982); Dorfman and Moffett (1987); George (1993); George and Maddox (1977); Gove, Style, and Hughes (1990); Kessler and Essex (1982); Kilty and Behling (1985); Shinn et al. (1989); Vinick and Ekerdt (1989).

7. Newsom and Schulz (1996).

8. Mutran, Reitzes, and Fernandez (1997). In an earlier study of older men and women ages sixty and older, Lee (1978) reports significant contributions of marital satisfaction to morale; however, the positive effect of marital satisfaction on morale was notably stronger for women than for men.

9. See, for example, Calasanti (1996); Quick and Moen (1998, 2002); Romsa, Bondy, and Blenman (1985).

10. See Han and Moen (1999a, 1999b); Moen and Han (2000, 2001).

11. See also Acitelli and Antonucci (1994); Dehle and Weiss (1998); Gilligan (1982); Helgeson (1994); Levenson, Carstensen, and Gottman (1993); Ross (1995); Williams (1988).

12. See, for example, Kim and Moen (1999); Moen, Kim, and Hofmeister (2001); Szinovacz (1996).

13. Ryff (1989).

14. We have performed general linear model (GLM) analyses testing the main effects of gender and life stage and the interaction effect between gender and life stage. In order to test whether there are significant differences between spouses, we have conducted a series of analysis of variance (ANOVA) tests within each life stage.

15. We conducted the analyses with ordinary least squares (OLS) regression. We first examine the influences of life stages on psychological well-being, with our two psychological well-being measures, personal growth and negative affect, separately regressed on sets of variables reflecting life stage. Education, income adequacy, and subjective health are included as covariates. Next we add work control, workload, and work hours, including interactions between the work hour variable and the other two work control variables, work control and workload, to test whether the impact of work control is contingent on the number of work hours. As can be seen in tables 8.1 and 8.2 (available at www.lifecourse.cornell.edu/about_time.html), only the interaction between work control and work hours is significant. Next, we test whether the two social support variables, family satisfaction and marital satisfaction, mediate any effects of work characteristic variables or contribute independent explanatory variance to psychological well-being above and beyond the influence of work characteristic variables, life stage variables, and other controls.

16. See the large body of work by Mel Kohn and colleagues (Kohn 1990, 1995; Kohn and Schooler 1973, 1978, 1983, 1985).

17. To help interpret the significant interaction effect between work control and work hours, estimates of dependent variable men's negative affect were calculated based on scores of the two predictor variables (work control and work hours) that were one standard deviation above (= high group) and one standard deviation below (= low group) the means of the relevant predictor variables. Regression coefficients from model 2 of table 8.2 were used.

18. See Bosma, Stansfeld, and Marmot (1998); Frese (1999); Kohn and Schooler (1973); Theorell and Karasek (1996); Thomas and Ganster (1995).

19. The finding confirms the theoretical and empirical work of others with regard to the association between social support and psychological well-being. See, for example, Acitelli and Antonucci (1994); Mutran, Reitzes, and Fernandez (1997); Levenson, Carstensen, and Gottman (1993); Newsom and Schulz (1996).

9. Success

1. Barley (1989); Breiger (1995); and Stovel, Savage, and Bearman (1996) provide good analyses of the concepts of careers and attainment.
2. See, for example, Brim (1992); Mead (1934); Gattiker and Larwood (1986, 1990); Rosenberg (1979).
3. See Goode (1960, 491).
4. See Clausen and Gilens (1990).
5. The concept of structural lag has been developed by Matilda White Riley. (1987; Riley and Riley 1994).
6. See Moen (1992, 1998); Clarkberg and Moen (2001).
7. See Elder (1978); Moen and Wethington (1992).
8. See Bandura (1982, 140).
9. See Pearlin et al. (1981, 340); Pearlin and Schooler (1978).
10. See Ross and Mirowsky (1989, 207). We hold that both the objective environment (in terms of resources and demands) and subjective perceptions (including a sense of success) operate in dynamic interplay, producing strategies of adaptation which, in turn, shape subsequent objective and subjective dimensions of the life course (Moen and Wethington 1992).
11. See Goode (1960, 433).
12. See Goode (1960, 434).
13. See, for example, Greenhaus et al. (1989); Hertz (1986); Higgins, Duxbury, and Irving (1992); Hochschild (1989, 1997); Ishii-Kuntz and Coltrane (1992); Marks and MacDermid (1996); Pleck (1985); Shelton (1992).
14. Williams and Alliger (1994). See also Barnett and Rivers (1996); Evans and Bartolome (1984a).
15. See Goode (1960, 485).
16. See discussions of one or both domains by Aldous (1996); Hill (1970); Kohli (1986); Kohli and Meyer (1986); Mayer and Schöpflin (1989); Riley (1987); and Wilensky (1960). Elder's (1998a) life course perspective draws on a body of work (e.g., Thomas and Znaniecki 1918–20) to emphasize the dynamic, age-related interdependence and synchronization of roles (and consequently resources and demands). Individuals of different ages may hold different assessments of their own success precisely because they occupy different family and work environments. They also have had distinctive historical experiences, possibly producing different expectations and different yardsticks by which they measure success.
17. See Ishii-Kuntz and Coltrane (1992); Shelton (1992).
18. See Althauser and Kalleberg (1990).
19. Note that this is a stylized version of the conventional life course (based on four ideal-type life stages) of married workers; we consider other stages, including those more off time, in the results section.
20. Wilensky (1960).
21. See, for example, Moen (2001).
22. See Moen and Wethington (1992); Becker (1981); Curtis (1986).
23. See Bandura (1982, 23).
24. See Elder (1998b); Elder, George, and Shanahan (1996); Barley (1989); Weiss (1990).
25. Karasek and Theorell (1990); Barnett and Brennan (1997).
26. Cournoyer and Mahalik (1995).
27. Goode (1960).
28. See, for example, Han and Moen (1999a, 1999b; Moen and Han 2000, 2001); Bielby and Bielby (1992).

29. These were modified from the 1992 National Study of the Changing Workforce (see Galinsky, Bond and Friedman 1993).

30. See Moen and Yu (1999).

31. Because these factors can differentially influence women and men, given their distinct roles, gender interaction terms were tested for all these factors. No interaction effects were determined for control, and this term was dropped from subsequent analyses.

32. Interaction terms were tested for all these factors in the preliminary analyses. In the analyses presented here, only the significant interaction of mastery is discussed; the others proved nonsignificant. All these variables are summarized and referenced in the appendix of this volume.

33. Middle class is operationalized as the respondent's having attended college but not necessarily having a college degree.

34. Multiple regression was used to estimate the various models. Tables with actual coefficients are available from the authors.

35. Hochschild (1997).

36. Note also the power of the model we have presented, which offers greater explanatory power than previous sociological studies of success, explaining as much as one-fifth to one-quarter of the variance in perceived success, as revealed by the R^2 statistics in table 9.2.

37. See, for example, Becker and Moen (1999).

38. Our findings suggest that both demands and resources are important in contemporary assessments of success. Evidence from *The Cornell Couples and Career Survey* reveals that the factors predicting success across domains are both similar and different—with perceived income adequacy and job security important across the board. Although perceived income and job security are key resources, actual income behaves in complex ways, sometimes even negatively predictive of perceived success. What is most common in the multivariate statistical models is the significance of work circumstances—apart from earnings—for feeling successful at work, at home, and in balancing both.

10. Managing Households

1. See Hochschild (1989); DeVault (1987, 1991).

2. See Mederer (1993); Shelton and John (1996).

3. See Hochschild (1997).

4. See Hays (1996).

5. See Heck, Winter, and Stafford (1992).

6. See Gross, Crandall, and Knoll (1980); Deacon and Firebaugh (1988); Heck, Winter, and Stafford (1992).

7. See Key and Firebaugh (1989).

8. See Heck, Winter, and Stafford (1992).

9. See Garrison, Pierce, and Tiller (1997, 65).

10. See Deacon and Firebaugh (1988); Heck, Winter, and Stafford (1992).

11. Garrison, Pierce, and Tiller (1997); Deacon and Firebaugh (1988); Heck, Winter, and Stafford (1992).

12. Heck, Winter, and Stafford (1992).

13. Duncan, Zuiker, and Heck (2000). Both groups score highest on the same items as the respondents in Heck, Winter, and Stafford (1992) study. The items include checking, adjusting, and demand response. However, Duncan, Zuiker, and Heck (2000) find through factor analysis that dual- and solo-role holders clearly used different management strategies.

14. See Heck, Winter, and Stafford (1992).

15. See Buehler and Hogan (1986).

16. Moen and Wethington (1992).

17. See Hochschild (1989); Moen (1992); Spain and Bianchi (1996).

18. Moen and Yu (1999, 2000).

19. See Kohn (1995).

20. Heck, Winter, and Stafford (1992); Deacon and Firebaugh (1988).
21. Heck, Winter, and Stafford (1992); Duncan, Zuiker, and Heck (2000).
22. Moen and Yu (2000).
23. See also Moen and Yu (2000).
24. Hunts et al. (2000, 110).
25. Furthermore, with respect to the importance of individual management items, these findings mirror those of Heck, Winter, and Stafford (1992) and Duncan, Zuiker, and Heck (2000).
26. Thus, the findings provide suggestive confirmatory evidence of the validity of a basic assumption of the family economics–home management approach.
27. See Heck, Winter, and Stafford (1992).
28. See Duncan, Zuiker, and Heck (2000).
29. Hays (1996).
30. Kohn (1995).

11. Turning Points in Work Careers

1. See Elder (1998c).
2. See Cohler (1982); Ross and Buehler (1994).
3. See for example Elder (1998c); Pearlin et al. (1981).
4. See Settersten (1999); Wethington (forthcoming).
5. Clausen (1995).
6. Elder (1985); Pickles and Rutter (1989, 133).
7. See Baldwin (2000, 3).
8. See Settersten (1999).
9. See Elder (1998c); Ross and Buehler (1994).
10. Clausen (1995, 1998).
11. Clausen (1998, 202).
12. See Brown and Harris (1978).
13. See Holmes and Rahe (1967).
14. See Wethington, Brown, and Kessler (1995); Wheaton (1999).
15. See Wethington, Kessler, and Pixley (Forthcoming); Mroczek and Kolarz (1998).
16. See Wethington (In press).
17 Clausen (1995).
18. See Wethington et al. (Forthcoming).
19. See Wethington et al. (Forthcoming).
20. See Becker and Moen (1999, 995).
21. See Becker and Moen (1999).
22. See Hochschild (1997).
23. The PTP data do not contain comparable measures of well-being.
24. The selection of events for analysis depends on previous research and the findings of our classifications of turning points and is constrained by the types of data available on events for the entire sample. Only *The Cornell Couples and Careers Study* data are used in these analyses.
25. *The Cornell Couples and Careers Study* may not show marital status differences because few of the respondents were not married.
26. No other group contrast was significantly different.
27. See Mroczek and Kolarz (1998).
28. See Ryff and Keyes (1995).
29. See Galinsky, Bond, and Friedman (1993).
30. See Schwartz, Groves, and Schuman (1998).
31. See Clausen (1998).
32. See Lazarus (1999).
33. See Hochschild (1997).
34. See also Wethington (In press).

12. Prioritizing Careers

1. See, for instance, Han and Moen (1999b); U.S. Bureau of Labor Statistics (1999).

2. In his review of the scholarship on relocation, Markham (1987) concludes that geographic mobility issues restrain some women from occupational advancement and that more couples will face difficult decisions about relocating as women become increasingly oriented toward career advancement.

3. Examining data from the National Longitudinal Surveys of Young and Mature Women, collected from 1967 through 1977, Spitze (1986) finds that, overall, wives' employment status had no effect on their families' likelihood of moving. Bielby and Bielby (1992), using the 1977 General Social Survey, demonstrate that wives were much more likely than husbands to express reluctance to move for their own careers and that wives' income had very little impact on husbands' predicted willingness to relocate. In scholarship conducted prior to the 1960s, this issue is largely ignored, presumably because the issue of whether decisions would favor the husband's career was taken for granted. *Husbands and Wives: The Dynamics of Married Living* (Blood and Wolfe 1960) is a classic examination of how husbands and wives make major decisions. Here, the list of decisions does not include whether or where to move or which job the wife will take, but only which house to take, which job the husband will take (decided "always" by 90% of the husbands) and whether the wife will work are considered as relevant.

4. Becker and Moen (1999), after examining the qualitative interviews of the Cornell study, report that in many dual-earner couples, at least one spouse experiences some type of scaling back at work in order to help manage family needs, such as having more time together or caring for children or elderly relatives.

5. Becker (1991).

6. Mincer (1978). See also the seminal work of Polacheck and Horvath (1977) on applying theory on individual migration to family migration.

7. See, for example, Blood and Wolfe (1960); Curtis (1986); Emerson (1976); Homans (1958).

8. Curtis (1986).

9. See, for example, Hochschild (1989); Risman and Johnson-Sumerford (1998); Sewell (1992).

10. Decisions that could potentially affect both spouses' jobs but do not involve the possibility of moving appear to be unusual, according to Pixley's (2002) research on career-prioritizing decisions among dual-earner couples in upstate New York.

11. This was true even after controlling for the effects of education and income predicted by economic models. See Bielby and Bielby (1992); Markham and Pleck (1986).

12. See Simon and Landis's (1989) analysis of the 1980 and 1985 Roper Poll surveys.

13. See, for example, Lichter (1982); Spitze (1986).

14. See, for example, Jacobsen and Levin (1997); LeClere and McLaughlin (1997); Morrison and Lichter (1988).

15. Lichter (1982, 55–56).

16. See Mincer's (1978) classic argument, which he supports using U.S. Census and Current Population Survey analyses.

17. See, for example, Ofek and Merrill (1997).

18. See, for example, Cooke and Bailey (1996); Jacobsen and Levin (2000); Spitze (1984); LeClere and McLaughlin (1997).

19. For a similar argument, see Gerson's (1985) account of how women's early attitudes and investments can be reversed by later circumstances, such as when traditional women found themselves divorced and recommitted themselves to their work roles.

20. Green (1997).

21. Gill and Haurin (1998).

22. See, for example, Ferber and Loeb (1997); McNeil and Sher (1999); Cutler (1995).

23. See Tesch et al. (1992).

24. In their classic examination of marital decision making, Blood and Wolfe (1960) report that the majority of Detroit-area women interviewed in 1955 said that their husbands make most types of household decisions, with the exception of managing the food budget.

25. For a more in-depth discussion of structural lag, see Riley, Kahn, and Foner (1994).

26. Interpretation of such a model must be cautious. Researchers of women's life paths, such as Gerson (1985), suggest that current attitudes could also have been influenced by past career decisions.

27. This subsample is drawn from the 811 heterosexual couples in which both spouses are currently working and who are defined as middle-class—that is, one or both are professionals or managers or have attended college. Eight couples were removed because one or both spouses have missing values for the perceived career hierarchy measure. Same-sex couples are not included, given the gender-specific nature of many of the hypotheses about couples' career prioritizing.

28. Recall that these men and women are not representative of the U.S. population. The sampling design deliberately selects for professionals and managers and is limited to dual-earner couples in the upstate New York area, who are not necessarily typical of couples from other areas, especially large urban areas. Couples in which both spouses are pursuing highly competitive or specialized careers tend to migrate to large metropolitan areas where they can both find suitable work. By contrast, the upstate New York cities and towns where these couples live bear little resemblance to the densely populated urban areas on either U.S. coast and may attract a different type of dual-earner couple. Looking at the qualitative data from *The Couples and Careers Study*, Becker and Moen (1999) note that strategies of scaling back at work to buffer the family from work demands—which they found to be common—can influence a couple's choice to live in this less-metropolitan region.

29. In comparing the distribution of current income for men and women in this sample across more detailed levels of initial educational attainment, these breaks were found to correspond to observed significant differences in income. Average incomes by educational category among men are: less than college, $56,858 (SD 25,935); bachelor's or master's, $69,622 (SD 27,698); and advanced professional degree, $83,534 (SD 28,763). For women in the same categories, the same figures are $31,497 (SD 19,781), $46,855 (SD 28,050), and $68,267 (SD 27,046), respectively. Note that the distinction between an MBA and other master's degrees (MA and MS) was embedded in the survey question and that no significant income difference was found for bachelor's versus (non-MBA) master's degree attainment among either men or women in this sample.

30. Standard deviations for age are 7.3 years for women and 8.0 years for men.

31. Job history data were collected for spouses' first major jobs and then for all jobs held at and since age thirty. In thirty-nine couples (5%), the marriage or cohabiting date occurred between one or both spouses' first job and his or her job at age thirty, meaning that their work-hours at the time cannot be determined. In addition, work hours were not given (responses of "don't know" or "refused") for the relevant jobs by one or both spouses in thirty couples (4%). Valid data on initial work hours are available for both members of 734 couples (91%).

32. We use this delineation of work hours to be consistent with other chapters in this volume. These categories connote nothing about benefits available to workers (such as sick time or overtime pay). Note that the terms "reduced," "regular," and "long" are intended to reflect observed averages in population work hours rather than a normative stance.

33. According to our calculations, based on tables summarizing findings from the March 1998 Current Population Survey, the husband alone was employed in 77 percent of the single-earner white married couples in the United States, the demographic group closest to that in our sample (note that when using labor-force participation rather than employment, the comparable figure is 79%). (These figures are taken from U.S. Bureau of Labor Statistics 1999).

34. Given the sampling design, the relationships found for these single-earner couples cannot be generalized, yet remain suggestive.

35. Relative risk calculations indicate that spouses' risk of being the same status (both reporting or both not reporting an opportunity) is 1.45 times that of being of different status (95% CI = 1.03 to 2.05).

36. All other factors being equal, individuals should be less likely to choose an option if it has negative consequences for their spouse's career than if the spouse has no career to affect.

37. The categorical model we use simultaneously assesses multiple logistic regression analyses, each comparing one category of the dependent variable against the omitted reference

category. As such, parameter estimates differentiate only between each category and the omitted category, not between dependent variable categories shown in table 12.4.

38. Models predicting husbands' reports of career priority and wives' reports of career priority separately were also assessed, but are not included here due to space limitations. The results are consistent with those found for the joint career priority measure. These tables are available upon request.

39. We tested models using a number of reasonable permutations of (and interactions among) the theorized factors. Variables that we found to not adequately predict variation in career hierarchy and that were removed include continuous variables representing age, age difference, initial work hours, initial work-hour differences, and the interaction between husband's and wife's (continuous) gender-role attitudes, categorical variables representing broader categories of initial work hours (e.g., working/not working) and more specific categories of initial education and education differences, traditional gender-role attitudes divided at the median, and the interactions of these categorical variables. The final models were selected based on model fit improvement indicated by the AIC (Akaike's Information Criterion).

40. Men and women who did not face career opportunities are used as the reference category.

41. Because of regression to the mean, this is probable despite assortive mating by education and occupational status. Even if a substantial proportion of professionals marry others who are similar to them in attainment, those spouses who are not similar are more likely to exhibit lower attainment than to exceed that of the (above-average) professionals.

42. Alternately, it could be argued that organizational membership influences career hierarchy reports if individuals change their minds about whose career had priority in major decisions based on the later (perhaps unexpected) outcomes of those decisions. The subsequent analysis thus rests on the assumption that self-reported career priority indicates (albeit imperfectly) an underlying, real pattern of decisions that favored one or the other spouse's career.

43. These analyses also use SAS CATMOD, with two categorical dependent variables: (1) employee of which of seven sampled organizations (run for wives and husbands separately); and (2) both spouses employed at one of these organizations, only the husband, only the wife, or neither.

13. Sunday Morning Rush Hour

1. See Moen and Wethington (1992).
2. See Smith (1998).
3. Hertel (1995).
4. See Bluestone and Rose (1997, 1998); Jacobs and Gerson (1998).
5. See Hertz (1986).
6. See Becker and Moen (1999).
7. See Becker and Hofmeister (2001).
8. See Hertel (1995); Luckmann (1967).
9. Lehrer (1996); Heaton and Cornwall (1989).
10. Lehrer (1995).
11. See Mueller and Johnson (1975).
12. See Hertel (1995); cf. Demerath (1965); Mueller and Johnson (1975).
13. Hertel (1995).
14. Roof and McKinney (1987).
15. Caplow et al. (1982).
16. See Gesch (1995).
17. See Hertel (1995).
18. See Becker and Hofmeister (2001).
19. See Becker and Hofmeister (2001).
20. Gesch (1995).
21. Hall (1995).
22. Sherkat (2000).
23. Hertel (1995).

24. See Becker and Hofmeister (2001).

25. See Degler (1980, 27). For a review, see Becker (1998).

26. Portes (1998, 3–4); Bourdieu (1985).

27. See Becker and Hofmeister (1999).

28. See Smith (1998); cf. Stolzenberg, Blair-Loy, and Waite (1995).

29. See Smith (1998); Hammond (1988).

30. We have grouped denominations according to classifications used by Smith (1987): Catholics; liberal Protestants; conservative Protestants; those in other, non-Christian faiths (too few in our sample to make further distinctions); and those not affiliated with any denomination or faith.

31. We asked spouses "with whom do you attend?" Respondents answered "alone", "with my spouse", "with my children but not my spouse", "together with everyone in the family", or "with friends."

32. See Becker and Hofmeister (1999, 2001); Becker and Dhingra (2001).

33. Wives' and couples' gender-attitude differences are significant at $p < .001$; husbands' gender attitudes are significant at $p < .05$.

34. We place husbands and wives who attend alone into one category because of the small numbers in those categories and for simplicity of presentation, but we discuss relevant gender differences in the text.

35. See Becker and Dhingra (2001); Becker (2001).

36. See Becker (forthcoming); Christiano (2000); Sherkat and Ellison (1999).

37. See Demerath and Williams (1992).

38. Moen (2001).

14. The New Technology Climate

1. See U.S. Census Bureau (2000a).

2. See U.S. Census Bureau (2000a).

3. See U.S. Census Bureau (2000b).

4. See Watt and White (1999—p. 1 for quotation).

5. Lewis and Cooper (1999).

6. An exception is research examining the effects of telecommuting (see Galinsky and Kim 2000).

7. See Papadakis and Collins (2001, viii), italics in original.

8. See Haddon and Silverstone (2000).

9. See Van Horn and Storen (2000). Van Horn and Storen define "teleworkers" as those "working at home, away from an employer's place of business, using information technology appliances, such as the Internet, computers, or telephones. Teleworkers include people who work at home full-time or part-time and those who work at a remote location other than their employer's central office full-time or part-time. Excluded from our definition are people who own home-based businesses and conduct much of their work from their private residences and the purely 'mobile workforce,' the traveling sales force and consultants of the 21st Century" (2000, 3–4).

10. See U.S. Department of Labor (1999); Moen (1992, 67).

11. See Van Horn and Storen (2000).

12. See Standen, Daniels, and Lamond (1999).

13. See Galinsky and Kim (2000, 245, 252, 261).

14. See Cintron (2000).

15. See Elder (1998a); Moen, Elder, and Lüscher (1995).

16. See Moen and Wethington (1992).

17. Moen and Wethington (1992).

18. See Almeida, Wethington, and Chandler (1999).

19. Galinsky, Kim, and Bond (2001) have found that employees who report using a range of information technologies outside the office are also more likely to report that they feel overworked.

20. See Wellman (2001).

21. See Nie (2001).

22. See Kraut, Kiesler, et al. (Forthcoming); Kraut, Patterson, et al. (1998).

23. Kraut et al. (1998).

24. This company was not one of the seven organizations highlighted in our study.

25. A study done by National Public Radio and the Kennedy School finds that fewer people sixty or older used computers, email, and the Internet compared with those younger than sixty (National Public Radio 2000).

26. Patterns of technology use by level of education and income are consistent with findings from national studies that have looked at computer and Internet use (Nie 2001; National Public Radio 2000; U.S. Census Bureau October 2000b).

27. See Tompkins (2000).

28. We used binary logistic regression to model IT use. Computations were performed using SPSS 9.0. Because the women and men in this study are married to one another, they do not represent independent observations, an important assumption of regression. Therefore, throughout this chapter, we estimate separate models for women and men.

29. Jan English-Lueck, an anthropologist, has proposed that families create "eco-systems" of technology that they use to navigate both work and home. In a series of qualitative interviews and ethnographic observations of families in Silicon Valley, she finds that "people don't just own or use individual devices . . . pagers, faxes, cell phones, telephone answering systems and computers are used together to serve the goals of individuals and families" (English-Lueck 1998).

30. The number of possible technology strategies that could be used ranges from zero to seven. See appendix for further documentation of this measure.

31. We use SPSS 9.0 to estimate the coefficients reported in tables 14.3 and 14.4. All OLS models control for education, negative affect (in negative models only), life stage, log of household income, organizational affiliation, occupation type, work hours, commute to work, and perceived control over work. See the appendix for further documentation of these measures.

32. With a p-value of .08, this result is only suggestive. In addition, models that include interaction terms (wife's level of technology use by husband's level of technology use) were tested and these interactions were not significant.

15. Alternative Employment Arrangements

1. See Cohany (1998); Segal (1996).

2. See Capelli et al. (1997).

3. The U.S. Bureau of Labor Statistics began tracking alternative employment arrangements in the 1990s. They define alternative employment arrangements as any employment arrangement that is arranged through an intermediary such as a temporary help agency or whose time, place, or quantity of work is potentially unpredictable (Polivka 1996). This definition does not include part-time work because part-time work cuts across both alternative employment arrangements and traditional work arrangements, which introduces the problem of double-counting. See also Spalter-Roth et al. (1997) and Blau, Ferber, and Winkler (1998).

4. See Bregger (1996); Cohany (1998); Blau, Ferber, and Winkler (1998).

5. See England (1999); Moen (1992); Bernard (1981); Moen and Yu (2000).

6. See Blossfeld and Hakim (1996); Blank (1990); Higgins, Duxbury, and Johnson (2000).

7. See Blank (1990).

8. See Feldman, Doerpinghaus, Turnley (1995); Steinberg (1994).

9. See Marler (2000); Rogers (2000).

10. Losocco (1997).

11. Kalleberg et al. (1997); Kalleberg, Reskin, and Hudson (2000).

12. See Cappelli, Constantine, and Chadwick (2000).

13. See Gattiker and Larwood (1988); Judge et al. (1995).

14. See Aryee, Chay, and Tan (1994); Gattiker and Larwood (1986); Han and Moen (2001); Peluchette (1993).

15. See Moen and Yu (1998); Gattiker and Larwood (1988); Judge et al. (1995).

16. Parasuraman, Purohit, and Goldshalk (1996).

17. We use information from the 792 couples in this study that have no missing data on variables of interest.

18. This criterion follows the definition of part-time work used by the U.S. Department of Labor.

19. For a table documenting the derivation of these types, please contact Janet Marler.

20. Education is measured by respondents' report of number of years of education completed after high school. Number of children includes all children in the family, across all ages, as reported by wives. Gender ideology is measured by a scale derived from respondents' answers to a number of attitudinal questions (see appendix).

21. See Gattiker and Larwood (1988); Judge et al. (1995). Economists generally use hourly wage instead of annual salary as the more accurate measure of an individual's success in the labor market because it controls for variance in hours worked and is a better measure of marginal price, but using this measure is problematic in a study of NSWAs, for which an accurate estimation of annual hours is not possible.

16. Moving toward Retirement

1. See Useem (1994, 49).

2. General research on interest in reduced work hours includes Clarkberg and Moen (2001).

3. See Quinn, Burkhauser, and Myers (1990).

4. In particular, the 1969–1979 Retirement History Survey, the 1992–2000 Health and Retirement Study, and the 1966–1990 National Longitudinal Survey of Older Men have been used for this purpose.

5. See Quinn, Burkhauser, and Myers (1990); Hurd (1996).

6. See Gustman and Steinmeier (1983).

7. Hurd (1996) provides an excellent discussion of why there is a minimum hours constraint; he refers to team production and fixed costs of employment (such as health insurance).

8. See Quinn, Burkhauser, and Myers (1990).

9. See Hurd (1996).

10. See Bodie (1990); Gustman, Mitchell, and Steinmeier (1994); Kotlikoff and Wise (1987).

11. See Commonwealth Fund (1993, 21).

12. Future waves of data collected for *The Cornell Couples and Careers Study* will tell us if our sample actually does reduce their work hours before retirement. We do know that 150 people in the total sample who report an intention to retire within the next ten years moved from full-time to part-time jobs at some point in their reported job history. Only two people (1.4 percent) chose to move from full-time to part-time at the age of earliest Social Security eligibility (age sixty-two) or later, whereas approximately 60 percent of the moves occurred before age forty. These people are not included in our sample due to our restriction of the sample to full-time workers, and, furthermore, we can only speculate as to who is involved in gradual retirement without knowing their specific intentions or actual retirement date.

13. Quinn and Burkhauser (1990) similarly report that in the Retirement History Survey older women who work full-time are more likely to prefer to shift to part-time than are older men who work full-time.

14. This is similar to findings about women retiring because of their husbands but not vice versa. See review by Kim and Moen (2001).

15. Heckman (1979). Selection issues arise because workers were only asked the question on interest in a reduced schedule if they said they expected to retire within ten years. The identifying variables in the first-stage probit (indicating expect to retire in ten years) are age and amount of savings. Because we always rejected the null hypothesis that selection influences results, only the uncorrected models are presented here.

16. On the one hand, having a young child in the home could cause a worker to want to spend less time at work and more time interacting with (or caring for) the at-home child. On the other hand, the workers in our sample work at least thirty-five hours per week; those with children at home have already chosen full-time work. Full-time work may play an especially important role

in their lives, perhaps as a source of income or for its intrinsic rewards (the pleasures of a challenging career). As such, they may have little interest in reduced hours.

17. Unfortunately, we cannot distinguish between the respondents' type of pension plan from our data.

18. Two other factors, health and prior job experiences, have been demonstrated to be important for actual retirement timing (Blau 1998). In our sample, unhealthy workers are likely to leave the workforce and are therefore not in the survey. Neither the respondent's nor the spouse's health were significant in our models of gradual retirement interest. Prior job experiences, including the number of past job changes and prior moves from full-time to part-time status, were also not significant.

19. In other words, age is used to identify the coefficient on lambda in the Heckman (1979) correction for sample selection bias. By implication, we are assuming that, conditional on intending to retire within ten years, age does not affect interest in reduced hours.

20. This conclusion is not contradicted by the observation that the coefficient on (household) income is significant for women, a measure that takes into account husbands' earnings.

21. We also considered the spouse's professional status in our models, but there are very few professional spouses in this subsample (nine husbands and seven wives).

22. This is consistent with past research on retirement behavior that suggests that family circumstances influence wives more than husbands (Henretta, O'Rand, and Chan 1993) and that retired couples do not view wives' retirements as influential for their husbands' retirement decisions, although husbands' impending retirements are considered influential for the wives' decisions (Smith and Moen 1998).

23. For research linking marital quality to retirement decisions, see Szinovacz and DeViney (2000); Moen, Kim, and Hofmeister (2001).

24. See Moen and Wethington (1992).

25. Of 229 possible couples (264 total referents minus the 35 spouses from our subsample), information is available for 162 couples.

26. Precisely, three-quarters are wives, with an average age of forty-eight (an age range of 20–68). Of the 86 percent that are currently working, they have an average of eight years of current job experience. In contrast, spouses intending to retire within ten years average fifty-two years of age (an age range 42–63) and have ten years of current job experience.

27. Note that each member of the couple did not always report the same household income, which leads us to average their reports together here and suggests to us that this difference in reporting might influence our results.

28. See Rhine (1978); Christensen (1989); Barth, McNaught, and Rizzi (1993). Also included in this strand are Brady et al. (1991); McCool and Stevens (1989); and Paul (1983, 1987).

29. Christensen (1989).

30. Details of the questionaire and additional results can be found in Hutchens and Dentinger (2000).

31. The same approach is used in Brady et al. (1991).

32. The interviewer did not probe why there was so little flexibility in the pension or why the organization could not change the pension. Perhaps the inflexible pension rules mask a deeper phenomenon. When an organization is trying to shed older workers, it is unlikely that staff time will be devoted to developing opportunities for gradual retirement.

17. The Case of Same-Sex Couples

1. See Allen and Demo (1995).
2. See Patterson (1995).
3. See Bronfenbrenner and Morris (1998).
4. See Bronfenbrenner (1979).
5. See Bem (1994).
6. See Yang (2000).
7. See van der Meide (1999).

8. See Human Rights Campaign Census Report (2000).
9. See Blumstein and Schwarz (1983).
10. See Kurdek (1994).
11. $F(3,34) = .371, p > .10$. Also, controlling for gender, the means are approximately 2.5, compared with 2.24 for the entire sample (where 1 = opinions do not differ and 4 = opinions differ a lot), which indicates a moderate level of disagreement between couples on average.
12. See Kim and Moen (1999).
13. See Diamond (2000); Kitzinger and Wilkinson (1995).
14. See Fassinger (1995).
15. See Savin-Williams and Esterberg (2000).
16. See Peplau, Veniegas, and Campbell (1996).
17. See Blumstein and Schwarz (1983).
18. See Blumstein and Schwarz (1983); Kurdek (1994, 1998); Peplau, Veniegas, and Campbell (1996).
19. See Kurdek (1998).
20. $F(2,43) = .466, p > .05$.
21. $F(3,87) = 0.786, p > .05$.
22. $F(3,94) = 2.775, p < .05$.
23. See Chan et al. (1998).
24. See Slater (1999).
25. See Julien, Chartrand, and Begin (1999).
26. $F(3,27) = 6.345, p, < .01$. This is borne out in post hoc analyses as well.
27. $F(3,27) = 5.277, p < .01$.
28. See Blumstein and Schwarz (1983); Peplau, Veniegas, and Campbell (1996).
29. See Carrington (2000).
30. See Horowitz, Weis, and Laflin (2001).

18. Institutionalizing Family-Friendly Policies

1. For foundational descriptions of the disjuncture between formal and informal organizational structure, see Selznick (1949), Gouldner (1954), and Blau (1955). Much contemporary work follows Meyer and Rowan (1977) in emphasizing the loose coupling between a ceremonial formal structure and informal but practical problem solving.
2. See Abrahamson (1996); Strang and Macy (2001).
3. See Easton and Jarrell (1998, 256).
4. See Shellenbarger (1992).
5. See Capowski (1996).
6. See Eaton (2001).
7. See MacDermid, Litchfield, and Pitt-Catsouphes (1999).
8. See Friedman and Johnson (1991).
9. See Kossek, Dass, and DeMarr (1994).
10. Despite the burgeoning literature on the benefits of family-friendly and work-life programs, Strang and Still (2001) report that work-life programs continue to be seen by top managers as having little impact on the bottom line and as having ambiguous cause-effect relationships.
11. See Goodstein (1994); Friedman (1990); Kossek, Dass and DeMarr (1994).
12. See Kelly and Dobbin (1999); Kossek, Dass, and DeMarr (1994); Milliken, Martins, and Morgan (1998).
13. We use the term "work-life" to refer to policies and practices that are part of an overall program to assist employees with meeting both work and personal demands. The term "work-life" is synonymous with "work-family," but has largely replaced it to emphasize the needs of individuals with few or no familial obligations but with other personal interests or responsibilities.
14. See Cole (1999) for a detailed analysis of the influence of the quality movement on U.S. business.
15. See Appelbaum and Batt (1994).

16. See Osterman (1995); Hewlett (1991); Goodstein (1994).
17. See Strang and Still (2001).
18. See Friedman and Johnson (1991).
19. See Cutcher-Gershenfeld, Kossek, and Sandling (1997).
20. See Friedman and Johnson (1991).
21. Friedman and Johnson (1991); Cutcher-Gershenfeld, Kossek, and Sandling (1997).
22. See, for example, Glass and Fujimoto (1995); Morgan and Milliken (1992); Bailyn (1992).
23. This is not an exhaustive list of all work-life innovations, but it does include the most common programs as well as many uncommon ones.
24. See Milliken, Martins, and Morgan (1998).
25. See Peters, Peters, and Caropreso (1990); Conference Board (1991).
26. See Friedman and Johnson (1991).
27. See Still (2000).
28. Programs such as job sharing and time off for volunteering were not asked of both employees and HR professionals.
29. We explored the possibility that many wrong answers were reported by nonprofessional employees who typically have less access to benefits, but in most cases the answers of nonprofessional employees were better aligned with HR accounts than those of professional employees.
30. See Williams (2000).
31. It is especially puzzling that some respondents answered that they used on- or near-site child care when their employer does not provide day care. Some respondents who have used company child-care referral services may believe the day-care centers are affiliated with the company. In addition, we suspect some may have responded affirmatively because they use day-care services that are on- or near-site, although they are not sponsored by the employer.
32. HR managers were not asked about dependent care leave, so we are unsure if it is formally offered; 42 percent of Citizens' Health employees report using it. Although we might be tempted to conclude that this implies that the policy exists, table 18.1 reports cases in which even larger percentages of employees said they use programs that do not formally exist.
33. See Morgan and Milliken (1992).
34. See Osterman (1995).
35. See Glass and Estes (1997).
36. Thomas and Ganster (1995).
37. See Glass and Fujimoto (1995); Morgan and Milliken (1992); Goodstein (1994); Kossek, Dass, and DeMarr (1994); Still (2000).
38. See Kalleberg and Van Buren (1996) for a careful analysis of the mechanisms underlying the observed effect of organizational size on job rewards.
39. See Goodstein (1994); Still (2000); Glass and Fujimoto (1995).
40. The two health-care organizations present quite different profiles because the study population included physicians at Citizens' Health and excluded them at Valley View. Valley View thus has the youngest and least-educated respondents in our sample, whereas respondents at Citizens' Health have an average of 17.5 years of schooling and (for men) the highest incomes in the sample.
41. See Kossek, Dass, and DeMarr (1994).
42. See Kanter (1977).

19. Work-Life Integration: Challenges and Organizational Responses

1. In an earlier study (Batt and Valcour 2003), we examine these issues for individual women and men in *The Cornell Couples and Careers Study*. In the present chapter, we extend our earlier work by incorporating a qualitative analysis of transcripts from fourteen focus groups conducted at the seven participating organizations in the study. In addition, we use regression analysis to assess how the work characteristics of one spouse influence the work and family-related outcomes of the other spouse.
2. See Zedeck (1992).
3. See Kanter (1977).

4. See Friedman and Galinsky (1992, 194).

5. See Hochschild (1997).

6. See Edwards and Rothbard (2000); Greenhaus and Beutell (1985).

7. See Brett and Yogev (1988).

8. See Pleck and Staines (1985).

9. See Brett and Yogev (1988).

10. Specifically, women who said their husbands had high security were more likely to be satisfied with their jobs. Their spouse's weekly work hours were positively related to men's job involvement and negatively related to women's job involvement. Spouse's income was negatively related to men's job involvement (Lambert 1991).

11. See Becker and Moen (1999).

12. See Friedman and Greenhaus (2000); Grimsley (2000); Mirvis and Hall (1996).

13. See Galinsky, Bond, and Friedman (1996); Glass and Estes (1997); Friedman and Greenhaus (2000).

14. See Kofodimos (1995); Osterman (1995); Galinsky and Johnson (1998).

15. See Galinsky and Johnson (1998).

16. See Rapoport et al. (2002); Bailyn (1993a); Bailyn et al. (1998); Lobel (1999); Rayman et al. (1999).

17. See Goff, Mount, and Jamison (1990).

18. See Kossek and Ozeki (1998).

19. See Dalton and Mesch (1990).

20. See Aryee, Luk, and Stone (1998).

21. See Baltes et al. (1999); Judge, Boudreau, and Bretz (1994); Lobel (1999).

22. See Christensen and Staines (1990); Lobel (1999).

23. See Pleck, Staines, and Lang (1980).

24. See Kingston (1990).

25. See Becker and Moen (1999); Catalyst (1998).

26. See Galinsky, Bond, and Friedman (1996).

27. See Raabe and Gessner (1988).

28. See Jacoby (1985); Osterman (1984).

29. See Raabe (1990).

30. See Galinsky, Bond, and Friedman (1996).

31. See Lambert (1991).

32. See Bailyn (1993b).

33. See Thomas and Ganster (1995).

34. See Rapoport et al. (2002); Bailyn (1993a); Bailyn, Rapoport, and Fletcher (2000); Perlow (1997).

35. See Cohen and Bailey (1997); Cotton (1993).

36. See Bailyn (1993b); Bailyn et al. (1998); Rayman et al. (1999); Appelbaum, Berg, and Kalleberg (2000).

37. See Barker (1993).

38. See also Epstein et al. (1999); Hill et al. (1998).

39. See Eaton (2000).

40. See Galinsky, Bond, and Friedman (1996).

41. See Burkett (2000); Rothausen et al. (1998).

42. See Shore (1998).

43. See Gutek, Searle, and Klepa (1991); O'Driscoll, Ilgen, and Hildreth (1992).

44. Expectations for long work hours can arise from occupational norms, the stated and unstated expectations of employers, and from the unconscious behavior of employees (Epstein et al. 1999; Perlow 1997).

45. See Bailyn (1993a); Perlow (1997).

46. This point has also been made persuasively by Bailyn (1993a).

47. See Lucero and Allen (1994).

48. Thomas and Ganster (1995).

49. We applied a natural logarithmic transformation to this variable to normalize it.

50. This approach is consistent with Thomas and Ganster (1995).

51. Supervisor support is a shortened version of the scale developed by Shinn et al. (1989). Two additional items, how frequently an employee's supervisor was critical of efforts to combine work and family and how frequently the supervisor held the employee's family responsibilities against him or her (both reverse coded) were not used in the scale because they failed to load on the same factor as the four items that were retained.

52. The decision-making autonomy scale is adapted from the 1997 National Study of the Changing Workforce (Bond, Galinsky, and Swanberg 1998).

53. The coordination scale adapted from Appelbaum, Berg, and Kalleberg (2000).

54. The negative affect scale is adapted from the John D. and Catherine T. MacArthur Foundation Network Study of Successful Midlife Development in the U.S. (MIDUS).

Appendix: Methodological Notes on *The Cornell Couples and Careers Study*

1. "Workers" refer to employees from one of the seven participating organizations. "Spouses/partners" refers to the spouses or partners of the workers.

2. Of the 932 referents, thirty-nine workers had left the organizations participating in our study between the time of initial contact and the time of the actual interview, thirty-three of those thirty-nine workers were working outside the participating organizations at the time of the interview, and the remaining six workers had retired.

3. This includes both referents and spouses who work for one of the participating organizations.

4. Moen and Yu (1999).

5. Moen, Sweet, and Townsend (2001).

6. Nakao and Treas (1990).

7. Nakao and Treas (1990).

8. Modified from Galinsky, Bond, and Friedman (1993).

9. Modified from Bond, Galinsky, and Swanberg (1998).

10. Modified from Bond, Galinsky, and Swanberg (1998); Galinsky, Bond, and Friedman (1993).

11. Modified from Bond, Galinsky, and Swanberg (1998); Galinsky, Bond, and Friedman (1993).

12. Modified from Bond, Galinsky, and Swanberg (1998).

13. Modified from Galinsky, Bond, and Friedman (1993).

14. Applebaum, Bailey, Berg, and Kalleberg (2001).

15. Modified from Bond, Galinsky, and Swanberg (1998).

16. Modified from Bond, Galinsky, and Swanberg (1998).

17. Thomas and Ganster (1995).

18. Shinn, Wong, Simko, and Ortiz-Torres (1989).

19. Welbourne, Johnson, Erez. (1998).

20. Modified from Galinsky, Bond, and Friedman (1993).

21. From Mid Life Development Inventory.

22. From Mid Life Development Inventory.

23. From General Social Survey, National Opinion Research Center.

24. From Mid Life Development Inventory.

25. From Mid Life Development Inventory.

26. From Mid Life Development Inventory.

27. Modified from Galinsky, Bond, and Friedman (1993).

28. From Mid Life Development Inventory.

29. Modified from Bond, Galinsky, and Swanberg (1998). Likert scale, not continuous.

30. Smilkstein, Ashworth and Montano (1982).

31. From Mid Life Development Inventory.

32. Modified from Galinsky, Bond, and Friedman (1993).

33. Modified from Bond, Galinsky, and Swanberg (1998).

34. Modified from Bond, Galinsky, and Swanberg (1998).
35. Modified from Bond, Galinsky, and Swanberg (1998).
36. Modified from Bond, Galinsky, and Swanberg (1998).
37. Heck, Winter, and Stafford (1992).
38. Modified from Galinsky, Bond, and Friedman (1993).
39. Modified from Galinsky, Bond, and Friedman (1993).
40. From General Social Survey, National Opinion Research Center.
41. From General Social Survey, National Opinion Research Center.
42. Adapted from the Organizing Religious Work Survey, 1997–98.
43. Cornell Retirement and Wellbeing Study.
44. Modified from Bond, Galinsky, and Swanberg (1998).
45. Cornell Retirement and Well-being Study.
46. Cornell Retirement and Well-being Study.
47. Cornell Retirement and Well-being Study.
48. Modified from Bond, Galinsky, and Swanberg (1998).

References

Abbott, Andrew. 1995. "Sequence Analysis: New Methods for Old Ideas." *Annual Review of Sociology* 21: 93–113.

Abbott, Andrew, and Emily Barman. 1997. "Sequence Comparison via Alignment and Gibbs Sampling: A Formal Analysis of the Emergence of the Modern Sociological Article." *Sociological Methodology* 27: 47–87.

Abbott, Andrew, and Alexandra Hrycak. 1990. "Measuring Resemblance in Sequence Data: An Optimal Matching Analysis of Musicians' Careers." *American Journal of Sociology* 96: 144–58.

Abel, Bruce J., and Bert Hayslip. 1987. "Locus of Control and Retirement Preparation." *Journal of Gerontology* 42: 165–67.

Abrahamson, Eric. 1996. "Management Fashion." *Academy of Management Review* 21: 254–85.

Acitelli, Linda K., and Toni C. Antonucci. 1994. "Gender Differences in the Link between Marital Support and Satisfaction in Older Couples." *Journal of Personality and Social Psychology* 67: 688–98.

Adams, Gary A., Lynda A. King, and Daniel W. King. 1996. "Relationships of Job and Family Involvement, Family Social Support, and Work-Family Conflict with Job and Life Satisfaction." *Journal of Applied Psychology* 76: 60–74.

Aldous, Joan. 1996. *Family Careers: Rethinking the Developmental Perspective*. Thousand Oaks: Sage Publications.

Allen, Katherine R., and David H. Demo. 1995. "The Families of Lesbians and Gay Men: A New Frontier in Family Research." *Journal of Marriage and the Family* 57: 111–27.

Allen, Tammy D., David E. L. Herst, Carly S. Bruck, and Marty Sutton. 2000. "Consequences Associated with Work-to-Family Conflict: A Review and Agenda for Future Research." *Journal of Occupational Health Psychology* 5: 278–308.

Almeida, David M., Elaine Wethington, and Amy L. Chandler. 1999. "Daily Transmission of Tensions between Marital Dyads and Parent-Child Dyads." *Journal of Marriage and the Family* 61: 49–61.

Althauser, Robert P. 1989. "Job Histories, Career Lines and Firm Internal Labor Markets: An Analysis of Job Shifts." *Research in Social Stratification and Mobility* 8: 177–200.

Althauser, Robert P., and Arne L. Kalleberg. 1990. "Identifying Career Lines and Internal Labor Markets within Firms: A Study in the Interrelationships of Theory and Methods." In *Social Mobility and Social Structure*, edited by R. Breiger, 308–56. Cambridge, UK: Cambridge University Press.

Altucher, Kristine. 2000. Changing Lives, Changing Plans: Stability of Childbearing Intentions and Gender in the United States. Working paper no. 00-07, Cornell Employment and Family Careers Institute, Cornell University, Ithaca.

Appelbaum, Eileen, Thomas Bailey, Peter Berg, and Arne L. Kalleberg. 2001. "Do High Performance Work Systems Pay Off?" In *The Transformation of Work*, edited by Steven P. Vallas, 85–107. Greenwich, Conn.: JAI Press.

Appelbaum, Eileen, and Rosemary Batt. 1994. *The New American Workplace: Transforming Work Systems in the United States*. Ithaca: ILR Press.

Appelbaum, Eileen, Peter Berg, and Arne L. Kalleberg. 2000. *Balancing Work and Family: Effects of High Performance Work Systems and High Commitment Workplaces*. Report to the U.S. Department of Labor, Washington, D.C.

Aryee, Samuel, Yue Wha Chay, and Hwee Hoon Tan. 1994. "An Examination of the Antecedents of Subjective Career Success among a Managerial Sample in Singapore." *Human Relations* 47: 487–503.

Aryee, Samuel, and Vivienne Luk. 1996. "Balancing Two Major Parts of Adult Life Experience: Work and Family Identity among Dual-Earner Couples." *Human Relations* 49: 465–87.

Aryee, Samuel, Vivienne Luk, and Raymond Stone. 1998. "Family Responsive Variables and Retention-Relevant Outcomes among Employed Parents." *Human Relations* 51: 73–87.

Assadian, Afsaneh, and Jan Ondrich. 1993. "Residential Location, Housing Demand and Labour Supply Decisions of One- and Two-Earner Households: The Case of Bogota, Colombia." *Urban Studies* 30: 73–86.

Bailyn, Lotte. 1992. "Issues of Work and Family in Different National Contexts: How the United States, Britain, and Sweden Respond." *Human Resource Management* 31(3): 201–8.

——. 1993a. *Breaking the Mold: Women, Men, and Time in the New Corporate World*. New York: Free Press.

——. 1993b. Work-Family Partnership: A Catalyst for Change. Working paper no. 3827-95, Sloan School of Management, Massachusetts Institute of Technology, Cambridge, Mass.

Bailyn, Lotte, Rhona Rapoport, and Joyce K. Fletcher. 2000. "Moving Corporations in the United States toward Gender Equity: A Cautionary Tale." In *Organizational Change and Gender Equity*, edited by Linda Haas, Philip O. Hwang, and Graeme Russell, 167–79. Thousand Oaks, CA: Sage.

Bailyn, Lotte, Paula Rayman, Maureen Harvey, Robert Krim, Robert Read, Françoise Carré, Jillian Dickert, Pamela Joshi, and Alina Martinez. 1998. *The Radcliffe-Fleet Project: Creating Work and Life Integration Solutions*. Cambridge, Mass.: Radcliffe Public Policy Center.

Baldwin, Wendy. 2000. "Information No One Else Knows: The Science of Self-Report." In *The Science of Self-Report: Implications for Research and Practice*, edited by Arthur A. Stone, Jaylan S. Turkkan, Christine A. Bachrach, Jared B. Jobe, Howard S. Kurtzman, and Virginia S. Cain, 3–8. Mahwah: Lawrence Erlbaum.

Baltes, Boris B., Thomas E. Briggs, Joseph W. Huff, Julie A. Wright, and George A. Neuman. 1999. "Flexible and Compressed Workweek Schedules: A Meta-Analysis of Their Effects on Work-Related Criteria." *Journal of Applied Psychology* 84: 496–513.

Bandura, Albert. 1982. "Self-Efficacy Mechanism in Human Agency." *American Psychologist* 37: 122–47.

Barker, James R. 1993. "Tightening the Iron Cage: Concertive Control in Self-Managing Teams." *Administrative Science Quarterly* 38: 408–37.

Barker, Kathleen, and Kathleen Christensen. 1998. *Contingent Work: American Employment Relations in Transition*. Ithaca: ILR Press.

Barley, Stephen R. 1989. "Careers, Identities, and Institutions: The Legacy of the Chicago School of Sociology." In *Handbook of Career Theory*, edited by Michael B. Arthur, Douglas T. Hall, and Barbara S. Lawrence, 41–65. New York: Cambridge University Press.

Barnett, Rosalind C., and Robert T. Brennan. 1997. "Change in Job Conditions, Change in Psychological Distress, and Gender: A Longitudinal Study of Dual-Earner Couples." *Journal of Organizational Behavior* 18: 253–74.

Barnett, Rosalind C., Nancy L. Marshall, Stephen W. Raudenbush, and Robert T. Brennan. 1993. "Gender and the Relationship between Job Experience and Psychological Distress: A Study of Dual Earner Couples." *Journal of Personality and Social Psychology* 64: 795–806.

Barnett, Rosalind C., and Caryl Rivers. 1996. *She Works/He Works: How Two-Income Families are Happier, Healthier, and Better-Off*. New York: HarperCollins.

Barth, Michael C., William McNaught, and Philip Rizzi. 1993. "Corporations and the Aging Workforce." In *Building the Competitive Workforce: Investing in Human Capital for Corporate Success*, edited by Philip H. Mirvis, 156–200. New York: John Wiley and Sons.

Batt, Rosemary, and P. Monique Valcour. 2003. "Human Resource Practices as Predictors of Work-Family Outcomes and Employee Turnover." *Industrial Relations* 42(2).

Becker, Gary S. 1981. *A Treatise on the Family*. Cambridge, Mass.: Harvard University Press.

———. 1991. *A Treatise on the Family*. Cambridge, Mass.: Harvard University Press.

Becker, Penny Edgell. 1998. "'Rational Amusement and Sound Instruction: Constructing the True Catholic Woman in the Ave Maria." *Religion and American Culture* 8(1): 55–90.

———. 2001. "It's Not Just a Matter of Time: How the Time Squeeze Affects Congregational Participation." *Journal of Family Ministry* 15(2): 11–26.

———. Forthcoming. "Religion and Family in a Changing Society." In *Religion and Family: Understanding the Transformation of Linked Institutions*, edited by Paul DiMaggio, Michèle Lamont, Robert Wuthnow, and Viviana Zelizer, 1–42. Series in Cultural Sociology. Princeton: Princeton University Press.

Becker, Penny Edgell, and Pawan Dhingra. 2001. "Religious Involvement and Volunteering." *Sociology of Religion* 62(3): 315–35.

Becker, Penny Edgell, and Heather Hofmeister. 1999. Work, Family, and Religious Involvement for Men and Women: "Family Values" or the Modern Family? Working paper no. 00-05, Cornell Employment and Family Careers Institute, Cornell University, Ithaca.

———. 2001. "Work, Family, and Religious Involvement for Men and Women." *Journal for the Scientific Study of Religion* 40(4): 707–22.

Becker, Penny Edgell, and Phyllis Moen. 1999. "Scaling Back: Dual-Earner Couples' Work-Family Strategies." *Journal of Marriage and the Family* 61: 995–1007.

Bellah, Robert N., Richard Madsen, William M. Sullivan, Ann Swidler, and Steven M. Tipton. 1985. *Habits of the Heart: Individualism and Commitment in American Life*. Berkeley: University of California Press.

Bem, Sandra L. 1994. *The Lenses of Gender: Transforming the Debate on Sexual Inequality*. New Haven: Yale University Press.

Bernard, Jessie. 1981. "The Good-Provider Role." *American Psychologist* 36: 1–12.

Beutell, Nicholas J., and Ursula Wittig-Berman. 1999. "Predictors of Work-Family Conflict and Satisfaction with Family, Job, Career and Life." *Psychological Reports* 85: 883–903.

Bielby, William T., and Denise D. Bielby. 1992. "I Will Follow Him: Family Ties, Gender Role Beliefs, and Reluctance to Relocate for a Better Job." *American Journal of Sociology* 97: 1241–67.

Blair-Loy, Mary. 1999. "Career Patterns of Executive Women in Finance: An Optimal Matching Analysis." *American Journal of Sociology* 104: 1346–97.

Blank, Rebecca. 1990. "Are Part-Time Jobs Bad Jobs?" In *A Future of Lousy Jobs?* edited by Gary Burtless, 123–65. Washington, D.C.: Brookings Institution.

Blau, David M. 1998. "Labor Force Dynamics of Older Married Couples." *Journal of Labor Economics* 16: 595–629.

Blau, Francine D., and Ronald G. Ehrenberg, eds. 1997. *Gender and Family Issues in the Workplace*. New York: Russell Sage Foundation.

Blau, Francine D., Marianne A. Ferber, and Anne E. Winkler. 1998. *The Economics of Men and Women at Work*. Upper Saddle River: Prentice Hall.

Blau, Peter. 1955. *The Dynamics of Bureaucracy: A Study of Interpersonal Relations in Two Government Agencies*. Chicago: University of Chicago Press.

Blood, Robert O., Jr., and Donald M. Wolfe. 1960. *Husbands and Wives: The Dynamics of Married Living*. Glencoe: The Free Press.

Blossfeld, Hans-Peter, and Catherine Hakim. 1996. "Part-time Work in the United States of America." In *Between Equalization and Marginalisation*, edited by Hans-Peter Blossfeld and Catherine Hakim, 289–314. New York: Oxford University Press.

Bluestone, Barry, and Stephen Rose. 1997. "Overworked and Underemployed." *American Prospect* 31(March–April): 58–69.

———. 1998. "The Macroeconomics of Work Time." *Review of Social Economy* 56: 425–41.

Blumen, Orna. 1994. "Gender Differences in the Journey to Work." *Urban Geography* 15: 223–45.

Blumstein, Philip, and Pepper Schwarz. 1983. *American Couples: Money, Work, Sex*. New York: William Morrow.

Bodie, Zvi. 1990. "Pensions as Retirement Insurance." *Journal of Economic Literature* 28(1): 28–49.

Boles, James S., W. Gary Howard, and Heather Howard. 2001. "An Investigation into the Inter-Relationships of Work-Family Conflict, Family-Work Conflict and Work Satisfaction." *Journal of Managerial Issues* 13: 376–90.

Bolger, Niall, Anita DeLongis, Ronald C. Kessler, and Elaine Wethington. 1989. "The Contagion of Stress across Multiple Roles." *Journal of Marriage and Family* 51: 175–83.

Bond, James T., Ellen Galinksy, and Jennifer E. Swanberg. 1998. *The 1997 National Study of the Changing Workforce*. New York: Families and Work Institute.

Bosma, Hans, Stephen A. Stansfeld, and Michael G. Marmot. 1998. "Job Control, Personal Characteristics, and Heart Disease." *Journal of Occupational Health Psychology* 3: 402–9.

Bourdieu, Pierre. 1985. "The Forms of Capital." In *The Handbook of Theory and Research for the Sociology of Education*, edited by John C. Richardson, 241–58. New York: Greenwood.

Bowen, Gary L. 1998. "Effects of Leader Support in the Work Unit on the Relationship between Work Spillover and Family Adaptation." *Journal of Family and Economics* 19: 25–52.

Brady, E. Michael, Richard H. Fortinsky, Kari Koss, Margaret Vishneau, and Mary Colombo. 1991. *Employers' Views on the Value of Older Workers: Final Report*. Human Services Development Institute, Edmund Muskie Institute of Public Affairs. Portland, Maine: University of Southern Maine.

Bregger, John E. 1996. "Measuring Self-Employment in the United States." *Monthly Labor Review* 119: 3–9.

Breiger, Ronald L. 1995. "Social Structure and the Phenomenology of Attainment." *Annual Review of Sociology* 21: 115–36.

Brett, Jeanne M., and Sara Yogev. 1988. "Restructuring Work for Family: How Dual-Earner Couples with Children Manage." *Journal of Social Behavior and Personality* 3: 159–74.

Brim, Gilbert. 1992. *Ambition: How We Manage Success and Failure throughout Our Lives.* New York: Basic Books.

Brines, Julie. 1994. "Economic Dependency, Gender, and the Division of Labor at Home." *American Journal of Sociology* 100: 652–88.

Bromet, Evelyn J., Mary A. Dew, and David K. Parkinson. 1990. "Spillover between Work and Family: A Study of Blue-Collar Working Wives." In *Stress between Work and Family*, edited by John Eckenrode and Susan Gore, 135–51. New York: Plenum Press.

Bronfenbrenner, Urie. 1979. *The Ecology of Human Development: Experiments by Nature and Design.* Cambridge, Mass.: Harvard University Press.

——. 1995. "The Bioecological Model from a Life Course Perspective: Reflections of a Participant Observer." In *Examining Lives in Context: Perspectives on the Ecology of Human Development*, edited by Phyllis Moen, Glen H. Elder, Jr., and Kurt Lüscher, 599–618. Washington, D.C.: American Psychological Association.

Bronfenbrenner, Urie, and Pamela A. Morris. 1998. "The Ecology of Developmental Processes." In *Handbook of Child Psychology, Theory*, Vol. 1, 5th ed., edited by Richard M. Lerner and William Damon, 993–1028. New York: John Wiley and Sons.

Brown, George W., and Tirril O. Harris. 1978. *Social Origins of Depression.* New York: Free Press.

Buehler, Ivan, and Janice M. Hogan. 1986. "Planning Styles in Single-Parent Families." *Home Economics Research Journal* 14(June): 351–62.

Burkett, Elinor. 2000. *The Baby Boom: How Family-Friendly America Cheats the Childless.* New York: Free Press.

Calasanti, Toni M. 1996. "Gender and Life Satisfaction in Retirement: An Assessment of the Male Model." *Journal of Gerontology* 51B: S18–S29.

Camstra, Ronald. 1996. "Commuting and Gender in a Lifestyle Perspective." *Urban Studies* 33: 283–300.

Capelli, David, Lauri Bassi, Harry Katz, David Knoke, Paul Osterman, and Michael Useem. 1997. *Change at Work.* New York: Oxford University Press.

Caplow, Theodore, Howard M. Bahr, Bruce A. Chadwick, Reuben Hill, and Margaret Holmes Williamson. 1982. *Middletown Families: Fifty Years of Change and Continuity.* Minneapolis: University of Minnesota Press.

Capowski, Genevieve. 1996. "The Joy of Flex." *Management Review* 85(March): 14–18.

Cappelli, Peter, Jill Constantine, and Clinton Chadwick. 2000. "It Pays to Value Family: Work and Family Tradeoffs." *Industrial Relations* 39: 175–98.

Carlson, Dawn P., and Perrewe, Pamela A. 1999. "The Role of Social Support in the Stressor-Strain Relationship: An Examination of Work-Family Conflict." *Journal of Management* 25: 513–40.

Carrington, Christopher. 2000. *No Place like Home: Relationships and Family Life among Lesbians and Gay Men.* Chicago: University of Chicago Press.

Carter, Mary Anne Taylor, and Kelli Cook. 1995. "Adaptation to Retirement: Role Changes and Psychological Resources." *Career Development Quarterly* 44: 67–82.

Catalyst. 1998. *Two Careers, One Marriage: Making It Work in the Workplace.* New York: Catalyst.

Chadwick, Bruce A., and Tim B. Heaton. 1992. *Statistical Handbook on the American Family.* Phoenix: Onyx Press.

Champoux, Joseph E. 1980. "The World of Nonwork: Some Implications for Job Re-Design Efforts." *Personal Psychology* 33: 61–75.

Chan, Raymond, Risa C. Brooks, Barbara Raboy, and Charlotte J. Patterson. 1998. "Division of Labor among Lesbian and Heterosexual Parents: Associations with Children's Adjustment." *Journal of Family Psychology* 12(3): 402–19.

Chan, Tak Wing. 1995. "Optimal Matching Analysis: A Methodological Note on Studying Career Mobility." *Work and Occupations* 22: 467–90.

Chen, Renbao, and S. Philip Morgan. 1991. "Recent Trends in the Timing of First Births in the United States." *Demography* 28: 513–33.

Christensen, Kathleen E. 1989. *Flexible Staffing and Scheduling in U.S. Corporations.* Research Bulletin no. 240. New York: The Conference Board.

———. 1995. *Contingent Work Arrangements in Family-Sensitive Corporations.* Boston, Mass.: Center on Work and Family.

Christensen, Kathleen E., and Ralph E. Gomory. 1999. "Three Jobs, Two People." *Washington Post,* 2 June, p. A21.

Christensen, Kathleen E., and Graham Staines. 1990. "Flextime: A Viable Solution to Work/Family Conflict?" *Journal of Family Issues* 11: 455–76.

Christiano, Kevin. 2000. "Religion and the Family in Modern American Culture." In *Family, Religion, and Social Change in Diverse Societies,* edited by Sharon K. Houseknecht and Jerry G. Pankhurst, 43–78. New York: Oxford University Press.

Cintron, Leslie. 2000. "The Implications of Telework for Work-Life Balance." In *Symposium on Telework and the New Workplace of the 21st Century.* Available from www.dol.gov/asp/telework/p3_4.htm; INTERNET. Accessed Jan. 30, 2002.

Clarkberg, Marin. 2000. "The Time-Squeeze in American Families: From Causes to Solutions." In *Balancing Acts: Easing the Burdens and Improving the Options for Working Families,* edited by Eileen Appelbaum, 25–36. Washington, D.C.: Economic Policy Institute.

———. 2001. "Understanding the Time-Squeeze: Married Couples Preferred and Actual Work-Hour Strategies." *American Behavioral Scientist* 44: 1115–36.

Clausen, John A. 1995. "Gender, Context, and Turning Points in Adults' Lives." In *Examining Lives in Context: Perspectives on the Ecology of Human Development,* edited by Phyllis E. Moen, Glen H. Elder, and Kurt Lüscher, 365–89. Washington, D.C.: American Psychological Association.

———. 1998. "Life Reviews and Life Stories." In *Methods of Life Course Research: Qualitative and Quantitative Approaches,* edited by Janet Z. Giele and Glen H. Elder, 189–212. Thousand Oaks: Sage.

Clausen, John A., and Martin I. Gilens. 1990. "Personality and Labor Force Participation across the Life Course: A Longitudinal Study of Women's Careers." *Sociological Forum* 5: 595–618.

Cohany, Sharon R. 1998. "Workers in Alternative Employment Arrangements: A Second Look." *Monthly Labor Review* 121(11): 3–20.

Cohen, Susan, and Diane Bailey. 1997. "What Makes Teams Work: Group Effectiveness Research from the Shop Floor to the Executive Suite." *Journal of Management* 23: 239–90.

Cohler, Bertram J. 1982. "Personal Narrative and the Life Course." In *Life Span Development and Behavior,* Vol. 4, edited by Paul Baltes and Orville G. Brim, 205–41. New York: Academic Press.

Cole, Robert E. 1999. *Management Quality Fads: How American Business Learned to Play the Quality Game.* New York: Oxford University Press.

Commonwealth Fund. 1993. *The Untapped Resource: The Final Report of the Americans over 55 at Work Program.* New York: The Commonwealth Fund.

Conference Board. 1991. *The Globalization of Work-Family Policies: Supplement to Work and Family Policies—the New Strategic Plan.* Report no. 949. New York: The Conference Board.

Cooke, Thomas J., and Adrian J. Bailey. 1996. "Family Migration and the Employment of Married Women and Men." *Economic Geography* 72: 38–48.

Coser, Rose L., and Gerald Rokoff. 1971. "Women in the Occupational World: Social Disruption and Conflict." *Social Problems* 18: 535–54.

Cott, Nancy F., and Elizabeth H. Pleck. 1979. *A Heritage of Her Own: Toward a New Social History of American Women.* New York: Simon and Schuster.

Cotton, John L. 1993. *Employee Involvement: Methods for Improving Performance and Work Attitudes.* Newbury Park: Sage.

Cournoyer, Robert J., and James R. Mahalik. 1995. "Cross-Sectional Study of Gender Role Conflict Examining College-Aged and Middle-Aged Men." *Journal of Counseling Psychology* 42: 11–19.

Cox, Harold, and Albert Bhak. 1978. "Symbolic Interaction and Retirement Adjustment: An Empirical Assessment." *International Journal of Aging and Human Development* 9: 279–86.

Cramer, James. 1980. "Fertility and Female Employment: Problems of Causal Direction." *American Sociological Review* 45: 167–90.

Crouter, Ann C. 1984. "Spillover from Family to Work: The Neglected Side of the Work-Family Interface." *Human Relations* 37: 425–42.

Crouter, Ann C., and Beth Manke. 1994. "The Changing American Workplace: Implications for Individuals and Families." *Family Relations* 43(2): 117–24.

Curtis, Richard. 1986. "Household and Family Theory on Inequality." *American Sociological Review* 51: 168–83.

Cutcher-Gershenfeld, Joel, Ellen Ernst Kossek, and Heidi Sandling. 1997. "Managing Concurrent Change Initiatives: Integrating Quality and Work/Family Strategies—Part III." *Organizational Dynamics* (winter 25): 21–37.

Cutler, W. Gale. 1995. "Hire Me, Hire My Husband!" *Research Technology Management* 38: 57–58.

Dalton, Dan R., and Debra J. Mesch. 1990. "The Impact of Flexible Scheduling on Employee Attendance and Turnover." *Administrative Science Quarterly* 35: 370–87.

Deacon, Ruth E., and Francille M. Firebaugh. 1988. *Family Resource Management: Principles and Applications,* 2nd ed. Boston: Allyn and Bacon.

Degler, Carl N. 1980. *At Odds: Women and the Family in America from the Revolution to the Present.* New York: Oxford University Press.

Dehle, Crystal, and Robert L. Weiss. 1998. "Sex Differences in Prospective Associations between Marital Quality and Depressed Mood." *Journal of Marriage and the Family* 60: 1002–11.

Demerath, Nicholas J. III. 1965. *Social Class in American Protestantism.* Chicago: Rand McNally.

Demerath, Nicholas J. III, and Rhys H. Williams. 1992. *A Bridging of Faiths.* Princeton: Princeton University Press.

DeVault, Marjorie L. 1987. "Doing Housework: Feeding and Family Life." In *Families and Work,* edited by Naomi Gerstel and Harriet E. Gross, 178–91. Philadelphia: Temple University Press.

——. 1991. *Feeding the Family: The Social Organization of Caring as Gendered Work.* Chicago: University of Chicago Press.

DeViney, Stanley, and Angela M. O'Rand. 1988. "Gender-Cohort Succession and Retirement among Older Men and Women, 1951–1984." *Sociological Quarterly* 29: 525–40.

Diamond, Lisa M. 2000. "Sexual Identity, Attractions, and Behavior among Young Sexual-Minority Women over a 2-Year Period." *Developmental Psychology* 36(2): 241–50.

DiPrete, Thomas A., and Margaret L. Krecker. 1991. "Occupational Linkages and Job Mobility within and across Organizations." *Research in Social Stratification and Mobility* 10: 91–131.

Dorfman, Lorraine T., and Mildred M. Moffett. 1987. "Retirement Satisfaction in Married and Widowed Rural Women." *The Gerontologist* 27: 215–21.

Drago, Robert, Robert Caplan, David Costanza, and Tanya Brubaker. 1999. "New Estimates of Working Time for Elementary School Teachers." *Monthly Labor Review* 122(4): 31–40.

Drobnic, Sonja, Hans-Peter Blossfeld, and Gotz Rohwer. 1999. "Dynamics of Women's Employment Patterns over the Family Life Course: A Comparison of the United States and Germany." *Journal of Marriage and the Family* 61(1): 133–46.

Duncan, Karen A., Virginia Solis Zuiker, and Ramona K. Z. Heck. 2000. "The Importance of Household Management for the Business Owning Family." *Journal of Family and Economic Issues* 21(3): 287–312.

Duxbury, Linda, and Christopher Higgins. 1994. "Interference between Work and Family: A Status Report on Dual-Career and Dual-Earner Mothers and Fathers." *Employee Assistance Quarterly* 9: 55–80.

Duxbury, Linda, Christopher Higgins, and Catherine Lee. 1994. "Work-Family Conflict: A Comparison by Gender, Family Type, and Perceived Control." *Journal of Family Issues* 15: 449–66.

Duxbury, Linda, Christopher Higgins, and Catherine Lee, and Shirley Mills. 1992. "An Examination of Organizational and Individual Outcomes." *Optimism: The Journal of Public Sector Management* 23: 46–59.

Eagle, Bruce W., Edward W. Miles, and Marjorie L. Icenogle. 1997. "Interrole Conflicts and the Permeability of Work and Family Domains: Are There Gender Differences?" *Journal of Vocational Behavior* 50: 168–84.

Eagle, Bruce W., Marjorie L. Icenogle, Jeanne D. Maes, and Edward W. Miles. 1998. "The Importance of Employee Demographic Profiles for Understanding Experiences of Work-Family Interrole Conflicts." *Journal of Social Psychology* 138(6): 690–709.

Easton, George S., and Sherry L. Jarrell. 1998. "The Effects of Total Quality Management on Corporate Performance: An Empirical Investigation." *Journal of Business* 71(2): 253–307.

Eaton, Susan. 2000. Work-Family Integration in the Biotechnology Industry: Implications for Firms and Employees. Ph.D. diss., Sloan School of Management, Massachusetts Institute of Technology.

——. 2001. If You Can Use Them: Flexibility Policies, Organizational Commitment, and Perceived Productivity. Working paper no. RWPO1-009, John F. Kennedy School of Government, Harvard University, Cambridge, Mass.

Edwards, Jeffrey R., and Nancy P. Rothbard. 2000. "Mechanisms Linking Work and Family: Clarifying the Relationship between Work and Family Constructs." *Academy of Management Review* 25: 178–99.

Elder, Glen H., Jr. 1978. "Family History and the Life Course." In *Transitions: The Family and the Life Course in Historical Perspective*, edited by Tamara K. Hareven, 17–64. New York: Academic Press.

——. 1985. "Perspectives on the Life Course." In *Life Course Dynamics: Trajectories and Transitions, 1968–1980*, edited by Glen H. Elder, Jr., 23–49. Ithaca: Cornell University Press.

——. 1992. "The Life Course." In *The Encyclopedia of Sociology*, edited by Edgar F. Borgatta and Marie L. Borgatta, 1120–30. New York: Macmillan.

——. 1995. "The Life Course Paradigm: Social Change and Individual Development." In *Examining Lives in Context: Perspectives on the Ecology of Human Development*, edited by Phyllis Moen, Glen H. Elder, Jr., and Kurt Lüscher, 101–40. Washington, D.C.: American Psychological Association.

——. 1998a. *Children of the Great Depression*. Boulder: Westview Press.

——. 1998b. "The Life Course as Developmental Theory." *Child Development* 69: 1–12.

——. 1998c. "The Life Course and Human Development." In *Handbook of Child Psychology*. Volume 1, *Theoretical Models of Human Development*, edited by William Damon, 939–91. New York: John Wiley and Sons.

Elder, Glen H., Jr., Linda K. George, and Michael J. Shanahan. 1996. "Psychosocial Stress over the Life Course." In *Psychosocial Stress: Perspectives on Structure, Theory,*

Life Course, and Methods, edited by Howard B. Kaplan, 247–91. Orlando: Academic Press.

Emerson, Richard M. 1976. "Power-Dependence Relations." *American Sociological Review* 27: 31–41.

England, Paula. 1999. "Thoughts on What We Know and Don't about Gender." In *Proceedings of the American Sociological Association Annual Meeting*, edited by Margaret Greer, 3–5. Chicago: Sex and Gender News.

England, Paula, and George Farkas. 1986. *Households, Employment, and Gender: A Social, Economic, and Demographic View*. New York: Aldine.

English-Lueck, Jan A. 1998. "Technology and Social Change: The Effects on Family and Community." In *COSSA Congressional Seminar*. Available from www.sjsu.edu/depts/anthropology/svcp/SVCPcosa.html; INTERNET. Accessed Jan. 30, 2002.

Epstein, Cynthia Fuchs, Carroll Seron, Bonnie Oglensky, and Robert Sauté. 1999. *The Part-Time Paradox: Time Norms, Professional Life, Family, and Gender*. New York: Routledge.

Evans, Paul, and Fernando Bartolome. 1984a. "The Changing Picture of the Relationship between Career and the Family." *Journal of Occupational Behavior* 5: 9–21.

———. 1984b. "The Dynamics of Work-Family Relationships in Managerial Line." *International Review of Applied Psychology* 35: 371–75.

Fagnani, Jeanne. 1993. "Life Course and Space: Dual Careers and Residential Mobility among Upper-Middle-Class Families in the Île-de-France Region." In *Full Circles: Geographies of Women over the Life Course, International Studies of Women and Place*, edited by Cindi Katz and Janice Monk, 171–87. London: Routledge.

Fassinger, Ruth E. 1995. "From Invisibility to Integration: Lesbian Identity in the Workplace." *Career Development Quarterly* 44: 148–67.

Feldman, Daniel, Helen I. Doerpinghaus, and William H. Turnley. 1995. "Employee Reactions to Temporary Jobs." *Journal of Managerial Issues* 7: 127–39.

Ferber, Marianne A., and Jane W. Loeb, eds. 1997. *Academic Couples: Problems and Promises*. Urbana: University of Illinois Press.

Ferber, Marianne A., and Brigid O'Farrell, eds. 1991. *Work and Family: Policies for a Changing Work Force*. Washington, D.C.: National Academy Press.

Fox, Marilyn L., and Deborah J. Dwyer. 1999. "An Investigation of the Effects of Time and Involvement in the Relationship between Stressors and Work-Family Conflict." *Journal of Occupational Health Psychology* 4: 164–74.

Frese, Mary. 1999. "Social Support as a Moderator of the Relationship between Work Stressors and Psychological Dysfunctioning: A Longitudinal Study with Objective Measures." *Journal of Occupational Health Psychology* 4: 179–92.

Fretz, Bruce R., Nancy A. Kluge, Shelly M. Ossana, Sharon M. Jones, and Marilyn W. Merikangas. 1989. "Intervention Targets for Reducing Preretirement Anxiety and Depression." *Journal of Counseling Psychology* 36: 301–7.

Friedman, Dana E. 1990. "Work and Family: The New Strategic Plan." *Human Resource Planning* 13(2): 79–89.

Friedman, Dana E., and Ellen Galinsky. 1992. "Work and Family Issues: A Legitimate Business Concern." In *Work, Families, and Organizations*, edited by Sheldon Zedeck, 168–207. San Francisco: Jossey-Bass.

Friedman, Dana E., and Arlene A. Johnson. 1991. *Strategies for Promoting a Work-Family Agenda*. Report no. 973. New York: The Conference Board.

Friedman, Stewart E., and Jeffrey H. Greenhaus. 2000. *Work and Family—Allies or Enemies?* New York: Oxford University Press.

Frone, Michael R., Marcia Russell, and Grace M. Barnes. 1996. "Work-Family Conflict, Gender, and Health-Related Outcomes: A Study of Employed Parents in Two Community Samples." *Journal of Occupational Health Psychology* 1: 57–67.

Frone, Michael R., Marcia Russell, and M. Lynne Cooper. 1992. "Antecedents and Outcomes of Work-Family Conflict: Testing a Model of the Work-Family Interface." *Journal of Applied Psychology* 77: 65–78.

Fulton, Philip N. 1983. *Public Transportation: Solving the Commuting Problem?* Washington, D.C.: Population Division, U.S. Bureau of the Census.

Galinsky, Ellen, and James T. Bond. 1998. *The 1998 Business Work-Life Study: A Sourcebook.* New York: Families and Work Institute.

Galinsky, Ellen, James T. Bond, and Dana E. Friedman. 1993. *The Changing Workforce: Highlights of the National Study.* New York: Families and Work Institute.

——. 1996. "The Role of Employers in Addressing the Needs of Employed Parents." *Journal of Social Issues* 52: 111–36.

Galinsky, Ellen, and Arlene A. Johnson. 1998. *Reframing the Business Case for Work-Life Initiatives.* New York: Families and Work Institute.

Galinsky, Ellen, and Stacy S. Kim. 2000. "Navigating Work and Parenting by Working at Home: Perspectives of Workers and Children Whose Parents Work at Home." In *Telework and the New Workplace of the 21st Century.* Available from www.dol.gov/asp/telework/p3_4.htm. Accessed Jan. 30, 2002.

Galinsky, Ellen, Stacy S. Kim, and James T. Bond. 2001. *Feeling Overworked: When Work Becomes Too Much.* New York: Families and Work Institute.

Ganster, Daniel C., and Marcy R. Fusilier. 1989. "Control in the Workplace." In *International Review of Industrial and Organizational Psychology*, edited by Cary L. Cooper, and Ivan T. Robertson, 235–80. London: John Wiley and Sons.

Garrison, M. E. Betsy, Sarah H. Pierce, and Vicky Tiller. 1997. "An Examination of the Construct Validity of Managing and Coping." *Family Economics and Resource Management Biennial, the Conference Proceedings* 2: 65–9.

Gattiker, Urs E., and Laurie Larwood. 1986. "Subjective Career Success: A Study of Managers and Support Personnel." *Journal of Business and Psychology* 1: 78–94.

——. 1988. "Predictors for Managers' Career Mobility, Success, and Satisfaction." *Human Relations* 41: 569–91.

——. 1990. "Predictors for Career Achievement in the Corporate Hierarchy." *Human Relations* 43: 703–26.

George, Linda K. 1993. "Sociological Perspectives on Life Transitions." *Annual Review of Sociology* 19: 353–73.

George, Linda K., and George L. Maddox. 1977. "Subjective Adaptation to Loss of the Work Role: A Longitudinal Study." *Journal of Gerontology* 32: 456–62.

Gerson, Kathleen. 1985. *Hard Choices: How Women Decide about Work, Career, and Motherhood.* Berkeley: University of California Press.

Gerth, Hans. H., and C. Wright Mills, eds. 1946. *From Max Weber: Essays in Sociology.* New York: Oxford University Press.

Gesch, Lyn. 1995. "Responses to Changing Lifestyles: 'Feminists' and 'Traditionalists' in Mainstream Religion." In *Work, Family, and Religion in Contemporary Society*, edited by Nancy Tatom Ammerman and Wade Clark Roof, 123–36. New York: Routledge.

Giele, Janet Z., and Glen H. Elder, Jr., eds. 1998. *Methods of Life Course Research: Qualitative and Quantitative Approaches.* Thousand Oaks: Sage.

Gill, H. Leroy, and Donald R. Haurin. 1998. "Wherever He May Go: How Wives Affect Their Husband's Career Decisions." *Social Science Research* 27: 264–79.

Gilligan, Carol C. 1982. *In a Different Voice.* Cambridge, Mass.: Harvard University Press.

Gilman, Charlotte Perkins. 1898. *Women and Economics.* Boston: Small, Maynard and Company.

Glaser, Barney G., and Anselm L. Strauss. 1973. *The Discovery of Grounded Theory: Strategies for Qualitative Research.* Chicago: Aldine.

Glass, Jennifer L., and Sarah Beth Estes. 1997. "The Family Responsive Workplace." *Annual Review of Sociology* 23: 289–313.

Glass, Jennifer, and Tetsushi Fujimoto. 1995. "Employer Characteristics and the Provision of Family-Responsive Policies." *Work and Occupations* 22: 380–411.

Goff, Stephen J., Michael K. Mount, and Rosemary L. Jamison. 1990. "Employer Supported Child Care, Work/Family Conflict, and Absenteeism: A Field Study." *Personnel Psychology* 43: 793–809.

Goode, William I. 1960. "A Theory of Role Strain." *American Sociological Review* 25: 483–96.

Goodstein, Jerry D. 1994. "Institutional Pressures and Strategic Responsiveness: Employer Involvement in Work/Family Issues." *Academy of Management Journal* 37(2): 350–82.

Gouldner, Alvin W. 1954. *Patterns of Industrial Bureaucracy*. Glencoe: The Free Press.

Gove, Walter R., Carolyn Briggs Style, and Michael Hughes. 1990. "The Effect of Marriage on the Well-Being of Adults." *Journal of Family Issues* 11: 4–35.

Green, Anne E. 1997. "A Question of Compromise? Case Study Evidence on the Location and Mobility Strategies of Dual Career Households." *Regional Studies* 31: 641.

Greenhaus, Jeffrey H., and Nicholas J. Beutell. 1985. "Sources of Conflict between Work and Family Roles." *The Academy of Management Review* 10(1): 76–88.

Greenhaus, Jeffrey H., Saroj Parasuraman, and Karen M. Collins. 2001. "Career Involvement and Family Involvement as Moderators of Relationships between Work-Family Conflict and Withdrawal from a Profession." *Journal of Occupational Health Psychology* 6: 91–100.

Greenhaus, Jeffrey H., Saroj Parasuraman, Cherlyn Skromme Granrose, Samuel Rabinowitz, and Nicholas J. Beutell. 1989. "Sources of Work-Family Conflict among Two-Career Couples." *Journal of Vocational Behavior* 34: 133–53.

Grimsley, Kirstin Downey. 2000. "Family a Priority for Young Workers." *Washington Post*, 3 May, p. E1.

Gronau, Reuben. 1977. "Leisure, Home Production, and Work—The Theory of the Allocation of Time Revisted." *Journal of Political Economy* 85: 1099–124.

Gross, Irma H., Elizabeth W. Crandall, and Marjorie M. Knoll. 1980. *Management for Modern Families*. 4th ed. Englewood Cliffs: Prentice-Hall.

Grzywacz, Joseph G. 2000. "Work-Family Spillover and Health during Midlife: Is Managing Conflict Everything?" *American Journal of Health Promotion* 14: 236–43.

Grzywacz, Joseph G., and Nadine F. Marks. 2000. "Reconceptualzing the Work-Family Interface: An Ecological Perspective on the Correlates of Positive and Negative Spillover between Work and Family." *Journal of Occupational Health Psychology* 5: 111–26.

Gustman, Alan L., Olivia S. Mitchell, and Thomas L. Steinmeir. 1994. "The Role of Pensions in the Labor Market: A Survey of the Literature." *Industrial and Labor Relations Review* 47(3): 417–38.

Gustman, Alan L. and Thomas L. Steinmeier. 1983. "Minimum Hours Constraints and Retirement Behavior." *Contemporary Policy Issues. Economic Inquiry* (suppl.) 3: 77–91.

Gutek, Barbara A., Sabrina Searle, and Lilian Klepa. 1991. "Rational versus Gender Role Explanations of Work-Family Conflict." *Journal of Applied Psychology* 76(4): 560–8.

Haddon, Leslie, and Roger Silverstone. 2000. "Information and Communication Technologies and Everyday Life: Individual and Social Dimensions." In *The Information Society in Europe: Work and Life in an Age of Globalization*, edited by Ken Ducatel, Juliet Webster, and Werner Herrmann, 233–57. Lanham: Rowman and Littlefield.

Hall, Charles. 1995. "Entering the Labor Force: Ideals and Realities among Evangelical Women." In *Work, Family, and Religion in Contemporary Society*, edited by Nancy Tatom Ammerman and Wade Clark Roof, 137–56. New York: Routledge.

Hammond, Phillip E. 1988. "Religion and the Persistence of Identity." *Journal for the Scientific Study of Religion* 27(1): 1–11.

Han, Shin-Kap, and Phyllis Moen. 1999a. "Clocking Out: Temporal Patterning of Retirement." *American Journal of Sociology* 105: 191–236.

——. 1999b. "Work and Family over Time: A Life Course Approach." *Annals of the American Academy of Political and Social Sciences* 562: 98–110.

——. 2001. "Coupled Careers: Men's and Women's Pathways through Work and Marriage in the United States." In *Careers of Couples in Contemporary Societies: A Cross-National Comparison of the Transition from Male Breadwinner to Dual-Earner Families*, edited by Hans-Peter Blossfeld and Sonja Drobnic, 201–31. Oxford: Oxford University Press.

Hanson, Susan, and Geraldine Pratt. 1992. "Dynamic Dependencies—a Geographic Investigation of Local-Labor Markets." *Economic Geography* 68: 373.

Hays, Sharon. 1996. *The Cultural Contradictions of Motherhood*. New Haven: Yale University Press.

Heaton, Tim B., and Marie Cornwall. 1989. "Religious Group Variation in the Socioeconomic Status and Family Behavior of Women." *Journal for the Scientific Study of Religion* 28(3): 283–99.

Heck, Katherine E., Kenneth C. Schoendorf, Stephanie Ventura, and John L. Kiely. 1997. "Delayed Childbearing by Education Level in the United States, 1969–1994." *Maternal and Child Health Journal* 1(2): 81–8.

Heck, Ramona K. Z., Mary Winter, and Kathryn Stafford. 1992. "Managing Work and Family in Home-Based Employment." *Journal of Family and Economic Issues* 13(2): 187–212.

Heckman, James J. 1979. "Sample Selection Bias as a Specification Error." *Econometrica* 47(1): 153–62.

Helgeson, Vicki S. 1994. "Relation of Agency and Communion to Well-Being: Evidence and Potential Explanations." *Psychology Bulletin* 116: 412–28.

Hendrick, C., K. S. Wells, and Martin V. Faletti. 1982. "Social and Emotional Effects of Geographical Relocation on Elderly Retirees." *Journal of Personality and Social Psychology* 42: 951–62.

Henretta, John C., Angela M. O'Rand, and Christopher G. Chan. 1993. "Joint Role Investments and Synchronization of Retirement: A Sequential Approach to Couple's Retirement Timing." *Social Forces* 71: 981–1000.

Hertel, Bradley R. 1995. "Work, Family, and Faith." In *Work, Family, and Religion in Contemporary Society*, edited by Nancy T. Ammerman and Wade C. Roof, 81–121. New York: Routledge.

Hertz, Rosanna. 1986. *More Equal than Others: Women and Men in Dual-Career Marriages*. Berkeley: University of California Press.

Hertz, Rosanna, and Nancy L. Marshall, eds. 2001. *Working Families: The Transformation of the American Home*. Berkeley: University of California Press.

Herzog, Anna Regula, James S. House, and James N. Morgan. 1991. Relation of Work and Retirement to Health and Well-Being in Older Age. *Psychology and Aging* 6: 201–11.

Hewlett, Sylvia A. 1991. *When the Bough Breaks: The Cost of Neglecting Our Children*. New York: Basic Books.

——. 2002. *Creating a Life: Professional Women and the Quest for Children*. New York: Talk Miramax Books.

Higgins, Christopher A., and Linda E. Duxbury. 1992. "Work-Family Conflict: A Comparison of Dual-Career and Traditional-Career Men." *Journal of Organizational Behavior* 13: 389–411.

Higgins, Christopher A., Linda E. Duxbury, and Richard H. Irving. 1992. "Work-Family Conflict in the Dual-Career Family." *Organizational Behavior and Human Decision Processes* 51: 51–75.

Higgins, Christopher A., Linda E. Duxbury, and Karen L. Johnson. 2000. "Part-time Work for Women: Does It Really Help Balance Work and Family?" *Human Resource Management* 39(1): 17–32.

Hill, E. Jeffrey, Brent C. Miller, Sara P. Weiner, and Joe Colihan. 1998. "Influences of the Virtual Office on Aspects of Work and Work/Life Balance." *Personnel Psychology* 51: 667–83.

Hill, Reuben. 1970. *Family Development in Three Generations*. Cambridge, Mass.: Schenkman Publishing.

Hochschild, Arlie. 1989. *The Second Shift*. New York: Avon Books.

———. 1997. *The Time Bind: When Work Becomes Home and Home Becomes Work*. New York: Metropolitan Books.

———. 1999. "The Nanny Chain." *American Prospect* 11: 32–6.

Hogan, Dennis P. 1978. "The Variable Order of Events in the Life Course." *American Sociological Review* 43: 573–86.

Holmes, Thomas, and Richard Rahe. 1967. "The Social Readjustment Rating Scale." *Journal of Psychosomatic Research* 11: 213–18.

Homans, George C. 1958. "Social Behavior as Exchange." *American Journal of Sociology* 63: 597–606.

Horowitz, Stephen M., David L. Weis, and Molly T. Laflin. 2001. "Differences between Sexual Orientation Behavior Groups and Social Background, Quality of Life, and Health Behaviors." *Journal of Sex Research* 38: 205–18.

Howell, Frank M., and Deborah Richey Bronson. 1996. "The Journey to Work and Gender Inequality in Earnings: A Cross-Validation Study for the United States." *Sociological Quarterly* 37: 429.

Hughes, Everett C. [1937] 1994. "Institutional Office and the Person." In *On Work, Race, and the Sociological Imagination*, edited by Everett C. Hughes, 136–45. Reprint, Chicago: University of Chicago Press.

Hughes, Diane, and Ellen Galinsky. 1994. "Work Experiences and Marital Interactions: Elaborating the Complexity of Work." *Journal of Organizational Behavior* 15: 423–38.

Hughes, Diane, Ellen Galinsky, and Anne Morris. 1992. "The Effects of Job Characteristics on Marital Quality: Specifying Linking Mechanisms." *Journal of Marriage and Family* 54: 31–42.

Human Rights Campaign Census Report. 2000. *Gay and Lesbian Families in the United States: Same-Sex Unmarried Partner Households. A Preliminary Analysis of 2000 United States Census Data*. 22 August 2001, Washington, D.C.

Hunts, Holly, Sharon M. Danes, Deborah C. Haynes, and Ramona K. Z. Heck. 2000. "Home-Based Employment: Relating Gender and Household Structure to Management and Child Care." In *Gender and Home-Based Employment*, edited by Charles B. Hennon, Suzanne Loker, and Rosemary Walker, 79–117. Westport: Auburn House.

Hurd, Michael D. 1996. "The Effect of Labor Market Rigidities on the Labor Force Behavior of Older Workers." In *Advances in the Economics of Aging*, edited by David A. Wise, 1–11. Chicago: University of Chicago Press.

Hutchens, Robert M., and Emma Dentinger. 2000. Gradual and Retire-Rehire Pathways to Retirement: Evidence from Seven Case Studies of Employers in Upstate New York. Working paper no. 00-13, Cornell Employment and Family Careers Institute, Cornell University, Ithaca.

Ishii-Kuntz, Masako, and Scott Coltrane. 1992. "Predicting the Sharing of Household Labor: Are Parenting and Housework Distinct?" *Sociological Perspectives* 35: 629–47.

Jacobs, Jerry. 1998. "Measuring Time at Work: Are Self-Reports Accurate?" *Monthly Labor Review* 121(12): 42–53.

Jacobs, Jerry, and Kathleen Gerson. 1998. "Who Are the Overworked Americans?" *Review of Social Economy* 56(4): 442–59.

———. 2001. "Overworked Individuals or Overworked Families?" *Work and Occupations* 28(1): 40–63.

Jacobs, Klaus, Martin Kohli, and Martin Rein. 1991. "Testing the Industry-Mix Hypothesis of Early Exit." In *Time for Retirement: Comparative Studies of Early Exit from the Labor Force*, edited by Martin Kohli, Martin Rein, Anne–Marie Guillemard, and Herman van Gunsteren, 67–96. New York: Cambridge University Press.

Jacobsen, Joyce P., and Laurence M. Levin. 1997. "Marriage and Migration: Comparing Gains and Losses for Migration for Couples and Singles." *Social Science Quarterly* 78: 688–709.

———. 2000. "The Effects of Internal Migration on the Relative Economic Status of Women and Men." *Journal of Socio-Economics* 29: 291–304.

Jacoby, Sanford. 1985. *Employing Bureaucracy*. New York: Columbia University Press.

Johnston-Anumonwo, Ibipo. 1992. "The Influence of Household Type on Gender Differences in Work Trip Distance." *Professional Geographer* 44: 161.

Johnston-Anumonwo, Ibipo, Sara McLafferty, and Valerie Preston. 1995. "Gender, Race, and the Spatial Context of Women's Employment." In *Gender in Urban Research*, edited by Judith A. Garber and Robyne S. Turner, 236–55. Thousand Oaks: Sage.

Jones, Fiona, and Ben C. Fletcher. 1993. "An Empirical Study of Occupational Stress Transmission in Working Couples." *Human Relations* 46: 881–903.

Judge, Timothy A., John W. Boudreau, and Robert D. Bretz. 1994. "Job and Life Attitudes of Male Executives." *Journal of Applied Psychology* 79: 767–82.

Judge, Timothy A., Daniel Cable, John Boudreau, and Robert Bretz, Jr. 1995. "An Empirical Investigation of the Predictors of Executive Career Success." *Personnel Psychology* 48: 485–508.

Judge, Timothy A., and Shinichiro Watanabe. 1994. "Individual Differences in the Nature of the Relationship between Job and Life Satisfaction." *Journal of Occupational and Organizational Psychology* 67: 101–7.

Julien, Danielle, Elise Chartrand, and Jean Begin. 1999. "Social Networks, Structural Interdependence, and Conjugal Adjustment in Heterosexual, Gay, and Lesbian Couples." *Journal of Marriage and the Family* 61: 516–30.

Juster, F. Thomas, and Frank P. Stafford. 1985. *Time, Goods, and Well-Being*. Ann Arbor: University of Michigan Press.

Kahn, Robert L., Donald M. Wolfe, Robert P. Quinn, J. Diedrick Snoek, and Robert A. Rosenthal. 1964. *Organizational Stress: Studies in Role Conflict and Ambiguity*. New York: John Wiley and Sons.

Kalleberg, Arne L., David Knoke, and Peter V. Marsden. 1995. "Interorganizational Networks and the Changing Employment Contract." *Connections* 18: 32–49.

Kalleberg, Arne L., Edith Rasell, Naomi Cassirer, Barbara F. Reskin, Ken Hudson, David Webster, Eileen Appelbaum, and Roberta M. Spalter-Roth. 1997. *Nonstandard Work, Substandard Jobs*. Washington, D.C.: Economic Policy Institute.

Kalleberg, Arne L., Barbara F. Reskin, and Ken Hudson. 2000. "Bad Jobs in America: Standard and Nonstandard Employment Relations and Job Quality in the United States." *American Sociological Review* 65: 256–78.

Kalleberg, Arne L., and Mark E. Van Buren. 1996. "Is Bigger Better? Explaining the Relationship between Organization Size and Job Rewards." *American Sociological Review* 61: 47–66.

Kanter, Rosabeth Moss. 1977. *Work and Family in the United States: A Critical Review and Agenda for Research and Policy*. New York: Russell Sage.

Karasek, Robert. 1990. "Lower Health Risk with Increased Job Control among White Collar Workers." *Journal of Organizational Behavior* 11: 171–85.

Karasek, Robert, and Tóres Theorell. 1990. *Healthy Work: Stress, Productivity and the Reconstruction of Working Life*. New York: Basic Books.

Kelly, Erin, and Frank Dobbin. 1999. "Civil Rights at Work: Sex Discrimination and the Rise of Maternity Leave Policies." *American Journal of Sociology* 105(2): 455–92.

Kessler, Ronald C., and Marilyn Essex. 1982. "Marital Status and Depression: The Importance of Coping Resources." *Social Forces* 61: 484–507.

Key, Rosemary J., and Francille M. Firebaugh. 1989. "Family Resource Management: Preparing for the 21st Century." *Journal of Home Economics* (spring 81): 13–17.

Kilty, Keith M., and John H. Behling. 1985. "Predicting the Retirement Intentions and Attitudes of Professional Workers." *Journal of Gerontology* 40: 219–27.

Kim, Jungmeen E., and Phyllis Moen. 1999. Work/Retirement Transitions and Psychological Well-Being in Late Midlife. Working paper no. 99-10, Cornell Employment and Family Careers Institute, Cornell University, Ithaca.

——. 2001. "Is Retirement Good or Bad for Subjective Well-Being? *Current Directions in Psychological Science* 10: 83–6.

Kingston, Paul W. 1990. "Illusions and Ignorance about the Family-Responsive Workplace." *Journal of Family Issues* 11: 438–54.

Kinnunen, Ulla, and Saija Mauno. 1998. "Antecedents and Outcomes of Work-Family Conflict among Employed Women and Men in Finland." *Human Relations* 51: 157–77.

Kirchmeyer, Catherine. 1992. "Perceptions of Nonworkers-to-Work Spillover: Challenging the Common View of Conflict-Ridden Domain Relationships." *Basic and Applied Social Psychology* 13: 231–49.

——. 1993. "Nonwork-to-Work Spillover: A More Balanced View of the Experiences and Coping of Professional Women and Men." *Sex Roles* 28: 531–52.

Kitzinger, Celia, and Sue Wilkinson. 1995. "Transitions from Heterosexuality to Lesbianism: The Discursive Production of Lesbian Identities." *Developmental Psychology* 13(1): 95–104.

Kofodimos, Joan R. 1995. *Beyond Work-Family Programs: Confronting and Resolving the Underlying Causes of Work-Personal Life Conflict*. Greensboro, N.C.: Center for Creative Leadership.

Kohli, Martin. 1986. "Social Organization and Subjective Construction of the Life Course." In *Human Development and the Life Course: Multidisciplinary Perspectives*, edited by Aage B. Sorensen, Franz E. Weinert, and Lonnie R. Sherrod, 271–92. Hillside: Lawrence Erlbaum.

Kohli, Martin, and John W. Meyer. 1986. "Social Structure and Social Construction of Life Stages." *Human Development* 29: 145–80.

Kohn, Melvin L. 1990. "Position in the Class Structure and Psychological Functioning in the United States, Japan, and Poland." *American Journal of Sociology* 95: 964–1008.

——. 1995. "Social Structure and Personality through Time and Space." In *Examining Lives in Context: Perspectives on the Ecology of Human Development*, edited by Phyllis Moen, Glen H. Elder, Jr., and Kurt Lüscher, 114–68. Washington, D.C.: American Psychological Association.

Kohn, Melvin L., and Carmi Schooler. 1973. "Occupational Experience and Psychological Functioning: An Assessment of Reciprocal Effects." *American Sociological Review* 38: 97–118.

——. 1978. "The Reciprocal Effects of the Substantive Complexity of Work and Intellectual Flexibility: A Longitudinal Assessment." *American Journal of Sociology* 84: 24–52.

——. 1983. *Work and Personality: An Inquiry into the Impact of Social Stratification*. Norwood: Ablex.

——. 1985. "Job Conditions and Personality: A Longitudinal Assessment of Their Reciprocal Effects." *American Journal of Sociology* 87: 1257–86.

Komarovsky, Mirra. 1964. *Blue-Collar Marriage*. New York: Random House.

Kossek, Ellen E., Parshatam Dass, and Beverly DeMarr. 1994. "The Dominant Logic of Employer-Sponsored Work and Family Initiatives: Human Resources Managers' Institutional Role." *Human Relations* 47(9): 1121–29.

Kossek, Ellen E., and Cynthia Ozeki. 1998. "Work-Family Conflict, Policies, and the Job-Life Satisfaction Relationship: A Review and Directions for Organizational Behavior Human Resources Research." *Journal of Applied Psychology* 83: 139–49.

Kotlikoff, Laurence J., and David A. Wise. 1987. "The Incentive Effects of Private Pension Plans." In *Issues in Pension Economics*, edited by Z. Bodie, J. B. Shoven, and D. A. Wise, 283–340. Chicago: University of Chicago Press.

Kraut, Robert, Sara Kiesler, Bonka Boneva, Jonathon Cummings, Vicki Helgeson, and Anne Crawford. 2002. "Internet Paradox Revisted." *Journal of Social Issues* 58: 49–74.

Kraut, Robert, Michael Patterson, Vicki Lundmark, Sara Kiesler, Tridas Mukopadhyay, and William Scherlis. 1998. "Internet Paradox: A Social Technology That Reduces Social Involvement and Psychological Well-Being?" *American Psychologist* 53: 1017–31.

Kurdek, Lawrence A. 1994. "Areas of Conflict for Gay, Lesbian, and Heterosexual Couples: What Couples Argue About Influences Relationship Satisfaction." *Journal of Marriage and the Family* 56: 923–34.

——. 1998. "Relationship Outcomes and Their Predictors: Longitudinal Evidence from Heterosexual Married, Gay Cohabiting, and Lesbian Cohabiting Couples." *Journal of Marriage and the Family* 60: 553–68.

Lachman, Margie E. 1986. "Locus of Control and Aging Research: A Case for Multidimensional and Domain-Specific Assessment." *Psychology and Aging* 1: 34–40.

Lachman, Margie E., and Suzanne L. Weaver. 1998. "The Sense of Control as a Moderator of Social Class Differences in Health and Well-Being." *Journal of Personality and Social Psychology* 74: 763–73.

Lambert, Susan J. 1990. "Processes Linking Work and Family: A Critical Review and Research Agenda." *Human Relations* 43: 239–57.

——. 1991. "The Combined Effects of Job and Family Characteristics on the Job Satisfaction, Job Involvement, and Intrinsic Motivation of Men and Women Workers." *Journal of Organizational Behavior* 12: 341–63.

Lazarus, Richard S. 1999. *Stress and Emotion.* New York: Springer.

LeClere, Felicia B., and Diane K. McLaughlin. 1997. "Family Migration and Changes in Women's Earnings: A Decomposition Analysis." *Population Research and Policy Review* 16: 315–55.

Lee, Gary R. 1978. "Marriage and Morale in Later Life." *Journal of Marriage and the Family* 40: 131–9.

Lee, Ronald, and Shelley Lapkoff. 1988. "Intergenerational Flows of Time and Goods: Consequences of Slowing Population Growth." *Journal of Political Economy* 96: 618–51.

Lehrer, Evelyn L. 1995. "The Effects of Religion on the Labor Supply of Married Women." *Social Science Research* 24: 1–21.

——. 1996. "The Role of the Husband's Religious Affiliation in the Economic and Demographic Behavior of Families." *Journal for the Scientific Study of Religion* 35: 145–55.

Levenson, Robert W., Lauren L. Carstensen, and John M. Gottman. 1993. "Long-Term Marriage: Age, Gender, and Satisfaction." *Psychology and Aging* 8: 301–13.

Levinson, David M. 1999. "Space, Money, Life Stage, and the Allocation of Time." *Transportation* 26: 141–71.

Levinson, David M., and Ajay Kumar. 1997. "Density and the Journey to Work." *Growth and Change* 28: 147–72.

Lewis, Suzan, and Cary L. Cooper. 1999. "The Work-Family Research Agenda in Changing Contexts." *Journal of Occupational Health Psychology* 4: 382–93.

Lichter, Daniel T. 1982. "The Migration of Dual-Worker Families: Does the Wife's Job Matter?" *Social Science Quarterly* 63: 48–57.

Lobel, Sharon A. 1999. "Impacts of Diversity and Work-Life Initiatives in Organizations." In *Handbook of Gender and Work*, edited by Gary N. Powell, 453–74. Thousand Oaks: Sage.

Loscocco, Karyn A. 1997. "Work-Family Linkages among Self-Employed Women and Men." *Journal of Vocational Behavior* 50: 204–26.

Lucero, Margaret A., and Robert E. Allen. 1994. "Employee Benefits: A Growing Source of Psychological Contract Violations." *Human Resource Management* 33: 425–46.

Luckmann, Thomas. 1967. *The Invisible Religion.* New York: Macmillan.

MacDermid, Shelley M., Leon C. Litchfield, and Marcie Pitt-Catsouphes. 1999. "Organizational Size and Work/Family Issues." In *The Evolving World of Work and Family: New Stakeholders, New Voices,* edited by M. Pitt-Catsouphes and B. K. Googins, 111–26. The Annals of the American Academy of Political and Social Sciences. Philadelphia: The American Society of Political and Social Science.

Madden, Janice Fanning. 1981. "Why Women Work Closer to Home." *Urban Studies* 18: 181–94.

Markham, William T. 1987. "Sex, Relocation, and Occupational Advancement: The 'Real Cruncher' for Women." *Women and Work* 2: 207–31.

Markham, William T., and Joseph H. Pleck. 1986. "Sex and Willingness to Move for Occupational Advancement: Some National Sample Results." *Sociological Quarterly* 27: 121–43.

Marks, Stephen R. 1977. "Multiple Roles and Role Strain: Some Notes on Human Energy, Time and Commitment." *American Sociological Review* 42: 921–36.

Marks, Stephen R., and Shelley M. MacDermid. 1996. "Multiple Roles and the Self: A Theory of Role Balance." *Journal of Marriage and the Family* 58: 417–32.

Marler, Janet H. 2000. Toward a Multi-level Model of Preference for Contingent Employment. Ph.D. diss., Department of Industrial and Labor Relations, Cornell University.

Marshall, Nancy L., and Rosalind C. Barnett. 1993. "Work-Family Strains and Gains among Two-Earner Couples." *Journal of Community Psychology* 21: 64–78.

Matthews, Anne M., and Kathleen H. Brown. 1987. "Retirement as a Critical Life Event: The Differential Experiences of Women and Men." *Research on Aging* 9: 548–71.

Maume, David J., Jr., and Paula Houston. 2001. "Job Segregation and Gender Differences in Work-Family Spillover among White-Collar Workers." *Journal of Family and Economic Issues* 22: 171–89.

Mauno, Saiji, and Ulla Kinnunen. 1999. "The Effects of Job Stressors on Marital Satisfaction in Finnish Dual-Earner Couples." *Journal of Organizational Behavior* 20: 879–95.

Mayer, Karl Ulrich. 1986. "Structural Constraints in the Life Course." *Human Development* 29: 163–70.

Mayer, Karl Ulrich, and Urs Schöpflin. 1989. "The State and the Life Course." *Annual Review of Sociology* 15: 187–209.

McCool, Audrey Carol, and George E. Stevens. 1989. *The Impact of Employee Benefits and Job Outcomes on the Employment of Older Persons in the Service Industries.* Orlando: University of Central Florida.

McLafferty, Sara, and Valerie Preston. 1997. "Gender, Race, and the Determinants of Commuting: New York in 1990." *Urban Geography* 18: 192.

McNeil, Laurie, and Marc Sher. 1999. "The Dual-Career-Couple Problem." *Physics Today* 52: 32–7.

Mead, George Herbert. 1934. *Mind, Self, and Society.* Chicago: University of Chicago Press.

Mederer, Helen J. 1993. "Division of Labor in Two Earner Homes: Task Accomplishment versus Household Management as Critical Variables in Perceptions about Family Work." *Journal of Marriage and the Family* 55: 133–45.

Meissner, Martin. 1971. "The Long Arm of the Job: A Study of Work and Leisure." *Industrial Relations* 10: 239–60.

Menaghan, Elizabeth. 1989. "Role Changes and Psychological Well-Being: Variations in Effects by Gender and Role Repertoires." *Social Forces* 67: 692–714.

Menken, Jane. 1985. "Age and Fertility: How Late Can You Wait?" *Demography* 22(4): 469–83.

Merola, Stacey S. 2001 Leisure and the Life Course: American Workers' Free-Time 1977 and 1997. Ph.D. diss., Department of Sociology, Cornell University.

Meyer, John, and Brian Rowan. 1977. "Institutionalized Organizations: Formal Structure as Myth and Ceremony." *American Journal of Sociology* 83: 340–63.

Milkie, Melissa A., and Pia Peltola. 1999. "Playing All the Roles: Gender and the Work-Family Balancing Act." *Journal of Marriage and the Family* 61(2): 476–90.

Milliken, Frances, Luis L. Martins, and Hal Morgan. 1998. "Explaining Organizational Responsiveness to Work-Family Issues: The Role of Human Resource Executives as Issue Interpreters." *Academy of Management Journal* 41(5): 580–93.

Mincer, Jacob. 1978. "Family Migration Decisions." *Journal of Political Economy* 86: 749–74.

Mirvis, Philip H., and Douglas T. Hall. 1996. "Psychological Success and the Boundaryless Career." In *The Boundaryless Career*, edited by Michael B. Arthur and Denise M. Rousseau, 237–55. New York: Oxford University Press.

Moen, Phyllis. 1992. *Women's Two Roles: A Contemporary Dilemma*. Westport: Auburn House.

———. 1994. "Women, Work and Family: A Sociological Perspective on Changing Roles." In *Age and Structural Lag: The Mismatch between People's Lives and Opportunities in Work, Family, and Leisure*, edited by Matilda White Riley, Robert L. Kahn, and Anne Foner, 151–70. New York: John Wiley and Sons.

———. 1996. "A Life Course Perspective on Retirement, Gender, and Well-Being." *Journal of Occupational Health Psychology* 1: 131–44.

———. 1998. "Recasting Careers: Changing Reference Groups, Risks, and Realities." *Generations* 22(1): 40–5.

———. 2001. "The Gendered Life Course." In *Handbook of Aging and the Social Sciences*, 5th ed., edited by Linda George and Robert H. Binstock, 179–96. San Diego: Academic Press.

Moen, Phyllis, Donna Dempster-McClain, and Robin Williams, Jr. 1989. "Social Integration and Longevity: An Event History Analysis of Women's Roles and Resilience." *American Sociological Review* 54: 635–47.

———. 1992. "Successful Aging: A Life Course Perspective on Women's Roles and Health." *American Journal of Sociology* 97(6): 1612–38.

Moen, Phyllis, Glen Elder, Jr., and Kurt Lüscher, eds. 1995. *Examining Lives in Context: Perspectives on the Ecology of Human Development*. Washington, D.C.: American Psychological Association.

Moen, Phyllis, and Shin-Kap Han. 2000. "Reframing Careers: Work, Family, and Gender." In: *Restructuring Work and the Life Course*, edited by Victor Marshall, Walter Heinz, Helga Krueger, and Anil Verma, 424–45. Toronto: University of Toronto Press.

Moen, Phyllis, and Shin-Kap Han. 2001. "Gendered Careers: A Life Course Perspective." In *Working Families: The Transformation of the American Home*, edited by Rosanna Hertz and Nancy L. Marshall, 42–57. Berkeley: University of California Press.

Moen, Phyllis, Deborah Harris-Abbott, Shinok Lee, and Patricia Roehling. 1999. *The Cornell Couples and Careers Study*. Cornell Employment and Family Careers Institute. Ithaca: Cornell University.

Moen, Phyllis, Jungmeen E. Kim, and Heather Hofmeister. 2001. "Couples' Work/Retirement Transitions, Gender, and Marital Quality." *Social Psychology Quarterly* 64: 55–71.

Moen, Phyllis, and Ken R. Smith. 1986. "Women at Work: Commitment and Behavior over the Life Course." *Sociological Forum* 1: 450–75.

Moen, Phyllis, Stephen Sweet, and Bickley Townsend. 2001. *How Family Friendly Is Upstate New York?* Ithaca: Cornell Employment and Family Careers Institute.

Moen, Phyllis, and Elaine Wethington. 1992. "The Concept of Family Adaptive Strategies." *Annual Review of Sociology* 18: 233–51.

Moen, Phyllis, and Yan Yu. 1998. "Does Success at Work Compete with Success at Home?" In *Proceedings of the Conference on Women's Progress: Perspectives on the Past, Blueprint for the Future*, 171–74. Washington, D.C.: Institute for Women's Policy Research.

———. 1999. "Having It All: Overall Work/Life Success in Two-Earner Families." In *Work and Family: Research in the Sociology of Work*, Vol. 7, edited by Toby Parcel and Randy Hodson, 109–39. Greenwich, Conn.: JAI Press.

———. 2000. "Effective Work/Life Strategies: Working Couples, Work Conditions, Gender, and Life Quality." *Social Problems* 47(3): 291–326.

Morgan, Hal, and Frances J. Milliken. 1992. "Keys to Action: Understanding Differences in Organizations' Responsiveness to Work-and-Family Issues." *Human Resource Management* 31(3): 227–47.

Morrison, Donna R., and Daniel T. Lichter. 1988. "Family Migration and Female Employment: The Problem of Underemployment among Migrant Married Women." *Journal of Marriage and the Family* 50: 161–72.

Mroczek, Daniel K., and Christian M. Kolarz. 1998. "The Effect of Age on Positive and Negative Affect: A Developmental Perspective on Happiness." *Journal of Personality and Social Psychology* 75: 1333–49.

Mueller, Charles W., and Weldon T. Johnson. 1975. "Socioeconomic Status and Religious Participation." *American Sociological Review* 40: 785–800.

Musick, Marc A., Anna Regula Herzog, and James S. House. 1999. "Volunteering and Mortality among Older Adults: Findings from a National Sample." *Journal of Gerontology* 54B: S173–80.

Mutran, Elizabeth J., Donald C. Reitzes, and Maria E. Fernandez. 1997. "Factors That Influence Attitudes toward Retirement." *Research on Aging* 19: 251–73.

Nakao, Keiko, and Judith Treas. 1990. *Computing 1989 Prestige Scores*. General Social Survey Methodological Report no. 70, Chicago: National Opinion Research Center.

National Public Radio. 2000. "Survey Shows Widespread Enthusiasm for High Technology." Available at http://www.npr.org/programs/specials/poll/technology; INTERNET. Accessed July 2, 2002.

Near, Janet P., Robert W. Rice, and Raymond G. Hunt. 1987. "Job Satisfaction and Life Satisfaction: A Profile Analysis." *Social Indicators Research* 19: 383–401.

Newsom, Jason T., and Richard Schulz. 1996. "Social Support as a Mediator in the Relation between Functional Status and Quality of Life in Older Adults." *Psychology and Aging* 11: 34–44.

Nie, Norman H. 2001. "Sociability, Interpersonal Relations, and the Internet." *American Behavioral Scientist* 45: 420–35.

O'Driscoll, Michael P., Daniel R. Ilgen, and Kristin Hildreth. 1992. "Time Devoted to Job and Off-job Activities, Inter-role Conflict and Affective Experiences." *Journal of Applied Psychology* 77: 272–79.

Ofek, Haim, and Yesook Merrill. 1997. "Labor Immobility and the Formation of Gender Wage Gaps in Local Markets." *Economic Inquiry* 35: 28–47.

O'Rand, Angela M., and John C. Henretta. 1982. "Delayed Career Entry, Industrial Pension Structure, and Early Retirement in a Cohort of Unmarried Women." *American Sociological Review* 16: 241–62.

Orrange, Robert. 1999. Women as Household Managers. Working paper no. 99-05, Cornell Employment and Family Careers Institute, Cornell University, Ithaca.

Osterman, Paul, ed. 1984. *Internal Labor Markets*. Cambridge, Mass.: MIT Press.

———. 1995. "Work Family Programs and the Employment Relationship." *Administrative Science Quarterly* 40: 681–700.

Pampel, Fred C., and Jane A. Weise. 1983. "Economic Development, Pension Policies, and the Labor Force Participation of Aged Males: A Cross-National, Longitudinal Approach." *American Journal of Sociology* 89: 350–72.

Papadakis, Maria C., and Eileen L. Collins. 2001. *The Application and Implications of Information Technologies in the Home: Where Are the Data and What Do They Say?* Arlington: Division of Science Resources Studies, National Science Foundation.

Parasuraman, Saroj, and Jeffrey H. Greenhaus. 1993. "Personal Portrait: The Life-Style of the Woman Manager." In *Women in Management*, edited by Ellen A. Fagenson, 186–211. Newbury Park: Sage.

Parasurman, Saroj, Yasmin S. Purohit, and Veronica M. Goldshalk. 1996. "Work and Family Variables, Entrepreneurial Career Success, and Psychological Well-Being." *Journal of Vocational Behavior* 48: 275–300.

Parker, Sharon K., Nik Chmiel, and Toby D. Wall. 1997. "Work Characteristics and Employee Well-Being within a Context of Strategic Downsizing." *Journal of Occupational Health Psychology* 2: 289–303.

Patterson, Charlotte J. 1995. "Sexual Orientation and Human Development: An Overview." *Developmental Psychology* 31(1): 3–11.

Paul, Carolyn. 1983. *Expanding Part Time Options for Older Americans: A Feasibility Study.* Los Angeles: Andrus Gerontology Center, University of Southern California.

——. 1987. "Work Alternatives for Older Americans: A Management Perspective." In *The Problem Isn't Age: Work and Older Americans*, edited by Steven H. Sandell, 165–76. New York: Praeger.

Pavalko, Eliza K. 1997. "Beyond Trajectories: Multiple Concepts for Analyzing Long-Term Processes." In *Studying Aging and Social Change: Conceptual and Methodological Issues*, edited by Melissa A. Hardy, 129–47. Thousand Oaks: Sage.

Pavalko, Eliza K., Glen H. Elder, Jr., and Elizabeth C. Clipp. 1993. "Work Lives and Longevity: Insights from a Life Course Perspective." *Journal of Health and Social Behavior* 34: 363–80.

Pavalko, Eliza K., and Brad Smith. 1998. "The Rhythm of Work: Health Effects of Women's Work Dynamics." *Social Forces* 77(3): 1141–62.

Pavese, Cesare. 1961. *The Burning Brand: Diaries 1935–1950.* Translated by A. E. Murch with Jeanne Molli. New York: Walker and Co.

Pearlin, Leonard I., Morton A. Lieberman, Elizabeth Menaghan, and Joseph T. Mullan. 1981. "The Stress Process." *Journal of Health and Social Behavior* 22: 337–56.

Pearlin, Leonard I., and Carmi Schooler. 1978. "The Structure of Coping." *Journal of Health and Social Behavior* 19: 2–21.

Peluchette, Joy Van Eck. 1993. "Subjective Career Success: The Influence of Individual Difference, Family and Organizational Variables." *Journal of Vocational Behavior* 43: 198–208.

Peplau, Letitia-Anne, Rosemary C. Veniegas, and Susan M. Campbell. 1996. "Gay and Lesbian Relationships." In *The Lives of Lesbians, Gays, and Bisexuals: Children to Adults*, edited by Ritch C. Savin-Williams and Kenneth M. Cohen, 250–73. New York: Harcourt Brace.

Perlow, Leslie A. 1997. *Finding Time: How Corporations, Individuals, and Families Can Benefit from New Work Practices.* Ithaca: Cornell University Press.

Peters, James L., Barbara H. Peters, and Frank Caropreso. 1990. *Work and Family Policies— The New Strategic Plan.* New York: The Conference Board.

Pickles, Andrew, and Michael Rutter. 1989. "Statistical and Conceptual Models of Turning Points." In *Problems and Methods in Longitudinal Research: Stability and Change*, edited by David Magnusson, Lars Bergman, Georg Rudinger, and Bertil Toerestad, 133–65. Cambridge: Cambridge University Press.

Pisarski, Anne, Philip Bohle, and Victor J. Callan. 1998. "Effects of Coping Strategies, Social Support and Work-Nonwork Conflict on Shift Worker's Health." *Scandinavian Journal of Work, Environment and Health* 24: 141–45.

Pixley, Joy E. 2002. Reports of Career Prioritizing in the Career Decisions Study. Paper presented at the BPW Academic Conference on Persons, Processes, and Places: Research on Families, Workplaces and Communities, 8 February, San Francisco.

Pleck, Joseph H. 1985. *Working Wives/Working Husbands*. Beverly Hills: Sage.

Pleck, Joseph H., and Graham L. Staines. 1985. "Work Schedules and Family Life in Two-Earner Couples." *Journal of Family Issues* 6: 61–82.

Pleck, Joseph H., Graham L. Staines, and Linda Lang. 1980. "Conflict between Work and Family Life." *Monthly Labor Review* 3: 29–32.

Polacheck, Solomon W., and Francis W. Horvath. 1977. "A Life Cycle Approach to Migration: Analysis of the Perspicacious Peregrinator." *Research in Labor Economics* 1: 103–49.

Polivka, Anne E. 1996. "Into Contingent and Alternative Employment: By Choice?" *Monthly Labor Review* (119 October): 55–74.

Portes, Alejandro. 1998. "Social Capital: Its Origins and Applications in Modern Sociology." *Annual Review of Sociology* 24: 1–24.

Potuchek, Jean L. 1997. *Who Supports the Family? Gender and Breadwinning in Dual-Earner Marriages*. Stanford: Stanford University Press.

Pratt, Geraldine, and Susan Hanson. 1988. "Gender, Class, and Space." *Environment and Planning D-Society and Space* 6(1): 15–35.

Preston, Valerie, Sara McLafferty, and Ellen Hamilton. 1993. "The Impact of Family Status on Black, White, and Hispanic Women's Commuting." *Urban Geography* 14: 228–50.

Quick, Heather, and Phyllis Moen. 1998. "Gender, Employment, and Retirement Quality: A Life-Course Approach to the Differential Experiences of Men and Women." *Journal of Occupational Health Psychology* 3(1): 44–64.

——. 2002. "Careers in Competition? The Orderliness of Spouses' Occupational Careers." Cornell Couples and Careers Institute, Cornell University, Ithaca. Unpublished manuscript.

Quinn, Joseph F., and Richard V. Burkhauser. 1990. *Retirement Preferences and Plans of Older American Workers*. Background paper no. 4. Americans over 55 at Work Program. New York: The Commonwealth Fund.

Quinn, Joseph F., Richard V. Burkhauser, and Daniel A. Myers. 1990. *Passing the Torch: The Influence of Economic Incentives on Work and Retirement*. Kalamazoo: W. E. Upjohn Institute for Employment Research.

Raabe, Phyllis H. 1990. "The Organizational Effects of Workplace Family Policies." *Journal of Family Issues* 11: 477–91.

Raabe, Phyllis H., and John C. Gessner. 1988. "Employer Family-Supportive Policies: Diverse Variations on a Theme." *Family Relations* 37: 196–202.

Rain, Jeffery S., Irving M. Lane, and Dirk D. Steiner. 1991. "A Current Look at the Job Satisfaction/Life Satisfaction Relationship: Review and Future Considerations." *Human Relations* 44: 287–307.

Rapoport, Rhona, Joyce K. Fletcher, Bettye H. Pruitt, and Lotte Bailyn. 2002. *Beyond Work-Family Balance: Advancing Gender Equity and Workplace Performance*. San Francisco: Jossey-Bass.

Rayman, Paula, Lotte Bailyn, Jillian Dickert, and Francoise Carre. 1999. "Designing Organizational Solutions to Integrate Work and Life." *Women in Management Review* 14: 164–76.

Repetti, Rena L. 1989. "Effects of Daily Workload on Subsequent Behavior during Marital Interaction: The Roles of Social Withdrawal and Spouse Support." *Journal of Personality and Social Psychology* 57(4): 651.

———. 1994. "Short-Term and Long-Term Processes Linking Job Stressors to Father-Child Interaction." *Social Development* 3: 1–15.

Repetti, Rena L., Karen A. Matthews, and Ingrid Waldron. 1989. "Employment and Women's Health." *American Psychologist* 44(11): 1394–1401.

Repetti, Rena L., and Jenifer Wood. 1997. "Effects of Family Stress at Work on Mothers' Interactions with Preschoolers." *Journal of Family Psychology* 11: 90–108.

Rhine, Shirley H. 1978. *Older Workers and Retirement*. New York: The Conference Board.

Riley, Matilda White. 1987. "On the Significance of Age in Sociology." *American Sociological Review* 52: 1–14.

Riley, Matilda White, Robert L. Kahn, and Anne Foner, eds. 1994. *Age and Structural Lag: Society's Failure to Provide Meaningful Opportunities in Work, Family, and Leisure*. New York: John Wiley and Sons.

Riley, Matilda White, and John W. Riley, Jr. 1994. "Structural Lag: Past and Future." In *Age and Structural Lag: Society's Failure to Provide Meaningful Opportunities in Work, Family, and Leisure*, edited by Matilda White Riley, Robert L. Kahn, and Anne Foner, 15–36. New York: John Wiley and Sons.

Rindfuss, Ronald R., C. Gray Swicegood, and Rachel A. Rosenfeld. 1987. "Disorder in the Life Course: How Common and Does It Matter?" *American Sociological Review* 52: 785–801.

Risman, Barbara J., and Danette Johnson-Sumerford. 1998. "Doing It Fairly: A Study of Post-gender Marriages." *Journal of Marriage and the Family* 60: 23–40.

Robinson, John P., and Geoffrey Godbey. 1997. *Time for Life: The Surprising Ways Americans Use Their Time*. University Park: Pennsylvania State University Press.

Rodin, Judith, Carolynne Timko, and S. Harris. 1985. "The Construct of Control: Biological and Psychosocial Correlates." In *Annual Review of Gerontology and Geriatrics*, edited by Carl Eisdorfer, M. Powell Lawton, and George L. Maddox, 3–55. New York: Springer.

Rogers, Jackie Krasas. 2000. *Temps: The Many Faces of the Changing Workplace*. Ithaca: ILR Press.

Romsa, Gerald, P. Bondy, and Morris Blenman. 1985. "Modeling Retirees' Life Satisfaction Levels: The Role of Recreational, Life Cycle and Socio-Environmental Elements." *Journal of Leisure Research* 17: 29–39.

Roof, Wade Clark, and William McKinney. 1987. *American Mainline Religion: Its Changing Shape and Future*. New Brunswick, N.J.: Rutgers University Press.

Rose, Damaris, and Paul Villeneuve. 1998. "Engendering Class in the Metropolitan City: Occupational Pairings and Income Disparities among Two-Earner Couples." *Urban Geography* 19: 123.

Rosenbaum, James E. 1984. *Career Mobility in a Corporate Hierarchy*. Orlando: Academic Press.

Rosenberg, Morris. 1979. *Conceiving the Self*. New York: Basic Books.

Rosenfeld, Rachel A. 1980. "Race and Sex Differences in Career Dynamics." *American Sociological Review* 45: 583–609.

———. 1992. "Job Mobility and Career Processes." *Annual Review of Sociology* 18: 39–61.

Ross, Catherine E. 1995. "Reconceptualizing Marital Status as a Continuum of Social Attachment." *Journal of Marriage and the Family* 57: 129–40.

Ross, Catherine E., and John Mirowsky. 1989. "Explaining the Social Patterns of Depression: Control and Problem-solving or Support and Talking." *Journal of Health and Social Behavior* 30: 206–19.

Ross, Michael, and Roger Buehler. 1994. "Creative Remembering." In *The Remembering Self*, edited by Ulric Neisser and Robyn Fivush, 205–35. New York: Cambridge University Press.

Rothausen, Teresa J., Jorge A. Gonzalez, Nicole E. Clarke, and Lisa L. O'Dell. 1998. "Family-Friendly Backlash: Fact or Fiction? The Case of Organizations' On-Site Child Care Centers." *Personnel Psychology* 51: 685–706.

Rousseau, Denise M. 1978. "Relationship of Work to Nonwork." *Journal of Applied Psychology* 63: 513–17.

Rouwendal, Jan, and Piet Rietveld. 1994. "Changes in Commuting Distances of Dutch Households." *Urban Studies* 31: 1545.

Rowe, John W., and Robert L. Kahn. 1998. *Successful Aging.* New York: Pantheon.

Rydstedt, Leif W., and Gunn Johansson. 1998. "A Longitudinal Study of Workload, Health and Well-Being among Male and Female Urban Bus Drivers." *Journal of Occupational and Organizational Psychology* 71: 35–45.

Ryff, Carol D. 1989. "Happiness Is Everything, Or Is It? Explorations on the Meaning of Psychological Well-Being." *Journal of Personality and Social Psychology* 57: 1069–81.

Ryff, Carol D., and Corey L. M. Keyes. 1995. "The Structure of Psychological Well-Being Revisited." *Journal of Personality and Social Psychology* 69: 719–27.

Savin-Williams, Ritch C., and Kristin G. Esterberg. 2000. "Lesbian, Gay, and Bisexual Families." In *Handbook of Family Diversity*, edited by David H. Demo, Katherine R. Allen, and Mark A. Fine, 197–215. New York: Oxford University Press.

Schor, Juliet. 1991. *The Overworked American: The Unexpected Decline of Leisure.* New York: Basic Books.

Schwartz, Norbert, Robert M. Groves, and Howard Schuman. 1998. "Survey Methods." In *Handbook of Social Psychology,* Vol. 2, edited by Daniel T. Gilbert, Gardner Lindzey, and Susan T. Fiske, 143–79. Boston: McGraw-Hill.

Segal, Lewis M. 1996. "Flexible Employment: Composition and Trends." *Journal of Labor Research* 17: 525–42.

Selznick, Philip. 1949. *TVA and the Grass Roots: A Study in the Sociology of Formal Organization.* Berkeley: University of California Press.

Settersten, Richard A. 1999. *Lives in Time and Place: The Problems and Promises of Developmental Science.* Amityville, N.Y.: Baywood Publishing.

Sewell, William H., Jr. 1992. "A Theory of Structure: Duality, Agency, and Transformation." *American Journal of Sociology* 98: 1–29.

Sharp, Clifford. 1981. *The Economics of Time.* New York: John Wiley and Sons.

Shellenbarger, Sue. 1992. "Lessons from the Workplace: How Corporate Policies and Attitudes Lag behind Workers' Changing Needs." *Human Resource Management* 31(3): 157–70.

Shelton, Beth A. 1992. *Women, Men and Time: Gender Differences in Paid Work, Housework, and Leisure.* New York: Greenwood Press.

Shelton, Beth A., and Daphne John. 1996. "The Division of Household Labor." *Annual Review of Sociology* 22: 299–322.

Sherkat Darren E. 2000. " 'That They be Keepers of the Home': The Effect of Conservative Religion on Early and Late Transitions into Housewifery." *Review of Religious Research* 41(3): 344–58.

Sherkat, Darren E., and Christopher Ellison. 1999. "Recent Developments and Current Controversies in the Sociology of Religion." *Annual Review of Sociology* 25: 363–94.

Shinn, Marybeth, Nora W. Wong, Patricia A. Simko, and Blanca Ortiz-Torres. 1989. "Promoting the Well-Being of Working Parents: Coping, Social Support, and Flexible Job Schedules." *American Journal of Community Psychology* 17: 31–55.

Shore, Rima. 1998. *Ahead of the Curve.* New York: Families and Work Institute.

Sieber, Sam D. 1974. "Toward a Theory of Role Accumulation." *American Sociological Review* 39: 567–78.

Simon, Rita J., and Jean M. Landis. 1989. "Women's and Men's Attitudes about a Woman's Place and Role." *Public Opinion Quarterly* 53: 265–76.

Slater, Suzanne. 1999. *The Lesbian Family Life Cycle*. Chicago: University of Illinois Press.

Smilkstein, Gabriel, Clark Ashworth, and D. Montano. 1982. "Validity and Reliability of the Family APGAR as a Test of Family Function." *The Journal of Family Practice* 15: 303–11.

Smith, Deborah B., and Phyllis Moen. 1998. "Spousal Influence on Retirement: His, Her, and Their Perceptions." *Journal of Marriage and the Family* 60: 734–44.

Smith, Tom. 1987. *Classifying Protestant Denominations*. General Social Survey Methodological Report 43. Chicago: National Opinion Research Center.

———. 1998. "A Review of Church Attendance Measures." *American Sociological Review* 63: 131–36.

Sørensen, Aage B., and Nancy B. Tuma. 1981. "Labor Market Structures and Job Mobility." *Research in Social Stratification and Mobility* 1: 67–94.

Spalter-Roth, Roberta M., Arne L. Kalleberg, Edith Rasell, Naomi Cassirer, Barbara F. Reskin, Ken Hudson, David Webser, Eileen Appelbaum, and Betty L. Dooley. 1997. *Managing Work and Family: Nonstandard Work Arrangements among Managers and Professionals*. Washington, D.C.: Economic Policy Institute.

Spain, Daphne, and Suzanne Bianchi. 1996. *Balancing Act: Motherhood, Marriage, and Employment among American Women*. New York: Russell Sage Foundation.

Spenner, Kenneth I., Luther B. Otto, and Vaughn R. A. Call. 1982. *Career Lines and Career*. Lexington, Mass.: Lexington Press.

Spillerman, Seymour. 1977. "Careers, Labor Market Structure, and Socioeconomic Attainment." *American Journal of Sociology* 83: 551–93.

Spitze, Glenna. 1984. "The Effect of Family Migration on Wives' Employment: How Long Does It Last?" *Social Science Quarterly* 65: 21–36.

———. 1986. "Family Migration Largely Unresponsive to Wife's Employment (across Age Groups)." *Sociology and Social Research* 70: 231–34.

Spitze, Glenna, John R. Logan, Genevieve Joseph, and Eunju Lee. 1994. "Middle Generation Roles and the Well-Being of Men and Women." *Journal of Gerontology* 49: S107–S116.

Staines, Graham L. 1980. "Spillover versus Compensation: A Review of the Literature on the Relationship between Work and Nonwork." *Human Relations* 33: 111–29.

Standen, Peter, Kevin Daniels, and David Lamond. 1999. "The Home as a Workplace: Work-Family Interaction and Psychological Well-Being in Telework." *Journal of Occupational Health Psychology* 4: 368–81.

Stanfield, Jacqueline Bloom. 1996. *Married with Careers: Coping with Role Strain*. Aldershot, UK: Avebury Ashgate Publishing.

Steinberg, Bruce. 1994. "An Insight into Customer Service and Recruiting: Profile of the Temporary Workforce." *Contemporary Times* (Summer): 53–54.

Still, Mary C. 2000. Work/Life Practices as Symbolic Innovation: A Longitudinal Examination of U.S. Companies. Paper presented at the Academy of Management, 8 August, Toronto.

Stolzenberg, Ross M., Mary Blair-Loy, and Linda J. Waite. 1995. "Religious Participation in Early Adulthood: Age and Family Life Cycle Effects on Church Membership." *American Sociological Review* 60: 84–103.

Stovel, Katherine. 1996. *DISTANCE*. Chapel Hill: Department of Sociology, University of North Carolina.

Stovel, Katherine, Michael Savage, and Peter Bearman. 1996. "Ascription into Achievement: Models of Career Systems at Lloyds Bank." *American Journal of Sociology* 102: 358–99.

Strang, David, and Michael W. Macy. 2001. "In Search of Excellence: Fads, Success Stories, and Adaptive Emulation." *American Journal of Sociology* 107: 147–82.

Strang, David, and Mary C. Still. 2001. Learning and Legitimacy in Organizational Emulation. Paper prepared for Strategic Management Conference, Stanford University Graduate Business School, 3 March, Palo Alto.

Szinovacz, Maximiliane E. 1996. "Couples' Employment/Retirement Patterns and Perceptions of Marital Quality." *Research on Aging* 18: 243–68.

Szinovacz, Maximiliane E., and Stanley DeViney. 2000. "Marital Characteristics and Retirement Decisions." *Research on Aging* 22(5): 470–98.

Szinovacz, Maximiliane, and David J. Ekerdt. 1995. "Families and Retirement." In *Handbook of Aging and the Family*, edited by R. Blieszner and V. H. Bedford, 377–400. Westport: Greenwood Press.

Tait, Marianne, Margaret Y. Padgett, and Timothy T. Baldwin. 1989. "Job and Life Satisfaction: A Reevaluation of the Strength of the Relationship and Gender Effects as a Function of the Date of the Study." *Journal of Applied Psychology* 74: 502–7.

Taylor, Mary Anne, and Lynn McFarlane Shore. 1995. "Predictors of Planned Retirement Age: An Application of Beehr's Model." *Psychology and Aging* 10: 76–83.

Tesch, Bonnie J., J. Osborne, D. E. Simpson, S. F. Murray, and J. Spiro. 1992. "Women Physicians in Dual-Physician Relationships Compared with Those in Other Dual-Career Relationships." *Academic Medicine: Journal of the Association of American Medical Colleges* 67: 542–44.

Theorell, Tores, and Robert A. Karasek. 1996. "Current Issues Relating to Psychosocial Job Strain and Cardiovascular Disease Research." *Journal of Occupational Health Psychology* 1: 9–26.

Thoits, Peggy A. 1983. "Multiple Identities and Psychological Well-Being: A Reformulation and Test of the Social Isolation Hypothesis." *American Sociological Review* 48: 174–87.

———. 1986. "Multiple Identities: Examining Gender and Marital Status Differences in Distress." *American Psychological Review* 51: 259–72.

Thomas, Linda T., and Daniel C. Ganster. 1995. "Impact of Family-Supportive Work Variables on Work-Family Conflict and Strain: A Control Perspective." *Journal of Applied Psychology* 80: 6–15.

Thomas, William I., and F. Znaniecki. 1918–20. *The Polish Peasant in Europe and America.* Chicago: University of Chicago Press.

Thompson, Cynthia A., and Gary Blau. 1993. "Moving beyond the Traditional Predictors of Job Involvement: Exploring the Impact of Work-Family Conflict and Overload." *Journal of Social Behavior and Personality* 8: 635–46.

Thomson, Elizabeth. 1997. "Couple Childbearing Desires, Intentions and Births." *Demography* 34(3): 343–54.

Tilly, Louise A., and Joan W. Scott. 1978. *Women, Work, and Family.* New York: Holt, Rinehart and Winston.

Tingey, Holly, Gary Kiger, and Pamela J. Riley. 1996. "Juggling Multiple Roles: Perceptions of Working Mothers." *Social Science Journal* 33: 193–91.

Tompkins, Wayne. 2000. "Rebels Ditch the Office's 'Electronic Leash'." *Ithaca Journal,* 28 August.

Tuma, Nancy B., and Michael Hannan. 1984. *Social Dynamics: Models and Methods.* Orlando: Academic Press.

Turner, Tracy, and Debbie Niemeier. 1997. "Travel to Work and Household Responsibility: New Evidence." *Transportation* 24: 397–419.

U.S. Bureau of Labor Statistics. 1996. *Employment and Earnings Characteristics of Families.* Washington, D.C.: U.S. Department of Labor.

———. 1999. *Selected Reports from the March 1998 Current Population Survey.* Available from www.census.gov/population/ww/socdemo/hh-fam.html; INTERNET. Accessed Nov. 16, 2001.

———. 2000. *Labor Force Statistics from the Current Population Survey, Series ID LFU601702.* Washington, D.C.: Bureau of Labor Statistics.

U.S. Census Bureau. 1975. *Historical Statistics of the United States: Colonial Times to 1970.* Washington, D.C.: U.S. Department of Commerce, Bureau of the Census.

——. 1977/1996. *Current Population Survey.* Washington, D.C.: U.S. Department of Commerce.

——. 1998. *Statistical Abstract of the United States.* Washington, D.C.: U.S. Census Bureau.

——. 1999. *Statistical Abstract of the United States.* Washington, D.C.: U.S. Census Bureau.

——. 2000a. *Fertility of American Women: June 2000.* Washington, D.C.: U.S. Census Bureau.

——. 2000b. *Home Computers and Internet Use in the United States: August 2000.* Washington, D.C.: U.S. Department of Commerce, Economics and Statistics Administration.

——. 2000c. *Statistical Abstract of the United States.* Washington, D.C.: U.S. Census Bureau.

U.S. Department of Labor. 1999. "Futurework: Trends and Challenges for Work in the 21st Century." Available at http: //www.bls.gov/opub/ooq/2000/Summer/art04.pdf; INTERNET. Accessed July 3, 2002.

Useem, Michael. 1994. "Business Restructuring and the Aging Workforce." In *Aging and Competition: Rebuilding the U.S. Workforce,* edited by James A. Auerbach and Joyce C. Welsh, 33–57. Washington, D.C.: National Council on the Aging, National Planning Association.

van der Meide, Wayne. 1999. *Legislating Equality: A Review of Laws Affecting Gay, Lesbian, Bisexual, and Transgendered People in the United States.* Washington, D.C.: The Policy Institute of the National Gay and Lesbian Task Force.

Van Horn, Carl E., and Duke Storen. 2000. Telework: Coming of Age? Evaluating the Potential Benefits of Telework. Paper presented at Symposium on Telework and the New Workplace of the 21st Century, U.S. Department of Labor, 16 October, New Orleans.

van Ommeren, Jos, Piet Rietveld, and Peter Nijkamp. 1997. "Commuting: In Search of Jobs and Residences." *Journal of Urban Economics* 42: 402.

Veen, Anne van der, and Gerard H. M. Evers. 1985. *Female Labour Supply and the Value of Commuting Time.* Groningen, Netherlands: University of Groningen, Institute of Economic Research, Faculty of Economics.

Vinick, Barbara H., and David J. Ekerdt. 1989. "Retirement and the Family." *Generations* 13: 53–56.

Vinokur, Amiram D., Penny F. Pierce, and Catherine L. Buck. 1998. "Work-Family Conflicts of Women in the Air Force: Their Influence on Mental Health and Functioning." *Journal of Organizational Behavior* 20: 865–78.

Wallace, Jean E. 1999. "Work-to-Nonwork Conflict among Married Male and Female Lawyers." *Journal of Organizational Behavior* 20: 797–816.

Ward, Russell A. 1993. "Marital Happiness and Household Equity in Later Life." *Journal of Marriage and the Family* 55: 427.

Watt, David, and James M. White. 1999. "Computers and Family Life: A Family Development Perspective." *Journal of Comparative Family Studies* 30: 1–15.

Weiss, Robert S. 1990. *Staying the Course.* New York: Free Press.

Welbourne, Thereas M., Diane E. Johnson, and Amir Erez. 1998. "The Role-Based Performance Scale: Validity Analysis of a Theory-Based Measure." *Academy of Management Journal* 41: 540–55.

Wellman, Barry. 2001. "Computer Networks as Social Networks." *Science* 293: 2031–34.

West, Candace, and Sarah Fenstermaker. 1993. "Power, Inequality, and the Accomplishment of Gender: An Ethnomethodological View." In *Theory on Gender/Feminism on Theory,* edited by Paula England, 151–74. New York: Aldine de Gruyter.

——. 1995. "Doing Difference." *Gender and Society* 9: 8–37.

Wethington, Elaine. 2001. "Contagion of Stress." *Advances in Group Processes* 17: 229–53.

——. 2002. "The Relationship of Work Turning Points to Perceptions of Psychological Growth and Change." In *Advances in Life Course Research: New Frontiers in Socialization,* edited by Richard A. Settersten, Jr. and Timothy J. Owens, 111–31. San Diego: Elsevier.

———. In press. "Turning Points as Opportunities for Psychological Growth." In *Flourishing: The Positive Person and the Good Life*, edited by Corey L. M. Keyes and Jon Haidt. Washington, D.C.: American Psychological Association.

Wethington, Elaine, George W. Brown, and Ronald C. Kessler. 1995. "Interview Measurement of Stressful Life Events." In *Measuring Stress: A Guide for Health and Social Scientists*, edited by Sheldon Cohen, Ronald C. Kessler, and Lynn Underwood Gordon, 59–79. New York: Oxford University Press.

Wethington, Elaine, Ronald C. Kessler, and Joy E. Pixley. Forthcoming. "Psychological Turning Points and the Midlife Crisis." In *Midlife in the United States*, edited by Carol D. Ryff and Ronald C. Kessler. Chicago: University of Chicago Press.

Wheaton, Blair. 1999. "Social Stress." In *Handbook of the Sociology of Mental Health*, edited by Carol S. Aneshensel and Jo C. Phelan, 277–300. New York: Kluwer Academic/Plenum Publishers.

Wilensky, Harold L. 1960. "Work, Careers, and Social Integration." *International Social Science Journal* 12(4): 543–60.

———. 1961. "Orderly Careers and Social Participation: The Impact of Work History on the Social Integration in the Middle Class." *American Sociological Review* 26: 521–39.

Wilkie, Jane Riblett, Myra Marx Ferree, and Kathryn Strother Ratcliff. 1998. "Gender and Fairness: Marital Satisfaction in Two-Earner Couples." *Journal of Marriage and the Family* 60: 577–94.

Willekens, Frans J. 1991. "Understanding the Interdependence between Parallel Careers." In *Female Labor Market Behavior and Fertility—A Rational Choice Approach*, edited by Jacques J. Siegers, Jenny de Jong-Gierveld, and Evert van Imhoff, 2–31. Berlin: Springer-Verlag.

Williams, D. G. 1988. "Gender, Marriage, and Psychosocial Well-Being." *Journal of Family Issues* 9: 452–68.

Williams, Joan. 2000. *Unbending Gender: Why Family and Work Conflict and What to Do about It*. New York: Oxford University Press.

Williams, Kevin J., and George M. Alliger. 1994. "Role Stressors, Mood Spillover, and Perceptions of Work-Family Conflict in Employed Parents." *Academy of Management Journal* 37: 837–68.

Williams, Linda B., Joyce Abma, and Linda Piccinino. 1999. "The Correspondence between Intention to Avoid Childbearing and Subsequent Fertility: A Prospective Analysis." *Family Planning Perspectives* 31(5): 220–27.

Yang, Alan. 2000. *From Wrongs to Rights 1973 to 1999: Public Opinion on Gay and Lesbian Americans Moves toward Equality*. Washington, D.C.: The Policy Institute of the National Gay and Lesbian Task Force.

Zedeck, Sheldon. 1992. *Work, Families, and Organizations*. San Francisco: Jossey-Bass.

Contributors

Kristine Altucher is a research associate in the Division of Nutritional Sciences at Cornell University. She received her Ph.D. from the Department of Development Sociology at Cornell University. Her research focuses on the influence of social policy on the well-being of women and their families over the life course. In addition to fertility decision making and work and family issues, her areas of interest include WIC, food security, and welfare reform. Her current work looks at patterns of food security and program participation over the life course.

Rosemary Batt is an associate professor of Human Resource Studies at the Industrial and Labor Relations School, Cornell University. She received her BA from Cornell University and her PhD from the Sloan School of Management, Massachusetts Institute of Technology. She was a Russell Sage Foundation Scholar in 2001–2 and received the Outstanding Young Scholar Award in 2000 from the Industrial Relations Research Association. Her research interests include service sector performance and competitiveness, work organization and teams, work-family balance, and labor market analysis. She has published numerous book chapters and articles in such journals as *Industrial and Labor Relations Review*, *Academy of Management Journal*, *Personnel Psychology*, *International Journal of Human Resource Management*, and the *British Journal of Industrial Relations*. She is coauthor of *The New American Workplace: Transforming Work Systems in the United States* (Cornell University Press).

Noelle Chesley is a doctoral candidate in the Department of Human Development at Cornell University and a fellow with the Cornell Employment and Family Careers Institute. Her research interests include the work-family interface, gender and the life course, and public and organizational policy. Her current research is concerned with assessing whether new information and communication technologies influence various aspects of life quality in contemporary working families.

Marin Clarkberg is an assistant professor in the Department of Sociology at Cornell University. In addition to her work on time use in dual-earner families, she is interested in the examining the ways in which employment shapes family building events, such as marriage, nonmarital cohabitation, and childbearing.

Steven W. Cornelius is a faculty member in the Department of Human Development at Cornell University and faculty associate in the Cornell Employment and Family Careers Institute. His research interests are in adult development and aging, with emphases on the study of cognitive aging, wisdom, and generativity.

Emma Dentinger is a doctoral candidate in the Department of Sociology at Cornell University and a predoctoral fellow at the Cornell Employment and Family Careers Institute. Her interests relate to work-family decision making among midlife workers and their spouses, particularly influences on and the effects of the timing and other characteristics of their retirements.

Penny Edgell is a professor in the Sociology Department at the University of Minnesota. She received her doctorate from the University of Chicago and also taught at Cornell University (1995–2002). Her work has focused on how the moral culture of religious institutions shapes decision making and conflict and how local religious communities foster social inclusion or exclusion along lines of race, gender, family form, and sexuality. Her new book on how congregations contribute to our understandings of "the good family," and how they foster work-family strategies, is forthcoming from Princeton University Press.

Francille M. Firebaugh is professor emerita in the Department of Policy Analysis and Management at Cornell University and a former dean of the College of Human Ecology at Cornell. She continues a long-time research interest in household work and management and its relation to paid work. She is a member of the Board of Directors of the Families and Work Institute in New York City.

Shin-Kap Han is an assistant professor of Sociology at the University of Illinois at Urbana-Champaign and faculty associate at the Cornell Employment and Family Careers Institute. He is coauthor of "Clocking Out: Temporal Patterning of Retirement" (*American Journal of Sociology*, 1999). His research interests are in the areas of social networks, economic sociology, organizations, and careers. He currently has several research projects in progress, among them projects on such topics as opportunity hoarding in the making of a class in Korea (1392–1910), music tastes, and social integration implications of immigrants' voluntary association membership.

Ramona K. Z. Heck is the Jonas Distinguished Professor of Entrepreneurship in the Department of Management of the Zicklin School of Business at Baruch College. She teaches and conducts research related to family businesses and the owning family's internal social and economic dynamics, the effects of the family on the family-business viability over time, the economic impact of family businesses on communities, minority business ownership, and gender issues within family firms. She received her doctoral degree from Purdue University and is a member the United States Association of Small Business and Entrepreneurship, Academy of Management, and National Council on Family Relations.

Heather Hofmeister is a senior research scientist and assistant professor on the GLOBALIFE project in Germany, directed by Hans-Peter Blossfeld. She received her doctoral degree from Cornell University in 2002 and was a pre-doctoral fellow at the Cornell Employment and Family Careers Institute during the writing of this book. Hofmeister's dissertation research on dual-earner couples' commuting won national recognition at the 2002 conference on Persons, Processes, and Places: Work, Family, and Community Contexts. Her research agenda centers on couple-level dynamics of work and family, considering geographic and social contexts across the life course.

Robert Hutchens is professor of Labor Economics at Cornell's School of Industrial and Labor Relations. He received his Ph.D. in economics from the University of Wisconsin in 1976, specializing in labor economics, public finance, and econometrics. He has written several papers on the economics of government transfer programs, with an emphasis on social security, unemployment insurance, and Aid to Families with Dependent Children. In recent years, his research has focused on long-term implicit contracts and on employer policies toward older workers. He has served as a policy fellow at the Brookings Institution, as an associate editor at the *Industrial and Labor Relations Review*, and as chairman of the Department of Labor Economics.

Allison Kavey is a doctoral candidate in the Department of the History of Science, Medicine, and Technology at Johns Hopkins University. She works on the portrayal of occult knowledge and mythology in vernacular texts and their contribution to the production of sixteenth-century England as an imperial imaginary.

Jungmeen E. Kim is an assistant professor of Clinical and Social Sciences in Psychology at the University of Rochester. Her research interests include stability and variability in personality development over the lifespan, risk and resiliency in development, and life-course studies of dynamic relationships among family functioning and psychological well-being.

Janet H. Marler is an assistant professor of Management in the School of Business at the State University of New York at Albany. She obtained her doctoral degree in Industrial and Labor Relations at Cornell University. In addition to her interest in alternative employment relationships and work and family careers, her research interests also focus on technology and compensation in human resource management strategy.

Stacey S. Merola received her doctoral degree from Cornell University and is a postdoctoral fellow at the American Sociological Association (ASA) and an adjunct faculty member at Trinity College in Washington, D.C. She is working with the Research Program on the Discipline and Profession at ASA. Her dissertation is titled *Leisure and the Life Course: American Workers Leisure, 1977 and 1997*. In addition to her ongoing interest in time use, some of her current research interests include how issues of work and family affect the occupational attainment of a cohort of recent sociology PhDs.

George T. Milkovich is the M. P. Catherwood Professor at the ILR School, Cornell University. Recently Ljubljana University in Slovenia and Zhejiang University in China elected him to their faculties. Understanding employment relationships and employee compensation has been his interest for over thirty-five years. He studies and writes about how people get paid and what difference it makes. Currently he is studying the effects of globalization on compensation and rewards. He is coauthor of the books *Compensation*, *Cases in Compensation*, and *Human Resource Management*.

Hyunjoo Min is a doctoral student of the Department of Sociology at Cornell University. Her research interests are in gender inequality in occupational attainments, with a special attention to the type of job transitions and gender gap in earnings over the life course.

Steven E. Mock is a doctoral student in the Department of Human Development at Cornell University and a predoctoral fellow at the Cornell Employment and Family Careers Institute. His broad research interests are in adult development and aging, focusing particularly on diverse family forms and their planning behavior, the experiences of same-sex attracted youths and adults, and religious involvement.

Phyllis Moen is Ferris Family Professor of Life Course Studies and a professor of Sociology and of Human Development at Cornell University, where she is a founding director of the Bronfenbrenner Life Course Center. As of fall 2003 she holds a Mcknight Presidential Chair in Sociology at the University of Minnesota. Her research focuses on gender and aging over the life course, including work-family transitions and trajectories, and is funded by the Alfred P. Sloan Foundation and the National Institute on Aging for life-course research. Her books include *Working Parents, Women's Two Roles*, and, as coauthor, *Examining Lives in Context, The State of Americans*, and *A Nation Divided*.

Robert M. Orrange is an assistant professor in the Department of Sociology, Anthropology, and Criminology at Eastern Michigan University. He was recently a postdoctoral associate with Cornell's Employment and Family Careers Institute. His research there focused on how dual-earner couples manage their household work and paid employment at various phases of the life course. Currently, his research and publications focus on the areas of work, family, leisure, social psychology and the life course. Prior to his academic career, he was an operations manager for a Fortune 500 industrial supply company.

Joy E. Pixley is an assistant professor in the Department of Sociology at the University of California, Irvine. She received her doctoral degree from Cornell University in 2002 and was a predoctoral fellow at the Cornell Careers Institute during the writing of this book. Her focus on career hierarchy is part of her ongoing interest in a life-course approach to patterns of work and family roles.

Patricia V. Roehling is an associate professor and chairperson of the Psychology Department at Hope College, in Holland, Michigan. From 1998 to 1999 she served as the director of research at the Cornell Careers Institute, where she is currently a faculty affiliate. Her research interests are in the area of the work-family interface, particularly work-family spillover, work-family policies, and the impact of work on family relationships. She has also published research in the areas of alcohol abuse and the adolescent-parent relationship.

Richard P. Shore is a visiting fellow at the School of Industrial and Labor Relations at Cornell University, as well as a faculty associate at the Cornell Careers Institute. His research interests include technology, change and economic downsizing, and labor and industrial relations. He was formerly executive director of the Institute for Labor Market Policies at the ILR School and was a policy analyst in the Office of the Secretary of Labor, Washington, D.C.

Mary C. Still is a doctoral candidate in the Department of Sociology at Cornell University and a former predoctoral fellow at the Cornell Careers Institute. Her interests are in organizational theory, diffusion of innovation, social networks, and gender and the life course. Her dissertation is a comparative diffusion study of work-life and Internet strategies in corporate America. With David Strang, she has studied benchmarking teams at a global financial services firm to understand innovation activities across numerous issue areas, including work-life.

David Strang is a professor of Sociology at Cornell University. His current research examines the diffusion of management practices within firms and across the business community. His projects include the study of mechanisms of interorganizational learning on benchmarking teams, the cross-national diffusion of a quality initiative within a global bank, and entry into and exit from total quality management (TQM) consulting.

Stephen Sweet is the associate director of the Cornell Careers Institute. His recent books, *College and Society: An Introduction to the Sociological Imagination* and *Data Analysis with SPSS: A First Course in Applied Statistics*, illustrate the theoretical and empirical application of sociological perspectives to the study of social life. He is currently studying job insecurity and its effects on working families.

Pamela S. Tolbert is a professor in the Department of Organizational Behavior, School of Industrial and Labor Relations at Cornell University and is serving as codirector of the Cornell Careers Institute for the 2003–04 academic year. She is broadly interested in processes of organizational change. Her current research includes studies of the use of tenure systems by higher education organizations, the changing gender composition of university faculty, and the determinants of men's and women's intraorganizational and interorganizational mobility.

P. Monique Valcour is a doctoral candidate in the Department of Organizational Behavior, School of Industrial and Labor Relations, Cornell University and a predoctoral fellow at the Cornell Careers Institute. She is interested in work-life integration and in how careers are affected by shifts in the composition of the workforce and the changing employment contract. She studies these issues from both the individual and organizational level. Her dissertation examines the effects of career strategy use, individual characteristics, work design, and human resource practices on objective and subjective career success.

Ronit Waismel-Manor is a doctoral student at the School of Industrial and Labor Relations at Cornell University and a predoctoral fellow at the Cornell Careers Institute. Her research interests are gender stratification, sociology of work and the family, alternative employment arrangements, and the origins and transformation of institutions.

Elaine Wethington is an associate professor of Human Development and of Sociology at Cornell University. Her major research interests are in the epidemiology of mental health and illness. She is the author of numerous papers on social support, life events and illness, and coping with stress.

Lindy Williams is an associate professor in the Department of Rural Sociology at Cornell. Previously, she has worked for the National Center for Health Statistics on the National Survey of Family Growth, and she has conducted research as a postdoctoral fellow at the University of Michigan's Population Studies Center. Her research focuses on family demography in the United States and southeast Asia. Recent topics include intergenerational decision making in east and southeast Asia and couple decision making and unplanned fertility in the United States and the Philippines. She also investigates methodological issues surrounding the integration of survey data with qualitative methods.

Sonya Williams is a research analyst with the Labor Market Information Division of the North Carolina Employment Security Commission. Her major research interests include labor markets, careers, and institutional structure and change. She has also served as a predoctoral fellow of the Cornell Careers Institute.

Index

Subject Index

Age, 83–89, 197; alternative employment arrangements and, 247–50; commuting and, 68, 73–74; in *Cornell Couples and Careers Study*, 346; family-friendly benefit use and, 303–8; information technology use and, 227–28; religious participation and, 206; success and, 138–39; *See also* Life stage *and* Retirement

Alternative employment arrangements, 242–48; and age, 247–50; defined, 243; and educational attainment, 248–50; and gender values, 244, 248–50; and income, 249–53; and job prestige, 249–51; and life stage, 247; and parenthood, 247–50; and success, 250–52, 254–56; trends, 242–44; and work hours, 249–50

Baby boomers, 2–3, 92; religious participation and, 206–7

Benefits. *See* Family-friendly policies

Birth spacing. *See* Childbearing *and* Family size

Careers: and age, 83–89; and baby boomers, 92; and childbearing, 94; coming out and, 282–84; commuting and, 68, 70; defined, 11–12; and divorce, 94; and educational attainment, 91–92; and employer type, 84–85, 88; and gender, 91; and geographical moves, 184, 186–87, 195; and income, 93; and job prestige, 84–86, 89–91; and job security, 93; and marriage, 93–94; and occupation type, 84–86, 89; research methods, 82–83; and success, 93; trends, 81–82, 183–84; turning points and, 179–80; and work status, 83–85, 87

Caregiving. *See* Childcare *and* Eldercare

Cell phone and pager use, 227, 233

Childbearing, 94; effect on commuting, 64–65; and educational attainment, 52; and employment, 50–51; effect on income, 143; timing of, 51–52, 55–58; as a turning point, 178–79; trends, 51–52, 58; *See also* Parenthood *and* Family size

Childcare: employer programs, 289–90; leisure time and, 46; same-sex couples and, 285; spillover and, 106, 114–15; strategies, 17–18; telecommuting and, 222; time spent by life stage, 40–42, 73–74; work hours and, 24–26

Childlessness, 58. *See also* Infertility

Chores. *See* Housework

Class, 205, 211

Cohabitation. *See* Marriage

Cohort. *See* Baby boomers

Commuting, 68, 70; and age, 68, 73–74; and childbearing,

Author Index

Endnotes are given as a chapter number followed by a period and the endnote number. Numbers given in parentheses refer to pages in the text referenced by the note. For example, n 8.9 (123) refers to chapter 8, endnote 9, which appears on page 123 of the text.